CW01572840

THE BARONY OF BURLEIGH

A History

Dorothy Thomson

THE BARONY OF BURLEIGH – A HISTORY

First edition. All rights reserved © Dorothy Thomson 2024

No part of this book (text, images, tables or other material) may be reproduced or transmitted in any form or by any means, electronic or mechanical, without written permission from the author.

The opinions expressed are those of the author. The author does not take any responsibility for errors or changes that occur after publication.

Cover by Chris Collins

ACKNOWLEDGEMENTS

THIS BOOK HAS TAKEN four years to come into being. I was visiting our lawyer on business and, as I was about to leave, I said that as my nine years of being Session Clerk at Orwell was ending, I now had the time to research the lands of Tillyrie and Burleigh, given to Sir Michael Balfour by King James II in 1456. The lawyer said, 'wait a moment' and returned with a battered box, asking me if I would like the title deeds of Tillyrie 1700 to 1830. It was a great start to the project.

They were on vellum and took some reading, even with magnification. My thanks to husband John for the help in deciphering them, after which we put the results onto the laptop. When the lawyers moved to new premises a while later I asked if he wanted more out of the way and he gave me the title deeds from 1830 to the 1950s, when my father bought Tillyrie from the Reids. It was most rewarding.

Having been born at Burleigh, played in the castle and lived in Kinross-shire for 71 of my 80 years, we were always surrounded by history. At school we had a wonderful Australian history teacher – she really brought to life characters and the consequences of their actions. In writing this I have 'met' many folk and travelled through time in their footsteps. It has been a pleasure.

My thanks to Dr Munro and the volunteers at Kinross Museum for their cheerful help, putting up with me looking for information, and keeping my enthusiasm going. Also to Esme Malcolm for proof-reading the ongoing chapters, and never giving up on it.

Thanks to Hannah Phillips and Chris Collins for editing, and all their time and patience after lockdown to produce the book, and to everyone who contributed photographs.

I hope you readers enjoy the travel through yesteryear and can see the times of the folk and the changes that challenged them.

Warmest regards

Dorothy Thomson

CONTENTS

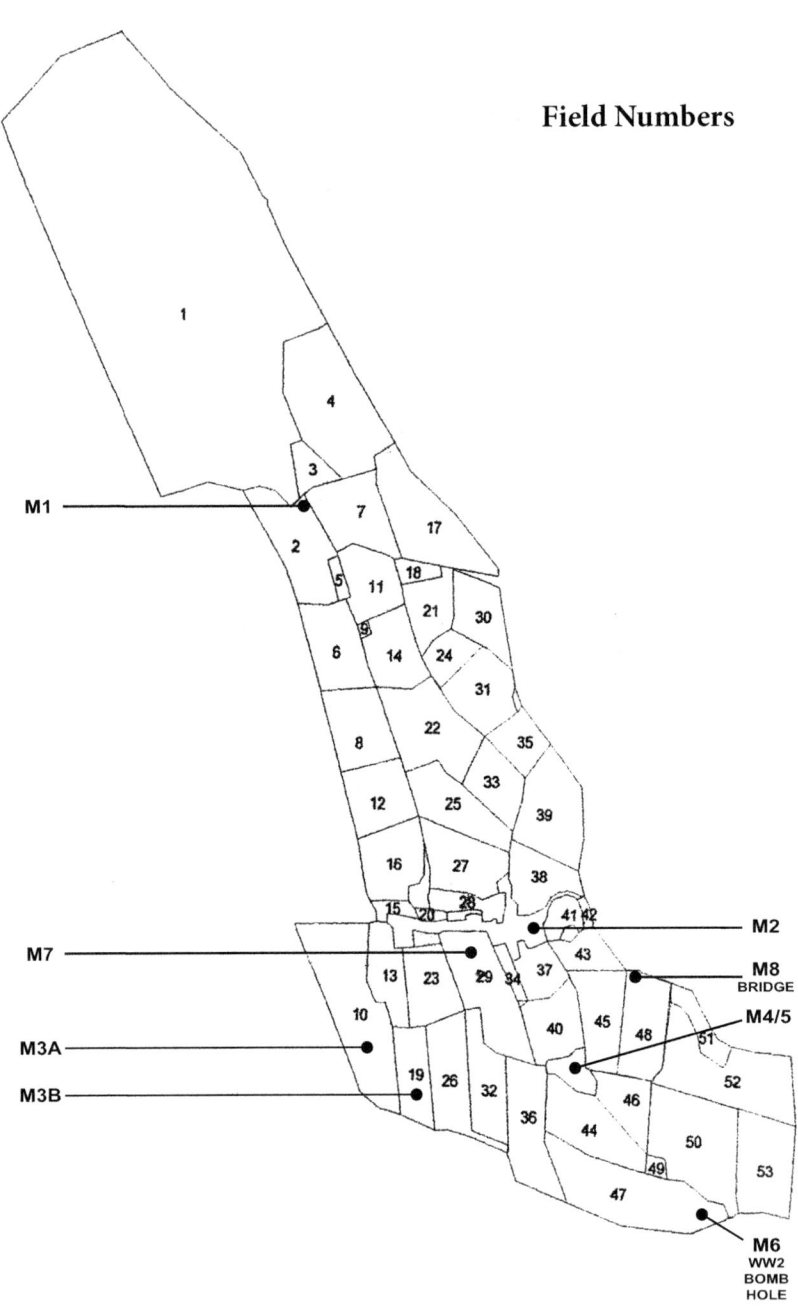

Field Numbers

Archaeology

There are a number of recorded archaeological features to be found on Tillyrie.

M1 Middle Bronze Age flanged axe (found 1874)

M2 Village of Upper Tillyrie and Farmstead

M3 Crop marks of ancient stockaged homes in the bottom half of the Seggie Field and Mucket Land. One in each field, parallel to each other. These are described as:

A) SETTLEMENT – a place, typically one which has previously been inhabited, where people established a community, or

B) SOUTERRAIN – a French word for underground. These structures are mainly associated with European Atlantic Iron Age. They were brought north from Gaul in the late Iron Age.

M4 Nether Tillyrie – a settlement and souterrain.

M5 Nether Tillyrie – a souterrain.

M6 The site of a bomb hole or land mine from the second world war in the Millgate Field. When the Germans were bombing the Forth Bridge, Rosyth dockyards and Grangemouth oil refinery, they could only get home safely fuel-wise if empty, so they discarded bombs as they circled to go home. Quite a few fell in Kinross-shire. This one is near the north-east end of the Millgate where the field narrows. Even after decades of cropping it is still a deep wide crater.

M7 Site of Greig Hall on an old map, at the top of the 40-acre field where the big sycamore tree stands. There is a well nearby nearer the road. The ornate wall tops and pillared gateway in the hamlet would be the entrance to Hall Greig.

M8 Bridge for a footpath from Nether Tillyrie to Holeton. The support stones for the bridge are still there, on the burn sides at the foot of the fields where the Tillyhenry Field meets the facing Holton Field. This would give access to the brothers Greig in Nether Tillyrie (Little Tillyrie) and Holton Farms.

During the dry summer of 1887 the surface water of Loch Leven was at an all time low, and the remains of an Iron Age crannog was seen by Kirkgate Park in Kinross.

Loch Leven is the largest glacial deposit lake in Europe. At the top of Tillyrie Hill the dyke built below the ridge separating the back hill from the lower grass and wooded hill facing south towards the loch has wee slithers of white in the stone, which I am informed happened when the Ice Age encased ex-volcanic crystals in the rock. Even 100 feet below, the field dykes (at the foot of the Spratis Muir etc) have none of these features on the same type of stones in the dykes.

Roman Influence

Although the Romans were in Britain from Julius Caesar's first expedition in late August 55 BC, until the final withdrawal in AD 410, they had very little influence in this area, having bypassed most of Fife and Kinross. There is evidence of a battle near Strathmiglo, but most of this area was not on their line of march/invasion.

The Roman Empire in the second century AD completely encircled the Mediterranean Sea, and stretched over 2,500 miles west to east from the Atlantic Ocean to modern Iraq, and nearly 2,000 miles from north to south from mid-Scotland to the Sahara Desert.

Under the Emperor Hadrian (117-138) there were no major new additions, though it would be 150 years before the contraction of the empire began. The Romans started to construct frontiers to define and protect their empire. The progress began in the first century and reached its apogee with the building of the Antonine Wall in the 140s.

Hadrian had the first wall constructed by his soldiers from Bowness in Cumbria to Wallsend in Northumberland, some 73 miles east to west and sea walls 26 and 50 miles down the coasts. When Hadrian came to the throne in 117 it was recorded "that the Britons could not be kept under control". The wall, as well as defining the edge of the Roman Empire, made sure all trade went through the gates and was taxed.

The legions, each 5,000 strong, were formed of highly trained and heavily armed infantry, with a small cavalry detachment. Each soldier was equipped with: distinctive armour formed of metal strips to aid flexibility; a sword; dagger; two spears and a rectangular shield. Legions were organised into ten cohorts, each 480 strong. Their length of service was 25/26 years; discharge appears to have taken place every other year. The legions formed the main building force, with auxiliary units undertaking work as well. The auxiliaries were not recruited from Roman citizens, but from peoples from frontier provinces. Auxiliaries normally wore mail shirts and were armed with sword, spears and oval shields. Each received Roman citizenship on retirement.

Pay was issued three times a year at special parades. Soldiers had to buy their own weapons and pay for a share of the tent used on campaign (the money would be regained on retirement, or by the sodier's heirs if he died earlier). Money was deducted for food and bedding, and the remaining money retained in a savings account managed by the standard bearer of the century. Potential recruits had to meet basic qualifications, that is: born free; pass a medical examination; and be at least 5ft 8-10in (1.75m). Also, they would normally be 18-21 years old.

A 1,000 cohort was divided into ten or six centuries. Each legion included surveyors, architect-engineers, masons, carpenters, even glaziers. They would each be allocated a section of about 3-4 Roman miles. Road making was the least favourite work for the soldiers.

On 10 July 138 the Emperor Hadrian died in his villa at Baiae near Naples, and was succeeded by Titus Aurelius Antonius, a 51-year-old wealthy, learned, thrifty man of moderation. He had no military experience, and it is thought he ordered the building of the Antonine Wall in Scotland to reflect a victory in Britain and give the new emperor military prestige.

The Veniconi in East Lothian and Northumbria were allied with Romans, with headquarters at Traprain Law, Castle Rock in Edinburgh, and Eildon Hills, trading successfully with the Romans. However, the Caledonians – who still used chariots and had foot soldiers with shields, spears, swords, and daggers – used hit and run tactics, the best approach to the well-disciplined Romans. Even so, none of the guerrilla wars waged in Britain against Romans were successful.

The Antonine Wall was built between Old Kilpatrick in the west and Carriden in the east. It ran through the narrowest part of Scotland, using natural defence in the geography, and running through a Central Valley much boggier than today, aiding the Roman position. The sea level was slightly higher 2,000 years ago than today, and mudflats extended well out at low tide. It crossed a well-farmed landscape too, and as Roman law respected property rights, they paid compensation for loss of crops.

Stone walls were bottomed 15 Roman feet wide (4.44m), with turfs 18x12in (45x30cm) and 6in (15cm) deep, making a wall approx 10ft (3m) high, with culverts crossing the stone base to prevent water ponding. There were 17 forts and the legionary strength would have been no more than 8,000 men, supported by auxiliary units who are recorded building forts. The construction was from local supply of timber, grass lands for turf, and local rough stone for foundations of the wall.

Clearance of the natural woodland of north Britain had already been underway for one or two centuries. However, with the arrival of the Romans, there was an increase in activity and within a generation much of the remaining woodland was removed. Therefore the Roman army would have crossed a landscape probably less woodland than today, and occupied by farms and divided into fields between lanes and tracks. The houses were usually wooden and round in shape though still spacious within. Sometimes the farm and its attendant yard were defined by a bank and ditch. Cattle pigs and sheep were raised, while crops included wheat, barley, oats and rye. The Romans were known to come annually from Hadrian's Wall to purchase grain in the rich Strathearn Valley.

Barrack blocks, stores barns, work shops, bath houses and latrines were mainly built with wood. The commanding officer's house would be of stone. He would be a member of the aristocracy and probably brought his wife, family and certainly slaves with him. The house was commensurate with his social standing, a stone courtyard surrounded by four ranges of rooms, with its own bath house.

Construction began in 158 and took 12 years, after having been forced to send legionaries to Germany and the Moorish war in North Africa before they returned and construction resumed.

The Antonine wall was abandoned in 180, as Hadrian's Wall was refurbished and troops gradually pulled back to there. It is possible that the abandonment may have taken as long as six years from the initial decision. Buildings with the forts were demolished, but the ramparts and ditch were left intact.

Battles were fought north of this 'last frontier' against the Caledonians and Maeatae for years after this, and outpost forts like 'Bertha' on the River Tay (just upstream from modern Perth) protected those provincials and their lines of communication living beyond it.

There was also a 50 acre (20ha) legionary fortress at Inchtuthil on the River Tay, which was erected in no more than two seasons in the late first century. As the Romans passed by Kinross-shire they did have hill-top forts on Benarty and Lomond Hills. Otherwise the Roman occupation had little effect on the Fife and Kinross areas as the roads north went further west, although it is recorded they found the population very aggressive, and avoided them.

In 1851 a hoard of 700-800 Roman denarii was found in a moss near Kinross. In the same year a boy in Portmoak, while reaping, found a Roman coin. In a search another 600 denarii were found all lying together as if they had been in a bag. At the same spot, an iron sword and a beautiful but imperfect silver ornament, thought to have formed the crest of a helmet, were found. It was thought to have formed the treasure of a soldier in the northern expedition of Sept. Severus in AD 208.

In 1854 a Roman urn was found at Craigton, able to hold four Scots pints.

Early Balfours

BALFOURS HAVE A LONG and distinguished history in Fife and Kinross. At the beginning of the 18th century, there were a greater number of Heritors in Fife than any other surname. The family of Balfour contained no less than 13 landed properties in these counties of the name *viz* Balfour of Burleigh, of Fernie, Dunbog, Denmile, Grange, Forret, Randerston, Northhank, Balburnie, Halbeath, Lawletham, and of Banktown. The branches of Balgarvie and Montwhanney were in the six most important in earlier times.

Sir William de Balfor, Knight Sheriff of Fife, who was witness to a charter by Sir Alexander circa 1200, received his castle and the lower part of the Strath-Orr from his grandfather and transmitted them to his son, Henry de Balfor, Knight Sheriff of Fife, who is mentioned in 1230-41, and left a son.

Sir John de Balfor, Knight Sheriff of Fife, was slain with many of the Barons of Fife at the sack of Berwick by Edward I on 8th March 1296, leaving two sons.

For two centuries the Scots and English had been on friendly terms. The Royals intermarried as did many nobles and lesser subjects. The Normans had been fully integrated into Scots society by marriages. Alexander II had married Joan, the sister of Henry III, and Alexander III married Margaret, daughter of Henry III, in 1251, the wedding taking place at York in unparalleled magnificence. She was sister to Edward who became King Edward I of England. The siblings were close friends and when Edward married Eleanor, a half-sister to King Alfonso of Spain in 1254, they toured Scotland with Alexander and Margaret. The Scots King and Queen were guests in London for Edward's coronation in 1274. By today's standards the landscape would seem thinly populated and unproductive. Thirteenth-century England had a population of three to four million people, and in Scotland a population of 400,000 people lived mainly in small villages and were obliged (either for their lords or for their own sakes) to till the soil in order to survive. Accurate maps were entirely unknown, and as the equator was held to be too hot a barrier to cross, beyond which life could not exist, therefore only the northern half of the spherical world was known.

Most nobles could read, but writing was thought a messy business (with ink and quill), and there were plenty dedicated clerical staff employed in households to do it. Currency was in pounds, shillings and pence. Twelve pennies equalled one shilling and there were twenty shillings in a pound. An unskilled labourer would earn one or two pence for a day's work, while a skilled craftsman would earn double that sum. A man who took home £20 a year was considered well off, and even earls rarely enjoyed incomes in excess of £5,000. The only type of coin in wide circulation was the silver penny, so even a small-sounding sum like £5 would need 1200 silver pennies. Money was also reckoned in marks, which were equivalent to 160 pennies or two-thirds of a pound. Earls were the only noblemen of rank, there were no dukes or marquesses then. Aristocrats could kill their non-noble inferiors with impunity, but did not kill or mutilate each other. In battle, captive imprisonment, ransom and release were the long-established conventions of warfare. Disinheritance, even more than death, was the rebel's greatest fear, for it entailed lasting shame and the end of their family's fortune. Consequently, it was an overlord's greatest threat.

The Great Seal of Alexander III

In Scotland, King Alexander III, a strong and successful king who established peace in his time, was unlucky with his family life in his later years. His good marriage came to an end with Queen Margaret's death in 1275. They had three children: the heir Prince Alexander, younger son David and Margaret (who married King Erik II of Norway). Sadly David the younger son died in 1281 and the heir Alexander in 1283. King Alexander III had no brothers or uncles to replace him if he died. At the age of 40 in 1285 he remarried, taking Yolande of Dreux to be his wife.

On 12th March 1286, in a terrible storm and despite being warned against travel, Alexander left Edinburgh after business to cross the Forth at Queen's ferry and continued towards Kinghorn where Yolande was waiting. Somewhere during this ill-advised journey he lost his escort, tumbled over a cliff and broke his neck. It was the next day at dawn that his body was found lying on the shoreline.

In the hope that Yolande was pregnant a regency council of six Guardians was formed of two earls, two bishops and two barons. Yolande's pregnancy was unsuccessful with the delivery of a stillborn daughter.

The heiress was now the daughter of the Queen of Norway, who had died in childbirth. Alexander and Edward had discussed previously the possibility of the three-year-old Princess Margaret of Norway marrying Edward's son Edward of Caernarfon. This was proposed again and the Scots were far from unhappy with the prospect. It promised an end to uncertainty since 1286 and the latent threat of further disorder. Negotiations started in earnest. The prenuptial agreement dragged on into 1290. Edward promised that Scotland should remain 'free in itself without subjection from the kingdom of England.' Pope Nicholas IV issued a bull giving dispensation for the marriage of the cousins.

The seven-year-old maid sailed from Norway, and Edward sent jewels for a welcome gift to her. The Scots magnates assembled at Scone Abbey in readiness for the enthronement of their new queen. In late September representatives of both nations rode to the north of Scotland to greet the Norwegian ship, which had unexpectedly put in at Orkney. Only then did they learn that Margaret had fallen sick during the voyage, maybe having eaten decayed food on board. In October they returned with the news of Margaret's death.

This death opened the question of succession, and the Guardians had to go back four generations to 1214 and King William the Lion to find an heir. There were two main contenders. Firstly, John Balliol, Scots on his mother's side, and whose claim came through her being the granddaughter of King William's brother David, Earl of Huntington (who died in 1219) through his elder daughter Margaret. John was the fourth son of Lord of Barnard Castle in Co Durham, and his brothers pre-deceasing him left him heir to his father's English estates. His father had fought with Henry II in battles and founded Balliol College in Oxford. When his mother Devorgilla died in 1290, he inherited her extensive Galloway estates and so had land in Scotland. John was in his early sixties but still had fine sensitive features and considerable intelligence.

The second contender was Robert Bruce, a grandson of Earl David of Huntington, and his claim was through his mother Isobel the second daughter of Earl David. He was a generation nearer King William than Balliol, but through the second daughter. He was one of the great magnates of England and vassal to King Edward I. Robert Bruce 'The Competitor' was an English lawyer, having been a judge and Chief Justice of the Peace in the reign of Edward's father King Henry III. He was also Earl of Carrick with land in Scotland, and the more obvious Scots candidate.

Support was split between the two camps and neither could impose a decisive settlement amongst Scotland's political community. Edward of England had enjoyed a good reputation as an international peacemaker in Europe for the last five years. On 7th October 1290 one of the Guardians, the Bishop of St Andrews, wrote to King Edward stressing the turmoil in Scotland and urged him to hasten north to prevent civil war, and give a friendly neighbourly choice of the candidates to be King of Scotland.

Edward's intentions were far from friendly or neighbourly. The death of the Maid of Norway robbed him of a rich prize, and within a few weeks he had lost his beloved Queen Eleanor. Edward now planned to reduce the king and kingdom of Scotland to his rule. Queen Eleanor of Castile, a smart and shrewd woman, never assumed political roles in England so there were no factions in her husband's court as there had been in his father's. She travelled everywhere with her husband, and had a calming and constructive effect on Edward, missing after her death on the evening of 28th November 1292, at just 49 years old.

Edward had promised the year before that Scotland would be left free and independent. The Guardians accepted a formula that Edward would control Scotland for a limited period. On 12th June the Guardians surrendered the Seal, along with the royal castles. Edward promised to keep the laws and customs of Scotland. The following day the Scots present swore fealty to Edward in his capacity of Scotland's temporary caretaker until a king was proclaimed. Edward then embarked on a tour of the heartlands, the prosperous royal burghs round the Firth of Forth: Haddington, Edinburgh, Linlithgow, Stirling, Dunfermline and St Andrews. By 2nd August he was back over the border at Berwick.

Edward chose John Balliol, the weaker character who could be manipulated into Edward's idea of reducing the kingdom of Scotland to his authority. On 30th November 1292 John Balliol was crowned King John I of Scotland at Scone. Edward did not attend. Before leaving for Scone John Balliol had sworn fealty to Edward, not only for his lands in England but also applied unambiguously to the kingdom of Scotland. This constituted a clear breach of Edward's earlier promise.

While Edward had been duping and bullying the Scots into submission, the Christian communities of the Holy Land had been driven into the sea. By May even Acre had fallen, and so ended the Kingdom of Jerusalem. Edward had been on an earlier crusade there and had meant to go on another when troubles at home allowed. All of Europe was shocked by the news.

In the summer of 1294 Edward had difficulty at home when the feudal right to provide the king with military service for a limited time was disputed and whether it applied to fighting overseas. It flared up again when asked to muster for war in Gascony against Philip of France, and almost caused rebellion amongst the sorely taxed English. The Scots and Welsh observed their 'self-appointed lord' struggling to cope with this crisis and realised the situation was an opportunity not to be missed. By the summer of 1295 the signs were unmistakable and the Scots found the courage that had failed their unfortunate King John I. In July the lords in Scotland imposed their will on John Balliol, depriving him of executive initiative. They sent representatives to King Philip of France and cemented a firm alliance on 23rd October. France and Scotland would attack Edward of England on two fronts.

Edward's reaction was to seize all property held by Scots in England. He then moved against Scotland using legalistic steps that he believed gave his actions legitimacy. King John I refused to surrender three of his towns and castles. This gave Edward his mandate to invade. On 16th December Edward declared his intention to march against King John I as he had 'violated the fealty he owed the English crown'. Edward, preparing this destructive rather than corrective campaign, advised his officials he would need £5,000 a week as he intended to recruit 1,000 mounted men and 60,000 foot soldiers, the largest army he had ever assembled. He shipped hundreds of tons of grain and food out of Ireland, despite the famine caused by poor harvests, and introduced taxes. Having failed to raise the troops from Ireland, he made the extraordinary offer to pay higher wages and pardon any crimes and debt to the crown for those willing to serve him in Scotland, which secured some 3,000 men, mostly infantry, and the largest force to sail from Ireland at that time.

Edward arrived at Newcastle on Tyne on 1st March 1296 to meet his giant army. The Scots had, unsurprisingly, not presented themselves. The English army marched to Wark and stopped for a Holy Week. On Easter Monday the Scots attacked nearby Carham, giving Edward the justification he needed for his invasion.

Berwick, on Edward's army arriving on 8th March, declined to surrender until a naval bombardment breached the wooden defences, and many stupefied citizens were indiscriminately put to the sword. A town refusing to surrender left itself open to be sacked. The 200-strong garrison eventually wisely accepted Edward's conditions of safety of life and limb, the right to retain their lands and possessions – even the right to go free, if they swore never to bear arms against him again. It was at this sacking of Berwick in March 1296 that John de Balfor, Sherriff of Fife was slain.

A day after the surrender of Berwick, Edward received a formal message from King John I, in which he renounced his fealty as 'extorted under violent pressure'. This was at the end of April. Edward sent the Earl of Surrey north, and he laid siege to Dunbar Castle, 30 miles from Berwick. The Scots army drew up on the crest of the Brunt Hill to the west of Dunbar. Surrey and his force charged across what looked to be flat land, to be surprised by a deep ravine behind what is now Spott Village, and the Scots army, inexperienced and undisciplined, charged down from their advantage, and were routed by the English co-ordinated assault. Scots soldiers perished by the hundreds and several nobles were captured. Edward arrived the next day and Dunbar Castle surrendered. Many more prestigious prisoners (including three earls) were taken. Elias de Spot signed the Ragman Rolls of 1296, obliging him to be loyal to Edward I, and received lands near Dunbar. Elias de Spot built a fortalice where two 60ft ravines meet, known as Spott Fortalice. The village is known as Spott,

Edward then captured the castles of Roxburgh, Jedburgh, Stirling and Edinburgh by mid-June. King John Balliol offered to resign as King of Scots and become an English earl, but Edward did not agree, and the Scots king was ceremoniously humiliated and 'unmade' on 8th July and, with other Scots leaders, was sent to the tower of London. Edward travelled taking hostages, and received homage as far north as Elgin. A parliament was held there and 1,000 Scots swore fealty to 'their new direct overlord'. The Scots were to have no king of their own from now. The elderly Robert Bruce was disappointed, having hoped when he supported Edward that he would get support from Edward to his claim to the throne. A new English-style administration was set up, based at Berwick. In charge would be the Earl of Surrey, the victor at Dunbar. John de Warenne, Earl of Surrey, a close friend of King Edward, was 61 years old and he did not relish the new duty as Scotland's Royal Governor as he found 'the Scottish weather unbearably awful', and he spent most of his time in the north of England.

The absence of the governor had a derogatory effect on the new administration, which by 1297 was struggling to cope with a multitude of problems caused by imposing itself on a country against its people's will. The regime was unpopular and seen as oppressive. When demands were made for the Scots to supply money and materials for Edward's war against France in May 1297 it was the last straw! Unrest and resistance boiled over into outright revolt.

Trouble started in Lanark when the sheriff was killed. Here we introduce William Wallace, the younger son of landowner Sir Malcolm Wallace of Ellersie and Auchenbothie in Ayrshire. Educated at Paisley Abbey, the best learning in the west of Scotland, William read, wrote, was an accomplished horseman with martial skills. He learned to fight with dirk and claymore, the latter his favourite weapon with its five foot double-edged blade and handle a foot long. This was worn in a scabbard strapped to the owner's back, unsheathed by reaching over his shoulder, a two-handed weapon dependent on the strength and skill of the user. William was about six foot seven inches tall, when most men were only five foot something. Described at the time as 'a skilful counsellor, compassionate in comfort, patient in suffering, a distinguished speaker who hated falsehood, deceit and treachery'. He was born about 1272/3, so was in his 14th year when disaster struck and Edward plunged Scotland into a sequence of events the changed the course of history.

In 1292 William had been fishing on the banks of the Irvine Water, and on his way home five Englishmen tried to steal his fish. In the ensuing fight one of the English, a man called Selby, was killed. For this William was declared an outlaw.

William was protected by his kinsman Wallace of Auchencruvie, and found refuge in Legen Wood near Irvine. Between 1293 and 1296 living in central Scotland often in the dense, vast Selkirk Forest, he learned the skills of generalship necessary to organise a relatively large force, and take on what was the most successful army in Europe. William possessed a considerable personal magnetism and charm. He was an impressive leader and his men adored him.

William's father was killed in an ambush by an Englishman called Fenwick, and in 1297 news came to William that Fenwick was back in south-west Scotland, escorting a treasure convoy from Carlisle to either Lanark or Ayr. Along with 50 men, William laid a trap for the convoy at Loudon Hill, ironically the very spot where Fenwick had killed Sir Malcolm Wallace five years earlier. Fenwick had an escort of 180 horsemen for the convoy, but William and his 50 men had surprise on their side. The Scots partially blocked the pass with boulders and rocks and fought on foot with spears and swords under the bellies of the horses. Fenwick himself tried to skewer William with his lance, but William side-stepped and sliced Fenwick off his horse. The success of the ambush gained Wallace two hundred horses (some pack animals laden with provisions and wine, as well as the armoured destriers of the knights and men-at-arms), armour, weapons and money. News of the battle spread like wildfire, and destroyed the myth that heavily armoured horsemen were invincible when confronted by a well-disciplined force, on ground chosen by the latter and used to best advantage.

The Sheriff of Clydesdale, in 1297 was Sir William Heselrig, a cruel man of whom many were afraid. He lived in Lanark. William Wallace had married Marion Braidfute, the 18 year-old heiress of Hugh Braidfute of Lamington, who had recently died. As William entered Lanark he was chased by Heselrig's men. Escaping from them, William took refuge in Marion's house. Heselrig marched on the house, and finding Wallace had escaped out the back to the woods, he had Marion seized and put to death. This atrocity, his father's death and the persecution of his mother (who died about this time) angered William and destroyed all restraint. William returned with his band to Lanark and broke into Heselrig's house. Finding him in bed, William killed him with a single stroke of his sword. The Scots then went on the rampage and killed many of the English.

While William Wallace was raising the land south of the Firth of Forth Andrew Murray was raising the north. Son and heir to Sir Andrew de Moray of Petty, who with his brother Sir William Moray (a very wealthy man) was captured at Dunbar and, along with young Andrew, were imprisoned. The older knights were sent to the Tower of London while Andrew, having been imprisoned at Chester Castle, managed to escape, arriving back in Moray in the spring of 1297. Sir William was set free by agreeing to fight for Edward in Flanders, but Sir Andrew chose to stay a prisoner rather than fight for England. His father in prison and his uncle effectively a hostage in English hands, it was perhaps rash for Andrew to raise the north. By April 1297 Andrew had raised the whole of Moray against a strong English presence in the area with garrisons in Inverness, Urquhart, Nairn, Forres, Elgin and Lochindorb.

The Morays were a powerful family of Celtic stock possessing seven extensive estates in the area and in Bothwell, Lanarkshire. His uncle David, younger brother of Sir Andrew and William, was a priest in Lanark and following the incarceration of his brothers he assumed the position of head of the family. He was appointed Canon of Elgin in 1298 and Bishop of Moray and Caithness a year later. He also achieved the founding of the Scots College in Paris in 1325. Moray was one of the few districts in Scotland in which the normal feudal system did not operate; its inhabitants owed their allegiance direct from the sovereign without the intermediary of a feudal superior. Thus the rising was in the name of King John I.

News travelled slowly in the 13th century. King Edward did not hear of the northern revolt until June, and was unaware of its leaders until much later. Edward was in Flanders when the news reached him, and was not planning to leave his wars there to mastermind the Scots situation. He sent the elderly, and in poor health Earl of Surrey, Warden of Scotland, to sort out the rebellions. As the winter of 1296 set in Surrey had taken himself south for his health, then delayed in making the move to Northumberland. On 14th June Edward ordered Surrey back to Scotland, but he didn't return until the end of July. Even then he lost time sending his grandson Henry de Percy to negotiate with the Scots.

In June William Wallace met up with Sir William Douglas at Perth and they advanced to Scone, a few miles to the north-east, where the English melted away, and the Justice there fled to Northumberland, abandoning a great quantity of goods and chattels. Scotland was in a state of tumult, the English troops in their castles in a state of virtual siege. Only those supplied by sea could be maintained against attack. The leading Scots in Ayrshire were summoned in the name of Edward to appear at a building known as The Barn, being used as a barracks on the outskirts of town. The Scots were heavily guarded and entered in single file, where a noose was slung over their heads and they were hung from an enormous beam running the whole length of the building. About 350 barons and knights were executed without trial, and bodies stripped and flung into the yard.

William Wallace had gone to Kinhace that day and thus evaded the trap, and on entering Ayr a woman from the Craufurd family told him the dreadful news. A few days later William Wallace and his band returned to Ayr. Having instructed the girl to mark the doors of the English inhabitants with chalk, he ordered these doors secured and then took the rest of his band to The Barn. There the Judge and a large company were sleeping off a late-night carousal, and placing brushwood all round the huge wooden building, Wallace torched it. The inmates perished and 140 troops were subsequently slain at their quarters in the Priory.

A rising by McDuff of Fife in June/July 1297 was speedily suppressed by the pro-English Earl of Strathearn. The Scots may have quarrelled and fought amongst themselves, but they were never going to knuckle down to any alien power, however benevolent. Ironically the English occupation probably gave the Scots a real sense of nationhood. Men of different races, languages, with different traditions found a common cause. By August Andrew Murray and William Wallace met up, and with mutual respect thereafter were joint commanders of the Scots forces.

The Earl of Surrey had at last arrived at Berwick, but to the frustration of Cressingham, who was in charge of the expenditure of the army, Surrey delayed taking submissions from Scots captives, which were deliberately drawn out by captives like Wishart and Robert Bruce. At last, at the end of August, Surrey reluctantly moved his forces north to relieve the siege at Stirling. 1000 horse and 50,000 foot came north to meet a second army from Carlisle of 300 horse and 850 foot under Percy: a well-equipped army which had never been defeated, and whose rank & file had confidence in their leadership.

Surrey marched the forces north to find Murray and Wallace waiting for him on the opposite side of the Firth of Forth near Stirling. The Scots were greatly outnumbered, thus the English presumed that, as at Irvine earlier, they would negotiate and surrender. However the celebrated answer was 'Go back, tell your people we have not come for the benefit of peace, but are ready to fight to avenge ourselves and free our kingdom.'

The wooden bridge over the river was narrow and horsemen could only cross two abreast, and there was only a narrow tongue of land at the north end of the bridge on which to manoeuvre once across. Surrey called a council of war but Cressingham, conscious of the enormous cost of a delay in feeding the army, argued for an immediate advance. At dawn on the morning of 11th September 1,297,500 foot soldiers, including the Welsh contingent, crossed the bridge. The Earl, recovering from his recent illness and exhausted, was still asleep. There was a moment of indecision and, in default of positive orders, the advance troops turned round and recrossed the bridge. Surrey dithered about attacking, and it was at 11am that the English cavalry began to cross the bridge but were attacked by the Scots army while their hosts were only half-formed. The Scots rushed towards the river, seized the bridge, and so divided the English army. The English already across, including Cressingham, were surrounded and killed.

William Wallace: from a painting c.1700

Those stranded on the south side of the river could only watch the slaughter happen. Surrey came out of his shock, ordered the bridge destroyed and rode hard the hundred miles to Berwick. This was the greatest crisis England had faced in 30 years. The Scots harassed the retreating English as far as Belton, near Dunbar, before wearying of the slaughter. The news reached London by 21st September, and the government had to settle factions to prevent a civil war, as the intolerable taxation of Edward's subjects was similar to the situation with King John and the Magna Carta.

Andrew Murray died on 7th November, from wounds sustained at Stirling Bridge, and Scotland lost a great general. His son, born after his death, grew up to become one of the staunchest supporters, as well as brother-in-law to King Robert the Bruce.

By October after Stirling Bridge the English were cleared out of Scotland and all the castles were recovered. William Wallace was issued documents as Joint Guardian of Scotland with Andrew on 11th October 1297, but with Andrew's death became the sole guardian in the name of King John I. He had the Great Seal of Scotland and was technically the regent for King John, who was still in captivity in the south of England. Many of the nobles were uncomfortable with the power this young man had, and many had changed sides so often it was hard to keep track of their momentary allegiances. The powerful Comyn family, closely related to King John, wavered in their alliance as if to further their own claims to the empty throne, and for this reason there was bad blood between the Comyns and the Bruce family.

Wallace led a raid in Northumberland as far south as Durham, in retaliation for the sack of Berwick.

While King Edward was on the continent he left his eldest son, the 16-year-old Prince of Wales as regent. He lacked the moral strength of his father and was already showing evidence of the traits and character defects that would one day topple him from his throne. In the virtual power vacuum, the rebellious barons came dangerously close to open revolt, and the church refused to pay the tax (of half a year's income) and repudiated its corporate fealty.

When the Scots magnates refused to attend a York parliament when commanded, or Newcastle a week later, a formidable army under Surrey crossed the border and relieved the siege of Roxburgh, where the starving and disease-riddled garrison had been on the point of surrender after a three-month siege. Edward wrote saying he was returning and to take no further action in Scotland. With the cost of maintaining the vast army, especially in winter, Surrey stood the northern army down and only kept the levies from the more distant counties and the Welsh contingent.

During the winter of 1297-8 Wallace had been busy with administration, organising the country into military districts and a plan to raise levies of all able-bodied males over the age of 16. After the Roman fashion, rather than the feudal style, every 4 men had a 5th called a quaternion, every 9 a 10th called a Decurion, every 19 a 20th, a 100 a centurion set over them and the 1,000 a chiliarch, so there was a proper chain of command. This did not endear him to the landowning classes and their feudal arrangements. William was drilling his foot soldiers, so large numbers could move in close order without colliding. Wallace invented the Schiltroun, forerunner of the square, that would dominate British infantry tactics to the end of the 19th century. The infantry were armed with 12ft spears and drilled until they formed a compact maze of bristling spears outwards in all directions, a fearful obstacle to cavalry.

Once invasion was imminent Wallace ordered the destruction of towns and villages in Berwickshire and Lothians. The population was evacuated north of the Forth and cattle driven into the hills. This scorched-earth policy was ruthlessly calculated to deny shelter and sustenance to the invader.

Edward returned from Flanders on 14th March 1298, and went to York to take personal control of the invasion. His planning was meticulous. The actual invasion was scheduled for 25th June. From mid-March elaborate plans were made for a depot in Carlisle, to where provisions would be shipped from Ireland. A large quantity of shipping was stationed at ports along the east coast of England to bring supplies to Berwick and Edinburgh as King Edward went victoriously north.

To test the strength of the Scots, the Earl of Pembroke and Sir John Siward crossed directly from Flanders to land in Fife with a substantial force, intending to split the Scots army in two. At first they met little opposition as they laid waste to a great deal of Fife, before running into William Wallace and his army on 12th June at the forest of Blackearnside near Abernethy. Here they engaged in a running fight, then a pitched battle with the invaders defeated. The Scots did have some losses. Sir Duncan Balfour, Sheriff of Fife and Sir Christopher Seton were killed and Sir John Graham badly wounded.

Edward reached Roxburgh on 24th June with 3,000 heavy cavalry, 4,000 light horse and 80,000 foot, the majority of the infantry paid troops recruited in Ireland and Wales, rather than feudal England. They met only burned ruins, bereft of crops or livestock. His long columns were vulnerable to Scots hit and run tactics, frequently from Dirleton, Tantallon and Hailes castles, which without siege engines were unconquerable. The situation was aggregated by shortage of provisions, only three ships eventually arriving at Dunbar. Edward advanced to Kirkliston and rested there for a few days, with no sight of the Scots army. Further advance was hampered for several days with no sign of the provision ships, the winds stopping them landing and the troops were placed on short rations.

Meanwhile the Scots besieged Carlisle to prevent supplies landing there. Such cavalry as Wallace could muster was commanded by John 'The Red' Comyn, nephew of John Balliol (and destined to dubious immortality as the man Bruce slew at Dumfries in 1306), and young Earl of Carrick, whose loyalty neither side could rely on.

While attacking the Annandale estates of the elder Bruce, King Edward had already foreclosed on his debts the previous winter and seized £650 worth of goods from his Essex estates. This was retaliation for young Bruce having failed to hand over his young daughter Marjorie to Edward as a hostage. It was the last straw for young Bruce who now threw in his lot with Wallace, holding Ayr Castle for the Scots, from where Bruce could control shipping on the Firth of Clyde and stop supplies from Ireland landing at Greenock and Glasgow.

Wallace's army came mainly from the bonnet lairds, squires, yeomen, farmers and peasantry, burgesses, craftsmen and labourers of towns and villages. They were called to arms in the cause of freedom to live without alien interference, rather than a lord's feudal bidding. They mainly came from Lothians and the Borders, displaced at this time. William Wallace, the Guardian of Scotland, was knighted about this time.

Edward at Kirkliston saw three ships arrive. Unfortunately the supplies were mainly wine, but to give the troops moral support he ordered it distributed to them anyway. This led to drunken fighting, some of which soon broke out between the Welsh and English infantry, the former threatening to side with the Scots. On 21st July spies reported the Scots were only 20 miles away. At dawn next day, after a night spent at Lintithgow half-expecting a Scots attack, the soldiers slept with their arms ready and the cavalry, instead of hitching the horses in lines, slept with them beside them, with shields as pillows and armour for blankets. Edward's groom was careless and the great war horse stood on the king breaking two of his ribs. In the dark rumour went round that the King was injured, so Edward, aged 58 and with broken ribs, mounted painfully and ordered the advance before dawn.

Wallace had never intended a pitched battle, but his plans were badly upset by the night advance of the English. He drew up his army and reluctantly ordered the deploy to battle formation. Although hurried he chose the ground well, a ridge above a small stream where the ground was heavy and boggy, impassable for heavy horses, about four miles south of Falkirk.

Edward hesitated before attacking, wanting his tired hungry troops to have a much-needed meal. The Barons objected and demanded immediate attack when there was only a small stream between them and the Scots. First Edward sent forward the Welsh archers but, still resentful over their rough treatment earlier, they refused to be treated as spear fodder. Therefore the knights charged but found what they had not earlier noticed, that green grass hid the boggy ground. The first wave went west to go round the bog and the second wave, going slower, went to the east. The Scots were facing roughly south and the English were advancing northwards. The Scots had drawn up into four schiltrons, circular and consisting of two ranks of men facing out with 12ft spears. The front rank crouched with the spears slanting upwards, the second rank stood with their spears inclined over the heads of their comrades. The spaces between the schiltrons were occupied by the Border bowmen commanded by Sir James Stewart. The cavalry were in the rear ready to give chase when the invaders broke.

This strategy has been criticised, but it was exactly the strategy used by the Duke of Wellington at Waterloo. The main difference between the battles two millennium apart, was that the artillery of 1815 was not as accurate or deadly as the English archery of 1298. It was not the heavy armoured cavalry that broke the schiltrons, but the Welsh and Lancastrian longbowmen. The longbow was a relatively new weapon, so deadly and capable of upsetting the tenets of medieval chivalry, it was at first condemned as illegal and regarded with the same horror reserved in a later age for poison gas used in the First World War.

Wallace's incessant drilling of his men paid off. The Schiltrons stood firm. The spearmen, to their credit, showed courage and resolution and against their wicked steel points all the gallantry and dash of the experienced cavalry came to grief. Edward committed the main body of his infantry, which had a considerable body of Lancastrian longbowmen, and their deadly arrows succeeded where the cavalry had failed. The shower of arrows and missiles thrown by foot soldiers crossing the stony ground did the damage. The Scots cavalry fled the field so were not there to assault the foot soldiers. As the hail of arrows and stones fell the schiltrons wavered and finally broke, thus enabling the English cavalry to charge and despatch the spearmen. The second wave of cavalry, which had worked round to the rear of the Scots, now charged into the fleeing spearmen. William Wallace and the remnants of his army withdrew to the north, many drowning trying to cross the River Carron. It was estimated 10,000 Scots were killed, including Sir

John Stewart, Sir John Graham and MacDuff of Fife. Although the battle was an English victory it was quite indecisive. Edward had succeeded in killing thousands of commoners but from the drop in his infantry wages he also lost a great many soldiers. Edward dismissed his foot soldiers and sent his cavalry to find the Scots fugitives.

Sir William Wallace resigned the Guardianship of Scotland after Falkirk, and for the next seven years went back to guerrilla warfare with his band of men, and made several visits for Scotland to the continent visiting Paris, Rome and Norway on behalf of the Scots government and cause. Robert Bruce, Earl of Carrick and John Comyn were joint Guardians of Scotland, despite their traditional hostility. The Scots had been allies of Philip of France since 1295, and when King Philip made peace with King Edward I, they expected to be included in the peace agreement, but Edward vetoed this. He did release John Balliol to the Pope's representatives. This gave the Scots heart, but the Bruce supporters were disappointed. Within a week of John Balliol's release the tension between the two Guardians boiled over at a meeting at Peebles on 19th August, when an argument broke out, then a fight. John Comyn leapt at the Earl of Carrick and seized him by the throat, reported an English spy.

The English commanders had a hard time. Supplies were constantly running low, wages were in arrears and garrisons threatened to desert or mutiny – all aggravated by the natives, who seized crops and horses as often as they could. Edward's first target was Stirling Castle which fell in two weeks. His second target was to capture Robert Bruce but, when Edward rode into Carrick, his quarry had flown. The Ayr rendezvous with Edward's fleet failed to happen and he was forced to cut short his operations. Even horses were dying from lack of food, although they would have provided some food for the troops. Records report that few of the horses made it back to Carlisle, which must have been a great loss, given the market value of a fully-trained battle charger. More men were dying of illness and disease than were being killed by the enemy. The 1298 campaign ending failed to subjugate the Scots. Edward marched by Jedburgh towards the border, crossing back to England in October. He knew only a full-scale invasion would suffice in Scotland.

At the end of July 1299 Philip of France made a permanent peace with Edward. The Prince of Wales was to marry Philip's daughter Isabella, the wedding to wait until the three-year-old child was old enough while Edward, a widower, was to marry Philip's 17-year-old sister Princess Margaret. A week after his wedding Edward ordered a muster in York for 12th November. He was determined he would conquer Scotland as he had Wales.

Supplies were stocked at Berwick and Carlisle. Few rallied to his muster. Edward had failed to sign charters and nobles even contested the traditional obligation of service based on tenure. In 1300 one Hugh Fitz Henry, a landowner in Shropshire was obliged by the terms of his tenure to serve the king with 'bow and arrow'. It was noted he saw the enemy, shot his arrow and went home.

The army finally mustered at Carlisle at midsummer 1300. 17,000 mounted men and the infantry was half the expected numbers, partly due to Edward's royal finances. The Welsh, who had formed 40% of the infantry at Falkirk, were ordered to stay at home. The strategy was to go up the south-west route by Dumfries and Galloway to north Ayrshire, laying waste to the Earl of Carrick's lands on the way.

An early success was a small victory at Caerlaverock on the Solway, when naval equipment caused the surrender of the castle. Then the war effort started to go wrong. The infantry deserted in droves and, on 27th July at Dumfries, orders were given that all fugitives be arrested. As the haemorrhage continued replacements were sent for.

The Scots wisely avoided battle and watched as the enemy evaporated. By the time Edward caught up with them half his army had gone. By the end of August Edward drew his depleted forces south of Dumfries at Sweetheart Abbey (founded by John Balliol's mother). The Archbishop of Canterbury arrived with a papal letter from Pope Boniface, ordering him to leave the Scots alone. Cold weather setting in and the army crumbling away, Edward dismissed the remaining troops and took ship south from the Solway Firth. The cavalry, obliged to serve at their own cost, stayed the course: it was the infantry, starved of food and wages, who deserted right from the start and ultimately destroyed the 1300 English campaign.

Edward stayed in Cumbria, joined by his wife Queen Margaret, newly delivered of a son (Thomas) born in Yorkshire. Edwards's last act before going south was, with distaste, to make a truce for six months with the Scots, scoffing at their suggestion of a permanent peace. He promised to return in the spring to lay Scotland to waste from sea to sea.

Edward of Caernarfon, Prince of Wales, was now a tall, good-looking 17-year-old, and his father decided to transfer some authority to him. In the new campaign he would be in charge of a separate army up the west and the King would go east and advance to meet in a pincer movement to Stirling. This was to be a decisive campaign in 1301.

A thousand landowners were summoned to muster along with 7,500 infantry drawn from Wales and the Marches, 650 horse from Ireland and 1,000 extra foot, induced by pardon from debt to the crown. The Prince of Wales made an impressive start and at midsummer marched straight up the western coast line to link up with the Irish allies. Bruce's castle at Ayr fell and so did his birth place, Turnberry Castle. The Scots mustered their forces at Loudoun Hill, and prevented the two armies uniting their armies on the Clyde coast.

Edward made slow progress from his base at Berwick, crossing inland and hacking his way through the vast Selkirk Forest. By 21st August he reached Glasgow. The two armies were now only twenty miles apart and in communication. The Prince of Wales never closed in as on 7th September a Scots army appeared outside Lochmaben and besieged the garrison there, causing the Prince of Wales to turn south to support the garrison. Edward was meanwhile beset with his familiar problem of dwindling resources. On 28th August crossbowmen and archers at Berwick mutinied, having had no wages for a month. By early September, when he began to besiege Bothwell's mighty stone fortress, two-thirds of Edward's infantry had deserted.

Two weeks later, having reduced Bothwell, Edward decided to go for broke and set out for Stirling with his remaining army. His officials tried to procure effective siege engines and other equipment to mount a siege, but with difficulty. In the end, short of supplies, Edward was forced to stop at Dunipace, six miles short of his target of Stirling and for three weeks he waited for fresh supplies, his anger mounting. The failure of the 1301 to 'reach an honourable, satisfactory conclusion', 'was not due to bureaucratic inefficiency but with executive impatience'.

The Scots regrouped in Selkirk Forest. Turnberry was seized by them and Ayr feared they were next. The Prince of Wales, his own army frittered away and the Irish allies long gone, having sailed home, was himself back in Carlisle. John Balliol had been released by the Pope and was now enjoying life in northern France. Philip was playing the Scots card and Edward called his bluff, agreeing to a peace if French troops defended his Scots gains, knowing the French would never send troops to Scotland. A peace was made in February 1302, leaving the Scots out on their own.

Edward had decided to winter in Scotland, and despite shortages he managed to sustain an impressive show of strength at Linlithgow, joined by the Prince of Wales and his Queen, delivered of another son, Edmund. The truce came to a successful conclusion for Edward, which meant his gains in Scotland were secure. The Pope, while keeping in with Edward, dropped support for Scotland.

Edward left no stone unturned in his preparation of his spring offensive. Every available financial recourse was squeezed and every source of manpower summoned. Ten thousand were demanded from the north of England, and 3,500 men embarked on 173 ships from Ireland, the largest naval force the island had ever seen.

Edward demanded of the Scots new obedience. Robert Bruce was ordered to turn out 2,000 foot and as many cavalry as he could muster. Fifty carpenters at Kings Lynn built a pontoon bridge of three different sized, each with drawbridges and giant crossbows. It took 30 ships to ferry them to the Firth of Forth. (It was never proved that this feat of medieval engineering was actually used.) The army mustering on the border in May reached Linlithgow on 6th June. They advanced north sweeping through Stirling to Perth, and followed the east coast, arriving in Montrose in late July, making rendezvous with provision ships there. All the while he destroyed everything in his path: hamlets, towns, and granges, barns both full and empty, taking plunder and burning. Edward hit hard because he knew his chances in a war of endurance were weak. By 23rd August he reached Aberdeen, where he had an anxious wait for his ships carrying coin to pay the infantry, already reduced to half the number he started with. By mid-September he was at the shores of the Moray Firth, the most northerly point of his devastating progress. A week later he laid siege to John Comyn's castle at Lochindorb, which fell in early October.

Comyn himself, the sole Guardian of Scotland, was still active in central Scotland raiding English positions with 100 horse and 1,000 foot soldiers. The Scots decided not to fight in open battle (as they had at Falkirk) but by attrition, victory going to the side that meted out the most damage, pain and suffering in the territory of the other.

In September it was hoped more Scots would come in to surrender to Edward. However, when those in question approached the English camp at Linlithgow and took one look at its starving Irish garrison, they concluded their enemies were on the verge of collapse, and went home again. Yet in spite of its apparent exhaustion English power prevailed.

Edward wintered his army by Dunfermline Abbey. On his return from harrying the north his forces were too weak to carry out his intention of taking Stirling Castle, but he made it clear he was not going to retire south again. While he settled in for the winter at Dunfermline, the Prince of Wales established his army at Perth. Both sites were important to the Scots, their kings buried at Dunfermline and crowned at Scone Abbey near Perth. Edward stole the Stone of Destiny, on which the Scots' kings were crowned at Scone, and had it placed at Westminster Abbey.

For seven years the Scottish Kingdom had been without a king. All that time they had fought in the name of King John Balliol, but now they were certain their king was not coming back. With winter setting in so did despair. John Comyn and his allies surrendered early in the new year of 1304, having negotiated a deal with Edward for no loss of life, limb, land or liberty. Edward had thought the Scots would be conquered in a summer but now, seven years later, these men had earned his respect. Comyn and 130 landowners knelt and swore allegiance to Edward in an especially convened parliament at St Andrews in March.

This only left Stirling Castle to be reduced. Edward sent for artillery from every quarter and ordered lead from as far as Perth and St Andrews to be stripped from church roofs to make counterweights to give the trebuchets their tremendous hurling power. Reducing the castle took months, and is one of the earliest records of 'Greek Fire' (i.e. gunpowder) used in Britain. After 12 weeks of bombardment the garrison indicated their willingness to surrender. However Edward had built a giant trebuchet, the work of 50 men for two months, and wished to see this machine, named 'War Wolf', at work, so insisted on no surrender until he had bombarded with it. Finally on 24th July a surrender was accepted with life and limb granted. Edward felt that he had finally subdued Scotland.

The terms of capitulation were remarkably lenient, probably because Edward was in an indulgent mood,

Sir William Wallace alone was not included in the peace, Edward placing a reward of 300 marks to the man bringing him Wallace's head. William went into hiding. Edward was implacable on a complete submission, an unconditional surrender by Wallace. William Wallace remained true to himself, the only Scots leader who never wavered in his allegiance to his King (John) and country, and would have found the surrender to the English king impossible. In March 1304 King Edward moved out of Dunfermline Abbey, ordering the Abbey destroyed as he left it, even though his sister and her husband, his friend, were buried there.

Sometime during that month the guerrilla band led by Sir William Wallace was defeated in a bloody encounter near Stobbo in Peeblesshire by a large English force. A fellow Scot tracked Wallace down and received 10 shillings as a reward. It was Sir William Wallace's last fight. Edward continued to harbour a vindictive grudge against Wallace. In February 1305 he released from custody Ralph de Halliburton, who had been captured at the siege of Stirling Castle. Put in charge of Sir John de Mowbray, one of the Scottish quislings now working for Edward, Hallliburton was returned to Scotland to hunt down the outlawed Sir William Wallace.

Scotland was struggling under the mailed fist of the conqueror. English sheriffs, provosts, sergeants, constables and tax-gatherers were busy repairing castles, re-fortification of burghs and restoration of their law and order. To this end the English depended on a large amount of spies from the native people. This was to prepare Scotland to be declared merely a 'land' and not a kingdom by September 1305. After Stirling fell Edward had detached 300 archers and a brigade of cavalry to go after William Wallace. Robert Bruce was appointed to help Sir John Segrave, the new Warden of Scotland. Bruce may have been playing a double game, and have sent messages warning the guerrillas of English movements. It was recorded in 1305 that Bruce came under suspicion and his arrest was imminent when he received warning, and fled from London.

Sir John Monteith had been taken prisoner at Dunbar, changed sides and fought for Edward in Flanders. In 1298 he returned to Scotland and espoused the national cause, certainly until 1303. He subsequently joined Edward once more and six months later was promoted to King Edward's service. He was chosen to apprehend Wallace because he was known to William, who was godfather to both of Monteith's sons.

Sir William Wallace was at Robroyston, a remote farmstead near Glasgow, where he expected a meeting with Robert Bruce. A spy in Wallace's band told Monteith, who moved in with sixty men while Wallace slept. The spy had removed Wallace's weapons, and Wallace was taken after fighting with his bare hands injuring many of his attackers. Conveyed south, Wallace was betrayed and handed over to Sir Segrave to take to London. As a reward for his night's dirty work Monteith received grants worth £100-£150 in annual rents, and he was appointed one of the ten Scots commissioners to attend Edward's parliament mid-September 1305, to negotiate regulations for the government of Scotland. On 16th June 1306 Edward gave him the revenues of the Bishopric of Glasgow, and the same day granted him the title and earldom of Lennox.

Sir William Wallace was taken south to London, mocked and humiliated on the way, arriving on the afternoon of 22nd August, and was housed in an Alderman's house. Next morning Wallace was taken to Westminster to a mock trial – his fate already decided. Placed on a bench with a laurel wreath on his head, there was no debate by the commissioners, no retiring jury, and apart for an outburst 'that he was no traitor as he had never sworn his oath to King Edward' but admitted the other charges, Wallace was not allowed any part of the trial. Wallace was sentenced for treason, the standard punishment for this (11th until 19th centuries) was to be hanged, drawn and quartered.

The sentence was carried out within the same day. Tied naked, face upwards, head pointing down towards the ground on a hurdle drawn by two horses, for four miles by a route chosen for maximum exposure to a scoffing crowd pelting him with offal, garbage and excrement as the hurdle bounced along the dusty cobbled streets. The hurdle finally came to a halt at what is now King Street in Smithfield. Wallace, barely conscious, had his legs unshackled and was dragged to the foot of the gallows. He requested a priest for his confession after which, his hands still securely bound behind his back, he was forced to mount the ladder.

Before the invention of drop gallows, hanging was an excruciatingly slow death by strangulation, which could take 20 minutes or more before the victim died. The hangman took care to ensure the running noose was at the side, and not at the back so the neck would not be broken. The executioner cut the rope before the victim went into his death throes, before being revived by having water thrown over them to ensure they were conscious. They were then castrated and a deep gash to the belly exposed the intestine which was then burned in front of them. Only then did the executioner reach into the chest cavity and pluck out the pulsating heart, and the body was then decapitated.

Sir John Segrave now had the difficult project of taking the body parts to their destinations. The head, dipped in pitch to preserve it, was placed on London Bridge; the right arm sent to Newcastle on Tyne, the left arm to Stirling, the right leg to Berwick and the left leg to Perth, all to be hung on display to show what happened to those who opposed King Edward of England.

Edward had just committed the supreme folly of giving the Scots a martyr. His death gave Sir William Wallace immortality, and his spirit rallied the people and made them a nation more surely than a decade of oppression. Exactly seven months later Robert Bruce, Earl of Carrick was crowned King of Scots.

In February 1306 Edward, aged 66 years and 8 months, had lived longer than any other previous reigning king of England. (Henry I died at 66 years and 7 months). Although he remained fit and healthy for his age, the constant Scottish Campaigns had left him feeling drained and in need of a long convalescence, but he had since rallied again and recovered his strength. A Crusade was being planned and Edward had a letter of invitation, and was looking forward to taking part in it. However, within the week news of a murder changed his plans.

Scotland was in confusion after a generation had been divided between the Bruce and Balliol claims to the throne. In February at the Franciscan Church in Dumfries two men had gone to talk. The conversation became an argument, a quarrel that ended in bloodshed. An impulsive unpremeditated act in which one drew a dagger and stabbed the other, his friends rushing into the church and finishing the victim off with their swords. The victim was John Comyn and the attacker Robert Bruce.

Robert Bruce's father had died and Robert was preparing to activate his claim to the Scottish throne. Comyn had been asked to join him and refused. Thereafter Bruce had to act fast. He rapidly secured control of the south-west of Scotland, rode into Glasgow where the Archbishop Robert Wishart absolved him of his crime, and produced the regalia and banner of the Royal Scottish arms urging him on to Scone. When Bruce arrived at Scone in March a sizeable number of nobles and clergy were assembled. He was crowned King Robert 1 of Scotland at Scone Abbey and Scotland proclaimed a kingdom once more.

When Edward heard about the proclamation he was incandescent with rage – this news might even have contributed to the sudden decline in his health. In the New Year he was in good shape for his age but by March was confined to Winchester for two months, and when he left in mid-May he had to be carried in a litter. Edward realised he must look to others to resume the struggle. Most contemporaries were gone (the Earl of Surrey had died in 1304 soon after his return from Scotland). The burden of leadership had to fall on the Prince of Wales. Their arguments of previous years would have to be forgotten. Edward, Prince of Wales was announced as commander of the main English army to assemble at Carlisle in July. To give the prince status he was knighted and granted Gascony.

The English advanced, scored victories and crossed the Forth. Bruce was almost captured at Methven near Perth; he retreated to the hills but many Scots were killed. Bruce sent his brother Neil to take his wife and daughter north to Orkney, while he went south-west.

Meanwhile Edward had set out to join his army, but after ten days had only covered thirty miles. He kept going for weeks in considerable pain. His reserves of clemency and mercy were exhausted and he thought his compromises to subjugate the Scots and his generosity were being flung back in his face. His only thought was for vengeance. He ordered his commanders to take no prisoners, neither noble nor clerical.

By mid-August King Edward was in Northumbria and very ill. He rested at Hexham Abbey, for two weeks lying motionless. He ominously made land over to his younger children from his second marriage, including the new baby daughter Eleanor. Then he rallied and the court made slow progress towards Carlisle. On 28th September 1306, it was decided King Edward should go no further. The court had reached Laner Coist Priory.

In any case the war was almost over. Scotland was under English control again and Bruce's womenfolk captured at Tain by some of the Balliol-Comyn cause and sent south to England. Neil was hung, drawn and quartered at Berwick, Athol condemned to a similar death in London (the only earl to be executed in England for 230 years). The Countess of Buchan, who had crowned Bruce, and his sister Mary were hung from specially constructed cages from Roxburgh and Berwick castles in all weathers as a spectacle to those who rebelled against King Edward.

In February 1307 a furious row erupted between King Edward and his son the Prince of Wales. Edward saw his son had an 'inordinate love for a certain Gascon knight Piers Gaveston'. The relationship was construed as homosexual and regarded by his subjects as inappropriate behaviour. King Edward's rage was not only at his son, or that of a dying man, but anger caused by the return of Robert Bruce at the start of February. Thomas and Alexander Bruce had led a raid in Galloway, and were captured. Both were hanged and beheaded, but Bruce himself evaded capture. It was not the caution of Edward's lieutenants that caused the difficulties, but the lack of restraint to which Edward had now urged on them. The English king's savage policy of revenge had driven many Scots, who may have submitted to English justice, into supporting his enemies.

Robert Bruce had left Scotland for Ireland in 1306 as an unpopular rebel, and returned in 1307 as a saviour. He repulsed the English in Galloway at Loch Trool and, although a minor English loss, their invincibility was dented. In the next two months he gained recruits and won victory at Loundon Hill on 10th May. The English commanders escaped but their invincibility was now shattered.

The Prince of Wales was in Dover saying goodbye to Piers Gaveston, who was now sailing into exile on the King's orders. and the Prince was in no hurry to return to the war zone.

King Edward inevitably ordered more troops and a new muster at Carlisle in July. His health declined again. He was now suffering from dysentery, the doctors using cordials and ointments to treat it. He passed his 68th birthday in mid-July. About 24th June, three weeks before the muster was due, and to still rumours of his death, King Edward ordered the advance of the assembled host (about half the expected men) with himself as leader instead of his feckless son. Rejecting a litter, the king mounted his war horse and rode out at the head of his army. He headed west out of Carlisle to sail across the Solway Firth, but after ten days had only covered six miles.

On July 6th he was forced to stop at Burgh by Sands, and in this windswept isolated settlement King Edward I of England spent his last night on earth. In the morning, as his attendants appeared to help him eat, he died in their arms. His death was kept a closely-guarded secret. The Prince of Wales had been sent a letter telling of his father's death on 11th July, but it was not until 20th July his rule was actually proclaimed at Carlisle. Edward II did come to Carlisle to lead the abandoned host, but in less than a month he was back in the south to deal with his father's funeral. England was in despair at the loss of King Edward, and had little faith in his son's ability to rule the country.

In Scotland the English failure was most dramatic and the legacy of bitterness lasted for centuries. The final decade of Edward's campaign had been cruel and harsh, throwing the Scots into the arms of his enemy Bruce. Before 1290 Scots christened their sons Edward. Robert Bruce's only surviving brother and Balliol's eldest son were both named Edward. By 1307 the Scots regarded Edward as the 'covetous King' of Merlin's prophecy. The swiftness with which English power in the British Isles contracted after Edward I's death was due partly to the incompetence of his successor, whose behaviour even before his coronation was giving much concern to his subjects.

Yet in Scotland itself the tide was turning. King Robert Bruce overcame his domestic opponents and consolidated his rule. English garrisons fell one by one under his forces.

In 1314, after mustering on 10th June at Berwick, an English army appeared north of the border to save Stirling Castle, which was under siege. In the summer of 1313 the English Governor, Sir Philip Moubray, made an agreement with Edward Bruce, commander of the besieging Scots, that 'if an English army had not relieved the garrison with a year he would surrender the Castle'. So Edward II stopped quarrelling with his barons in order to save Stirling Castle. This challenge would force the Scots into the open to fight a pitched battle, the kind of battle the English had a better chance of winning. The English host consisted of two thousand mounted knights and fifteen thousand infantry, including the son of the murdered Comyn. A fleet of ships from almost every English port sailed off shore accompanying the army northwards.

King Robert I had an army of five thousand spearmen and archers and five hundred knights, on lighter horses than the English war horses. The men had fought for the last seven years under their King Robert and respected him. They mustered at Torwood south of Stirling. The English, approaching from the south, would have to cross the Bannock burn in its narrow defile. Sir Philip Moubray would break the rules of the time, having made his agreement that, if he attacked from the castle, he would be considered as a 'false knight'.

The Scots were looking east towards the River Forth, over the broad flat carse of Stirling, then known as the Pows. Although parts were dry in summer it was covered by peat bogs and burns, of which Bannockburn was by far the biggest. The Scots dug small pits on the sides of the road the English would come along, filling the ditches with sticks and grass which would cause the English knights to have to bunch up.

On Saturday 22nd June the Scottish scouts sighted the English army approaching Falkirk. They had travelled from Berwick five days earlier with little rest, marching twenty miles a day, but the troops were in good shape.

The Scots had moved into positions at New Park, nearer Stirling. They were arranged in four divisions, the vanguard under Randolph; two others under Edward Bruce and Sir James Douglas, while Robert Bruce commanded the rear himself. Out of sight in the valley the camp followers were safely settled.

The English were led by the Earl of Gloucester, Constable of England, and the Earl of Hereford, their vanguard made up of dashing young and eager knights. Seeing the Scots appearing to retreat, they spurred their horses towards the enemy. One such eager young knight, Henry de Bohun sped clear of the others and made straight for King Robert. Robert was mounted on a palfrey, not his war horse, so de Bohun saw him as an easy target and charged. Robert, on the smaller and more nimble horse, avoided the great war horse's charge and, wheeling round and standing in his stirrups, he hit de Bohun a deadly blow with his axe, breaking both the axe and the English knight's skull. This was only part of a short skirmish between the English vanguard and the Scots rear guard and when Edward Bruce's division joined in the English were forced back.

Meanwhile about 300 English knights under Sir Robert Clifford set off over the carse to try to ride round the Scots flank. King Robert, seeing the situation, quickly sent Randolph to halt them and near St Ninian's Kirk the Scots spearmen formed a schiltron. The English could not resist this chance to wipe out some of the enemy, charged but could not break the ranks. Some were knocked off their horses; many were captured or fled back to their own lines. Twice in one day the Scots infantry had thrown back the English cavalry. This raised the morale of the Scots army.

King Edward II had arrived with the rest of the English army but the men and horses needed food and rest. During Sunday evening the English army began to cross the Bannockburn on open ground down the carse and rested. In the half-light of midsummer's eve there was little sleep for the English soldiers. They were rather depressed because of the two defeats in one day and the chance of an attack before dawn.

If they had only known the Scottish leaders were planning to retreat to the west when Alexander Seaton changed sides and came to King Robert, telling him the state of the English army. King Robert then decided to stay and fight. During the night the English cavalry moved up to the firmer ground of the carse, between Bannockburn and Pelstream. King Robert saw that his enemies were now in a narrow space and ordered the advance to address the situation. The Scots advanced at dawn, in their four divisions. The English could hardly believe the Scots army were risking an open battle, mere spearmen against an army of horseman. Hurriedly they made ready.

The fighting began with each side firing a salvo of arrows, the English long-bow superior to the Scots bows, and at the start the English scored heavily. As Bruce's men advanced and the English vanguard charged, the Scots formed a schiltron and threw them back. Under the stress of the Scots resistance the English disintegrated and their commander, the Earl of Gloucester, was killed. Now Randolph and Douglas moved up with their divisions against the rest of the English army, but so pressed together were the English between Bannockburn and the Pelstream they got in each other's way. Relentlessly the Scottish schiltrons pressed forward and helplessly the English cavalry stumbled and floundered. Some of the English archers managed to pull themselves out of the struggling mass of horses and knights, but King Robert had foreseen this danger and sent Sir Robert Keith with his five hundred light cavalry to charge them. Once the English archers were knocked out of the battle the Scots victory was assured. Now Bruce unleashed his men from Carrick and the Isles, who aggressively plunged into the fray with shouts mainly in Gaelic. The English were thrown back into even greater confusion amongst the streams and pools of the carse. Then worse, a fresh army seemed to appear which annihilated the English army. King Edward II, who had fought gallantly alongside his troops, was persuaded to flee for safety. Off he went, Douglas in hot pursuit, and with no refuge to be had at Stirling rode fast to Dunbar and took ship for Berwick.

The assumed fresh army were the camp followers come to see how the battle was going, but the tide turned, and the close run battle became a colossal defeat for the English. Many were killed as they fled south, the nobles more fortunately being held to ransom. The Earl of Hereford as released in exchange for King Robert's wife and daughter, his sister and Bishop Wishart of Glasgow. Over £200,000 of valuable equipment (equivalent to millions today) was captured, and Stirling Castle surrendered to King Robert. They did not realise it at the time but this battle made the Scots a free people again. They had vindicated their right to independence.

The English could not admit to this, and it was not until 1328 that they recognised that Scotland was an independent country, by which time Edward II had been put off the throne, brutally murdered, and his young son Edward III crowned. The Scots sent a letter to the Pope in 1320 declaring their determination; it was called the Declaration of Arbroath. A peace was eventually made and Edward III's sister Joan married King Robert's son David. The English agreed to return the Stone of Destiny, but the citizens of London refused to release it.

Robert the Bruce, King Robert I, ruled wisely. He died on 7th June 1329 at Cardross in his new house on the shores of the Firth of Clyde.

SIR MICHAEL BALFOUR of Balfour, Knight Sheriff of Fife, sat as a Baron of Parliament at Ayr on 6th April 1315, along with David de Balfour. David and Malcolm de Balfour attended the Parliament at Cambuskenneth on 6th November 1314. His son John succeeded him. Sir John's daughter Janet succeeded as her brother Sir John Balfour of Balfor died without issue in 1375. She was made a ward of the Crown, and given in marriage to Sir Robert de Betun, and their descendents are the Bethunes of Balfour.

Sir John Balfor, whose daughter had married Robert de Bethune, had a brother Adam, who married the granddaughter of Macduff, brother of Colbane Earl of Fife and obtained with her the lands of Pittencreiff. He died of wounds received at the Battle of Durham in 1346, and was buried at Melrose.

His son Sir Michael Balfour was brought up by his kinsman Duncan, 12th Earl of Fife, who in 1353 gave in exchange for Pittencrieff the much more valuable lands of Montwhanney. The Countess Isabella, daughter of Earl Duncan, also bestowed many grants upon her "cousin" Sir Michael. At her death Sir Michael should have succeeded as her nearest heir. However the Regent Albany, brother of her second husband, obtained the earldom in virtue of a disposition in favour by the countess. Sir Michael died in 1385. His eldest son Michael of Mountwhanney had a son, Sir Lawrence of Strathmore and Montwhanney. Sir Lawrence and his wife Marjory had three sons: George (his heir), John of Balgarvy and David of Carraldstone or Carriston.

James Balfour, son of Sir John Balfour of Balgarvey, obtained in 1451 from King James II the lands of Denmylie, in the parish of Abdie, Fife. The lands had originally belonged to the Earls of Fife and fell to the Crown on the forfeiture of Murdoch, Duke of Albany. This James Balfour was slain at the siege of Roxburgh, soon after the death of James II. In 1460 a charter, granted by King James III in favour of John Balfour, his son, who married Christian Sibbald, daughter of Peter Sibbald of Rankeillor, and fell with his sovereign James IV at the Battle of Flodden in 1513.

His elder brother Michael Balfour of Balfour died in 1490 leaving a son David, who died in 1527, and it is with his son John we pick up the story.

Balfour of Burleigh and Tillyrie

In 1445-6 Sir John Balfour was granted the lands of Balgarvie by King James II. Balgarvie Castle was located near Cupar, Fife. (It was much later sold to Earl Melville, and was demolished circa 1938-40.) Sir John and his wife Margaret both held office in the Royal Household. Sir John died in 1542.

Their son Michael received a Feu Carter of the lands of Burleigh and Tillyrie in 1456. In 1502 the same Michael received Charters of the lands of Monchester, Dullatur and Portbank, and in 1506 the lands of Easter and Wester Balgarvie with Mill of Sleoch near Bannockburn. On his marriage to Agnes, daughter of Forrester of Corstorphine in 1512, he also acquired the lands of Shanwell in Orwell Parish.

In 1469, at the age of eighteen, King James III married Margaret of Denmark and Norway and the lands of Orkney and Shetland came to Scotland as her dowry.

Sir Michael probably built a wooden manor house at Burleigh, and started building a stone Tower House in the late 1480s. This was finished about 1500 and still stands today.

Castles were first built in France in the 900s. Until this time battles were fought on foot, but horses were introduced into the equation and knights started to ride them into battle. Having twice in my life been run down by galloping horses it is a frightening experience and one to be avoided, so this must have been alarming to the infantry. Castles (from the Latin 'castellum' meaning a camp or building fortified for defence) were then built for shelter, defence and quarters for the population and their animals. They were also a statement of strength and the right to rule.

Stone castles were introduced into England with the Norman invasion in 1066. Norman knights had been welcome in Scotland since the time of King Macbeth (1040-1057). However it was not until the Canmore brothers Alexander I and David I came home from captivity in England and brought many Norman knights north with them (approx 1100-1153) that stone castles became more prolific. The brothers had been south in the court of King William II, then his son Henry I married the Canmore's sister Edith, and Alexander married Sybil, daughter of Henry

BALFOURS OF BURLEIGH

SIR WILLIAM BALFOR OF STRATH-ORR *inherited from his grandfather*

SIR HENRY DE BALFOR *Sheriff of Fife*

SIR JOHN DE BALFOR - *died at sack of Berwick march 1296*

John

Son Died   Daughter (*Ward of Court M=Bethune*)

Adam *m=Granddaughter of Earl Of Fife*

Michael Balfour of Pittencreiff

Michael Balfour of Mountwhinney *d. 1385*

St Lawrence of Strathmore and Mountwhinney *m=Marjory*

George (*Heir*)   John of Balgary   David of Carrieton

Michael *d1490*

James of Denmylie *d1460, siege of Roxburgh*

John *m= Christine Sibbald; d1513, fell at Flodden*

David

Sir John Balfour of Balgarvie *d1542 m=Margaret*

Sir Michael Balfour of Burleigh, Tillyrie, East and West Balgarvie etc

Sir Michael Balfour, Coronel of Fife = Christian Bethune

Lady Margaret, Heiress of Burleigh = Sir James Balfour of Pitendreich *d1583*

Michael, 1st Lord Balfour   Alexander   Henry   William   David   and 3 daughters

1: Margaret Adamson

2: Margaret Lundin

Lady Margaret Balfour *heiress of Burleigh* = Robert Balfour (*nee Arnot of Fernie*) 2nd Lord Balfour

John 3rd Lord Balfour = Isobel Balfour of Pitcullo   Jean   Margaret   Isobel   daughter

d.27. 2.1697

Robert = Margaret Melville   John   Henry   Margaret   Aemilia   Jean   Susan   Anne

4th Lord *d1723*

Robert   Lady Margaret   Lady Mary = Sir Alexander Bruce of Bennetmaster of Burleigh *d1757*

Mistress Balfour of Burleigh *d1769*   of Kennet *d1758*

I. Both brothers had rich lands in England and had been educated in the Norman style. With this in mind the Tower House became popular in Scotland.

History had limited use of castles for war as stronger castles called for better siege machines and, as ever, man was inventive in doing this. Moats were built to prevent mining under the castle and bringing down the walls. The mangonel used since Roman times was modified in the 10th century by the Chinese to a triangular frame called a 'perrier', the throwing arm like a see-saw with a pivot close to the end of the beam sending the missiles skywards. The Arabs in the 12th century refined this to a more sophisticated version called a 'trebuchet', which had a large counter weight and could silently hurl massive loads long distances depending on the size of the machine. When cannons were invented they sounded the death knell of castles in battle, especially with the mortar pieces able to lob grenades of hollow iron balls 12 inches in diameter and 200lbs in weight, packed with gunpowder and lit by a fuse, which exploded inside the castle sending shrapnel flying in all directions, killing or maiming everything in a wide radius. (It did require skill from the gunner to judge how to fire it, and how long to make the fuse!) Not always reliable, they put the fear of death and panic into the defenders. Battles began to be fought in open fields, and castles were less about defence after that and more about status and homes.

King James II was the first Scottish monarch to have cannon, 'such an instrument called a gun' came as part of his wife's dowry from her native Flanders. James was very interested in cannon, Mons Meg in Edinburgh Castle being a favourite of his. This interest over the years eventually caused his death at Roxburgh. On 3rd August 1460 one of the wedges used to strengthen the iron bands round the barrel broke, flew in the air and struck the watching king in the face, killing him. He was not yet 30 and left Scotland with another minority heir.

So when Sir Michael built his Tower House or 'Barmkin', defence was less of

Mons Meg

The Tower House built by Sir Michael. Watercolour by Dorothy Thomson

an issue than status and a home. He could have windows in the outside walls, the walls five feet thick instead of twelve, the entrance at ground level with no port-cullis just a strong iron gate or 'yet', and the parapet walk without high stone loops to protect defenders while shooting, and the moat several yards from the walls of the tower. Tower Houses were built to be self contained, having not only bed-rooms, but also a hall, kitchen and storerooms. The vaulted basement remains, with turnpike stairs up from the entrance gate, and fireplaces, toilets, and indi-cations of where timber floors were built in the rooms above. It was three storeys high with a garret or cap-house giving access to the parapet walk. The views must have been stunning, and the completed Tower House a strong statement of wealth and power, and a state of art in its day.

The King in Scotland gave permission for castles to be built, giving land to knights to administer and protect the lands and people in times of peace, with local extensive police powers including the power to mutilate or even execute criminals. Unlike the English system where courts were all central to the King, in Scotland the king is King of the Scots, not of Scotland, and the king worked with his nobility, with local courts. Also, and unlike the English kings, the Scots king had no annual income from taxes. There was an explosion of castle building in the 15th and 16th centuries under the Stewart kings.

The son and heir to Sir Michael and Agnes nee Foster was another Sir Mi-chael of Burleigh, who was Coroner of Fife. In 1566 he received a Charter for half the lands of Kinloch on his marriage to Christian, daughter of John Bethune of Creich. They had one child, Margaret.

Margaret Balfour, heiress to the Barony of Burleigh, married the second son of Balfour of Pitendreich, and that is a chapter on its own.

Sir James Balfour
1525 – 1583

"Religion, because of the hatred it engenders, is difficult."

James Balfour was one of the most perplexing and difficult to judge people in the reign of Queen Mary. Born in 1525, he was the second son of Sir Michael Balfour of Montquannie and Pittencrieff. Sir Michael was lineally descended from the Sir Michael Balfour who obtained the lands of Montquannie in exchange for the lands of Pittencrieff by charter from King David II in 1353. He was a cousin of the Earl of Bothwell, and an early convert to Protestantism.

Sir Michael had four sons: Michael Baron of Montquannie, Commenter of Melrose and progenitor of Balfour of Trenaby in Orkney; James of Pittendreich, Gilbert, Governor of Orkney in 1567; and Robert who was granted the provisory of Kirk o' Field in 1566. They were second cousins to the Earl of Bothwell.

They were living in a turbulent time in Scottish history. The Reformation was causing shock waves throughout Europe and the death of King James V after Flodden left a baby girl as his heir, as a prize for power through marriage.

Cardinal Beaton

The first we hear of young James Balfour is in connection with two religious murders. By 1540 the Protestant Reformation began to be felt in Scotland, and religious affiliations became identified with political issues. The invention of the printing press spread word as never before. Catholics wanted to continue and strengthen the 'auld alliance' with France, and the Protestants wanted a closer relationship with the now Protestant England.

The trouble began when the 'heretic' George Wishart, a successful reforming preacher, was strangled and burned to death at St Andrews in February 1546, on the orders of Cardinal Beaton. On 28th May a group of Protestant landowners from Fife burst into Beaton's palace, hauled him from his bed and murdered him, stuffing his genitals into his mouth then throwing him in a barrel down the bottle dungeon of St Andrews Castle. The brothers James and Gilbert Balfour were implicated in this revenge murder.

The Protestant protesters held out for a year in St Andrews Castle, until French ships sailed in and bombarded them into submission. Amongst the prisoners taken and sentenced to two years as galley slaves were John Knox, a follower of Wishart, and James Balfour. The latter bought his freedom in 1549 by converting to Catholicism, for which Knox never forgave him, and called him 'an apostate and a traitor'.

The Martyrdom of George Wishart

When released Balfour trained for the law and became an outstanding ecclesiastical lawyer and judge. In 1561 Queen Mary appointed him Lord of Session and Clerk of Register in the Council in Edinburgh.

He married Lady Margaret Balfour, heiress to the Barony of Burleigh, and took the title thereafter in her name. They were to have three sons and six daughters in their long and seemingly happy marriage.

He was reputed to be a notorious blasphemer and cynic. Knox said he 'neither feared God nor loved virtue'. Sir James seemed to use religion to further his own ends. Reputedly he was untrustworthy, treacherous and corrupt and, like Regent Moray, good at covering his own tracks. The kingdom fought and Scots lords flexed their power in self-interest. It was a dangerous time to in which to live.

In 1561 Queen Mary appointed her Privy Council of 16 members, including Lord James Stewart (Regent while she had been in France), Maitland and seven others who would be prominent in her future, i.e. Duke of Chatelherault, Earls of Bothwell, Huntly, Argyll, Morton, Glencairn, Errol, along with Montrose, Marischa, and Lord Erskine. Huntly, a cousin of sorts to Mary, his mother being a bastard daughter of James V. James Stewart was her half-brother, and Argyll was married to Mary's only half-sister Jean Stewart. James IV left a prolific amount of bastards.

Mary I, Queen of Scots

Earl Morton was head of the powerful Douglas family. Robert Douglas of Loch Leven had acquired the lands of Kirkness (Kinross-shire) from the Prior of St Serfs, who in turn had received the lands from King Macbeth in 1095. Robert Douglas was killed at the Battle of Pinkie in 1547, and his eldest son inherited the barony, soon afterwards succeeding to the Earldom of Morton to be the 6th Earl Morton. He was a staunch Protestant and a pensioner of Queen Elizabeth of England. Said to be witty in worldly affairs and policy, he was crafty, illiterate, sadistic, unscrupulous and avaricious. The Queen was often repulsed by his uncouth and often brutal manners. He was also active and a good manager but his private life was tragic as his wife, having borne him ten children all of whom died young, she succumbed to insanity for the last two decades of her life. Earl Morton was a cousin to Lennox through Douglas' marriage to the dowager Queen Margaret Tudor a generation earlier.

Lord Darnley was the elder son of the Earl and Countess of Lennox, with a claim to the English crown, like Queen Mary, through their mutual grandmother Margaret Tudor. Cecil, the English spymaster, thought Darnley a 'political lightweight and a weather cock'. In 1564 when Darnley wished to go north to Scotland, Cecil thought Queen Elizabeth would get the blame for sending 'such a plague into Scotland' if he married Queen Mary, but would prove less dangerous to England than a foreign Catholic prince and may prove himself a liability to the Scots.

Darnley arrived in Scotland in February 1565 to woo Queen Mary. A tall (six feet two inches when the average height of men was then five feet six), he was slim and athletic with fair cropped hair, clean shaven and handsome in an effeminate way. This teenager was a good lute player, an elegant dancer who wrote poetry and a man of letters proficient in Latin and French. On the other hand, when bored or thwarted he became spoilt, wilful, petulant, immature and, at his worst, grossly uncouth. In fact he was unreliable and unstable with a violent temper, haughty, proud and very weak, being easily led.

Queen Mary was in Fife in February and Lord Darnley struggled through snow and winter weather to see her on the 17th at Wemyss Castle. Attracted by their mutual link to the English throne, Queen Mary found his attractive person pleasing as he courted her. The engagement was finally announced in May 1565. Moray and some of the Scots lords led a revolt on 1st July against the marriage to a catholic; this was encouraged and funded by Queen Elizabeth. They failed to capture Mary at Perth and rallied at Stirling on 6th July under Argyll. Mary and Darnley meanwhile went to Seton, then back to Edinburgh. On 12th July the Queen issued a proclamation that she did not intend to make any alterations to the state of religion in Scotland to settle rumours and fears of the Protestant population. Hearing this, Moray raised an army in the west and marched on Edinburgh. Mary summoned her lieges to arms and sent to Paris for the Earl of Bothwell to return, as he had always been loyal to the crown.

On 22nd July Mary created Darnley Duke of Albany, and had their banns published in St Giles Kirk, the Cannon Gate Kirk and the Chapel of Holyrood. Feeling she would be in a stronger position to deal with the rebels when married, the Queen wrote to the Pope protesting her determination to restore the Catholic Church in Scotland, asking for a disposition to marry her cousin Darnley and the Pope's support for her in Scotland. In this resolve she had the support of Darnley, Lennox, Rizzio and Clerk Register Sir James Balfour of Burleigh.

Having inherited Burleigh through his wife, Sir James speedily ingratiated himself with Darnley and had him often to stay at Burleigh to hunt and fish. In July 1565 Darnley persuaded the Queen to admit Sir James to the Privy Council. It was through the influence of Darnley that Sir James came to political prominence.

Their marriage arranged for 29th July, the Queen had Darnley publicly proclaimed King of Scots, which should legally have had the consent of Parliament, so causing offence, anger and further resentment with the Lords.

Early at dawn on 29th July Queen Mary was conveyed by Athol and Lennox to the Chapel Royal at Holyrood for a Catholic service of marriage. Mary then went on to mass but Darnley, careful not to offend the Protestants, did not go but waited for Mary in rooms. A 16-course banquet was held in the great hall in the afternoon, followed by dancing.

Henry Stuart, Lord Darnley

Queen Mary continued to pursue the rebels, and from 7-10th September was in Dunfermline Abbey raising support. Then, after a stop at Loch Leven Castle (which they had visited on honeymoon) to see Lady Douglas (Moray's mother, who had been a King's mistress before marrying Sir William Douglas), the queen demanded their loyalty and respect for her position.

On 12th September at Falkland Palace, the Queen imposed a Declaration of Obedience on all barons and gentlemen of Fife. After staying at St Andrews, she visited Dundee, Perth, Innerpeffray Abbey and on 16th September lodged with Ruthven, then returned to Dunfermline Abbey on 17th September, before returning to Edinburgh. There she was free of Moray's influence and ready to rule with the support of her chief advisors Athol (an honourable man and loyal to Queen Mary), Lennox and Bothwell.

The disposition from the Pope for the cousins to marry did not reach Edinburgh until September. Bothwell, who had always been loyal to Regent Queen Mary of Guise, the Queen's mother, now arrived back in Edinburgh from Paris, and was re-appointed Lieutenant-General of the Borders. Bothwell was one of the few Scots lords not in the pay of Cecil in England and had hatred of the English. He kept the borders loyal from expected English invasion. By 6th October Moray and the rebels were defeated at Dumfries, Moray fleeing to England.

The Lords were increasingly bitter that the Queen was taking advice from her Italian secretary Rizzio, and lesser men like Balfour. With the majority of the

David Rizzio

Lords hostile to Darnley, Lennox his father, Bothwell and Rizzio, Queen Mary was in a precarious situation of which she was unaware.

To make matters worse, only a few months into their marriage relations between Darnley and Mary were already deteriorating. The Queen increasingly saw the defects in Darnley, realising she had married a wilful, haughty, vicious bully, who was often drunk and a weak character. He also antagonised the Lords and further alienated them from her. Darnley's attitude and insolence to the Queen, and his vile temper, finally finished her respect for him. He was often away hunting and hawking at Peebles, Fife and Kinross-shire.

Darnley wanted the Crown Matrimonial more than anything else and was disillusioned with the marriage, mainly because of the Queen's refusal to bestow it upon him. (This would have made him king in his own right should anything happen to the Queen). His resentment festered, and he blamed the Queen's secretary Rizzio for her failure to bestow it.

On 31st October the English ambassador to Scotland, Randolph, reported to Cecil at the English court that Queen Mary was with child. About this time in early November the Queen suffered from great pains in her side and was confined to bed. Darnley stayed away hunting and hawking in Fife and Kinross. By 1st December Queen Mary had recovered, and was taking a great deal of exercise.

The Queen and Darnley were reunited at Linlithgow Palace, but Darnley was not pleased that the coming child excluded him from ever succeeding to the throne. It was not an overly joyous time. On Candlemas day Mary and Darnley attended high mass together at Holyrood. Bothwell and the other Lords went to hear Knox preach in St Giles.

In the New Year a plot to murder Rizzio was hatched by a group of Protestant lords, who believed Rizzio was in the way of Moray's return. According to Melville it was conceived by Morton, Ruthven and Lindsay with the Douglas's, who drew Darnley into it by playing on his jealousy of Rizzio and his conviction that it was Rizzio who prevented him having the Crown Matrimonial. All the Lords were anxious to see Moray return.

On 9th February Cecil, in a letter from Maitland, heard of the plot. Ambassador Randolph also knew, but the English did not lift a finger to prevent it. The plan included the Queen being taken to Stirling Castle as a prisoner and held there until after the birth. Darnley was to receive the Crown Matrimonial. Moray and the other exiled lords were to return, pardoned and reconciled with Darnley, who would then exert himself to maintain the Protestant church.

Morton and Ruthven wanted Rizzio killed in either his own chamber or the garden, playing tennis, or even publicly hanged. Darnley insisted that Rizzio be murdered in the Queen's presence at her own table. This was not just a vicious revenge, but in the hope that it would cause a miscarriage or Mary's death in childbirth, leaving him with the Crown Matrimonial as King in his own right. Darnley played into the lords' hands for they could charge him with this treason, which carried the death penalty. The plotters had to act before Parliament met again, as that was when the exiled lords would be attainted.

Knox, who had often spoken against Rizzio, knew of the plot and apparently gave it his blessing. Those not involved in the plot included Bothwell, Huntly, Athol, Balfour, Glencairn, Mar, Seton and Livingston, none of whom were aware of what was planned.

On the fatal evening of 10th or 11th May some of the Lords who had been in attendance on the Queen prior to the supper party – Athol, Tullibardine, Fleming, Livingston, Balfour and the Bishop of Ross – were allowed to leave the palace. Mary later told Archbishop Beaton that the plotters had meant to hang Balfour, as they thought it was him that was working to keep Moray in exile. Ruthven however said that Balfour had leave from the King to depart after supper from Holyrood. It is highly unlikely Darnley would have let them murder one of his most influential supporters.

The conspirators burst into the Queen's apartments. Darnley held Mary from behind with Ker of Fawdenside holding a pistol against her stomach. Rizzio was then stabbed by the others as he clutched the Queen's dress. Rizzio was murdered by multiple stabbings. The Queen, shocked and in fear of her own life, knew by nightfall that she was to be a captive and was in great danger. Told that Moray was on his way back to Scotland, she was left confined to her rooms with the dowager

James Stewart, Earl of Moray

Countess of Huntley and a few female servants for company.

Some loyal lords hearing the disturbance eventually managed to help Queen Mary escape by the garden. Darnley, capitulated by fear, came too and they all rode for safety, first to Seaton, then on fresh horses to the castle at Dunbar some 30 miles away. Bothwell in the borders and other loyal lords including Athol, Balfour, Bishop Leslie, John Hume, John Maxwell and Lord Herris massed a muster of 4,000 men and at Haddington on 18th March they were joined by Glencairn, Rothes, Maitland and some rebels seeking and receiving pardon.

On 20th March the Queen issued a writ summoning Morton, Ruthven, Lindsay, Fawdenside, George Douglas and 63 others to appear before the Privy Council to answer for their crimes on pain of outlawry. Morton was deposed as Chancellor and replaced by Huntly. Balfour replaced James MacGill as Clerk. Athol, Seton, Livingston and Fleming made up the strength of the new Privy Council.

Queen Mary's reputation suffered due to the murder of Rizzio and the prestige of the Crown was diminished. The public now became aware of the rift between the royal couple, which in itself was a scandal. The Queen could have had Darnley executed for treason but she needed to ensure that there was no doubt about her child's legitimacy. Darnley appeared before the Privy Council and signed a declaration that he had never counselled, consented or assisted in Rizzio's murder. He had only agreed without the Queen's consent that Moray be allowed to come home.

For the sake of the unborn child and her reputation Mary let it appear as if they were reconciled. While saying she 'forgives and forgets all', the Queen was bitterly hurt and convinced her life had been in danger. She understandably wanted as little contact with her husband as possible. On 29th March Morton and 60 others were outlawed, their lands and possessions seized by the crown. Moray as usual was playing a double game, asking Cecil in England to protect his friends as the fugitive lords fled south. When Darnley's declaration of innocence was heard of by the outlawed conspirators they were raging and determined to have their revenge.

By 2nd April Mary and Darnley were virtually estranged. On 18th June Queen Mary went into labour at Edinburgh Castle, and after 24 hours was delivered of a healthy son, James. Darnley visited Mary and desired to see the child. Mary had Darnley publicly declare the child James as his son.

James Hepburn,
4th Earl of Bothwell

At this time Darnley's chief ally in Scotland was Sir James Balfour. On 7th June Ambassador Randolph reported that 'Balfour was out of favour' and that 'Balfour's credit with the Queen is reflected in his friendship with Darnley'. Queen Mary granted Balfour's brother Robert the provisory of Kirk o' Fields houses between 5th and 10th December. Some think with hindsight this sinister, but it was not until several weeks later, and after other houses were rejected, that the King was lodged there.

At Craigmillar Castle in early December, Moray and Maitland devised a plot to rid themselves of Darnley which involved Argyll, Huntly, Bothwell and others. A bond was drawn up. Ormiston stated that Bothwell told him 'the subtle devious lawyer Sir James Balfour was enlisted to draw up the bond'. It would have been strange for Balfour to have instigated the plot against his fellow Catholic, unless he wished to distance himself from the disgraced King, or unless Balfour was playing a double game, which is possible. There have been theories that Balfour was, in fact, in league with Darnley to destroy the Protestant establishment in Scotland and he was luring them into a trap. It is important to keep this in mind when looking into Balfour's movements in the following weeks. The document signed by all in the plot is known as The Craigmillar Bond.

Prince James was christened in a Catholic ceremony at Stirling and a pardon issued after the baptism to Morton and his fellow rebels. Only two were exempt from the pardon, George Douglas and Ker of Fawdonside. Once back in Scotland the Lords had a score to settle with Darnley. The Queen put a condition on their return, to protect Darnley, that the lords involved could not come to court for two years.

Mary departed for Christmas with Lord Drummond at Drummond Castle. Darnley stole away to the safety of Lennox' heartland near Glasgow and there underwent treatment, as he was 'eaten up by a loathsome skin disease and general foulness of the body', probably syphilis.

Mary had been looking into an annulment of her marriage to Darnley but was warned by friends across Europe that this would alienate the English catholics, many of whom thought his a better claim to the English throne than hers. There is no evidence Queen Mary ever contemplated freeing herself from Darnley other than by legal means. When Maitland suggested that other ways might be found, she insisted that they must not conflict with her honour or conscience.

Maitland, newly married and staying in East Lothian at Lethoington (Lennoxlove) rode over to Whittinghame to meet Bothwell, Morton, and a cousin of Morton called Archibald Douglas. Married to Bothwell's sister Jean the latter was a minister of the kirk with few virtues to qualify for the calling, he included treason, murder, espionage and forgery among his talents. They traditionally plotted the murder of Darnley under a old tree in the grounds of Whittinghame.

In January Darnley, in an unusually trusting mood, agreed to return with the Queen to Edinburgh to complete his cure, trusting she would protect him. She had offered to resume full marriage rights if he came, and he had schemes of his own to bring to fruition.

For his health and safety the Queen arranged for Darnley to recuperate in the healthier air and security of Craigmillar Castle outside the city. Prince James was at Holyrood. He could not be put at risk of any infection from Darnley. She must have hoped that given time and Darnley improving his behaviour the Lords would grow to tolerate him. Darnley had at least one spy at court and it was thought to be Sir James Balfour.

The Pope's ambassador Morette arrived in Edinburgh on 25-26th January. Moray received him and Maitland stayed in Edinburgh to entertain him. Sir James Balfour lent his house in the Cannongate to Morette during his visit. Balfour, a Catholic and a friend of Darnley, may have been acting as the latter's agent.

Bothwell left Edinburgh on 24th January for the Borders. As part of his court duty he oversaw the lodging at Craigmillar Castle as he passed en route to Liddesdale. Bothwell returned on January 29-30th to his chambers in Holyrood Palace (two rooms connected by a turnpike stair overlooking the gardens, previously occupied by Lord Ruthven.)

Queen Mary and Darnley approached Edinburgh on 31st January 1567 having left Glasgow on the 27th. At the last moment, whether from fear of imprisonment or murder once in the castle walls, or Craigmillar being inconvenient to his own plans, Darnley declined to stay at Craigmillar Castle. It was then decided that he could go to the old Provost's Lodge at Kirk o' Fields, a country house near the city with fresh air, where he could recover his health. The hasty preparations to make it ready for Darnley's reception confirms this last minute change of plan.

The big question of who chose Kirk o' Fields is crucial. It was expected that at Kirk o' Fields Darnley would occupy the Duke of Chatelherault's mansion – however, it was occupied. Darnley was therefore sent to the Old Provost's house, which he disliked. Kirk o' Fields was not the Queen's choice. It was claimed by an English spy that it was Darnley himself who chose the site, advised by Sir James Balfour as his brother owned the house. The change of venue was against the Queen's wishes; she still wished Darnley to stay at Craigmillar Castle. Darnley did not want anyone to see him in his present condition, until he had undergone a course of medical baths in private.

If Balfour was Darnley's accomplice in his treasonable schemes, his purpose in suggesting Kirk o' Fields may have been a sinister one. It is significant that it was after Morette's arrival Balfour may have been working in tandem with Morette and Darnley conspiring with them, and with the Protestant Lords.

On 8th February Queen Mary announced she would ratify the Treaty of Edinburgh which she had resisted for some time, and sent Robert Melville to London to open negotiations the next day. It is highly unlikely she would be contemplating murdering her husband at such a crucial time.

By 9th February Balfour had left Edinburgh. His departure may be significant. Having seen Darnley safely installed in Kirk o' Fields, and Morette in his town house, he may have felt it prudent to go home to Burleigh.

Sunday 9th February was the last Sunday in Lent, therefore a day of joy and feasting. The Queen had a full programme of engagements planned. Darnley began his last day of convalescence by hearing mass. Moray excused himself from court using the illness of his wife as a reason, and left immediately for St Andrews. Meanwhile Darnley had his last medical bath, doubtless looking forward to returning to Holyrood the following morning.

The Queen had a busy schedule planned, including the wedding of one of her ladies, the preparations filling the morning and she attended the farewell banquet for Morette in the afternoon. She visited Darnley in the evening, making it clear that after the wedding reception she would be staying at Holyrood overnight. Back at Holyrood the Queen met with some of her officials that she had been too busy to see earlier, including her Captain of the Prince's Guard (Bothwell) and her master of the Queen's Guard (Traquer) to make arrangements for the Prince's security as Darnley was coming to Holyrood next day.

The plot to murder Darnley was masterminded by Maitland and Moray. Maitland was the active partner, and Moray the passive one, but the ultimate beneficiary. There was little time to arrange the deed because of the Prince's christening and Darnley's illness. The aim was to rid Scotland of this troublesome Catholic activist and implicate their enemy Bothwell, if possible. Gunpowder was decided upon by the Lords on 7th February, so all the evidence would be destroyed and it would be easier to blame Bothwell. The gunpowder was either brought by Bothwell from the supply at Dunbar Castle, or purchased by Balfour and stored in his town property but it was not on hand before this date.

The conspirators would have to wait until Bonkil the cook had left the house at Kirk o' Fields and the cooking fires cooled, as the heat might have ignited the powder. To have brought about the destruction that it did, it would have been essential for the gunpowder to be packed well between the stones of the vault, where the ceiling was low (thus compressing the powder and increasing the power of the explosion), and hidden in secret places in the foundations of the house. The east gable wall was left standing and the back door of the New Provost Lodging was damaged, so it might be that the vaults beneath the eastern end of the Chambers, where the ceiling is higher, were also mined to effect maximum damage.

There was a theory that it was Darnley with Lennox and Balfour who were plotting the explosion at Kirk o' Fields, in an attempt to murder some of the Lords and maybe Mary too. The flaw is Darnley had no guarantee the Lords would visit him there. The theory hinges on Darnley expecting Mary and the Lords visiting after the wedding at Holyrood. However the evidence shows that the Queen made it clear she was not returning after the wedding, so there would be no misunderstanding by Darnley.

The surroundings in which Darnley found himself indicated surprise and haste. He had few servants, no armed support and none of his friends nearby. Balfour had left Edinburgh and Lennox was in Linlithgow (said to be waiting for news of a coup).

Ker of Fawdenside was waiting with mounted men near Kirk o' Fields on the night of the explosion, his intention to give aid and help to Darnley but Ker like Douglas had reason to revenge himself for Darnley's betrayal after the Rizzio murder.

Darnley may have been woken by suspicious noises outside, maybe caused by the assassins' rapid retreat after having lit the slow burning fuse, or armed men around the house. Convinced he was in danger and fearing no time to lose, Darnley panicked, woke Taylor his valet, and begged him to help him leave the house. Together with a rope and chair they climbed out of the window on the Flodden wall, and lowered themselves to the ground some 14 feet below. Darnley took a dagger and Taylor a cloak for himself. They had tried to wake other servants, but time was against them and self-preservation took first place.

They either fell or jumped during the 14-foot drop from the window, which would account for his broken ribs and internal injuries found at the post mortem. It is supposed they were both blown clear by the explosion, which would explain Darnley's injuries. There is evidence of an explosion throwing men clear and found in different places unmarked but it is inconceivable that several objects and clothing were found neatly beside them. Douglas's men were in the area and, gunpowder being an unreliable weapon, Douglas was perhaps there in case it did not kill the victims. Witnesses said a voice was heard calling 'Pity me kinsman, for the love of him who had pity on all the world', and suggested Douglas strangled him.

Those who saw the bodies were at a loss to know how Darnley died. There were no burns, no marks of strangulation or violence, no fractures or bruises. Near the bodies lay a chair, a length of rope, a dagger, Darnley's furred nightgown and a cloak. His clothes were not burned or marked with powder, but seemed to have been put there by chance or hand. The postern gate had been left open as an escape route. Norton was not in Edinburgh that night and refused to be involved. There is no evidence Huntly was present. Female witnesses in Black Friars Wynd saw 11 men before the explosion and 13 afterwards. Lennox claimed later that there were 50 men surrounding the house that night.

There is no question most Scots lords hated Darnley, and even those not involved in the plot would not have lifted a finger to save him. They were not pre-pared to tolerate any restoration of his influence. It looked as if the Queen and Darnley were to be reconciled, so the plan laid at Craigmillar had to be speedily carried out.

The Queen was informed after the bodies were found, and her grief at the death of her wayward husband hit her hard. She kept to her rooms all day. The murder left Mary stricken and emotionally shattered. Fearful for her own life for months afterwards, she was not functioning normally and her judgement, not always good at the best of times, utterly failed her. The Privy Council met in an emergency meeting, deliberating how to apprehend the traitors who had com-mitted the deed. Court mourning was proclaimed for 40 days.

The post mortem on Darnley the following morning found one of the King's ribs was broken, by the distance of a fall or jump, and he had suffered grave inter-nal injuries. It was concluded he had been blown into the garden by the explosion.

Some minor people were put on trial, tortured, hung and quartered, but no person of rank was tried. Hardly surprising as the conspirators were mainly run-ning the country! The outcome of the Kirk o' Field murder of Darnley was that Moray gained the political strength he desired, and was able to formally estab-lish the Reform religion in Scotland. It was not the throne Moray craved but the power. He had always thought had he been legitimate he would have been King and had been an able Regent before and after this time. It is unlikely it was in-tended to harm the Queen. Maitland had prevented her from staying at Kirk o' Field the fatal night, and Moray later did not execute Mary or do away with her when he did have the opportunity.

Balfour returned to Edinburgh on the night of 26th February, furtively ac-companied by thirty horsemen but dismounting outside town and entering by a secret way. He was 'hateful to the people' as rumours and placards placed on the Tolbooth were spreading about both his and Gilbert's involvement in Darnley's murder.

Sir James Balfour's role in the murder conspiracy is one of the most obscure and mysterious. Balfour was pragmatic as far as religion was concerned. Having embraced Protestantism early in life, and changing to the Catholic faith to buy freedom from the galleys, he used religion as it served his interests. Having come into political prominence through his friendship with Darnley, he was soon ad-mitted to the secret councils of the Lords. Although not involved in the Rizzio murder, he profited from it. There is only circumstantial evidence that Balfour was involved in Darnley's schemes. It may infer he played a double game to safe-guard his own position with whoever triumphed. However there is ample tes-timony that Balfour was involved with his relation Bothwell in the plot to kill Darnley, and Melville said they were great companions.

By 17th March the Queen was committed to send Bothwell and others named by Lennox to trial. Balfour was one of those named. On 21st March a council was held with Bothwell present, but not Balfour, who appeared to have maintained a low profile. The trial was set for 12th April.

On 19th April a report was made of a murder and burial in secret of a servant of James Balfour, presumably to keep him quiet, in case his conscience bothered him. 'Balfour for fear keeps to his house, especially at night, under great watch and guard'. In the wake of the placards that continued to link him to the King's death, Balfour doubtless feared reprisals from vengeful citizens.

Queen Mary

Parliament met that day and Queen Mary ratified the Act of the Reformation of Parliament of 1560, which she had previously refused to do. Next day the Queen sought refuge at Seton for the fourth time since Darnley's death. She was later joined by Bothwell, Maitland and Patrick Bellenden. It was here that Bothwell produced a bond signed at Ainslie's Tavern by many Lords, while well lubricated by Bothwell's hospitality, agreeing to support Bothwell marrying the Queen with her consent. Bothwell then proposed marriage to the Queen.

Queen Mary rejected the proposal on several accounts. Taking into consideration he was already married, a Protestant and a mere subject, such a marriage would prejudice future relations with England. She remained adamant even when Maitland and Bellenden pressed her to accept Bothwell.

In mid-April after seeing her son at Stirling and enjoying a few days with him, the Queen and 30 courtiers were returning to Holyrood when Bothwell with 800 armed Borderers rode up to them and surrounded the court party. To avoid bloodshed the Queen went with Bothwell, but managed to send a message with James Bothwick to Edinburgh for help. However the provost of Edinburgh feared for the Queen's life if they rallied.

Bothwell and his party lost no time, riding hard the 40 miles to Dunbar Castle. Melville, who was with Queen Mary at Dunbar that day, said Bothwell boasted that 'he would marry the Queen, who would or would not, yea whether she would herself or not.'

The Queen was further harassed to marry Bothwell, but was in no mood to yield. Bothwell sought her out in private, and continued to press his suit. Mary persisted in her refusal of his suit. Bothwell ignored the rebuff, and according to Melville, Bothwell raped the Queen, laying her open to dishonour and illicit pregnancy, with the consequent loss of reputation.

Mary, still in weakened health, wearied and broken, and well aware she was in Bothwell's power, had no choice but to capitulate. 'We were constrained to yield our consent, yet against our will,' she said years later to the Pope.

The Queen was still held at Dunbar when Bothwell's divorce came through on 26th April. Many of Mary's loyal subjects now turned against her. Desperate for fear of pregnancy and the subsequent scandal, which would cost her the throne, and being held prisoner, she had no choice but to do her captors' bidding.

Bothwell's abduction of the Queen gave the Lords the pretext they needed to move against him. On 1st May the unlikely coalition of Morton, Argyll, Atholl, Tullibardine and others met at Stirling and entered into a new bond to liberate the Queen, preserve the life of Prince James, and bring the King's murderers to justice, especially Bothwell.

News of Queen Mary's abduction and rape reached the English court. Lennox urged Queen Elizabeth to support the Lords but she would not approve of rebellion against another Queen. She did offer to have Prince James brought up in England.

Meanwhile Sir James Balfour was installed as Governor of Edinburgh Castle by 6th May. Bothwell, thinking Balfour was trustworthy and perhaps as a price for his silence, appointed Balfour to the position. That day the castle guns fired a magnificent salute as Bothwell and the Queen entered Edinburgh, the Queen on horseback and Bothwell on foot leading the horse by the bridle as if she were his prisoner. That night the couple stayed in Edinburgh Castle, where the Queen had troops stationed outside her room, ensuring she could not speak to anybody without Bothwell's knowledge.

The banns were read at St Giles on 11th May. On the 13th the Confederate Lords sent word to the Queen that unless she discharged her soldiers and paid heed to her nobles, they would not obey her commands.

There were reports of friction between Mary and Bothwell. He was jealous and would hardly allow Mary to look at or speak to anybody. He was even offended about a horse the Queen gave to the Lord of Arbroath. Mary was offended that Bothwell's ex-wife was still living in his Crighton Castle. Despite this the marriage contract was concluded and signed by witnesses (Huntly, Maitland, Flemming, Lindsay, Bellenden and Herries among them.)

On the eve of his marriage Bothwell had doubts about the loyalty of Balfour – with good reason as time would prove Balfour was determined to side with the winning faction. On 14th May Hepburn of Beanston, a Bothwell supporter, was appointed Governor of Edinburgh Castle. Acting on behalf of the Confederate Lords Melville told Balfour to refuse to part with his post, as he might be instrumental in saving Prince James. Balfour then refused to leave Edinburgh Castle so had control over the city of Edinburgh. Bothwell had no choice but to leave Balfour there or cause a bloody reaction. Alienating Balfour would prove to be Bothwell's gravest mistake.

On 15th May Queen Mary and the Earl of Bothwell were married in a Protestant ceremony. The bride wore widow's weeds, as she had for her marriage to Darnley, being the widow of the late King of France. At the wedding breakfast the couple sat at each end of a long table, where they and the guests ate in silence.

Although Mary had showered Darnley with gifts at their wedding, her only gift to Bothwell was some fur for his nightgown, which had come from one of her mother's cloaks.

Next morning Mary said to ambassador du Croc (who had diplomatically avoided the wedding) that she 'could not rejoice nor would ever again, but only wished death'. Bothwell made no comment, but Mary was suicidal. Her distress was evident before the wedding night. She may have suspected she was pregnant, which was a disaster as far as she was concerned, and later became an insurmountable barrier to ending the marriage.

Bothwell presided over a somewhat reduced Privy Council on 15th May. The Queen never bestowed the title of King on Bothwell, but his actions left none in doubt who wielded the power. Two days later du Croc reported that 'Queen Mary was the most changed woman to face, that in so little time, without extremity of sickness they have seen,' Mary suffered fainting fits now brought on by stress. Du Croc added that Balfour was to carry letters to the English court. Perhaps by this means Balfour was got rid of for a while.

Queen Elizabeth believed Bothwell had not only murdered Darnley, but was a danger to Prince James. In Scotland the Queen's marriage was an outrage. Even Spain and her French relations deserted Mary. No allowance was made for her health or her state of mind after the traumatic events of the previous year – two murders followed by abduction and rape – or that she was a virtual prisoner.

By June supporters were deserting her and, as Holyrood could not be defended, Bothwell decided to move to Edinburgh Castle but Balfour refused to admit them, having thrown in his lot with the Lords on their warning that he would be found as guilty as Bothwell if he supported the Royal couple. It is thought Balfour made a deal with the Lords granting him freedom from prosecution for his part in Darnley's murder if he joined them. Balfour had agreed to hold Edinburgh Castle for the Lords on the condition that the Laird of Grange (Kirkcaldy) would protect him should the nobility change their minds. This was betrayal as whoever held Edinburgh Castle held the city.

Bothwell and Queen Mary were trying to raise an army. On the 12th June the Confederate Lords entered Edinburgh with no trouble from the castle garrison. Next day Balfour committed the ultimate treachery. He sent a message to the Queen saying 'take to the open field, and march directly on Edinburgh, so as to meet the insurgents on the road.' He assured her they would keep their ground for a moment, especially when they knew that he had declared against them, and would open fire upon them. If she did not do so he would be compelled, he said, to come to terms with the Lords. But he had already joined the Lords, who now had gathered 4,000 men.

Queen Mary left Dunbar with 600 horsemen and three cannon, meeting Bothwell and 1600 men at Haddington. On 15th June Bedford reported in England that Queen Mary was with child, and the Lords were moving against only Bothwell.

The two armies came together on 15th June at Carberry Hill, seven miles east of Edinburgh, on a hot day, overlooking the River Esk. Both sides were reluctant to fight, so spent the day parleying. Du Croc attempted to mediate but unsuccessfully. At the end of the day, wishing to avoid bloodshed of her subjects, the Queen asked the Lords to state terms necessary for her surrender. Maitland and Atholl did not want to face her, so Kirkcaldy of the Grange met her and assured her if she put herself in their hands, they would let Bothwell go free until such time as Parliament decided.

Bothwell had no option but to go, leaving Mary in the hands of the Lords. Letting Bothwell go was a solution that suited the Lords, who had no wish to bring him to a trial which may have revealed their own involvement in the late King's murder.

At their parting Bothwell told Mary that Morton, Maitland and Balfour with others had killed the King and gave her his copy of the Craigmillar Bond. It must have been a shock for the Queen. The Lords later took this copy of the bond from her.

Mary, dirty and dishevelled, exhausted and faint was taken back to Edinburgh and kept in a fortified house called Black Temple. Confined under guard, her reign was effectively over.

After two days in which she never ate, Mary was returned to Holyrood and was just sitting down to a meal when Morton abruptly told her to make ready to move. With no time to pack, she stood up in a silk nightdress and a cloak. Lindsay and Ruthven were waiting with horses, and with two chamber women and an escort they set out to an unknown destination.

Riding west they crossed the Firth of Forth at Leith and rode fast and hard for Kinross. At Loch Leven the Queen was bundled into a rowing boat and taken across the water to Loch Leven Castle. The Queen was not put in the royal apartments but, in a state of exhaustion, was conducted to a ground floor room not in keeping with her rank. Next day Morton left her in the charge of the brutal Lindsay and hostile Ruthven.

Loch Leven Castle was owned by the Douglas family, but had enjoyed quasi-royal status since the 14th century, having been visited by successive Scottish monarchs. Mary had stayed there herself with Darnley. Sir William was Mary's nephew, Morton's cousin and Moray's half-brother. His mother had been mistress to King James V and wife to Douglas, who was gifted the castle and lands on his marriage by the King. Lady Douglas's daughter with Sir William Douglas was married to Lindsay. There is no evidence of her being spiteful to the Queen. After the first month of captivity Queen Mary was moved to the more suitable two rooms on the third floor of the tower and was allowed to walk in the gardens.

Sir Nicholas Throckmorton, who had been the English Ambassador in Paris while Mary was Queen of France, was sent as courier from Queen Elizabeth. He was denied access to Queen Mary, but managed to smuggle a note to her inside Robert Melville's scabbard. Throckmorton warned Mary of the public anger against her, and urged her to reject Bothwell. She replied she was with child and would rather die than divorce and make the child a bastard and lose her honour.

Loch Leven Castle painting bequeathed to Kinross Museum (artist unknown)

The Queen miscarried twins between 20th and 23rd July, suffering a severe haemorrhage which confined her to bed in a weakened state. When he heard of the miscarriage Throckmorton again urged her to reject Bothwell as she was no longer pregnant. He was afraid the Lords would do away with her, and urged her to abdicate if it would save her life, reminding her that the abdication would be illegal, having been made under duress, so invalid once she was free.

On 24th July, while the Queen was still bedridden from the miscarriage, Lindsay, Ruthven, Robert Melville and two others seized the opportunity and rowed out to Loch Leven with an instrument of abdication for the Queen to sign. Despite her weakened state, only able to sit up with difficulty, she was spirited enough to refuse to sign the abdication. She urgently requested her case was put before Parliament. Lindsay manhandled the Queen and brutally threatened to cut her throat if she did not sign. Mary took Throckmorton's advice and signed the abdication and a paper appointing Morton as Regent, but repeatedly protested that as she was under duress she would not be bound by the signed documents. Queen Elizabeth refused to negotiate with the Scottish Lords as long as their Queen was in prison.

Wasting no time the Lords had Prince James crowned as King James VI at Stirling on 19th July. It was the first time the ceremony was concluded according to Protestant rites. Knox, now back in Scotland, preached the sermon.

Morton returned to Edinburgh to an enthusiastic welcome by those who thought him their Protestant leader on 11th August. He immediately took control of the government.

By 13th August Balfour had resigned the governship of Edinburgh Castle and handed it over to Kirkcaldy of the Grange, 'for a large grant of money and church land, and acquaintance of all concern in Darnley's murder'. He left in harmony with the Lords, and was later made President of the Court of Session.

On August 15th Moray had a meeting with the Queen in Loch Leven Castle, and again the next day when he was more tolerant. He told her she could not have her liberty, but assured her that her life was safe. However if she made trouble he could not save her.

Bothwell in the meantime had tried unsuccessfully to raise support in the south and west, and was rejected in the north as well. On 14th August he was off the coast of Shetland but Grange and Tullibardine had sailed north to find him. Bothwell had failed to attend the Council for trial on 17th July, and was declared an outlaw and stripped of all lands and goods in his absence. Almost captured off Shetland, Bothwell sailed for Orkney. However Gilbert Balfour, brother to Sir James, was Bailiff of Orkney and foiled attempts by Bothwell to land and establish a base there.

Bothwell and his followers then took to piracy, harrowing English and Danish shipping, before sailing north to Norway. Here luck failed Bothwell again, as he was recognised and betrayed by an ex-mistress and captured. He was then sold by the Norwegian King to the Danish King as a political pawn.

In September one of her ladies-in-waiting, Mary Seton, was allowed to join Queen Mary in Loch Leven Castle. However there was little privacy as the dowager Lady Douglas insisted on sleeping in the Queen's room. Fortunately the Queen did not know that Morton had instructed Lady Douglas to kill Mary if anyone attempted to rescue her. In December 1567 Moray, Morton and Balfour visited the Queen but showed such disregard for her state that the meeting was frigid. The Queen was particularly contemptuous of Balfour, who had betrayed her twice, and called him an 'arch traitor' to his face, which caused him to retire behind the other Lords embarrassed.

On 2nd May, in the absence of Sir William Douglas, a young relative George Douglas of Kirkness, helped Queen Mary escape from Loch Leven Castle. She was met on the loch shore by Seton, Alexander Hepburn and Lord Claude Hamilton, one of Chatelherault's sons. They fled to the safety of Seton Castle at Longniddry.

Moray, in Glasgow, was 'sore amazed' when he heard of her escape and issued a proclamation calling the lieges to arms. Sir William Douglas was suicidal.

Mary led a growing force to Cadzow Castle near Hamilton, and Archbishop Hamilton helped draft a strong proclamation repudiating her abdication and reassuring her lawful sovereignty. The Queen now had nine earls and bishops, 18 barons, 14 commentators and 90 lairds, who all signed the Hamilton Bond to restore Queen Mary to her throne.

Moray had an army of 4,000 men led by the invincible Kirkcaldy of Grange. They inflicted a crushing defeat on Mary's less able force at the Battle of Langside outside Glasgow. Believing her cause lost, Queen Mary fled the field with Herries,

Flemming, Livingston and a dozen others, riding south-west to Dumfries and Galloway. They tried to persuade the Queen to flee to France where she had lands and an income, but she made the fateful decision to flee to England, convinced Queen Elizabeth would support her cause and help her.

A congress of 49 nobles met at Perth on 25th July. They dismissed Queen Mary's request for an annulment on the grounds that it was impious. They were afraid that if she married again a husband would dominate her. They vowed that Queen Mary would never return to Scotland as Queen or co-regent, or even as a private person. Balfour surprisingly was amongst the nine who voted to restore the Queen to her throne. He had already fallen foul of Moray. Maitland also declared for Mary, relations between him and Moray now poor.

In September Maitland was arrested at Stirling and Moray intended to imprison him in the fortress of Tantallion, but Kirkcaldy of the Grange rescued him and took him to the safety of Edinburgh Castle. Balfour was another arrested at this time. Accused of involvement in Darnley's murder, he was released on the condition he agreed to answer a summons to trial when required. This summons never came, perhaps a secret arrangement made between the Lords and Balfour.

By 1570 many nobles were disaffected by Moray's rule, and on 23rd January James Hamilton of Bothwell Haugh, assassinated Moray as he rode through the streets of Linlithgow. James Hamilton then fled to France.

The unofficial leader was now Morton. However England feared a Catholic movement in Scotland and forced Lennox on the Lords as regent. Lady Lennox and their surviving son Charles were kept by Queen Elizabeth as hostages for Lennox's behaviour.

Maitland, feeling safe now Moray was dead, left the refuge of Edinburgh Castle, which Grange continued to hold for Queen Mary. Balfour also stayed loyal to Queen Mary, if only in self interest, for Lennox was after his blood.

Lennox took Dumbarton Castle and Fleming escaped to France, but Archbishop Hamilton was hung 'in his eccesiatical robes'. Lennox was elected Regent (the fourth since Mary was deposed) which provoked Grange into publishing an act against Lennox, and again civil war broke out. On 4th September, 1571 Lennox was assassinated during a Hamilton coup, being shot during an attack on Stirling Castle.

An ailing Mar replaced Lennox, but he died after dining with Morton at Dalkeith on 28th October 1572. In January 1573 Queen Elizabeth at last recognised James VI as king of Scotland, and that she had no intention of returning Queen Mary.

Morton, now Regent, proved secretive, ruthless and avaricious but did restore stability to Scotland, while being friendly with England. Argyll established his loyalty to the Lords and was made Lord High Chancellor. He died in 1574. Balfour came to terms with the new Regent and obtained the reversal of his forfeited lands and property, having been attainted in 1571. However Balfour proved something of an embarrassment to Morton. Many were offended that Balfour enjoyed the benefit of pacification. In 1573 Balfour went to France and Spain, where he tried to raise support for the restoration of the Catholic faith in Scotland.

On 10th February 1573 Morton reduced the last bastion of resistance for Queen Mary at Blackness Castle, leaving him free to tackle Edinburgh Castle. With English siege guns and an English army led by Sir William Druary the castle was attacked. After 13 days of bombardment the stronghold surrendered.

On 29th March 1578 Athol and the new Earl of Argyll brought off a coup against Morton. However Morton had no thought of giving up power and, by June, he raised a counter-coup to regain control of the 11-year-old King but did concede that Athol and Argyll assist him in government. When Argyll died unexpectedly, in April 1579, Morton was suspected of poisoning but nothing was ever proved.

Bothwell died miserably and completely mad in a Danish prison on 14th April 1578.

Balfour, having been declared forfeit and in the Netherlands, by March made it known that he had evidence to incriminate Morton in the murder of Darnley and would produce it in return for permission to re-enter Scotland, unmolested and restored to his Scottish estates. The offer was made to Morton's enemies who were again looking for a reason to topple him. Balfour was trying to ensure his own safety from Morton, but Morton was not only alive but in power, and had to be neutralised.

Queen Mary was also interested in Balfour's evidence and on 18th March asked Archbishop Beaton to secure possession of it, especially the Craigmillar Bond that Morton was supposed to have signed. Balfour sent the Queen such evidence as he had, but it did not include the Craigmillar Bond. The Queen asked the Archbishop to play along with Balfour in the hope that more documents could be extracted from him.

On 15th December Captain James Stewart, a royal favourite, accused Morton of conspiring in Darnley's murder. Morton contemptuously dismissed the charge. However Morton was later angry enough to draw his sword, and was arrested and confined in Edinburgh Castle, before being transferred to Dumbarton Castle in January.

'Loved by none, hated and envied by many, they looked through their fingers to see Morton fall.' He was tried on 1st June at the Tolbooth in Edinburgh. Balfour testified against him, but failed to produce the Craigmillar Bond (which he may never have had). Morton was found guilty, declared forfeit and condemned to be hung, drawn and quartered. However, young King James commuted the sentenced to decapitation. On 2nd June Morton was beheaded in the Grass Market, on a guillotine called 'The Maiden', which he himself had introduced from Halifax as a more humane method of execution.

King James VI was 15 years old on 19th June 1581, and assumed personal rule. Protestant Lords led by William Ruthven, Earl of Gowrie, kidnapped the King and forced him to banish Lennox, who fled to France and died there in 1583. The King escaped and asserted his authority to rule in June 1583. In May 1584

Gowrie was executed and King James received the dubious 'casket letters', which then vanished. Parliament passed an Act in 1600 (after the next generation of Ruthvens also plotted treason), that the name Ruthven be abolished for all time.

John Knox died in 1572 aged 58.

Sir William Maitland of Lethington (now Lennoxlove near Haddington), Secretary of State to Mary of Guise and Queen Mary, died in 1573 either from a wasting disease or poison.

Queen Mary asked her son King James VI for the head of Lindsay, but James contented himself with imprisoning Lindsay in Tantallon Castle, where he died in 1589.

Kirkcaldy of the Grange, who held Edinburgh Castle for Queen Mary, bombarded by English siege machines, surrendered on a promise of a pardon by Morton but was hanged by him in 1573.

Queen Mary was implicated in the Babington Plot in 1586, and beheaded on 8th February 1587.

Queen Elizabeth I of England, Scotland, Wales and Northern Ireland died 26th March 1603.

King James VI of Scotland inherited the English throne on Queen Elizabeth's death, and moved south with his family to London. The local economy suffered for a long time when the court moved south, as there were no longer court activities in and around Falkland and Dunfermline so the local economies, foods, dressmakers, weavers, horse-markets and many others felt the pinch.

Sir James Balfour, who had almost certainly been implicated in the plot to murder Darnley, died in his bed at Burleigh Castle in 1583. He had served all parties, deserted all, yet had profited by all. Although attainted twice he recovered his title and lands, and was one of the few of the conspirators in the murder of Darnley who met a peaceful end.

Sir James Balfour is credited with being the author of the well known collection of decisions entitled 'Balfour's Practicks or A System of the More Ancient Law of Scotland', a voluminous work which remained in manuscript until 1754 when it was published in a folio volume of 684 pages, and continued to be used by practitioners until superseded by 'Stair's Institutes'.

Sir James had a long marriage to Lady Margaret Balfour, who must have been a good manager, running the estate, playing hostess to his guests and bringing up their five sons and three daughters when he was so occupied over the years. They extended the Tower House into a Courtyard House, fashionable at that time. With more peaceable times defence was not so important, so homes were being built for entertaining and as a statement of the owner's importance.

With less fear of attack, ornamentation was a crucial factor. Permission would be granted by the monarch to build, and wings were added to the Tower House to form a square. The Tower House was joined to the extension on the

Built by Sir James & Lady Margaret Balfour, this is how the courtyard at Burleigh may have looked.
(watercolour by Dorothy Thomson, from a Scottish National Heritage drawing)

west with a wall pierced by a round-topped arch entrance, with a second storey above and joined to a round tower on the corner. Wings were constructed to the north, south and east to complete the square. There would be an entrance on the east, probably as the south met the east wings, and there was also another tower mentioned in the 19th century, probably on the join of the north and east wings,

Burleigh Castle before 1818 when the walls fell after a flood and an earthquake. This is the only photograph showing the extension. Photo: Dr Munro, Kinross Museum

referred to as the East Tower. A drawing of the suggested house is mounted on a board outside Burleigh Castle today by Historic Scotland.

The new Courtyard Castle was finished in 1582, indicated by the engraved date and the initials SJB and MB for Sir James and Lady Margaret, to be found on the north gable of the round tower still standing. The two-storey gateway has, within its strong course, hood-mould over the gateway a moulded surround formally containing a heraldic panel. The wall is an excellent example of a small-scale but refined architectural sophistication of its period in Scotland.

Every room was built with a purpose. The buttery was for storing wine and ale, as water was too unsafe to drink. Ale went off quite quickly and, as with bread being baked every few days, ale was brewed regularly. The alcohol content was low in the small beer and it was drunk by the whole household. Wine was only for the 'top table'. The hall for entertaining and dining would be near the kitchens. There would be two long tables the length of the hall with benches on the wall side only of the tables, for the ease of the servants serving meals. There was a raised platform at one end of the hall, across which stood a shorter top table for the family and important guests, who had individual chairs. Those sitting at the long tables would be in social order depending on their status, the highest nearest the top table, and the salt cellar was placed halfway down the length of the tables, hence the term above or below the salt.

Meat of all sorts was the most expensive, so a status food. Hunting supplemented the diet, supplying venison and expensive game birds (partridge and pheasant). Fish was second in distinction, and could be salted, pickled or kept in ponds in the grounds for winter consumption. Vegetables grown in the ground were thought only fit for peasants to eat, as were most cheeses. Spits were used for roasting. Spices, almonds, raisins and honey were used in cooking.

There was now accommodation for the staff and followers in the new wings, so they no longer slept in the hall when the meal

and tables were removed. The house was controlled by the wife, and staff would include a butler, cook, chaplain, huntsman, lady's maid, governess, household servants and gardeners. There would also be stables for the horses and grooms and most likely hawks and falconers, and a doo-cot for pigeons as a source of fresh food in the winter.

A revolution in the glass industry in the mid-1500s meant glass was available in larger sheets and at a cheaper price, opening up a boom in larger windows and glass was no longer just for the privileged few. In the 17th century fire furnaces were introduced and made a dramatic technological change, again making glass available to even more of the population.

The castle Sir James and Lady Margaret built was a particularly fine picturesque example of Scottish Baronial architecture of the period. An avenue of trees was planted to the west to mark the official approach to the castle, and there were probably orchards and gardens to the south.

The Children of Lady Margaret and Sir James Balfour

"If you live without making a difference,
what difference does it make that you have lived?"
Felix Francis

Sir Michael was heir to his father in 1583, and later became the first Lord Balfour. He had a charter of the lands of Netherton of Auchinhuffs in Banffshire on 28th October 1577, and another of the barony of Burleigh on 20th October 1606, to his heirs – male whatever, carrying the name and arms of Balfour etc. He was President of the Court of Session, and had charters for the barony of Montwhannie, Kirberster, and several other lands and baronies. James VI honoured him with the title of Lord Burleigh by letters patent dated Royston in England 7th August 1606. Sir Michael was then James's ambassador to the Duke of Tuscany and the Duke of Lorraine. He was created a lord of Parliament under the same title at Whitehall on 10th July 1607. His lordship was subsequently sworn of the Privy Council. On 7th September 1614, a charter was granted to Michael, Lord Balfour of Burleigh, and the barony of Kilwinning, with the title of Lord Kilwinning,

His lordship first married Margaret Adamson and then, in 1591, Margaret, daughter of Lundie of Lundie, with whom he had a daughter, also Margaret. 'He was a man of good parts, and much esteemed by King James VI.' 'Being a man of great skill and knowledge in the management of state affairs, he was employed in several foreign negotiations, and acquitted himself with honour and reputation.'

The terms of the 'heirs – male' must have been changed to 'heirs –general' for his daughter to succeed him. Afterwards he got a charter under the great seal 'Michael Balfour, dominio Balfour de Burleigh, terrarium bariniae de Kilwinning, etc, to whom, et haeredibus et assignatis quibuscunque', dated 7th September 1614.

Lord Burleigh died in 1619. In the same year Margaret Balfour succeeded her father as Baroness Balfour of Burleigh. At an earlier date the 1st Lord Balfour

The Balfours had eight children: five boys and three girls.

Michael: *the eldest son, succeeded his parents, and became the first Lord Balfour of Burleigh under King James VI.*

Alexander of Balgarvie: *of whom there are several descendents in the male line still existing.*

Sir Henry: *a General in the United Provinces, and served under the Prince of Orange with great reputation.*

William: *went to Ireland and married the Hamilton heiress to Glenally, assuming her name. One of their descendents was created Lord Glenally.*

David: *was a captain in his brother Henry's regiment, and perished at sea going over to Holland.*

Eldest daughter: *married Sir Michael Arnot of that ilk.*

Middle daughter: *married Henderson of Fordell.*

Youngest daughter: *married Barclay of Collairny.*

had adopted Robert Arnot of Ferny as his son. Margaret married Sir Robert (*nee* Arnot), second son of Arnot of Ferny, Chamberlain of Fife, who had changed his name to Balfour and, in her right, became possessed of the Lordship of Burleigh.

It is said that immediately upon his marriage Sir Robert received a letter from the Crown, entitling him to also succeed to the honours and certainly it was he who enjoyed them for he made a great figure in Scotland as Lord Burleigh. During the civil war in the time of King Charles I, he was deeply engaged on the Parliament side, and had a great share of all public transactions of these troublesome times. This Sir Robert, 2nd Lord Burleigh, was president to the Parliaments that met in 1640 and early 1641 and was made Privy Counsellor during the life by that Parliament, which met in November that year.

He was president to the committee for trying malignants in the north, *anno* 1644, one of the committee of estates *anno* 1645, also one of the committee, bringing in public money and felling malignant's lands, *anno* 1646. After the murder of King Charles I, he was one of the Colonels of Fife for putting the kingdom in a posture of defence, *anno* 1649, and the same year was one of the last committee of estates, one of the Commissioners of Exchequer, and one of the Lords of the Solemn League, and had several private meetings with Cromwell *anno* 1648.

'The Troubled Times' in Scotland of 1639 to 1651, covering the unrest of the Covenanters in Scotland and the English Civil War, then after the execution of Charles 1 the differences between the two kingdoms, were all in his lifetime. Remember that all tenants in the baronies had to do 40 days annually, fighting for their landlord if called. So when Lord Balfour, a Colonel for Fife, raised troops, then men from Tilly-rie, Burleigh and other lands within the Barony would be part of his troops.

The Scots signed the National Covenant on 28th February 1638, an outward affirmation of Scottish adherence to the reform church. James VI was king of both countries, and recognised only too well that Scotland had its own law, language and custom. King Charles I had no such inhibitions, having been born in Dunfermline but been south since the age of three. His able elder brother Henry, educated to be heir to James, died at 19, having swum in the Thames and caught an infection; leaving the 10 years younger Charles as heir.

Charles never fully appreciated the all-important differences between his two kingdoms, and lacked the pragmatism that underpinned his father's governance. The Scots Parliament comprised of four collegiate 'Estates':

- **The Nobility**
- **Lesser Tenants or Landowners** serving as representatives for each shire
- **Representatives of the Royal Burghs**
- **Representatives of the Kirk**

It was the latter that proved controversial. Before the Protestant Reformation it was the bishops spiritual who sat in Parliament in Scotland but ousting bishops in favour of Calvinist presbyteries, gave this Estate and power into the hands of ministers who owed no allegiance but to their God. Charles's notion of power and authority of the bishops and his political ineptitude resulted in the campaigns of Generals Leslie, Fairfax, Cromwell and Montrose.

There was no standing army at this time; regiments were through necessity levied by local noblemen and lairds, under the old fencible system. By law, irrespective of status, all men between 16 and 60 were liable to turn out as required for up to 40 days service. In 1639 instructions were circulated for the forming of local committees of war. They were to manage a preliminary muster to establish the extent of available manpower, then whittle them down to a manageable pool of young and unmarried men fit for service, then to levy one man in four and form into regiments. The local committees were responsible for clothing, equipping, feeding and paying them for 40 days. One regiment in 1644 was to supply; two shirts, breeches, coat, stockings and a bonnet, bands and shoes and to be paid six (Scots) shillings each a day and, for every 12 men, a baggage horse and cooking utensils. If their services were required beyond the 40 day period, responsibility for them passed to central government, often with different results.

Infantry were expected to be equipped either as pikemen or musketeers, the former armed with a five-metre long weapon and often body armour. The length of the pike was calculated to outreach a cavalryman's lance. Pikemen were offensive shock-troops, to push back the enemy and break their formation. Successful attacks depended on the accompanying musketeers first winning the fire-fight. The major problem was that in wet weather the matchlock was very susceptible to misfiring, so that in damp conditions the slow-match often did not burn hotly enough to ignite dry gunpowder. On the other hand the matchlock rifle was comparatively cheap, robust, soldier-proof and in good weather quite reliable, and in trained hands could fire twice in a minute. It was accurate up to 50 metres, and the ounce of soft lead ball was very effective at stopping the enemy. Heavy guns were useful for siege work, but of little importance on the battlefield, being quite immobile and, once in place, not very effective.

Cavalrymen were undoubtedly useful. There were two types of horse soldier: cuirassiers or heavy cavalry, armoured from head to foot and carrying swords and pistols; harquebusiers, or light cavalry, wore protective leather coats with a corselet or breastplate and helmet, but were armed with a carbine in addition to sword and pistols. The Scots loaded themselves with excess pistols. The harquebusiers were the model for Cromwell's 'ironsides' troops in later years. The Scots generally had smaller horses than their English allies. The light cavalry were used in support and scouting.

General Alexander Leslie was called home to Scotland after serving first in Holland then Sweden for 30 years with distinction, before retiring with the rank of Field Marshal and a fair fortune. He invited other veterans back to Scotland to train and lead county levees. The Earl of Montrose and General Leslie worked together for the Covenanters putting down outbreaks in the north for the royalists. However there was still a reluctance in Scotland to disturb the long-continued peace.

In August 1640 General Alexander Leslie led a Scots army across the border, crossing the river Tweed at three points. He was working in conjunction with Parliamentary generals Fairfax and Cromwell in the south, Montrose having diced for the honour took the first regiment to Cornhill to cross the Tweed. The others crossed at Wark and Carham. At the time Lord Burleigh was president of the Parliament in absence of a commissioner for the King and continued in that office until 1641. He was also one of the commissioners for negotiating the treaty of peace in both 1640 and 1641, and Privy Councillors constituted by that Parliament.

General Leslie had victories at Newburn on 20th August, and Newcastle on Tyne surrendered on the 28th. It was Sir Robert Douglas of Kirkness who took the surrender of Newcastle on Tyne, so perhaps some Balfour troops were there too, if neighbouring Kirkness was prominent. The Treaty of Ripon started on 26th October, acknowledging the independence of the Kirk, a protracted process that took almost a year until signed and ratified on 10th August 1641. The Scots army was then disbanded on 27th August, except for three regiments.

Encouraged by the Scots' successful defiance, on 28th October there was a Catholic rebellion in Ireland, to the horror of the Protestants, many of whom were slaughtered. The three surviving Scots regiments, who were not disbanded, were immediately despatched to Ulster under General Leslie, now Earl of Leven. The Westminster Parliament were to request another further seven regiments to be raised. While willing to pay for an army for specific purposes they were afraid the King would be tempted to use it on his political opponents at home. Then at the beginning of January the King over-reached himself attempting to arrest five leading MPs. Both Parliament and the mob against him, Charles fled on 10th January to London and the English Civil War began.

The Civil War and Lord Balfour 1643-1663

ON 19TH JANUARY the Earl of Leven again led the Scots army over the border, and arrived outside Newcastle on 3rd February. England had a difficult time, both sides trying to muster sufficient forces to actually fight each other, and was at stalemate in summer 1643. So both looked elsewhere, the King to Ireland and Parliament to Scotland. De-

General Alexander Leslie, 1st Earl of Leven

spite the public differences between King and Covenanters in 1661, the Scots and English Parliamentarians were still natural political allies and in June 1643 the Parliamentarians made formal approaches to the Committees of Estates in Edinburgh. This eventually led to the Solemn League and Covenant in September and a definitive Treaty of Assistance on 29th November, committing Scotland to provide an army of 18,000 foot, 2,000 horse, 1,000 dragoons and a competent train of artillery. Hence the Scots marched over the border again.

The invasion began on frosty roads but by 24th January a thaw set in and melted waters, swelling rivers and turning roads to mud. The guns, shipped to nearby Blyth, did not arrive until 7th February. The indecisive Battle of Corbridge was fought on 19th February, Leven moving on again. South Shields fell on 20th March. In heavy snow the Scots moved on, meeting the Royalist Marquis of Newcastle on 23rd March at Bolton Hill. The wet ground and winter weather were bad for cavalry and the fight began at 5pm, in failing light with musketeers. The battle fought in darkness for the possession of the north ended inconclusively. At daylight the Marquis only stayed long enough to get his guns and wounded away. Five days later rested and re-equipped, Leven moved south. By 8th April and in improving weather, Leven took up another strong position south of Durham, only to find Durham abandoned.

The Royalists were utterly destroyed when outnumbered two to one at Selby on 11th April, and this left the way wide open to York for Leven and the Scots army. The Marquis of Newcastle rushed south to try and defend York. Leven pursued for a while but on 16th April instead rendezvoused with a Parliamentarian army under the command of Lord Fairfax at Weatherby. In the siege of York and the Battle of Marston Moor, which ended the English Civil War, the Scots did not fight as an independent force but in a triple alliance with the Northern Associated forces under Lord Fairfax and the Eastern Association forces under the Earl of Manchester and Oliver Cromwell. Leven was regarded the senior partner in the battle and it was he who ordered the grandly titled Army of Both Kingdoms to draw up on Marston Moor on 1st July 1644 to intercept the approaching Royal army, led by the King's nephew Prince Rupert.

The Civil War did not end at Marston Moor but it was won there. Without Leven's march to Newcastle, and ruthless pursuit of the Marquis of Newcastle and the Royalists to York, the Army of Both Kingdoms would not have fought at Marston Moor. There can be no doubt the victory was due to the Scottish element. However as Leven and his troops only stayed to see the surrender of York and returned north again to deal with unfinished business at Newcastle, and an expected crisis back home in Scotland where James Graham, now Marquis of Montrose, was leading a Royalist rebellion, they never got the credit they deserved.

Montrose's support for the Covenanter movement earlier had been sincere. Now he recognised that Scotland had a greater danger from the ambition of Archibald Campbell, Marquis of Argyll – who, when his Catholic father died in 1638, had become one of the main leaders of the Covenanting movement.

Montrose had ridden north from Oxford as the King's Lieutenant-General, with an army of two hundred cavalry of Scots mercenaries and English levies, crossing the border at Carlisle. On 27th June Alasdair MacColla sailed from Waterford in Ireland, landing at Ardnamurchan on the west coast of Scotland. He and his 2,000 men marched to Blair Athol to meet up with Montrose.

Montrose with the Royalist army met the government army at the open moorland of Tibbermore, west of Perth, on 1st September 1644. Montrose had as large an army as his opponents. The government troops were commanded by Lord Elcho, whose Fife levies were split as some were with Lord Balfour serving as garrison in Aberdeen. He was supported by Sir James Scott of Rossie on the left and the Earl of Tullibardine on his right. The battle went to the Royalists, who were able to re-equip themselves.

The Royalist army went on to Dundee, which refused to surrender so they marched north towards Aberdeen. At Aberdeen Montrose and his Irish troops summoned the city to surrender. The magistrates and Lord Balfour, commanding of a force equal to Montrose's force, refused to surrender the city. Provost Leslie of Aberdeen and Lord Balfour of Burleigh were able to assemble an army built around the regiment of regulars from Fife (and Kinross-shire) commanded by Lieutenant-Colonel Charles Arnot and the Aberdeen Militia commanded by Major Arthur Forbes. Between them they may have had 1,000 well-armed men, and fencibles under Udny between 1,500-2,000 foot and 300 horse. As at Tibbermore they were untried troops, and they suffered from a fatal lack of effective leadership under fire.

At the ensuing battle half a mile from the city on the 12th September Lord

Balfour was defeated. South and east of Craibstane Ridge, only the 'demise of the Fife Regulars' was exaggerated as they turned up again soon afterwards serving under General Baillie. As Aberdeen had not surrendered it was open to sacking and was plundered for two days before Montrose withdrew. Argyle was only three days away, trying to catch him.

On 7th August, after the surrender of York on 16th July, with the Scots army refreshed they marched north again. David Leslie with most of the horse went west to secure Carlisle, while dealing with remaining Royalists in Cumberland and Westmorland on the way. The Earl of Calender had Newcastle under siege. Leven and the Earl arranged for 3,000 colliers to undermine the defences. Ammunition came south by ship from Scotland. Newcastle fell on November in October. The city had a virulent typhus plague and unfortunately many soldiers carried it home to Scotland.

Having hustled the Royalists out of Aberdeen, Argyll harassed Montrose and the Royalists until he caught them unawares at Fyvie on 28th October. Skirmishing went on between the sides for three days before a shortage of fodder for his horses forced Argyll to give up. Montrose plundered Turriff then went west, but his army was melting away. By 6th November Montrose fled south to Blair Athol. Despite the victories at Tibbermore and Aberdeen the raising of Royalists in numbers had failed to take off. Argyll settled his men in as fighting in Scotland was unlikely in winter and it would be sufficient to end the Royalist movement. Argyll and Leven met in Edinburgh for a conference.

Alasdair MacColla, Montrose's Irish ally, came storming in from the west, burning and devastating the Campbell lands at the start of winter, forcing hundreds of starving homeless families out into bitter snows. Even Argyll's own burgh of Inveraray was included by 13th December. In undignified flight Argyll fled to Dumbarton in search of an army. There he met with Baillie who had returned from Marston Moor, but Baillie refused to take orders from Argyll, who then went north again with borrowed levies to stiffen his own and Baillie left with the rest to Perth.

On 1st February 1645 Montrose was trapped in the Great Glen with Argyll holding both ends. In midwinter Montrose led his men in an incredible march up over the mountains, a steep 300 metre climb, and down the steep decline into Glen Turret. In the early hours of 2nd February they marched for 36 hours climbing through hills in midwinter covering many miles, before arriving exhausted into Inverlochy. They now were to fight an army twice their size.

The last few hours of darkness were spent skirmishing in the woods. Argyll watched safe and warm on his galley off shore, giving command to the experienced soldier Sir Duncan Campbell of Auchinbrec. Montrose won the day, and the power of Clan Campbell was all but shattered for a generation. This brought great numbers of recruits to the Royalists. By March Montrose had about 3,000 infantry and, for the first time, was able to field an effective cavalry and many experienced fighters.

After this Montrose led the Scots government a merry dance, occupying Elgin in March, then Dunkeld. Baillie finally surprised Montrose at Dundee, forcing him to retreat to Arbroath, with Baillie's men too exhausted by the forced march from Perth to take advantage of the situation. Many of Montrose's men went home once safely back in their hills, reducing the force to only 500 men. Baillie attacked him at Crieff and chased him down Strathearn. Montrose rendezvoused at Doune Castle and Cardross House with Lord Aboyne, home from breaking out of Carlisle and MacColla at Deeside.

Baillie was hampered by interference from the Committee of Parliament attached to the army. Lord Balfour of Burleigh was one on this committee, which through the dissensions of its leaders frustrated the army command. The Royalists had victories at Auldearn on 8th May and Alford on 2nd July. At the latter Baillie had at least six regiments of regulars including Lord Elcho, so the 'Fifers' were there. This was an important victory for the Royalists as the King had been beaten at Naseby a few weeks earlier and Montrose was trying to relieve the pressure for him.

Montrose then led a raid on Perth where a parliament was being held to discuss the typhus plague that had been brought to Edinburgh from Newcastle by soldiers. Establishing himself in Methven Wood, Montrose mounted a series of fairly ineffectual skirmishes for a week before Baillie and Hurry chased them out Again, as at Dundee, the pursuit was poor because Hurry's cavalry failed to move fast or determinedly enough.

William Baillie, a professional soldier all his life, had served in the Netherlands and Sweden. He then came home to Scotland and served under Leven at Marston Moor, before taking over as Commander-in-Chief on Argyll's resignation. In his own mind at least 'those in front of him might be his opponents, but his enemies were behind him'. By the summer of 1645, Baillie was becoming increasingly irascible and exasperated by his failure to trap Montrose in Methven, caused by what he regarded as constant political interference in military operations, and he handed in his resignation on 4th August. As neither Hurry nor Lindsay would touch the job, although his 'demission' was accepted he was instructed to serve out his notice until 8th September when Robert Munro would be brought back from Ireland to replace him. From then on the directing of the war would be by Parliament or Committee of Parliament, and the actual management and execution of directions by the Commander-in-Chief. Baillie now had the Committee members quite literally riding at his elbow and interfering in day-to-day management. However, with his stubborn and increasingly uncooperative attitude it would be wrong to think of Baillie as an entirely innocent victim.

As Montrose pushed south again, Baillie made a fortified camp at Bridge of Earn, but the Royalist army moved west and crossed to the river Forth at Mills of Forth above Stirling on 11th August. Delayed by another fall-out with his political masters, and by the Fife infantry brigade who had taken the opportunity to go home, it was 14th August before his force crossed Stirling Bridge.

The Royalists were making for Glasgow and camped at Kilsyth. On arrival, Argyll came to Ballie's camp and, with the rest of the Committee, insisted on an immediate advance. The ground ahead was unsuitable, being riddled with eighteenth-century coal and iron workings, and a reservoir for the Forth and Clyde Canal. It also concealed a deep glen. Their Lordships ordered the ground be scouted. Meanwhile Baillie with Lord Elcho and Lord Burleigh had gone to the right hand of the regiments, when Baillie was called by the rest of the Committee. Baillie requested Burleigh and Elcho go with him, conjecturing they would advise removing, which they did. The Committee on seeing the advantage may be with the enemies in their present position, voted to withdraw to the hill nearby.

In the Battle of Kilsyth with his front line overwhelmed, and Lauderdale's regiments dispersed by the Royalist cavalry, Baillie galloped to find the reserves, only to find them gone too. MacColla's Highlanders were fully occupied in dealing with Ballie's regulars and the Gordon Foot routed Leslie's Fife Brigade. It was all over very quickly, and the whole army completely disintegrated. It was a difficult time for the three Fife regiments. Dissolved into a panic-stricken rabble, they were pursued for miles by exultant clansmen, and hundreds were ruthlessly cut down. Argyll fled to Berwick, and the Earl of Lanark abandoned Glasgow. Montrose sent cavalry to Edinburgh, and moved his infantry to Glasgow. He called a Parliament to meet there on 20th October, as Edinburgh still had the plague. MacColla went to Kintyre with personal ambitions to recover the lands of yesteryear. The Gordons marched home to protect their own country against a threat from local Covenanters. Montrose then went to Dalkeith and on 7th September moved to the borders where he hoped to get support cavalry. In Galashiels he waited, but to his disappointment neither the Earls Home or Roxburgh appeared. By 10th September, Montrose heard at Jedburgh that Lieutenant-General David Leslie had passed through Berwick days earlier with four regiments of infantry and six regiments of cavalry.

Leven with his rested army had spent much of the year in the north of England. The English Parliament wanted him to join them at Chester, but the state of affairs in Scotland was very critical, especially after Auldearn and Leven was reluctant to move far from the border. However, the English alliance needed to be maintained, so he compromised by crossing the Pennines into Westmorland, which allowed him to cover David Leslie's blockade of Carlisle. A Royalist danger to Yorkshire seemed imminent, so Leven again crossed the Pennines and rendezvoused with Lord Fairfax at Doncaster, where he learned the end of the war was not far off. On hearing of the disaster of Kilsyth, Leven headed for Scotland.

Meanwhile Montrose left Jedburgh, moving west to avoid David Leslie's army (who were looking for Royalists in Gladismuir) and made for Galashiels via Soutra. On 12th September Montrose reached Selkirk, and while the main army settled in to camp approximately three miles down the Ettrick Water at Philiphaugh, many officers found softer accommodation in the nearby town. Montrose had meant to pull out at dawn but, having been up late writing despatches to be sent to the King, he overslept. The single patrol sent out reported there was no sign of the enemy within 15 miles, and therefore no need for urgency.

The government army, warned by Amisfield, was concerned the Royalists would escape due to the thick foggy conditions. Leslie was closing in with a larger army, which he divided in two, half attacking Selkirk and the rest the Royalist camp. The battle started at 10am on 13th September 1645. The large body of Royalists, mainly untrained and inexperienced, camped on the haugh. Most of their officers were still in Selkirk, trapped there by half of the Parliamentary army. The Royalists troops scattered all over the haugh, too bewildered to make battle formations. The veteran Irish fled, realising the battle lost, while many were caught trying to get to their own baggage. The fog only added to the confusion. Leslie had his Irish prisoners shot, and the camp followers were also murdered. Senior officers amongst the prisoners were executed in the end.

Montrose was reunited with Inchbrackie at Dunkeld, but appeals to MacColla were unanswered. So with 200 cavalry and 800 foot, Montrose marched to link up with the Gordons but family rivalries were keeping them busy. Returning to Dunkeld, Montrose tried threatening Glasgow in a vain attempt to save the lives of the Royalist officers. Gradually the noose was tightening round Montrose and his men. Montrose took refuge in Speyside. He obeyed the King's order to 'disband all your forces', dismissing his men at Rattray on 30th July 1646 and, with an agreement of safe conduct, left Scotland by September.

Huntley also submitted, then raised his clan in response to secret orders from the King 'to have a force ready in anticipation of his return to Scotland'. Huntly was not captured until November 1647. MacColla escaped back to Ireland, and the last 176 Royalist soldiers surrendered at Dunveg Castle on 5th July 1647.

When King Charles I ordered his followers to lay down their arms, he was a 'guest' of the Scots army. The New Model Army in England amalgamated the remains of the previous three armies of Fairfax, Manchester and Cromwell into a single fairly large, organised, trained and equipped army. This had sharpened the differences between the Presbyterians and Independent factions in the English Parliament as to who should nominate officers for the new army, there being too many available for the reduced army. The Scots entered the war to secure their revolution by curbing the King's power and establishing the Presbyterian Church in England. That was the agreement with the Parliamentarians. However, failure to exploit their part in the victory at Marston Moor to advantage meant that the following year the Independents' Army, which had comprehensively defeated the King and destroyed his remaining army, made it obvious that a negotiated settlement was no longer necessary, and neither were the Scots. When the Scots army had served its purpose for them, the English wanted rid of it. King Charles thought to take advantage of the situation by surrendering to the Scots whom he trusted more than others. He rode into their camp and surrendered to the Earl of Leven in person. The King endured half a year of boredom in the Scots camp, plagued by lengthy sermons and prayers from Presbyterian ministers. Not having seen his beloved wife for two years, when she had left for France, he missed her greatly.

When Newark surrendered Leven swiftly marched north to avoid the New Model Army getting between him and Scotland. Both he, his army and the King were safe at Newcastle by 3rd May. Here they remained until the first instalment of the outstanding subsidy money was paid by the almost bankrupt English Parliament on 30th January. When the Scots left Newcastle making for home, the King was ruthlessly left behind, on the condition that no harm would come to him from the English Parliament.

In 1647 the Scots too were to remodel their army. The muster on January 1646 outside Newark revealed Leven's forces comprised 4,136 horse and 2,836 foot, exclusive of officers. The cavalry was reduced to 15 independent troops of horse and three of dragoons. Just seven infantry regiments were wanted, each with 800 men in eight companies, two of which were Highlanders. Argyll and the Kirk Party ensured it was their men, headed by David Leslie. Of the foot, nearly all were conscripts, and some were veterans who had been levied as fencibles, some as long ago as 1643, to serve for 40 days. They refused to march out of Dunblane until they received their arrears of pay. When they did move on 17th May it was to avoid the plague.

The basic problem was that English and the Scots went to war not to abolish the power of the Crown but to harness it. However, Charles I's uncompromising attitude was making it clear that he was pushing the English Parliament to the limit. The Scots Parliament was divided in two main factions. Argyll's Kirk party, which had the support of ministers, was prepared to see the King humbled if he would not take the Covenant and establish Presbyterianism in England. Hamilton's party, which included most of the nobility, was more concerned with the preservation of the existing social order, even if it meant accepting compromises on religion.

On 23rd March 1648 two officers declared for the King at Pembroke. Riots began in London, and a rising in Bury St Edmonds. The Second Civil War had begun.

The Scots Parliament ratified mobilisation on 2nd March, but it was 4th May before it was ordered, by which time the English danger was extinguished. It was noted in Scotland that many rising for the King were Cavaliers and many were Catholics who would never accept Presbyterianism as a price for Scots intervention. On 12th June Scots dissidents, who had moved counties to avoid the levies, gathered on Mauchline Moor near Kilmarnock only to be cut down by the Earl of Callander on the orders of government. Ten or twelve were killed and approximately 50 injured.

On 8th July the Scots army crossed the border with 3,000 horse and 6,000 infantry under the command of the Marquis of Hamilton along with Baillie, Lauderdale, Callender and Langdale. At Kendal, Monro was in charge of the Irish troops who wanted him as their commander, but when he refused to take orders from either Baillie or Callender, an exasperated Hamilton ordered him and his Irishmen to wait for the artillery train to come from Scotland. Hamilton moved on and, still not knowing where he was going and what he hoped to achieve, called a council of war at Hornby on 9th August. This decided, Lambert of the

English Parliament Army was at Pontefract and, unknown to them, Cromwell had rendezvoused with Lambert at Weatherby. Poor communication in a strung-out army, where the infantry were 20 miles behind the cavalry, the Scots were decimated piecemeal by Cromwell over two wet days near Preston. Hamilton evidently lost the head and fled the battle. Langdale was abandoned and left to his fate, while Baillie and Callender did at least try to form battle lines. On 19th August Baillie parleyed for peace. 1,712 soldiers laid down their weapons and surrendered 75 colours.

Hamilton fled south and, avoiding murder by his own men, surrendered at Uttoxeter on 25th August. He was tried under his English title as Earl of Cambridge and executed. Callander, Middleton, and Langdale escaped to Holland. Baillie and other officers were eventually released but the rank and file were sold abroad for service in the Low Countries.

In late August there was a rising of Covenanters in the west after hearing the news of the Scots army destroyed at Preston. Several thousand from Ayrshire and Lanarkshire were led by earls Loudoun, Eglinton and David Leslie. David Leslie seized Stirling Castle without a fight on 8th September. The Estates hurriedly ordered Munro to hold Carlisle and Berwick, and Hamilton's brother, the Earl of Lanark, to assemble others at Jedburgh. Munro then rendezvoused with Lanark and captured Linlithgow to block any Covenanter assistance from the west, but were well placed to receive their own regiments from the Royalist north. A truce was patched up, both sides agreeing to halt all military movements. Argyll's forces were approaching Stirling from the west. Monro scattered Argyll's levies, thus the two sides stood glowering at each other from Stirling and Edinburgh.

This stalemate was broken by Cromwell, who rode up to Edinburgh at the head of a cavalry brigade. He declared that Argyll either dealt with the Engagers (Royalists) or Cromwell would do it for him. After a series of truces, they all agreed to a negotiated settlement at the Treaty of Stirling 27th September 1648. It agreed that no Engager accepting the treaty was to be injured in life, estate, title or freedom, but those holding public office were to refrain from exercising their duties until a full parliament, to be held in January 1649, settled all outstanding civil matters. Under the treaty the Engagers had to surrender Stirling, Carlisle (still held by the Earl of Callender's men) and Berwick by 1st October. Argyll and Leslie agreed to disband all but 1500 of their men by that date, and both sides agreed to send home the rest of their troops.

Lord Balfour had opposed the 'engagement' to march into England to rescue the King, and was one of those who effectively dissuaded Cromwell from invading Scotland in 1648. Lord Balfour had several private meetings with Cromwell. Balfour was one of the last Committee of Estates and Lord of Treasury in 1649, and credited with being one of the chief contrivers to the 'Solemn League'.

Cromwell went south again, satisfied that both sides had stepped back from the brink and a sensible outcome had been reached. What the Scots had not expected was the execution of the King in London on 30th January 1649. With that the rules changed.

The immediate reaction to the execution was relatively restrained. In 1649 the Scots Parliament was dominated by supporters of the Kirk Party and, while controlling the King was something of an innovation, disposing of awkward ones was not. King James I's mother, Queen Mary, had after all been executed by her cousin in England. James VI was proclaimed King of Scots before inheriting the English throne and becoming James 1. Charles II was proclaimed in Scotland as King of Scotland and England in the style of his recently executed father. Scotland was wrong in this. They had every right to proclaim their own king, but in declaring him as king of Eng-

Oliver Cromwell

land was not in their remit and would be reactionary to the English. However, the prince would not be allowed to set foot in Scotland, far less crowned, unless he took the Covenant and accepted his late father had fatally resisted. The English anger was mollified for a while; they had more pressing business in Ireland.

King Charles II was in Holland and in an effort to improve negotiations with the Estates and hurry them along, Charles unleashed the long-feared foreign invasion. So, in September 1649, a pathetically small force of Scots and English Royalists, and more Danish and German mercenaries, sailed for Orkney. They took the town of Kirkwall but, while safe there, it was too remote from Edinburgh to influence decision-making. In March 1650 Charles raised the stakes by sending the feared James Graham, Marquis of Montrose, back home to Scotland to secure enough support for Charles so that, once he returned, he would not have the humiliating terms of the Kirk party.

Montrose established his headquarters at Thurso by 12th April. It comprised a few reluctant Orcadians with the original mercenaries and a number of local gentry dutifully rallied to the King's standard, but they had few clansmen with them. Leaving a 200-man garrison to defend Thurso, Montrose marched south, pausing to capture Dunbeath Castle, and leaving 100 men to hold it. He failed to take Dunrobin, so then moved inland to Lairg, and down the Kyle of Sutherland to Carbisdale arriving late on 25th April. Leaving garrisons behind and caution being a break with the past, but Montrose had not yet learned the importance of proper scouting and communication, and that time spent on reconnaissance is never wasted. On Sunday 27th May at Cardale this shortcoming finally found him out again.

Leslie was known to be south mustering at Brechin Muir two days earlier, and Montrose thought there was only a single troop of enemy cavalry within his area. Thinking it too good an opportunity to miss, Montrose broke camp and went after the cavalry sensing an easy victory. The government troops under Lt-Col Archibald Strachan had veteran cavalry totalling 230 men with 36 musketeers under a quartermaster. He marched north from Inverness and was joined at Tain by 400 levies. At a council of war at Tain some of Strachan's officers piously said they would not fight on the Sabbath, but with Royalists approaching nearby they put aside their scruples. Using his single troop of horse as bait, Strachan sprang his ambush at 3pm, riding down the small 40-horse Royalist cavalry, and the survivors were driven back on the Orcadian levies, who threw down their arms and ran. Montrose escaped from the battlefield, but pursued west and alone in unfamiliar territory he was soon captured. He was taken to Edinburgh and, as he had been sentenced back in 1644, there was no need for a trial. Montrose therefore was executed on 21 May.

At a standstill, all his plans failing, Charles II sailed from Holland. Reluctantly he signed the Covenant on 23rd June, and on 24th came on land at Speyside on the Scottish Government Terms, for which he never forgave them and he never set foot in Scotland again. It is said the king was entertained at Burleigh Castle on 16th August 1650 on his way from Perth to Edinburgh.

The English government at Westminster thought the settlement with Charles II a sign of weakness. They failed to appreciate the difference between English and Scottish kingship. The King of Scotland was King of the Scots and many of his nobles were hereditary owners of their lands while the King of England, since the Norman invasion, gave out titles and land owned by the crown and had the right to confiscate them, hence was King of England. They therefore feared a Scots invasion and on 12th June 1650, three weeks after Montrose was hanged, and a week before King Charles II landed in Scotland, they acted. Lord Fairfax and Oliver Cromwell (returned from campaigning in Ireland) were appointed to command a new field army as General and Lt-General respectively. Initially Fairfax assumed this was a precautionary move and he was only to command should the Scots invade, but within a week Parliament declared its intention of invading Scotland first. This was too much for Fairfax, and he had sufficient scruple to refuse the charge. Oliver Cromwell, with no scruples, was on 26th June created Lord-General instead.

Despite the obvious signs that the English were preparing for war, including buying horses in markets both sides of the border, the Scots Government was still trying avoid it. Not until 25th June was full mobilisation of the army decreed in order to defend Scotland. Lord Balfour, under the act of putting the kingdom in a posture of defence, was one of the colonels for the county of Fife and in the same year was nominated one of the commissioners of the Treasury and Exchequer.

In 12 years of conflict the fencible system had effectively collapsed, and government was reduced to simply demanding a certain number of men levied from each Sherriffdom. The Barony of Burleigh and Tillyrie was in the Sherriffdom of Kinross, but was often included in the Fife men when Lord Balfour was in command. To fill old regiments and mix veterans with recruits, the government ordered on 25th June the levy of 9,749 foot and 2,880 horse. The Border levies were reluctant to go north with their homes in danger of the invasion, and the west was problematic as opposition to the King was greatest in that area and made it difficult to source levies. Fife, Perthshire, Linlithgow and Clackmannan were most successful. Any who had marched as king's men or Engagers, or otherwise rendered themselves odious to the Kirk Party were purged as ungodly. Unsuitable officers were often appointed due to these purges. Leven took advantage of the purges by having as many of the veteran officers already serving in 1649 appointed.

The invading English army crossed the border at Berwick with 16,354 men on 22nd July and, meeting no resistance, got through the trappy gorge at Cockburnspath, arriving safely at Dunbar on 26th July. Cromwell stopped to assess the situation. The Scots had followed their usual scorched-earth plan, driving away all the stock and burning or hiding everything that would sustain the enemy. Also of concern to Cromwell were the 15 ships, including four men-of-war to support his army, which had not yet arrived at Dunbar and supplies were low.

Cromwell pushed on to Haddington, just beyond where he encountered Leven's outpost line. The English cavalry under Lambert were unable to penetrate Leven's cavalry screen, and the Scots continued to fall back steadily. On 29th July the English army at last uncovered the main body of the Scots army, causing first Lambert then Cromwell to halt in dismay. For the first time Cromwell realised Leven was not going to meet him in open battle, but had elected to dig in his raw army behind a line of forts and entrenchments stretching all the way from Edinburgh to the River Forth, along the line of the present Leith Walk. Cromwell recognised a formal front assault was out of the question, and tried to tempt Leven out to fight with no success. The weather turned bad and his men only had makeshift bivouacs in the pouring rain.

The wet weather and lack of provisions forced Cromwell back to Musselburgh. The Scots harried Lambert and his exposed rearguard. About 4am on 31st July, Major-General Robin Montgomerie took 800 hand-picked cavalry belonging to his and Sir James Hackett's regiments. By posting a few English Royalists at the front of the column, the familiar accents misled the pickets into thinking the approaching troops friendly until it was too late. Lambert's foot managed to let off a few rounds of shot and this seemingly was enough to see off Hackett and his men. Sir James Balfour remarked 'Sir James Hackett received a grate fryte at skirmishe with the enemy, he should haue secondit the L Generall, bot turnit and never lowesid a pistol against the enimey, bot tooke him to the speed of his horse heels'.

At midnight on 5th August Cromwell pulled his army back to Dunbar, as the ships bringing supplies were prevented from landing at Musselburgh due to the bad weather. An even greater mistake was having gambled on good weather and a swift campaign. He had not brought tents for the army and, having underestimated the Scots weather, the army now suffered accordingly. The tents were at last landed at Dunbar and issued to the soldiers, but already the foul weather and scarcity of provisions were producing an appallingly high rate of sickness.

On 11th August Cromwell made another attempt to bring Leven's army to open battle. He swung south and west of Edinburgh (approximately where the city bypass is today) in an attempt to reach the Forth at Queensferry and cut Leven off from Stirling. His lack of transport meant he could only carry three days' supplies. Initially seizing a strong position on the Braid Hills, he sent a letter to his old colleague David Leslie wanting a peace, which produced a meeting of officers on the sands between Leith and Musselburgh. David Leslie, while declaring abhorrence of the King, was not prepared to change sides. Negotiations failing and supplies used up, Cromwell next day again fell back to Musselburgh. Leven blocked him at Corstorphine Hill. Cromwell stormed a minor outpost at Redhall, then Leven blocked his path at Gogar. Thinking things looked promising as the Scots appeared to be standing in the open, Cromwell prepared to attack. Only when he realised that both ends of Leven's flanks were secured by boggy ground and the invitingly open front was not only boggy but also covered by artillery, Cromwell decided not to attack in the uninviting conditions. He moved back to Musselburgh and on 31st August once again made for Dunbar.

Leven and Leslie had drilled hard and improved the efficiency of the raw levies. They personally had overseen two successive purges of unsuitable officers. Cromwell showed no inclination to stand and face the Scots but hurried off to Haddington, where again his rearguard was attacked as it approached. On a cloudy afternoon there were hours of fighting before Colonel Charles Fairfax's foot repulsed the Scots. Early next day Cromwell, prayers said, lined up his exhausted army into battle order in an open field to the south of Haddington. The baggage and sick were sent back to Dunbar. At 10am, after waiting four hours in which no enemy came, Cromwell also made for Dunbar 12 miles away. A poor, shattered, hungry and discouraged army was pursued by the Scots and the rearguard had hard work to secure the weak foot that were not able to keep up the march. They drew near Dunbar towards night, the Scots ready to fall upon the rear when two guns played on them and so they drew off and left that night.

While Cromwell's rearguard was being actively harried by the Scots cavalry, the greater part of Leven's army slid east. Part of the Scots foot went south to Cockburnspath to defend the gorge on the Berwick road. The main party of the Scots army secured the adjacent heights of Doon Hill with a great view overlooking Dunbar, the road south to Berwick and the surrounding countryside. Cromwell's army was trapped, and a battle seemed unavoidable. Leslie slept that night of 2nd September at Spott House, a fortalice at the foot of Doon Hill.

It is difficult to know the strength of Cromwell's army at Dunbar. The 16,354 men who crossed the border with him on 22nd July had shrunk to about 12,080 by 3rd September. The lack of tents and exposure to Scottish wet weather caused the loss of many. About 2,000 men, who were sufficiently ill or injured, had been evacuated by sea. The rest must have died. There were still about 1,000 sick with the army. In battle the sick normally stayed in camp, but if the army was trying to break out (as was apparent next morning) every man fit to walk or sit in a saddle must be taken with them. Cromwell said afterwards that his army consisted of fit men of 7,500 foot and 3,500 horse.

We were told in history that the Church Ministers in their black flowing robes told the Generals to go down and smite the enemy. That is rubbish and takes no account of reality and the tactical range of weapons. To stop Cromwell retreating down the Berwick road it was more effective to seize Broxmouth House where the road crosses the Broxburn, and it took time to provoke a response from the English. The range of the guns was ineffective from Doon Hill and to stop the English army and Cromwell's escape south, they would have to be moved to Meikle Pinkerton, about a mile and a half from where the guns were. The guns began to move shortly before sunrise on 2nd September, but it was not until 4pm that the artillery and baggage were finally brought down to Meikle Pinkerton Farm. The length and complexity of the move once again emphasised the unmanageable position of the original hilltop site, and heavy weapons in battle were impractical as they took so long to move.

Meanwhile Cromwell brought his army from Dunbar to form a battle line on the north side of the Broxburn ravine. Leslie, wary of being attacked before his men were properly deployed, arranged his own battle line along the south side of the burn. The Broxburn is not deep nor broad and runs down a fairly wide valley with ravine sides, itself a significant military obstacle, particularly as the north (English) side of the ravine is higher than the southern side and largely dominates it. Consequently, by nightfall on 2nd September, most of Leslie's infantry were still uselessly positioned to the left of the Berwick road with an all but impassable ravine directly in front of them. Nevertheless Leslie had firmly blocked the Berwick road. Cromwell knew he was in trouble. There is no doubt the poor, shattered, hungry and discouraged English army was pretty well at the end of its tether. Major General Lambert vetoed the motion to ship out the foot and horse, as it would take too long and they would lose the baggage. Lambert forcefully and inspirationally advocated an assault on the Scots position, with the object of turning Leslie's right wing and pinning their army against the steep sides of Doon Hill and destroying them. That was what happened eventually next morning.

Cromwell was trying to break out to Berwick, even putting the baggage wagons up front. There were only three places to cross the Broxburn: Brands Mill, the main crossing on the Berwick Road, or the flat area between Broxburn House and the sea. Cromwell sent his cavalry on to the flat area, but needed control of the Berwick road. The weather remained very wet, and Cromwell rode on a little Scots horse all night by torch light through every regiment encouraging his troops. If the early morning attack failed the army would have to surrender.

The Scots army maintained an alert as night drew on, but at midnight permission was granted for all but two of the musketeers in a company to put out their slowmatch burners for their rifles. The troops found whatever shelter they could in the newly harvested corn fields, while many officers and the cavalry sought their tents. Two days later Leslie said bitterly that had the officers stayed with their troops that night, he might easily have won the fight. As it was, the Scots were unprepared at 4am when Cromwell manoeuvred and secured the crossing points of the Broxburn. Scattering the first line of the Scots cavalry, the English cavalry attacked the Scots infantry, even managing to do damage amongst the tents, before the Scots counter-attacked and halted the onslaught. Regimental commanders Sir William Douglas of Kirkness and Lt Col David Wemyss were both killed, and a great many colours were captured. Lumsden managed to drive Lambert back over the Broxburn, and the outlook was bleak for Cromwell and the breakout, but Cromwell persevered.

Leaving the Broxburn for the higher ground by Little Pinkerton, Lambert's regiment fought petty skirmishes with straggling remnants of Lumsden's Brigade. Meanwhile Cromwell fought and destroyed the Scots cavalry and crossed the Broxburn on the flat by the sea. Cromwell and Lambert halted their victorious troops and took the momentous decision to surround the Scots army and defeat them, instead of breaking out and heading for Berwick. The Scots were hemmed in between the Broxburn and the base of Doon Hill and, as the sun rose, Cromwell seized the chance, pushing his cavalry around the flank of Lawyer's position and into the rear of the Scottish infantry. By 6am the Scots army was defeated. Some managed to escape by crossing the Broxburn at what is now Doon Bridge, others escaped by Cockburnpath or over the Lammermuirs. Most of the prisoners and colours were taken in the final phase of the battle.

Amongst the Scots army at Dunbar was Lord Balfour of Burleigh, nominated to command a regiment in the second levy from Fife. A colour taken by the English bore his black and white crest. After the hard time the Fife Regiment had at Kilsyth, Balfour's men were consolidated with the Kirkness men. The brigade must have been a fairly strong one, for between 15th and 22nd July 2,700 men should have mustered for service in Fife. A proportion of them were put out as horse which would have brought the theoretical total to some 2,100 men, and even allowing for the usual wastage there must still have been about 2,000 men in the ranks at Dunbar. Balfour, while admitting many foot were taken prisoner, noted in his journal that there were 800 or 900 killed at the Battle of Dunbar.

After resting for two days (reputed to have his headquarters at Spott House) Cromwell accepted the surrender of Edinburgh on 7th September. The castle held out until the 23rd, but by this time Leslie has fallen back to Stirling. Cromwell came to Stirling but, unable to take the castle without a siege and there being little stomach for it in his army, retired again to Edinburgh. The Scots had a catastrophic military defeat at Dunbar, but from the English point of view it was an inconclusive victory that had not that achieved their aims, except their own deliverance from impending defeat. For although beaten, the Scots army was not destroyed.

In October there was as attempted Royalist coup in Perth. King Charles II had moved from Dunfermline to Perth, and here he dithered and cancelled the uprising, until persuaded that everyone was already too deeply committed. He

Battle of Dunbar, 1650 (opp)

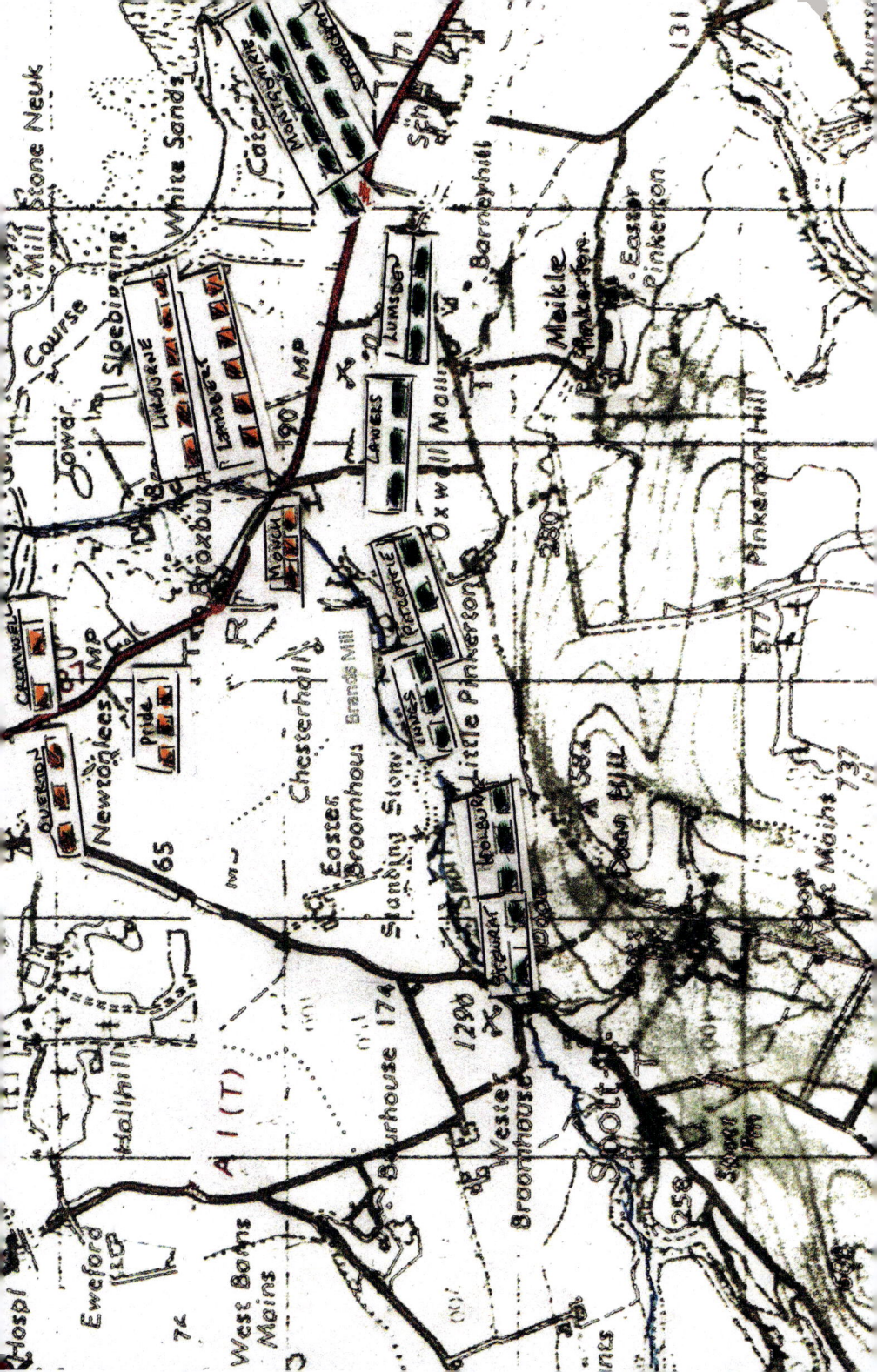

fled eastward to Glen Clova. Confusion reigned, many not knowing the Perth coup had been aborted. Erskine of Dun and Atholl had 2,000 men just north of Perth. The committee of Estates begged the king to return and eventually Robin Montgomerie caught up with him and persuaded him to go back to Perth to get his supporters to disband.

Lambert put down a rising at Hamilton in late November and Edinburgh Castle surrendered on 23rd December. William Dundas, in charge of the castle and summoned by Lambert to surrender it, asked for time to consult with the Estates. Lord Balfour recorded that 'the Estates for their part rather than weakened by the recent defeat of Westlanders (at Hamilton) responded firmly'.

It made no difference to the discredited Kirk Party that, after Dunbar, David Leslie's hastily realignment with the Royalists enabled Charles II to be crowned at Scone on 1st January 1650.

On 4th February Cromwell with Lambert and the cavalry went west intending to cross the Forth at Stirling, but at Kilsyth on 6th February the weather closed in, and a council of war was called. As the waters were impassable they returned to Edinburgh. In the damp Cromwell fell sick. It started off as a bad cold and rapidly became something worse, which took two months to recover from. The war continued at lower levels and Cromwell, by April, pushed west to try and secure the area once and for all. Glasgow, won back again by Cromwell, was occupied and another attempt was made to cross the Forth at Stirling. A month later a shortage of supplies forced Cromwell back to Edinburgh to meet shipping and supplies from London but, exhausted again, Cromwell took to his bed. His men were overstretched and the position in the west tenable only as long as the local population were at least passively sympathetic. Once patriotism and age-old loyalties won over religion and the Kirk, the west was lost. By the end of the month Dumfries and Hamilton had been abandoned by Cromwell's men.

There followed Royalist victories at Linlithgow in April and Paisley in May, before the defeat at Inverkeithing in July. Lambert had ferried troops across the Forth at Queensferry to a camp at Ferry Hills near Pitreavie Castle by Inverkeithing. Cromwell marched from Stirling and the Scots were routed. One of the Scottish brigades was that of Colonel Charles Arnot. Sadly, Scots regiments were caught on the open slopes of Pitreavie Castle and hundreds of Highlanders were killed. Sir James Balfour recorded that the Scots lost 800 men in total in the battle. Cromwell then marched towards Perth, stopping overnight at Kirkness House by Loch Leven. His hostess being Dame Isabel Lady Kirkness, the widow of Colonel Sir William Douglas (who was injured at the battle of Dunbar and died of his wounds in captivity), the welcome was somewhat frigid. When she greeted him with a kiss on the cheek, Cromwell remarked 'There are those who kiss on the cheek who would bite off the nose'. Perth surrendered on 2nd August, just as soon as Cromwell's engineers drained the wet ditch surrounding the defences.

On the early morning of 17th July Col Robert Overton, with 2100 troops, sailed from Leith to Burntisland and marched to the Ferry Hills. Cromwell tried to tempt Major-General John Leslie out of Inverkeithing to fight in the open. Failing, he sent Lambert to deal with Inverkeithing. By Sunday Lambert had three regiments of cavalry and four of foot up on Ferry Hills, all ferried over from Leith. The Scots were drawn up on castle hill near Pitreavie Castle. They stood ready for battle for an hour-and-a-half when Lambert heard from Cromwell that reinforcements were coming from Stirling to help the Scots. A real scrap evolved. The Scots cavalry and lances made it tough for the English, but in the end were routed by the reserve led by Lambert himself. The Scots scattered Lambert's troopers, hounding them and slaughtering many. Sir James Balfour recorded losses of 800 Scots.

Balfour Burleigh regimental standard, 1650

Shy of fighting in the open since Dunbar, David Leslie made no attempt to engage Cromwell but reluctantly agreed with King Charles II the desperate notion of marching into England, in a vain attempt to rally the English Royalists. On 31st July 1651 they marched out of Stirling, 14,000 strong. Crossing the border by Carlisle on 6th August, closely tailed by Colonel Monck, they made it to Worcester. Lord Derby, who was to have instigated a pro-royalist insurrection in Lancaster-shire, was wind-bound on the Isle of Man. On 24th August the King tried to muster the old county militia, ordering all men aged 16 to 60 to muster at Derby two days later. Surprisingly 1,000 men did appear. Cromwell reached Evesham by 27th August with 25,000 troops. The attack was on 3rd September, the anniversary of the Battle of Dunbar. The Royalists were defeated, with Cromwell accounting for 3,000 dead and 8,000 prisoners, who were shipped to the American plantations.

At Worcester the war was lost but not quite over. Stirling surrendered to Monck on 6th August 1651, Dundee was sacked on September 1st and Aberdeen occupied after a fight a week later. A cavalry charge raid on Alyth secured the remains of the Committee of Estates, including old Leven, leaving Scotland defeated and leaderless. The last of the Royalist army commanded by the Marquis of Huntly and Earl Balcarres capitulated on 21st November and 3rd December respectively. The surrender of the Bass Rock and finally Dunotter Castle in May 1652 ended fighting. Ironically, it was the same army of occupation led by George Monck which eventually brought about the restoration of King Charles II – and Scotland's independence.

When Archibald Campbell, first Marquis of Argyll, was arrested and tried in Edinburgh in 1661, Lord Balfour was cited as a witness at the trial "to prove words spoken by him in Parliament". He was excepted from the Act of Indemnity the following year and fined £1,111 Scots. Lord Robert did not long survive this penalty for he died in 1663 'being ane auld man he departed out of this life at Burley, and was interned at his local parish kirk, in the nicht time'.

The civil wars, through battle casualties and war-borne diseases, led to the deaths of an estimated 190,000 of the five million English population, and 60,000 of the one million Scots. The Irish population of 1.4 million in the same period was, through warfare, plague and exile, reduced by about 600,000.

Lord Balfour was one of the last Committee of Estates and Lord Treasury to the Scots Parliament in 1649. He was one of the chief contributors to the Solemn League. He died at Burleigh on 10th August 1663. A councillor and a soldier, better as a politician than a soldier, he nevertheless served his country with all of his energy through a troublesome time in history, never losing sight of the big picture. He lived to see King Charles II reinstated in 1660. His wife Margaret died in June 1639, and is also interned at Orwell Kirk, the old parish kirk by the loch side at Orwell village (the church was moved to Milnathort in 1729). They had four daughters and one son.

Lord John Balfour
to Mistress Margaret Balfour
of Burleigh

Margaret and Robert Balfour had five children.

John: *3rd Lord Balfour and heir to the barony.*

Jean: *married David, 2nd Earl of Wemyss*

Margaret: *married Sir James Crawford of Kilburnie*

Isobel: *married Thomas Lord Ruthven*

The youngest   *married her cousin Arnot of Ferny. There were no children*
daughter   *from their marriage and title then went to her brother Lord*
                      John Balfour of Burleigh.

John, the third Lord Burleigh, spent his younger years in France where he was wounded. When passing through London on his return home in 1649 he married, without his father's consent, Isobel, daughter of Sir William Balfour of Pitcullo, Lieutenant of the Tower of London. His father, with the view to having the marriage annulled, got it proposed to the General Assembly, Edinburgh the same year, but no answer was given to the application. Lord John fought at the battle of Drumclog under Claverhouse.

The Covenanters in Lanarkshire were on the verge of rebellion and, in defiance of the Government at large, The Hon my Lord Balfour and Sir William Bruce of Loch Leven were ordained as elders at Orwell Church on 30th July 1682.Lord John, 3rd Lord Burleigh died on 27th February 1697.

Lord John and Isobel had a large family of three sons and five daughters.

Robert	*Heir to the barony and 4th Lord Burleigh*
John Balfour of Ferny,	*Lieutenant-colonel in the reign of James VII. He had two sons: Arthur, (father of John Balfour of Ferny), and John who inherited by entail to the estate of Captain William Crawford, whose name and arms he assumed, and left issue.*
Henry of Starr *(1691)* and **Dunbog** *(1697)*	*The third son, who was a Major of Dragoons, and one of the representatives of the county of Fife in the last parliaments of Scotland, in which he warmly opposed the union. He mar-*

ried Elizabeth Oliphant, widow of George Bannerman of Dunbog by 1697, and thereby acquired the title of Dunbog. He participated in the Jacobite Rising in 1715 in a similar rank in the Jacobite Army. Major Balfour fought at Sheriffmuir and the Siege of Preston. It was at the latter that the Jacobite Army was surrounded and surrendered. Major Balfour presumably escaped from Preston as he was captured at Carlisle. As he had committed an act of rebellion, his lands were forfeit to the crown. However, the lands were restored to his children in 1720 and 1728. Married to Margaret Porterfield, they had three sons: Henry of Dunbog, their heir, 4th July 1730, followed by sons Robert and David. Henry of Star died on 11th September 1765 and Henry of Dunbog was his heir, who on 10th September 1765 was granted a Charter of Dunbog. Thus Henry sold Dunbog to the Dundas family in 1766. The most famous member of this branch of the family was Major General Nisbet Balfour of Dunbog (1743-1823) who fought in the American War of Independence and in the Napoleonic wars.

Margaret *(1630-1660)*	*married Andrew, Lord Rollo and had issue.*
Aemilia	*married John Malcolm of Innertail, had issue.*
Jean	*married to 1. Oliphant of Gask; 2. Sir Robert Douglas of*

Kirkness, who was educated at the bar passing out as an advocate, and was 'Commissioner of Supply' in 1685, '89, '90-95 and 1704, envied for these appointments. There is a letter from her brother delighted at her delivery of a baby. He wrote from 'Doublin' after the battle of the Boyne where he was serving with King William. They were the last Douglas of Kirkness buried at (old) Portmoak Kirk in 1724 under the family pew, with a plaque on the wall above.

Susan	*married to Robert Douglas of Strathendry and had issue.*
Anne	*married Captain Robert Sinclair. No issue.*
Robert, 4th Lord Burleigh	*married Margaret Melvil, daughter of George, Earl of Melvil. Robert was constituted one of the commissioners for executing the office of Lord Register of Scotland, anno 1686.*

As Master of Burleigh, he was one of the Commissioners for the University of St Andrews. In the reign of King William and Queen Mary, who had taken the throne to uphold the Protestant faith in Britain, they had lived in a society which, although Protestant, lived in peace with all types of Protestant faiths, and even employed Catholics in the Netherlands. The King was quite happy with the Episcopalian church in England, and failed to understand the Scots Presbyterian

attitude and the desire to purge the Episcopalian church and have their faith recognised as the Church in Scotland. The Scots in the 'Bishops and Covenanters'
conflict (1688 – 1691) made life difficult for the King to establish himself. William
was often away fighting wars in Ireland and later in France, and at times quite
misunderstood the situation in Scotland.

The Presbyterians eventually won the right by law to have their Church made
the National Scots Church. In July 1690 a special visitation of universities, col-
leges and schools was set up to see that beside being 'of pious, loyal and peaceable
conversation' and 'of good and sufficient literature and abilities for their respec-
tive employment' they should also submit to the government of the church now
established by law, should subscribe to the Westminster Confession of Faith and
swear the oath of allegiance to their majesties. On 23rd July, at a meeting in Glasgow, the commissioners formed into four committees for Glasgow, Edinburgh, St
Andrews and Aberdeen universities.

The Presbyterians had an element of extremists as well as moderate members.
The Episcopal had an element who still thought James VII was their king and had
many Jacobites in their number. It was a very complicated country. The city of
Edinburgh was flourishing as a cultural centre for medicine, law and science.

The Commissioners for the University of St Andrews had four earls and 13
others including, after the earls, the Master of Burleigh. They met again on 20th
August. The commission for St Andrews was led by the Earl of Crawford, who
behaved particularly roughly to the staff. Under Crawford's leadership at St Andrews the committed Jacobite principals and regents were purged.

In September 1697 a Robert Balfour is mentioned as an elder at Orwell
Church. In 1699 there was a great dearth and scarcity of food in the country, and
my Lord Balfour supplied three and a half bolls of 'bear' (a type of barley meal)
distributed by elders Robert Balfour and James Reid (of Tillyrie) to 20 named
poor, who received a measure of meal each. Lord Burleigh gave annually to the
Orwell church for the poor in the parish and in times of stress was approached
for more.

In March 1707 my Lord Balfour attended the synod of the Church in Dunfermline.

Between the years 1698-1700 there occurred an important event in Scotland's
history, one that happened in the 4th Lord Burleigh's lifetime and affected every
class of Scottish society, the ramifications influencing important happenings
thereafter.

Mr William Paterson, a Scot, who started the Bank of England in London,
came north with a plan to start a colony for Scotland in Panama. Once a colony
was established, with help from Dutch engineers a canal would be cut across the
narrow isthmus of land between the Caribbean Sea and the Pacific Ocean. A fortune could be made as shipping would no longer have to go by the long and dangerous tip of South America.

Scotland was in dire need after two reigns of tyranny and turmoil, the rule of

Sir William Paterson

favourites far away in London and neglect of the national welfare. Commerce was at a standstill, the treasury was empty and there were over 200,000 beggars and homeless vagrants in the land.

Mr Paterson asked for a Company of Scotland for Trading to Africa and the Indies, to plant Scots colonies with sole trading rights and monopolies, with subscribers. Naming Africa and the Indies was to divert attention from the scene in America, as there were fears that the English, French, Dutch and Spanish would see them as rivals, and try to stop them, or be annexed to the English crown.

Spain held most of the American mainland in the area, with small Portuguese and Dutch colonies, but in the very south of Central America is a narrow isthmus of land, shaped like the letter S. It was little known or esteemed, for its Carib coast was swampy and flat with no fair prospects, and there was so much good land elsewhere for the taking thousands of miles in each direction. Venturing inland, Paterson had found fair country a few miles beyond the swamps, and a great bay with a narrow hidden mouth leading into it, for an anchorage and port. Paterson found this isthmus between the Gulf of Darien and the Pacific Ocean, in some places only 30 miles wide, no more than the Forth–Clyde Canal.

Unclaimed by any nation, and with a charter from King William, it would hold potential for unimaginable riches. The wealthy nations of Europe drew their wealth from the Indies, the Spice Islands, China and Peru. All were on the Pacific Ocean, so ships had to sail two thirds of the world to reach them, further because Africa and India had to be circumnavigated too. China to Britain was 13,000 miles, East India 11,000 and Peru 16,000, yet to cross the Atlantic is only 4,000 miles.

With a canal the journey would be halved and the storms of the longer trips avoided. Help would be asked of the Dutch to fashion the canal, the land being as flat as Holland where the Dutch were expert at building canals. Ships would not have to be unloaded and haul cargo, but sail right through. This would be a toll gate of the oceans and Scotland holding the key. [1]

---

1   *Two hundred years later America dug the Panama Canal under President Roosevelt, directed by a descendant of William Paterson.*

King William was always looking for the money for his foreign wars and, as a Scots colony would pay direct to him and not the English treasury, he was willing to grant the Charter, but no other help. An estimated budget of £300,000-£500,000 would be needed for shipping, provisions and arms for the colonists and the first year's trade goods and so on. This was a huge sum for impoverished Scotland. Everyone was to be involved, however, from £1,000 from the wealthy to a few pounds from poorer folk. Some nobility invested £3,000, but it took time to collect and investors from England had to be repaid for it to be a Scots company. Orders went out for two new ships at Hamburg and Amsterdam, and a third vessel was bought from Leith merchants.

In July 1698, great crowds saw them off at Leith, with Highlanders and Lowlanders strongly represented – something hitherto unknown and not approved by some. The large crafts *Caledonia*, *St Andrews*, and *Unicorn* with cargo ships *Dolphin* and *Endeavour* sailed with the first 1200 settlers, militia and their gear. The two cargo ships transporting livestock, stores, provisions, trade goods etc sailed out of Leith led by Mr William Paterson. The English Parliament, East India Company and London merchants were hostile to the venture. King William, involved on the continent once more, was less than interested in Scotland.

The five ships reached the Gulf of Darien safely on 3rd November, in fair order and good morale despite a couple of deaths on the long cramped voyage and the efforts of the English warships to intercept them. There was no opposition to their landing, indeed they were welcomed by the local Indians, the more so as they offered to buy all the land the Indians would sell (usually Europeans just took the land as if having a right to do

Coat Of Arms of the Scottish Trading Company

so). They erected hutments, warehouses and port facilities, and built a stronghold called St Andrews on high ground behind the settlement. They had brought 50 cannon which were moved into the fort. Cheap and eager Indian labour facilitated this initial construction work and they called the colony New Caledonia.

Having chosen a level area of land at the head of a sheltered bay with good anchorage, they found their provisions unsuitable for the hot climate. Until they could grow their own corn there were shortages. Missions were sent north to the English colonies to purchase the required supplies. However it was discovered that orders from London to all English Governors specified that there was to be no trade or intercourse with the new colony, that the Scots were rebels against the King of England, and were to be treated as foes. So the mission returned empty-handed.

An allegation was made by Spain that Panama was theirs and they attacked the settlement, but were successfully beaten off. King William's present policy of harmony with Spain to keep the balance of power in Europe saw the English fleet watching the attack giving no support to the settlement.

Two weeks later a vessel was sent from Scotland with freight, and on 2nd August two more vessels were dispatched. In September a convoy of four ships set sail with arms, munitions, 1300 men, mainly military, and four ministers (one of the two previous ministers having died and the other being ill.) These sailed from the west coast to pick up Campbells at Bute and avoid the lurking English warships in the North Sea.

In late January 1700 William Paterson himself returned to Scotland, broken in health but not in spirit. New Caledonia had been abandoned. The original settlers had given up, surrendered to English pressure, were under-nourished, sick and disillusioned. What had been lacking was food and provisions. Stores sent were often unsuitable for the climate. They had expected to buy food from neighbouring colonies and islands until their own crops and cattle multiplied, but the Spanish, Dutch and French would not sell, and the English had been forbidden to have dealings with them. Their site abandoned they sailed to New York. Three hundred died before they left and another 300 on the voyage to New York. Of the original 1200 only 500 were left. They lost two ships en route to New York in a storm.

The second 1300 men arrived to find the site abandoned and, after being attacked by a large Spanish fleet sent especially from Seville, an English squadron again standing by and watching. Campbell of Finab, with his trained fighters, defeated a force six times their number. However it would take more than a military victory to convince this second party that they could succeed where the others had failed and gone.

The company had no more money. Already in debt, it had used half the coinage in Scotland and failed. Disappointment, disillusionment, resentment and anger were the reactions back in Scotland. The main wrath was against England and King William. There was talk of outright war and of separation of the Crowns.

In 1702 King William was thrown from a nervous horse and broke his collarbone. He died a few days later. His sister-in-law, the second daughter of King James II, ascended the throne as Queen Anne.

After the death of Queen Anne's last child the English Parliament settled the Crown on Sophia, daughter of Elizabeth, the daughter of Charles I. This brought the throne to the House of Hanover through the female line of Stuarts.

The English treasury had been desperately mismanaged, and bled by King William's European wars. It needed the Bank of England and, therefore, William Paterson. Paterson tried to get a payment to Scotland equivalent to losses on the Darien Affair, but had to agree it would only be given if Scotland agreed to the Union of the Parliaments and George of Hanover as King of Britain.

Commissioners were appointed to treat for such a union and on the nomination of the Queen (Anne) in both countries. It was a rough wooing. The English Parliament passed an act in 1705 saying 'unless by the following Christmas, the Scots Parliament had agreed to settle the succession to the throne in the same way as was already settled by England, namely the Electress Sophia of Hanover or her son George, then a state of hostility would exist between the two realms.'

In consequence, all natives of Scotland in England, Ireland or any of the colonies, would be treated as aliens, including those presently serving in the armed forces. All Scottish goods and commerce, such as coals, linen, cattle and the like, would be excluded from entering England, and no English goods or arms would enter Scotland. The Towns of Berwick, Carlisle and Newcastle would be fortified and garrisoned and regular regiments sent to line the border, with Northern militia put on a war-footing.

Scots seethed. A Convention of the Estates was called. Twenty five members concluded that the Union with England was inevitable and pointless to oppose. Others wanted a federal parliament, with national legislation still handing domestic matters, law, trade and commerce. This would leave Scotland reasonably free and independent in her affairs while allowing the benefits of the English connection. The motion to have the Union was carried at the Estates meeting on 28th June 1705 in Edinburgh.

Under this agreement grants for losses from the Darian Affair were paid to those voting for the union. This included Montrose, Argyll and the Kers of Cesford, all of whom were created Dukes, the latter Roxburgh received a grant of £10,000 which built his castle at Floors. They and others were members of the Westminster Parliament.

Robert, 4th Lord Balfour of Burleigh, died in 1713. He and his wife had three children:

Robert   *master of Burleigh;*

Margaret   *now representing the family;*

Mary   *married Alexander Bruce of Kennet Esq, and had issue.*

Robert, only son of the 4th Lord Burleigh, seems to have been a spoilt, selfish boy. As a young teenager of 12, he took a notion to Miss Henderson of Middleton and tried to abduct her when she was working in a field with her father. John Henderson was killed with a pitchfork defending her. No charge of homicide ever came to court; this may be due to his age and the influence wielded by the powerful Balfour family. John Henderson was buried at old Orwell Kirk and at the foot of the gravestone is carved a pitchfork and a Bible reading from the book of Job, chapter 14: 'Man that is born of a woman is of few days, and full of trouble. He cometh forth like a flower, and is cut down: he fleeth also as a shadow, and continueth not'.

Five years later this precocious, violent-tempered lad was in trouble again. This time Janet Thomson, his sister's governess and niece of Rev Andrew Thom-

John Henderson's grave

son, Minister in Milnathort, was the object of the Master of Burleigh's attention. Disapproving strongly of the attachment, his father sacked the governess and the love-sick youth was sent to Europe to further his education and overcome the calf-love. Before leaving, however, Robert made the girl swear to wait for his return, vowing to seek her out and kill her husband if she married.

On his return in 1707 Robert found Janet had married Henry Stenhouse, an Inverkeithing schoolmaster, in 1705. Filled with fury, Robert rode to the school and shot young Stenhouse through the shoulder. Stenhouse died ten days later.

Robert escaped to Burleigh but with a £200 reward for apprehending him; £14 10s Scots contributed by Orwell Church Session towards the cost of his pursuit. He was captured two years later, tried in the High Court Justiciary in August 1709, and found guilty of murder. He was sentenced to be beheaded on the maiden (an early form of guillotine) at Edinburgh on 6th January 1710. Margaret his sister helped him escape. Dressed in her clothes, he escaped from his cell in the Tolbooth before the sentence was carried out. History does not record how Margaret managed to untangle the ramifications. Such was the power of the Balfours, no attempt was made to re-arrest the culprit.

In 1708 a invasion by the French known as 'Entreprise d'Ecosse' planned to land 5,000 to 6,000 French troops to help local Jacobites restore James Francis Edward Stuart to the British throne, instead of his half-sister Anne. They assembled in February at Dunkirk and were joined by Prince James himself on 9th March. However they were delayed until 17th March by the Prince catching measles. In the lighter but faster 30 privateers and 5 warships they set out, despite a gale that kept the British Navy out of their way. They arrived at Fife Ness on the Firth of Forth on 25th March.

This build-up of French troops and their sailing caused much concern at home in Britain, with movement of Jacobites gathering at Perth and Hanoverians at Stirling. A detachment of Hanoverian soldiers at Crieff were hastily marched over the Ochils by Tillyrie Hill to the Forth.

The French were eventually chased out of the Firth of Forth by the arrival of the British warships and for two days made for the Moray Firth. Not finding a place to disembark they made for home, and most ships made it back to Dunkirk.

In the May 1708 general election, the first since the Union of the Parliaments, this unrest helped the pro-war Whigs to a majority and they cemented the power of the Godolphin–Marlbourgh ministry and the continuation of war.

In 1713 Lord Robert, 4th peer of the line, died and, having disowned his son, he left the estate of Burleigh to his brother John of Ferny. However the 'Mad Master of Burleigh' did inherit the title and was the 5th Lord Burleigh. At the time he was abroad, having fled the country in 1710, but according to the Session Minutes of Orwell Parish Church he returned to live at Burleigh, showing little sign of mending his ways. Two cases are listed against him for paternity recognition of children born to women of the parish which were investigated by Orwell Kirk Session. At least one was proved, but no action was taken against him. Margaret Simpson, daughter of David Simpson, a Milnathort blacksmith, was brought to bed of a child in 1709 and, not being married, was called to Session. Margaret named the Master of Burleigh as the father.

Robert, Lord Robert (now the 5th Baron of Burleigh), was present at the meeting in Lochmaben on 29th May 1715, when the Old Pretender's health was drunk at the Mercat Cross. The following year he was 'out' in the rebellion, fighting at the Battle of Sheriffmuir for which he was attainted by Act of Parliament, and on 13th November 1715 was convicted of high treason and sentenced to death. Once more he escaped prison and managed to lay low until 1717 when the government passed an Act of Grace and Free Pardon. Thus this wild and lecherous man, who had murdered twice and twice been sentenced to death, walked free. This he did this for another 40 years, leading a quieter life before dying in Edinburgh on 20th March 1775 and being buried at Grey Friars.

Meanwhile Colonel John Balfour of Ferny, to whom his brother, the late 4th Lord Balfour, had left the Burleigh Estates, also came out in the 1715 Rebellion, and was also attainted. Attainder was a breathtakingly inequitable form of punishment, finding an accused guilty by Act of Parliament rather than a trial. His basic 'right' for a man to be tried by his peers was completely circumvented, as Parliament simply enacted his guilt into law, denying him the ability to plead his case or have a judgement reached by any court but that of Parliament. All those attainted lost every title, castle, piece of land, and income that they owned. Hereditary right was utterly ignored, as was any form of legal purchase. Their titles and properties now belonged entirely to the Crown. At the stroke of a pen even the most powerful man in the land could be made penniless and a common outlaw, as were his allies.

Rob Roy MacGregor, a drover by trade, an honourable occupation whereby vendors let him take their cattle hundreds of miles south, and trusted him with negotiating a good price and bringing them back the money. Trists at Crieff and Falkirk were the 'big' ones and drove roads existed all over the country. There was an annual Trist at Cuthil Muir, where there was an inn before markets were established in Milnathort. Rob Roy was not publicly on either side in the civil

Rob Roy MacGregor

war, but was suspected to be spying for the Hanoverians, and this following the only mention of him fighting for the Jacobites. But he may have been on a mission of his own when, on January 4th 1716, 134 MacGregors mustered at the ruins of Falkland Palace to rob and pillage through Fife, denying the Hanovarian cavalry food for their horses. The Hanoverians retaliated by advancing a garrison of a few hundred troops into Burleigh Castle to control the area; mainly Swiss and Dutch mercenaries hired by the hundreds to support the Hanoverian cause. Rob Roy and the MacGregors retired from Falkland Palace to Doune on 30th January. At this time Burleigh Castle would have been the property of the Crown having been forfeited the year before.

The Crown sold forfeited lands by public roupe until 1723. Margaret Balfour, eldest daughter of the late 4th Lord Balfour, bought the Burleigh and Tillyrie Estate back. She was known as 'Mistress Balfour, Lady Burleigh' and, but for the attainder, would have been Lady Balfour in her own right. She ran the estate

wisely until her death in 1769 leaving her worldly goods to the poor of the Parish of Orwell. Some lands of Tillyrie were sold by her to her tenants in her lifetime.

After 100 years the letters patent of the peerage were discovered at Kennet by Alexander Hugh Bruce, a descendent of Mary Balfour who had married Sir Alexander Bruce of Kennet and died in 1758. Ten years later, when he attained his majority, his claim to the peerage of Balfour of Burleigh was allowed by the House of Lords, the attainder of 1715 having been reversed by Act of Parliament in 1869. This made him the 10th Lord Balfour of Burleigh, although only the sixth to have borne the title. In the 1970s while in the Forth Valley Pony Club our children Mark and Jean received their prizes from Lord Balfour and his lovely wife at an Area Tetrathlon near Kincardine. It was a special moment for me, as secretary looking on, with our family connection to Burleigh.

Burleigh Castle would have been deserted by the late 18th or early 19th century, *(see the chapter Graham to Montgomery),* when the Kinross and Burleigh Estates were inherited by Lady Helen Montgomery nee Graham on the death of her father Thomas Graham, or when Thomas inherited the Kinross estate from his brother George.

Castles deteriorate rapidly once abandoned. Without maintenance of gutters, drains and roofs they become roofless and damp, open to the weather and ravaged by time. In 1816, after floods in the spring, there was an earthquake on 12th August at 11pm in Kinross-shire, and the following year in a terrible storm the east tower and a wall at Burleigh Castle fell down. This with the local population taking advantage of available stone, to recycle it into houses and farm buildings, reduced the survival of the castle. Only the Tower House, adjoining entrance wall and round corner tower have survived. The round tower is in good repair, and it was still lived in by farm workers in 1930 *(see chapter John Lawrie).*

Michael Balfour,
Tenant, Over Tillyrie
1681 – 1816

"Michael Balfour his testimonial was obtained bearing his abode in Arngask Parish two years and a half from grace he removed at ye term of Martinmas 1613 free of scandle, ye session ordered a testimonial to be given William Horn at Drumgarton."
(Reported to Orwell Session, 1st December 1695.)

On 5th June 1702 at the monthly session meeting of Orwell Kirk, it states that Alexander Balfour in 'Tillireie', and John Black in 'Tilliewhalley' are to join the Session as elders.

'On 5th July John Black of Tilliewhalley and Alexander Balfour in Meikle Tilliere ye oversight of that toun in conjunction with James Reid ye elder yr.

'On 14th September 1707, Alexander Balfour was appointed ruling elder to attend ye predbrie Wednesday next. Which he did as appointed.

BALFOUR TENNENT TY FAMILY TREE

Alexander Balfour   session mins 1681+
Michael Balfour   Seasine 1736
Alexander= Bethia Wilkie.   Doc 1783
Michael   (doc 1893)
     (doc 1816 selling to Robert Reid)

Alexander

On 7 July of the same year, Session discussed the recent order from Westminster for deacons to be made in the churches. Unanimously they agreed that such an officer should be chosen, 'yet yr in they may find their government to be more consonant to scripture rules'. They agreed to name to the office John and Andrew Black, Henry Laury in Drunzie, and Henry Simpson in Tulliry, 'James Reid and Alexander Balfour to speak to them'. In August the Blacks asked for more time to consider it. By 3rd November all but one had refused and the other had not replied. No deacons were therefore appointed.

On 12th June 1708 the four elders chosen to distribute the 'moy' to the poor were Alexander Balfour, James Reid, Robert Arnot and John Simpson. In these days the Laird (i.e. Balfour of Balfour) paid for the Minister and School, and collections on the Sundays were given to needy causes and the poor.

The key to the box with the moneys for the poor was kept by rotation by chosen elders. In 1710 it fell to Alexander Balfour, James Reid, John Simpson and Robert Arnot.

In 1712 Alexander Balfour and John Simpson were sent to David Greig in Little Tillyerie to see if he would accept the office of elder. David at first accepted, but declined before the edict was served.

There is a Seasine "in favour of Michael Balfour granted by Lady Margaret Balfour of Burleigh on 24th January 1736, in the reign of our sovereign Lord George II, by the grace of God King of Great Britain France and Ireland Defender of the Faith in this 9th year."

This refers to Michael Balfour tenant in Over Tillery, having and holding his Charter of the form of sale after mentioned, made and granted by Margaret Balfour of Burleigh in favour of the said Michael Balfour and his heirs.

"All and hail arable land as well outfield and infield grafts crofts mosses Muirs meadows pasturages commonly brid tominsots and hail parks, lying in the Barony of Burleigh and Sheriffdom of Kinross."

"From the Tofts down a bank below the riggings known as Gardales, and over the Clifts rigs, down to their banks on the Nether Clifts."

James Reid portioner of Over Tillery, Ballie in that part, James Rutherford (acturney for Michael Balfour)) were mentioned along with witnesses George Reid, Tenant in Over Tillery, Andrew Rutherford (servant to James Rutherford) and Andrew Paietdale.

The next document is in 1783, by which time Margaret Balfour of Burleigh had died in 1769 and the estate had be sold on twice.

An Instrument of Sasine dated 14.1.1783 in the reign of King George III. First is a Precept Clare Constal commissioner of George Graham esq of Kinross in favour of Alexander Balfour portioner of Over Tilleray.

Together with the said lands both great and small, they said Alexander Balfour, lawful eldest son and heir to the deceased Michael Balfour that he is of lawful age; the foresaid lands with the perinents are beholden to the said George Graham and his heirs.

For yearly payment by Alexander Balfour and his heirs to George Graham Esq. the sum of £115 6/8d Scots at Martinmas and Whitsunday by equal portions, and 8 capons, 2 hens, 2 long carriages, the carriage of 10 loads of coals from Kelty Heugh to Burleigh House, 4 shear dargs, 20 threaves of straw yearly. To be paid and performed at the ordinary times of year conform to use and want. Also there shall be yearly demands of their carrying their grindable victuals to the mill at Milnathort, and paying the ordinary multure prices as there are use and want, and yearly paying that part of the upkeep of the foresaid mill, dam and dykes and drawing stones and water to the said mill when required. Winning and leading home their part of the hay grown yearly in the meadow of Burleigh, where it is cut yearly as has formally been in use, carrying stones, lime, sand, timber, and other materials to the house yard of Burleigh as they shall be required and performing all other carriage services conform to use and want.

And paying to me the sum of £60 13/4d money in lieu of the double of the Fue at Entry to each heir to the said lands, which is the hereby declared to be the valued rent of the said lands in all time coming and all the other burdens exaction or demand that can be anywise required or forth of the said lands by persons whatsoever.

Then the Sasine on 18th July 1783 confirming the former regarding the room of land. The public notary Mathew Young in Tilleray, and David Honeyman a weaver in Tilleray Ballie, and John Graham clerk for George Graham. Published and registered 13.3. Witnesses were John Grieg, David Greig and James Stewart.

There followed ten years later, on 29th March 1893 a Disposition from Alexander Balfour to Michael Balfour his son.

Alexander Balfour portioner of Over Tillyrye for the love favour and affection which I have and bear Michael Balfour my eldest son. Do by these present (with and under the reservations burdens and provisions after mentioned) give grant alienate and dispose to and in favours of the said Michael Balfour and his heirs all and whole of that my room of land in Over Tillyrye.

But reserving always to me during all the days of my lifetime the possession of that piece of land called the Croft, comprehending four rigs and gelding together also with the ward and back yard with the dwelling house and offices presently built there on., and also that part of the commonly of Athrons which fell my share in the division of the said commonly. Which houses are to be kept in a habitable and tenanable condition, and the lands be dunged, plowed sown harrowed and the crop cut down and carried to the barnyard and to and from the mill by the said Michael Balfour and his foresaid at seasonable times.

And further the foresaid Michael Balfour shall be bond and obliged as by acceptation hereof, they bind therein to graze a horse to me along with their horses incase I shall chuse to keep one, and if not to keep one to furnish and provide me with a horse to ride upon when I occasion for the same, with the sowing of one peck of linseed yearly along with his own.

Also the carriage of what coals I shall stand in need of yearly from the Coalhill, and carry home 12 loads of turfs yearly.

Providing always that I shall not chuse to keep the ward then in that case Michael Balfour binds and obliges him to keep two cows to graze and herd with his cows.

Which prostrations the said Michael Balfour binds and obliges himself to perform to Bertha Wilkie, my spouse, all her life in case she survive me, excepting only in it shall not be in her power to keep a horse or retain ward in the lue of which she shall have a horse to ride upon whenever required, and two cows grassed and herded along with those of Michael Balfour's, and declaring the said burdens & provisions shall not commence or be payable until the term of Martinmas next, when he is to enter to the possession of the said lands, and I bind and oblige myself and my heirs to the above.

Written upon stamped paper by John Peat of Kinross and me at Tillrye 3rd October 1793, between 2 and 3 of the afternoon, witnessed by the said John Peat writer, Thomas Henderson (servant to me) Alexander Balfour. David Bukstin Shoemaker in Tillrie to Mr Balfour, James Reid & David Mailler shoemaker in Tillyrie.

The last document involving this family of Balfour is a Disposition in 1816 by Michael Balfour in favour of Robert Reid of the field or croft of land in Over Tilleray.

Michael Balfour portioner of Over Tillyeray, heritable propricctor of the lands and others after disposed, in consideration of £1,400 sterling, instantly advanced and paid to me by Robert Reid residing at Over Tillyery, eldest son of George Reid portioner there, as the agreed price and value of the field or croft after disposed.

Therefore I have Sold and disposed all and whole of the field or croft in Over Tillyeray, which is situated to the south of the road leading from Tillyeray to Seggie, bounded by as follows, On the North by the said road, on the East and West by Hall Greig property of Alexander Greig, and on the South by the property of John Thomson of Segue, and is part of the room of land in Over Tillyeray fued by the Honourable Mrs Margaret Balfour of Burleigh in 17

In which field or croft of land above disposed I hereby bind and oblige myself to the said Robert Reid, upon payment of £6:10/- at the term of Martinmas yearly, which is hereby declared the full compensation for all time fue duties and other burdens.

Witnesses Alexander Balfour, Michael Balfour and John Murray.

So ends this family connection with Tillyrie, although this Michael Balfour did have a son called Alexander.

BALFOUR to GRAHAM
and MONTGOMERY
1700s-2020

L ady Margaret Balfour of Burleigh died on 12th March 1769 aged 84. General Irwin purchased the Castle and Estate of Burleigh.

John Irwin was born in 1728, the son of General Alexander Irwin and his wife Catherine. Educated in Ireland, he was as a schoolboy made an ensign in his father's regiment, the 5th Foot, then later given a year's furlough to go on the Grand Tour in France and Holland. On his return in December 1749 he married Elizabeth, youngest daughter of Hugh Henry of Straffan, Kildare. Sadly she died in April 1750. In 1753 he married Anne, daughter of Sir Edward Barry of Dublin, who died in 1767 in Gibraltar. He married for a third time to Caroline, who outlived him.

He was a page of honour to Lionel, First Duke of Dorset, Lord Lieutenant of Ireland 1730-1737. This connection with the Sackville family was to last all his life. He was Member of Parliament for East Grinstead 1761 on Sackville interest and became a close friend of Lord George Sackville, whose political line he followed implicitly, voting with the opposition until 1774 and afterwards with government. His only recorded speech was on a trivial subject. He was re-elected until retiring in 1783, but his attendance was always irregular. Burk called him 'a good-humoured, well-behaved man' while Charles Fox regarded him as 'a fop, but good-humoured'. The final comment was from Wraxall: 'his person, manners and conversation were all for the drawing-room, where he seems to be in his native element. It was impossible to possess finer manners without any affection, or more perfect breeding'. John was said to be a favourite of King George III, and was well-known in French society.

He held offices in the armed forces: in 1738 an ensign in the 5th Foot; Captain in 1745; Major in 1751; Lieutenant Colonel (1752) and Colonel (1761). He saw service on the coast of France in 1758, and in 1760 with Prince Ferdinand of Brunswick in Germany. His regiment was disbanded in 1762, and John was three years without military employment. In June 1765 he was offered the post as Major General the Governorship of Gibraltar, which he having 'hoped for other work',

MONTGOMERY FAMILY TREE

JAMES (SIR) 1ST BT. Lord Chief Baron of the Exchequer (d.1803) m *Margaret*, daughter of Robert Scott of Killearn

---

William d.s.p 1800

JAMES (Sir) 2nd Bt b.1766–d.1839
m (1) *Elizabeth*, daughter of 4th Earl of Selkirk
m (2) *Helen*, daughter of Thomas Graham of Kinross

Archibald of the Whim b.1771 –d.1846

Robert b.1775 d.1854

James b.1811–d.1883

Helen m William Forbes Mackzie of Portmore (d.1870)

Elizabeth m James Kerr Williamson (d.1784)

GRAHAM (Sir) 3rd Bt b.1823–d.1901
m Alice Hope Johnston

John Hamilton of Newton b.1824–d.1911

Thomas Henry b.1828–d.1879 m Anna Maria Elphinstone

Anne

Flemming (b.1835–d.1840)

Alice
m (1) 1885 2nd Duke of Buckingham
m (2) 1894 Earl of Egerton

Helen m 1870 4th Earl of Temple

Lucy d.1881

Evelyn m 1892 Sir Robert Dundas

JAMES (Sir) 4th Bt b.1850 d.1902 Fell from the Flying Scotsman

BASIL (Sir) 5th Bt b.1852 d.1928

CHARLES (Sir) 6th Bt. (Rev) b.1855 d.1879

Arthur Cecil b.1858 d.1885

HENRY (Sir) 7th Bt b.1857–d.1947
m.1882 Maud Purvis Russell

Herbert b.1861–d.1944 m.1899 Janet Anson (issue)

Violet d.1944

Walter b.1881–d.1928
m (1) 1880 Mary, daughter of Sir Thomas Moncrieff (divorced)
m (2) Theresa Verschoie (no issue)

Graham   **Percy**   **Cecil**

Lena b.1882–d.1957

John

BASIL (Sir) 8th Bt. b.1884–d.1904
m.1915 Amelia Richards

Keith b.1896–d.1954 m 1930 Cynthia Maconochie-Welwood

Mary b.1912

Ethel b.1887–d.1919 m George Balfour Kinear

Clem b.1900 d.1979

Rachel b.1916   **Sheila** b.1923

DAVID (Sir) 9th Bt. b.1931 m.1956 Delia Reid d Dec 2019

Anthea b.1935

Andrew b.1967–d.1971

Caroline b.1959 m 1983 Nicholas Liddle

Davina b.1961 m 1987 Humphrey Butler

Iona b.1972 m Ben Roper Lee

Laura b.1974 m David Redvers

James b.1957 m 1983 Elizabeth Evans

Edward b.1986 m.2018 Flora Nichol   **Iona** b.1988

Lucy   Alexander   Harriet

Bertie   Hector

Arthur   Isla   Tommy

Charlie   Hubbie   Fenella

did until November 1767. On his return he was made Colonel of the 57th Foot, then Lieutenant General in 1772 and was Colonel-in-Chief from 1775 until 1782. He was Colonel 3rd Horse (later named the 6th Dragoon Guards) in 1782 and General in 1783. He and his second wife had their portraits painted by Sir Joshua Reynolds in 1761. Sadly Ann died at Gibraltar in 1767.

He was living at Queen Anne Street, London after 1771, and installed as a Knight of the Bath in 1779. He maintained a lavish establishment and was popular with all classes.

In the General Election of 1775 he contested unsuccessfully the seat for Kinross. Probably through the influence of the Sackville family, he was given command in Ireland. When affairs became difficult in Ireland Lord North wrote to the King 'Lord North thinks himself obliged to repeat to His Majesty that he in every quarter that Sir John Irwin, though well-esteemed as a gentleman, is not in great estimation as a general, and the world is very uneasy about his having command in Ireland in such a perilous moment as the present'. The King replied 'to move him would be a disgrace to an amiable man. But if the advice had been to send a good general below him he would hear good advice' No change was made and Irwin handled a dangerous situation better than might be expected.

Lord Carlisle, Lord Lieutenant in Ireland, wrote to the government on 30th June 1781: 'You have sent our Commander-in-Chief over. There is a great scrape as to money matters, for the other day some official letters were landed before me addressed to Sir James Irwin to repay a large sum owing to Government, which I fear he is by no means prepared for.' Wraxall wrote 'No income, however large could survive his expenses, which never being restrained within any reasonable limits, finally involved him in irretrievable difficulties.' When Lord North's administration in Ireland ended Sir James returned to Piccadilly and resumed his seat in the House of Commons.

The loss of his appointment in March 1782 ruined Sir John financially and he was obliged to exile himself in France to rent a chateau in Normandy. With no expectation of a return to the UK he retired from Parliament. In a letter to a friend dated 4th July 1784 he appears to be living in great poverty. The king is said to have sent him £1,000, but he was obliged to move to Parma, where he was a friend of the Duke and his consort Duchess Arabella. He died in May 1788. King George III sent the widow Caroline £500 for the two children and herself to return home. Caroline died on 27th August 1805.

The Burleigh Barony was sold to Thomas Graham in 1779.

Thomas Graham esq, having lived in Benares, India where he and his brother John, helped by their mother's brother Sir William Mayne with appointments, worked in the East India Company as a Bengal Civil Servant and a member of the Board of Revenue. He was also a partner in a private firm of Thomas Graham, John Mowbray, Robert Graham and William Skirrow. Thomas rose to be head of the Board of Revenue in Bengal. John worked in the service of the Supreme Council of Bengal. John died in 1776 while crossing from Marseilles to Lisbon.

Thomas married Ann Paul in India and, on their return to Britain, bought the manor of Burleigh.

George Graham, elder half-brother to Thomas, had initially gone to Jamaica where he worked as a planter but, after 1770, he joined his two younger half-brothers in India. They all appear to have made large fortunes. On his return to Britain, George worked as a merchant in London, and in 1777 bought Kinross House and estate in Kinross-shire. A distant relative of Bonnie Dundee, his branch of the family had originally come from Dunfermline.

This barony had been the property of the Douglas (Earls of Morton) family since 1390, when Henry Douglas received it as a wedding present from King Robert III, but their loyalty to the Jacobite cause left them financially troubled in the 1640s, and forced them to sell the estate. It was then bought by Sir William Bruce, Surveyor-General to King Charles I, who worked on Holyroodhouse Palace for the King and Thirlestane Castle for the Duke of Lauderdale. He built the beautiful Kinross House between 1679 and 1686. To raise finance when building the house, Sir William granted feu charters to many of the former tenants, with a feu paid annually to the 'superior of the land' and a grasson or lump sum also. The older house of the Douglas family was demolished in 1723 and the stone recycled in other buildings. Sir William became heritable Sheriff of Kinross-shire, and a great benefactor to the area. He died in 1710.

His heirs were two branches of the Bruce family. A complex deed of entail left to one family the Barony of Arnot and to the other the Estate of Kinross. The cost of upkeep on the large house was unsustainable by the Kinross Bruces. In 1770 there was a meeting of landowners and mill owners to discuss the lowering of Loch Leven to give a regular water supply to the mills and create drainage to lands. Nothing came of this at the time. The estate was sold it in 1777 to George Graham esq.

George had an illegitimate son, James Graham, but James did not inherit Kinross House when George died in 1801. Instead it passed to George's half-brother Thomas. James contested the will, which resulted in expensive law suits. Thomas and Ann had three children. Their son, born in 1784, was brought up by his aunt, Mrs Templer of Shapwick. He unfortunately lost his life in 1808 when, on his way to India, he was killed by pirates at the 'taking of the Kent'.

Thomas inherited the Kinross Estate from George in 1801 but, after his son's death, was left with only his two daughters as heirs. He left the joined Burleigh and Kinross Estates to whichever of his daughters produced a son first. The elder daughter Ann married her cousin the Rev G H Templer, Rector of Shapwick (son of George Templer and his wife a sister of Ann Paul); they had a daughter called Sophia. Helen, younger daughter of Thomas and Ann, married Sir James Montgomery of Stobo Castle, Baronet and MP for Perthshire. They became the parents of a son, and brought the estates to the Montgomerys of Stobo Castle, Stanhope and Peebles, who thus represent the Grahams of Kinross. The two estates will now be referred to as the Kinross Estates. Thomas Graham died in 1819.

Helen was the second wife of Sir James Montgomery (2nd Bart of Stobo Castle 1766-1839), who had been married on 1st August 1806 to Lady Elizabeth Douglas of Dunbar, daughter of the 4th Earl of Selkirk. A widower with the death of Lady Elizabeth on 28th October 1814, Sir James married Helen Graham on 13th May 1816. They had three sons (Graham, born 1823, John 1824, Thomas Henry 1828), and two daughters, Anne (born 1818 and died aged 17 in 1835), and Margaret, born in 1820.

Sir James was the son and heir of James Montgomery, who bought the Stobo Estate from the Murrays of Tweedsmuir in 1767. James was a judge, who served as Lord Advocate and Lord Chief Baron of the Scottish Exchequer from 1775. He was created a Baronet in 1801. He had been the last resident of Queensberry House in Edinburgh's Canongate, and kept a black servant called Hannibal. He was an undistinguished Lord Advocate in Pitt's second ministry, the possessor of a sinecure worth £610 year and a 'steady adherent' of the 1st and 2nd Lords Melville. He built Stobo Castle between 1805-1811. Like his father, he was on intimate terms with 'Old Q', the degenerate 4th Duke of Queensberry, who on his death in 1810 left him a legacy of £20,000. Sir James continued to sit unopposed for Peeblesshire, until retiring for health reasons in 1831.

Sir James inherited the estate and commissioned a new house from architect Archibald Elliot, constructed in 1811. It was reconstructed in the castellated style in 1848.

In his will, having died on 27th May 1839, he left all his property to his eldest son, successor and residuary legatee Graham Montgomery, Conservative member for Peeblesshire 1852-1868 and Selkirk & Peebles 1868-1880. To his daughter Mary Flemming (1820-1840), he gave £10,000, his second son John Basil (1824-1911) £20,000, to his third son Thomas Henry and his brother Robert £1,000.

Sir Graham Montgomery, shown here in an 1897 portrait by J Lorimer

Sir Graham Montgomery, 3rd Baronet (9th July 1823-2nd June 1901) attended Oxford University and graduated with a Master of Arts degree. On 10th April 1845, he married Alice Hope Johnstone (1830-1890). They had four sons: James in 1850, Basil (5th baronet) 1852, Charles (6th baronet), Arthur Cecil 1856-1887 and four daughters Alice 1885 (married 2nd Duke of Buckingham, Earl of Egerton & Tatton), Helen 1870 (married 4th Earl of Temple), Lucy 1881 and Evelyn 1892 (married Sir Robert Dundas of Arniston).

Sir Graham was only 16 years old and a minor when his father died in 1839. Trustees were appointed to run and improve the estate before his majority in 1844. The Agricultural Revolution had not yet begun and the gross annual income of £1705 was barely enough to cover the upkeep of the estate and Kinross House. Kinross Estate commissioned Edinburgh surveyor John Bell to map and explore the possibility of lowering the loch surface, draining poorly drained land and reclaiming land around the loch. The map produced in 1808 shows the prospect if the water was lowered either 2.5 or 5 feet. This map exists today, and a copy is in the Kinross Marshall Museum.

The cost of lowering the loch at £4,000 was too expensive for the Kinross Estate to do on its own, so a meeting was arranged with the mill owners and land owners along the River Leven. The mill owners were not receptive to the idea. In 1828 mill owners were complaining about lack of water in dry months, so Kinross Estate raised the idea again of lowering Loch Leven with sluices to regulate water flow. By 1824 land owners down the River Leven including General Balfour of Balburnie, James Balfour of Whittingham & Balgonie along with Sir James Montgomery as prime movers, persuaded the mill owners of the benefits to manufacturers and their tenants of the scheme at a meeting on the loch shore in October. The first commissioner to the project was Dr Andrew Coventry, who farmed his mother's estate at Shanwell in the parish of Orwell. An MD at Edinburgh University he became their first Professor of Agriculture in 1790 at 28 years of age. He was sworn in on 11th July 1827 as commissioner for the Leven Improvements.

An Act of Parliament was passed on 21st June 1827 to allow the scheme

Loch Leven Sluices opened in 1830.

to happen. In 1830 Kinross Estate employed schoolmaster and part-time surveyor Robert Burns-Begg to produce maps, both of estate farms and any land that would be reclaimed, as a result of lowering Loch Leven. Surveyors estimated approximately 1,566 acres of land round Loch Leven and along the sides of the River Leven would benefit. About 52 farms in Kinross-shire would have improved drainage. Agriculture was under pressure due to the vast increase in population caused by the industrial revolution that had been ongoing since the mid-1700s, and the 1742 Bounty Act which accelerated the growth of the Scottish linen, spinning and weaving industries. With improved roads and railways inland sites flourished as markets became available, and the settlements of Kinross, Milnathort, Leslie and Markinch flourished as London and Europe became viable markets. The population of Kinross-shire went from 5,936 in 1801 to 9,072 in 1831. Food production also had to be revolutionised to feed this population. The Leven River supplied 40 mills in 1828: meal mills, flax mills, waulk mills, paper mills, sawmills, bleachfields, spinning mills, iron foundries, malt mills, skutching mills, snuff and barley mills all shared the water from the 16-mile River Leven which powered their mills between 1813 and the mid-1830s.

Kinross Estates, who had put forward the greatest security for borrowing to build the sluices and lower the loch, made legal arrangements with landowners that all land recovered round the loch was their property in 1827. They also bought back land from the Arnot estate. The Bruces of Arnot, having no incentive for fishing or land improvement with the imminent lowering of the loch, had sold land to Ferguson of Raith – who, in turn, sold it to Adam of Blairadam. In 1825 the Kinross Estate bought back this land from Adam of Blairadam. The factor of the estate at this time was Mr John Campbell. Boundary stones were arranged round the pre-lowering property of Kinross Estate in July 1828, and a marking stone was cut at Kinross between 1828 and 1830 to mark the height of the loch. Work began on the 32ft-wide cut on 1st July 1828. The labourers were mainly lowland Scots and Irish working with picks, spades, shovels, mallocks and pinches. Gale force winds in June and floods in July 1829 did extensive damage to works, and in 1830 the entrance for the sluice had to be realigned to more stable ground to the north. All this slowed down progress. Sir James Montgomery became impatient as he wished work finished by the autumn so he could work on improving the reclaimed land in the spring.

On Christmas Day 1830 a large crowd gathered to see the opening of the sluices at the west end of the loch. By gradually reducing the water level between 1.5 to 3 inches a day, the loch was slowly but surely lowered by 4.5 feet. It had taken not two but three years to build, due mainly to weather conditions, but at last it proved beneficial to landowners and mill owners. They were never all going to be happy all the time, but for four decades it was very successful. However, it was massively more expensive than had been budgeted and it took two more Acts of Parliament (in 1831 and 1835) before the books on the project were finalised in 1849. The commissioner Andrew Coventry died in December 1830, leaving a serious financial crisis to the Trustees of the Leven Improvements. They met and

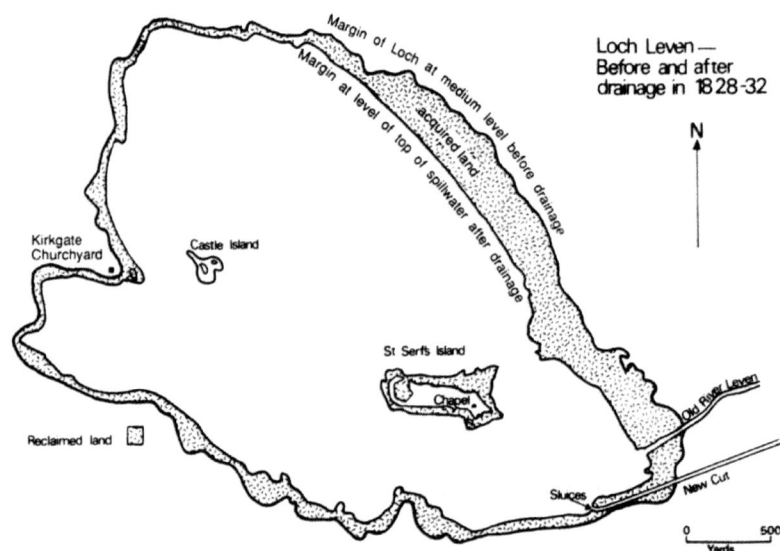

Loch Leven —
Before and after
drainage in 1828-32

N

Source: "Plan of Lands lying around Loch Leven" by Martin and Birrell (1827) updated by Johnson and Adie (1832)

set up a committee under the chairmanship of Mr John Greig of Lethangie to deal with the crisis. The mill owners tried to take control of the sluices in 1831 but were repulsed by the Trustees of the Leven Improvements.

The loch had been reduced from 4,638 acres to 3,543 acres. It was estimated that Kinross Estates recovered 612 acres of land round the loch side and 50 acres were added to the islands of St Serf, Castle and Reed Bower. East of Portmoak, where the loch is shallower, 441 acres were formed. Balado, Cleish, Drum, Carnbo and others also benefited from the lowering of the loch, and drainage increased the quality and quantity of agricultural land in the county.

Sir James Gordon Henry Graham-Montgomery, 4th Baronet, (1850-1902), inherited the title when the 3rd Baronet died in 1901, but he died in 1902 falling, according to family legend, from the 'Flying Scotsman' train.

Sir Basil Templar Graham-Montgomery, 5th Baronet (1852-1928), Baron Stanhope from 1902-1928, was the son of the 3rd Baronet and Alice Hope John-stone, who succeeded his brother. He invented a pattern of leather web gear similar to the Sam Browne belt that became part of the dress uniform for Rifle Regiment officers. He reached the rank of Lieutenant-in-Service of the 60th Rifles, gaining the rank of Honorary Lieutenant-Colonel in the service of the Kinross-shire Vol-unteer Regiment.

In 1844, on attaining his majority, a public dinner was partaken in Kirk-lands Hotel in honour of the occasion. On 17th July a fete was held at Kinross

House when thousands turned out to give a hearty welcome to Sir Graham on his first Kinross-shire visit after obtaining his majority. The tenants and feurars were among the guests, and a procession was marshalled when Hammermen and Weavers' standards were hoisted. The procession, accompanied by the Kinross and Milnathort Instrumental Bands, marched to Gougyranet where Sir Graham's carriage was met. In it were himself and his brother and loud cheering accompanied them all the way to Kinross. The entertainment broke up at 9pm, after escorting Sir Graham to Kirklands Inn and giving him three cheers. At Thomanean a long bonfire was lit, whiskey-toddy, porter and bread were liberally supplied to several hundred people, and the fun kept up until the early hours.

On 5th June 1845 Sir Graham received a Crown Charter confirming his right to the barony of Kinross, including lands, castle, lake and fishing.

He married first Mary Katherine Moncrieff (1858-1910), daughter of Sir Thomas Moncrieff of that ilk, 7th Baronet Moncrieff and Lady Louisa Hay-Drummond, on 26th October 1880. They had two children, Walter Basil Graham-Montgomery (1881-1928) and Lena Graham-Montgomery (1882-1958), but were divorced in 1905. His second marriage was to Theresa Blanche Verschoyle, daughter of Lt-Col Henry William Verschoyle, on 6th June 1905. They had no offspring. He died on 4 October 1928 aged 76.

Sir Basil opened up Kinross House in 1902, after almost a century of the family living at Stobo. He restored the gardens in Edwardian style, setting off the beautiful house.

Sir Basil took over the management of Loch Leven, encouraging and improving the fishing. Poaching with nets had taken its toll in the 19th century and the number of eels and pike had increased to the detriment of the trout. These were brought under control, and the tributaries to the loch provided excellent natural spawning grounds over coarse gravel for the trout. In their combined 150 miles trout flourished in the loch. The lowering of the loch had been expected to reduce catches of trout, but it turned out to have no reduction in the catch of fish, and these catches increased as time went on. In 1874 the loch had been leased to professional anglers who formed the 'Loch Leven Angling Association Ltd'. They sold 300 shares for £10 each to raise the capital to fund boats and equipment to hire and in 1867 to build a hatchery and rearing pond. Between 1909 and 1968, 30,000 trout were taken in a season. Sir Basil also built piers at Kinross, Castle Island and St Serf's Island.

In 1928 Sir Basil inaugurated the first Annual International Angling Competition on Loch Leven. The loch, now renowned worldwide for the fishing and the quality of the trout, meant this was a great success.

Walter Basil Graham Montgomery OBE, DL was the only son of the 5th Baronet of Stanhope. Educated at Eton and Cambridge, he chose service in the Diplomatic Corps as his career. He came to live at Kinross House with his father in 1902, and was known locally as Mr Walter. He took a lively part in local government. A councillor, for six years he was head of the burgh, and held positions

Kinross House and Gardens looking towards Loch Leven Castle

as County Commissioner, Deputy Lieutenant, and Chief of the Special Constabulary. He also sought Parliamentary honours, but was defeated in his ambition by the redistribution of seats when the old division of Clackmannan and Kinross was abolished. As Provost he discharged his duties with an ability which was unusual and well applied, and his forbearance in stressful arguments around the table won him respect and endorsed him to those whose opinions, political and otherwise, differed from his own.

In 1924, he was one of those who organised the Wembley Exhibition, and a few years later the Craigmillar Castle Pageant. This resourcefulness and ability in these fields were recognised, but ill-health plagued him, and compelled him to resign from heading the organising of the Glasgow Exhibition.

The Boy Scout Movement was in its infancy during his early years, and his energetic approach to furthering its cause throughout Britain was contributory to its success, for he spared neither time nor expense to advance its cause. He had a patient understanding of the boyish mind, and even where there was little intelligence, he was able to make something of what material he had to work with. His compassionate mind did not allow him to berate a boy for carelessness or inattention. Kinross Boy Scouts were taken to St Serf's Island at least once for a camping trip.

Unfit to take an active part in the First World War, he served as Military

The Courtyard with Kinross House behind (Photos: Kinross House)

Representative of the Country. To this kind-hearted man, gentle in his manner and attitude to other people, his duties must have often been distasteful to him, for they entailed his exercising judicial decisions when interviewing those whose principles were such that they refused to take part in a war which they abhorred for its senseless killing of their fellows. His kindly and understanding heart stood Mr Walter in good stead, and his decisions were fair and just, according to the circumstances of the moment.

A member of the Jolly Beggars Club, he seldom missed an annual meeting and was elected president in 1921. He was also greatly interested in the historical aspect of Loch Leven, and was an authority on its birdlife. A well-known figure during the 1921 and 1926 strikes, as Commander of Special Constables he was often seen patrolling the area in his car. Later he reverted to a motor-scooter, the first seen in the locality. When he died, the scooter was submerged in the loch; no other person would ever ride on it.

Kinross-shire was desolated in 1928 by the death of this heir to the Barony. His short life proved his worth and the county was enriched by his good works. In Walter Graham Montgomery's death Kinross-shire lost one of its most venerated and distinguished sons. He pre-deceased his father, who died in October the same year.

The 6th Baronet was Rev Sir Charles Percy Graham-Montgomery *(d 1930)* another son of the 3rd Baronet and Alice Hope Johnstone. He was educated at Winchester and Emmanuel College, Cambridge, graduating with a BA in 1880,

113

and MA in 1884. Ordained deacon in 1880 and priest in 1883, he held a succession of clerical posts, ending as Vicar of St John's Taunton from 1903 until his retirement to Stobo Castle in 1915. He succeeded to the Baronetcy on 4th October 1928.

He married firstly Minnie Gertrude Compton Walker, daughter of Major-General Chamberlain Walker in 1887. They had two children:

Graham John Graham-Montgomery	*(1894-1917) Captain in the Hampshire Regiment, killed in action 1917:*

Percy Cecil Graham-Montgomery *(1898-1915)*.

Both sons died in their father's lifetime.

His second marriage was in 1923 to Rose Kathleen Sullivan. There was no issue.

Sir Henry James Montgomery was the 7th Baronet (1859-1947). He was the eldest son of Captain Thomas Henry Montgomery (*d*1879) of Hattonburn, Milnathort and the Honourable Anna Maria Elphinstone (*d*1914) third daughter of the Honourable James Drummond Buller-Fullerton-Elphinstone and sister of Lord Elphinstone of Carberry Tower, Midlothian. Captain Thomas Henry Montgomery had noticed Hattonburn Estate when it came up for sale at a set price of £15,000 in 1867, and remaining unsold. He purchased it for £15,520 later that year, and the locals found satisfaction that he was going to set up residence there.

Sir Henry James Montgomery married Mary Maud Russell (1862-1947*),* daughter of Thomas Purvis Russell of Warroch, on 12th September 1882. He legally assumed the additional names Purvis–Russell in 1906, on his wife's succeeding to Warroch, Kinross-shire on the death of her father in 1907.

They had five children:

Sir Henry James, 7th Bart	*b.1859 d.1947*
Mary Gertrude Montgomery	*d.1912;*
Sir Basil Purvis-Russell-Montgomery, 8th Bart	*b.1884;*
Lt- Col Henry Keith Purvis-Russell–Montgomery*	*b.1896 d.1954;*
Clementine Helen Maud Purvis-Russell-Montgomery	*b.1900 d.1979;*
Ethel	*b.1887, m.1913 George Balfour Kinnear (d.1919) with whom she had a daughter, Kitty Sutton.*

Sir Henry James, 7th Bart, was educated at Trinity College, Glenalmond in Perthshire, then Jesus College, Cambridge University. He held office as Justice of the Peace for Kinross-shire. He succeeded as 7th Baronet Montgomery of Stanhope, Peebles in 1930, and held the office of Lord Lieutenant of Kinross-shire in 1934.

His eldest son Sir Basil succeeded as 8th Baronet (25 Sept 1884-1964) He married Amelia Richards in 1915 and they had two daughters, Rachel and Sheila. Sheila married John Griffith in 1945 and they had two daughters.

Lt-Col Henry Keith Purvis-Russell-Montgomery, second son of the 7th Bart and Mary Maud Purvis-Russell, was educated at Rugby School in Warwickshire, then Jesus College, Cambridge. He gained the rank of Captain in the Royal Highlanders (Black Watch) and fought in the First World War. He was wounded in the battle of Salonika in 1915.

The Battle of Salonika was fought on the Macedonian Front. When a Bosnian Serb assassinated Archduke Franz Ferdinand of Austria, Austria Hungary attacked Serbia in August 1914, but failed to overcome the Serbian resistance. In November 1914 the Ottoman Empire entered the war to side with the Central Powers (Bulgaria, Austria-Hungary and Germany) against the Allied forces (Serbia, France, UK, Russia until 1917, Italy 1916-18, and Greece 1916-17). Their defeat at Gallipoli in 1916 and the Russian defeat at Gorlice-Tarnow in 1915 demonstrated the strength of the Central Powers. An attempt by the Allies to aid Serbia in the autumn of 1915 came too late and with insufficient force to prevent its fall. Eventually a stable front was established from the Albanian Adriatic coast to the Struma River, pitting a multinational force against the Bulgarian Army. This Macedonian Front remained quite stable until the great Allied Offensive in September 1918, which resulted in the capitulation of Bulgaria and the liberation of Serbia.

In 1930 Sir Henry Keith Purvis-Russell Montgomery married Cynthia Louise Winifred-Welwood, daughter of John Allan Maconochie-Welwood and Winifred Louisa Drummond. She lived in Kinross House until 2003.

The couple had two children:

Basil Henry David Montgomery *(9th Bart)*   *b 1931*

Veronica Mary Anthea Montgomery   *b 1935.*

Sir Henry Keith held office as Deputy Lieutenant (DL) of Kinross-shire in 1937. He gained the rank of Lieutenant-Colonel in the Black Watch (Territorial Army). He also held the office of Lord-Lieutenant of Kinross-shire in 1944, and was appointed Officer, Order of the British Empire (O.B.E.) in 1944. He was a Director of Kinross Estate Company.

Major and Mrs Keith Montgomery of Hattonburn were great supporters of local community projects, and one of their particular interests was Milnathort golf course, opened in 1910. When the Milnathort course was being built Mrs Montgomery arranged for Joe Anderson, the first professional at Craigie Course, Perth to give advice on the layout of bunkers. Major Keith made a donation to defray expenses. In 1911 they supported fundraising for the first pavilion, prizes for juniors as well as flowers from Hattonburn supplied to every function. When raising funds to purchase the course outright in 1924, a Grand Bazaar was held at Hattonburn House, when Mrs Montgomery's persuasive and organising skills led to the outstanding success of the fete.

His sister, Miss Clementine Montgomery, became Scottish Lady Champion at Turnberry in 1924, receiving a telegram of congratulations from her local Milnathort Golf Club. Miss Clementine took part in many exhibition matches, and was Lady Captain on the 50th anniversary of the club in 1960, when her nephew Sir David was Captain. Sir David, when he officially opened the new clubhouse in 1981, presented a trophy which is a replica of the Scottish Ladies' Championship Trophy won by Miss Clementine in 1924.

Lt-Col Henry Keith Montgomery died on 1st October 1954. His son Sir Basil Henry David Montgomery, usually known by his middle name David succeeded as 9th Baronet. He was educated at Eton and gained the rank of officer (1949) in the Black Watch.

While serving in the Black Watch he was posted to the Peacekeeping Force in Berlin. Surrounded by the Russian army, the badge worn by the British Forces was a black circle on a red background, indicating the national settings. The British Forces were quartered in the Smut Barracks, in the Spandau district of Berlin. During this posting Sir David was, for some time, in-charge of the important political prisoners imprisoned in the nearby Spandau Prison. This building had been the home of the SS Panzer Division and after the Nuremberg Trials at the end of the Second World War housed convicted Nazi war criminals including Rudolf Hess. The building was dismantled after Hess's death and is now a shopping centre.

Aged only 23, Sir David was called home in 1954 on the unexpected death of his father and expected to take over the estate and its complex responsibilities – a daunting task. He tells a lesson on human management and thinking when, with the long-serving factor Mr Johnston going round the crops, Sir David enquired why the wheat straw was burned after use on the potato pits and not used to bed the cattle courts. Mr Johnston replied the wheat straw was not used for the cattle. A week later Mr Johnston said to Sir David that he had been 'thinking that the

wheat straw could be reused from the potato pits to bed the cattle courts', which was thereafter done. Sir David also valued the requested advice from tenant John Lawrie, with whom a mutual respect lasted a lifetime.

In the 1970s, when the plans were published for the new motorway to straddle Kinross-shire on its way from the Forth Bridge to Perth and the north, there was no way to connect the lands of the estate at Burleigh to Hattonburn, cut off by the planned route. Sir David requested John Lawrie in Burleigh to write indicating his departure from the tenancy of Burleigh, and that the farm then needed access to the estate land at Hattonburn. This resulted in the building of the flyover outside Milnathort, to Hattonburn, Netherton and to Glenfarg by Duncreivie.

The Laird: Sir David Montgomery

Sir David Montgomery

Sir David was Deputy Vice-Lord-Lieutenant of Kinross-shire from 1966-1974. He also held the office of Deputy Lieutenant of Perth and Kinross-shire in 1975. He was awarded the honorary degree of Doctor of Law by Dundee University in 1977, was Chairman of the Forestry Commission (1979-1989) and Chairman of Trustee Municipal Mutual Insurance (1980-1996). He became Lord Lieutenant of Perth & Kinross in 1995.

Sir David married Delia Reid, the twenty-year-old daughter of Admiral Sir John Peter Lorne Reid and Jean Dundas, on 5th April 1956. The young couple set up home at the Home Farm, then Kinross House, and again at the Home Farm. Their wedding was a great occasion: the tenants were invited and the county thrived as it recovered from the war. Life was stable and seemed full of hope again.

Together they bought the Green Hotel, famous for golf on the two home courses and the wonderful fishing on Loch Leven. There were 38 boats on the loch, all in great demand. Unfortunately cormorants arrived at the RSPB reserve; uncontrolled, these seabirds found easy pickings and ate more trout than were bred

The Green Hotel c1949 dates back to the 18th century. It was a traditional coaching inn, hosting stagecoaches that ran between Queensferry and Perth, allowing for a change of horses.

Fishing boats on Loch Leven

for fishing. This put the boats and boatmen out of business. Since then, with no trout being put into the loch, the cormorants have reverted to their natural environment of the sea. Lady Montgomery established the popular Shop at the Green, well stocked with quality goods. Kinross House was the venue for a very special ball to celebrate the Queen's Silver Jubilee in 1977, when we locals danced the night away in the ballroom, enjoying the hospitality and surroundings. The grounds were opened on the second Saturday of August from 1956 to 2010 for the Kinross-shire Agriculture Show. Many Christmas charity events were held in the house, and the gardens were open to the public for the pleasure of many.

The Green Hotel built a swimming pool in the late 1960s and the local community was able to access to it through a pool club, Kinross Otters, and as private individuals. Kinross Otters, with members from every corner of the county, is still going strong, competing to a high level and giving children enjoyment and the satisfaction of achievement. It is now located in the since-developed Loch Leven Leisure Centre.

Another even bigger venture was the Green Hotel ice-rink, opened in September 1978. Curling had been played for centuries as the weather dictated.

Curling on Loch Leven (1970s)

Grand Matches were held when the lochs at Linlithgow, Menteith and Loch Leven had strong enough ice. Ponds were built for the game and even fields were frozen over to create shallow ice. However, the indoor rinks brought a full season of guaranteed ice, and a boost to the local clubs in the Loch Leven Province. The number of clubs increased and the competitions with them. The atmosphere was electric during the games and a dram at the bar afterwards enabled the competitors to share their ups and downs. This ensured the ice rink was always busy. However, when Jack Frost was in the right mood the Kinross Club were still keen to have a game outside. Before the Green Hotel ice rink opened, the locals had to go to Perth, Kirkcaldy or Haymarket in Edinburgh to hire ice for a game. Sir David Montgomery presented a silver cigarette box in 1965 to be played for in a knockout competition.

Sir David and Lady Montgomery also gave land to create one of the first hospices in Scotland for children with life-limiting conditions; to have holidays, to give their carers a break and for the children and their families to have their final days in understanding conditions. Called Children's Hospices Across Scotland (CHAS), the facilities are tremendous. The charity is supported by volunteers with a few professional staff. They also have two charity shops in Kinross.

This charming couple had six children.

James David Keith Montgomery	*b1957 heir to the baronetcy. Married Elizabeth Lynette Evans in 1983.*
Caroline Jean Montgomery	*b1959. Married Nicholas John Kestell in 1983. A son and two daughters, Lucy, Alexander and Harriet.*
Davina Lucy Montgomery	*b 1961. Married Humphrey Martin Butler. Two sons, Bertie and Hector.*
Andrew Peter Montgomery	*b1967, d1971*
Iona Margaret Montgomery	*b1972. Married Ben Roper-Lee and have three children, Arthur, Isla and Tommy.*
Laura Elizabeth Montgomery	*b 1974. Married David Redvers of Tweenhills, Hartpury, Gloucestershire.*

They have established one of the best studs in the UK, and David attracted the attention of Sheikh Fahad bin Abdullah Al Thani, who selected him as his racing manager, for both his extensive breeding and racing enterprises. David and Laura have three children; Charlie, Hubbie, and Fenelica.

Heir, James David Keith Montgomery was educated at Eton and Exeter University. He gained the rank of Captain (1976) in the Royal Highland Regiment (Black Watch). He retired from the military in 1986. James married Elizabeth Lynette Evans, daughter of E. Lyndon Evans on 24 September 1983. They resided for a while at Tillywhally House, then Kinross House and, now at Burleigh House.

They have two children. Their son, Edward Henry James Montgomery

James and Elizabeth Montgomery

(*b1986*), was educated in Yorkshire where his parents were living at the time, then Eton. He entered the Parachute Regiment and has served widely, including spells in Afghanistan. He attained the rank of Major and is now with the Ministry of Defence in London. He married Miss Flora Nichol in 2018. Their first child, a son named Benji, was born just before Christmas 2019 to the delight of all.

Their daughter, Iona Rosanna Montgomery (*b1988*) was educated at Craigclowan, Kilgraston and Oundle in Northamptonshire. She is now a successful milliner with a business in London.

The Laird and Lady Montgomery moved back to the Home Farm, where they had lived when they first married. This charming house, set in a beautiful garden, sits behind Kinross and overlooks Loch Leven, being reached by a drive that winds through the golf courses. Sadly, Lady Montgomery died in 2019.

Kinross House was sold in March 2011 to Yorkshire businessman Donald Fothergill. He opened the house as a venue for conferences and weddings, with the gardens his particular interest.

Benji Montgomery

Jamie and Elizabeth moved into Burleigh House, adding a kitchen-living room wing. It is quite fitting that a story starting with the Barony of Burleigh now sees that same family again living at the house which, along with the Home Farm, they still own today.

Edward Montgomery

GREIG of LITTLE TILLYRIE and HALL GREIG
1712-1912

Orwell Session records state that in December 1712 David Grieg in Little Tillyrie was asked to be an elder and accepted, but declined before edict in 1713.

On 7th October 1731 John Greig in Lethangie bought the lands of Little Tilloray from Lady Margaret Balfour of Burleigh for 2,200 merks Scots, to be beholden to Lady Balfour in 'feu as expressed'. The 'Ballie of that part specially constitute for the transaction was David Greig portioner of Meilke Tillory. Witnesses for the Seasine were John Henderson schoolmaster in Milnathort and John Deas merchant in Perth lawful son to John Deas in Lethangie'.

John Greig in Lethangie is mentioned in November 1823 as authorised by the Heritors to get a new schoolroom built for Kinross Parish. The plans and documents are in the Heritors' Box in Kinross Museum. On 5th April 1797/8 he paid one shilling for the Dog Tax Rolls.

In 1830 the Kinross Corn Market Company was formed by subscription and used the site of the removed parish church until 1935. John Greig in Lethangie had three shares. He was named as being present at a meeting in 1831 to consider the plan to build a proposed building for the company.

When Loch Leven was lowered in 1829-30, Lethangie benefitted with acres of land drainable and improved. However the loch-side, by agreement, belonged to the Kinross Estate. In 1827 in the list of trustees providing security for the loan of £13,600 from the National Bank of Scotland, Sir James Montgomery is quoted at £5,000, much the largest security put forward. John Greig of Lethangie put forward £400, much the same as six other landowners around the loch. Mill owners also put forward security.

In December 1830 when the sluice was opened, the Commissioner was at death's door, and the financial situation was critical. The Trustees of the Leven Improvement formed a committee to take the project forward, under the chairmanship of Mr John Greig of Lethangie.

GRIEG FAMILY TREE

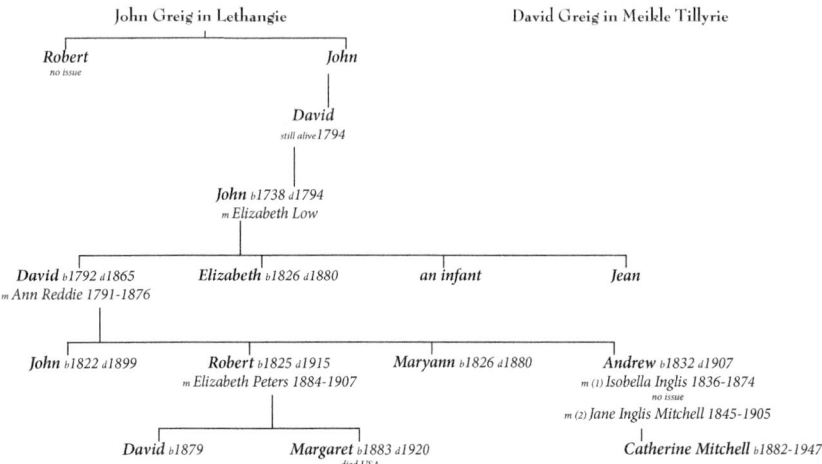

John Greig in Lethangie · David Greig in Meikle Tillyrie

Robert *no issue* · John

David *still alive 1794*

John *b1738 d1794* m Elizabeth Low

David *b1792 d1865* m Ann Reddie 1791-1876 · Elizabeth *b1826 d1880* · an infant · Jean

John *b1822 d1899* · Robert *b1825 d1915* m Elizabeth Peters 1884-1907 · Maryann *b1826 d1880* · Andrew *b1832 d1907* m (1) Isabella Inglis 1836-1874 *no issue* m (2) Jane Inglis Mitchell 1845-1905

David *b1879* · Margaret *b1883 d1920 died USA* · Catherine Mitchell *b1882-1947*

A Sasine on 7th January 1737 granted the room of land in Little Tillyirey to John Greig, son and heir to the deceased John Greig in Lethangie, and of deceased Robert Greig his eldest lawful son. There had been a document in 1731 giving Robert and John interests in life rent of the land conjointly.

John Greig died without issue and left his brother David heir to the lands by disposition on 31st December 1747. David was designed tenant in Little Tilliry at the time. The witnesses were James Reid of Berrybray in Tillyiry and Robert Arnot portioner of land and merchant in Milnathort.

David's son, John, manager of the Coltnese Iron Works at the time of the 1860 disposition, inherited the lands of Little Tilliyiry, and lived life as a land proprietor. This John Greig in 1794 made a disposition in favour of his son David.

All and whole of the lands of Little Tillyrye after my death. Reserving always to David Greig my father that part of the Commonly of Aithrons set apart to him with the division of that commonly and his life rent of the several parts of the foresaid town and lands specified in the disposition in my favour 28th March 1782." If he happens to leave a widow reserving her life rent and provisions contained in the said disposition". Obliging David Greig to pay my father David Greig whatever sum I am resting him by bill or otherwise, also whatever sum I may be owing for servants wages at my death.

To make payment to each of Elizabeth and Jean Greig my daughters the sum of £100 sterling at the first term of Whitsunday or Martinmas after my death. Also to furnish Elizabeth Low my spouse such a house and yard in Tillyiry as the tutors (guardians) undernamed shall judge

suitable to her station, and keep a cow for her summer and winter, with carriage of twelve cartloads of coal annually to be paid by her at the hill; and she obliges herself to maintain, cloth and educate Elizabeth and Jean till sich time as they shall arrive at the age of twelve years for which she will receive the due and legal interest from all provision left by me to them. But declaring that in case of the said Elizabeth Low shall enter into a second marriage, then she shall forfeit all the provisions in her favour, and Elizabeth and Jean shall be under the management of the tutors named hereafter.

David Greig and his heirs convey rents moults and duties of the foresaid subject from and after my death, with full power to uplift, receive and discharge rents and everything I could have done myself.

I nominate David Low tenant in Fairneybarns, Henry Greig of Milna-thort Mill and William Tod tenant in Holtown to be tutors and curators to my said children, or such as within years of minority at the time of my death, declaring any two a quorum.

Reserving always full power and liberty to at any time in my lifetime to alter or cancel these presents.

Witnesses David Low of Vain, and Robert Greig Student of divinity at Tillyre. John Peat writer (lawyer) in Kinross.

John Greig died at Tillyrie in 1794, his father still being alive. John's son David Greig (1791-1865) then inherited the lands of Little Tillyre and Hall Greig.

Hall Greig, (once the lands of Alexander Balfour) was land that had been owned by David Greig and his wife Elizabeth before his death in 1801. It was left in trust to their eldest son Alexander Greig, and there is a charter from Thomas Graham Esq of Kinross & Burleigh in favour of Alexander on 26th May 1816. Alexander and spouse left it in trust to their trustees in favour of Mr Thomas Robertson, an accountant in Edinburgh in 1834. A disposition in 1837 was in favour of creditor (of Alexander Greig) Robert Neilson of Hilton of Burleigh, who in turn by deed left it in favour of Rev James Neilson Palmer, an Episcopal Clergyman then residing at Millfield House, Edmonton, in life rent and James Neilson Palmer his son, in feu. The deed of settlement was issued on 27th December 1849, and a charter from Sir Graham Graham Montgomery of Stobo BT, was issued in favour of James Nelson Palmer, Rector of Braemore, Hampshire, in life rent and his son James, in feu, on 23 February 1852. Then on 17 May 1875 the Rev James Nelson Palmer residing at Bembridge Isle of Wight, son of the former mentioned Rev James Nelson Palmer left Hall Greig to John Greig of Tillyrie by disposition.

David was christened at six days old in Orwell. He married Anne Readdie *(1791-1876)* daughter of Robert and Mary *(nee* Brown) Readdie in Orwell Church. They had seven children, the older children born at Nether Tillyrie (or Little Tillyrie, both names now being used.) and younger ones including Robert in Kinross.

Eliza	*(1818-1820)*
Mary Anne	*(March 1818-1886)* married Hugh Laird 23rd December 1838 in Kinross.
An unnamed infant	who died 1821.
John	*(1822-1838)*
Robert	*(1825 to 1915)* A merchant.
David	(1828-1856)
Andrew	*(1830)* Farmer in Holeton. Married 1) Isabella Inglis *(1838-1874)* and 2) Janet Inglis Mitchell *(1845-1905)* a daughter Catherine Mitchell Greig *3.1.1882.*
Catherine	married Henry Robertson Stark of Ruddon Grange, Elie, and is buried in Orwell Graveyard.

The Common land for the Tillyries and Tillywhally called "commonly" were on the hill part of the Ochil Hills north of the said farms, referred to as Athrons in some documents. At some previous time this common land was divided between the relevant properties. On 3rd December 1812, David Greig for £220 sterling sold to George Reid of Upper Tillyrie "that portion of my said lands of Nether (Little) Tillyrie being the hill part including the parts called the Glach. Bounded by the lands of Holton (belonging to David Walker Arnott esq of Arlary) on the East, the lands of Tillywhally being the hill part of that farm on the North, and the said George Reid's own land on the West and South parts, all in the parish of Orwell and Shire of Kinross." This was subject to the feu duty, ministers stipend and school master's salary and other public burdens due and payable forth and in all-time coming, as was normal in these times. The disposition was witnessed by John Thomson, portioner of Seggie, and James Stocks of Lathro, and signed at Lathro on the above date.

There was a search of Incumberances affecting Little Tillerye belonging to David Greig Esq in 1817. It was recorded by David Greig writer (lawyer) in Edinburgh that there were no incumberances in the general records. There is a record of a loan of £1,000 from James Robertson, tobacconist in Edinburgh to David Greig, with the lands of Little Tillyrie as security on 22nd October 1816. There is also a sasine for the Rev David Greig of Lochgelly with security for £500 from David Greig of Little Tillerye with land as security dated 28th January 1817.

David died suddenly at the age of 74 in December 1865 of apoplexy. It was reported his death "removes from the district the last of the Bar Lairds, who have filled up so much of the history of our county. Mr Greig was held in great respect and his practical knowledge made him a valued Councillor and arbiter. His funeral was a large and impressive one". Anne lived on, dying on April 8th 1876 of congestion of the lungs and debility at 85.

David left his lands to his eldest son John, who farmed there until his death on January 29th 1899. In John's lifetime the lands of Hall Greig and Meikle Tillyrie came into this branch of the family (in May 1875). These were later to be described together as Nether Tillyrie. In 1730 a David Greig was recorded in Meikle Tillyrie, acting as Ballie when John bought Little Tillyrie. He may have been a brother or relation of John Grieg in Lethangie.

John, in turn, left all Nether Tillyrie to his brother Robert, a merchant residing at St Ronans, Kinross. Robert married Mary Eliza *nee* Peters on 5th November 1878. They had two children; the elder David born at Nether Tillyrie on 17th August 1879, and their daughter Margaret was born in 1883. Robert was described as a successful businessman and a partner in Messrs Todd and Company, a general draper and mercers company in Limerick. He had retired by the time he was 50 years old.

In the records of Kinross Curling Club a meeting was held of the Kinross-shire Curling Society on 17th February 1818 at 'Mrs Donaldson's Inn at Kinross Green'. The minutes state the club had a tradition that had existed for many generations but no written records were kept. A committee of seven worthies was formed to prepare the old established rules, ascertain the possible antiquity of the game, make a list of the present members and generally regulate the affairs of the society. Robert Greig was one of the seven chosen members, and they came back on the 7th March with a copy of the rules. The Club celebrated 350 years of curling in 2018.

Robert's sister Mary Anne married Hugh Laird in 1836. Hugh was a solicitor who owned a large amount of land at Cottarfauld, Kinross. He gave Robert land to build a house there in 1873. This was built, and Hugh died in 'Cottarfauld Villa' in June 1882. This house Robert later owned, renaming it St Ronans, moving in during 1891. There was still a thriving family of Greigs living there until 2018, when they downsized and the house was sold.

Robert paid off the borrowings, taking out a further bond from Mrs Catherine Dick, widow of the deceased former innkeeper in Glenfarg, for the £1,500, on 27th February 1899. In security were the lands of Tillyrie called Hall Greig, lying to the south side of the public road from Upper Tillyrie to Seggie. This land was at one time owned by Alexander Balfour and leased to his son Michael Balfour. On a map from the 1700s Hall Greig is named where the old sycamore tree stands in the north end of the 40-acre field, where there is also a well. The north dyke of the 40-acre field has a fancy wall, tile topped, and the gateway has stone pillars. The 40-acre field came with Nether Tillyrie lands when bought from the Greigs by the Reids as we will later see. Also in security were the eight-merk land of Tillyrie comprising the part called Tomarron. Also the whole of Meikle Tillyrie formerly tenanted by James Rutherford (but excepting the lands bought by George Reid of Upper Tillyrie), bounded on the west and south by the lands of Seggie, on the east by the lands of Upper Tillyrie and on the north by the service road leading from Upper Tillyrie to Seggie. All of these were formerly the property of David Greig of Tillyrie.

There are documents in 1884 between John Greig and his brother Andrew Greig of Holton for a water supply to Nether Tillyrie House and cottage from the Bent Well spring on Holton, and again in 1911. Also one about a wayleave agreement over Tillyrie to Holton for an electric supply in the early 1900s. The stone uprights of a bridge over the Hattonburn, (the march between Tillyrie and Holton), are still there at the foot of the Tillyhenry field and the 'Field Facing Holton', where a grass track goes down the field. The Holton bridge was used for communication between the brothers Greig in years past and Miss Reid used it up to the early 1970s, but the bridge itself has since been washed away in a storm.

Robert prepared to sell Nether Tillyrie and in 1904 had published 'Articles and Conditions of the Roupe and Sale of the Lands of Little Tillyrie and Hall Greig.'

> 1. All and whole of the lands of Little Tillyrie with houses biggings yards arable lands out fields and in fields tofts crofts mosses muirs meadows and haill pertinents & privileges. Sometime possessed by the deceased David Greig and John Greig his son.
>
> 2. All and whole of that part and portion lying south of the public road from Upper Tillyrie to Seggie and all and whole of those parts called Hall Greig, sometime possessed by Alexander Balfour.
>
> 3. The whole of the 8 merk land of Over Tillyrie comprehending that part called Tomasson, formally possessed by George Reid tenant, with houses etc.
>
> 4. The whole of those parts portone of the lands of Meikle Tillyrie with houses etc, formally possessed by James Rutherford tenant therein.
>
> Which lands above described are to be exposed to public roupe and sale by Robert Greig esq of Tillyrie and Hall Greig aforesaid, resident at St. Ronans, Kinross. Articles and Conditions underwritten at 18 George Street Edinburgh on 19th June 1904.
>
> The lands upset price £9,000 or such price as specified.
>
> If more than one offers then one shall exceed the least by £25.
>
> The Entry of the purchaser shall be at the term of Martinmas 1904, and the purchaser shall have right of rents to become due after that date, and shall bear interest at 5% per annum during non payment.
>
> The highest and last offer shall be prefered, and shall be bound if required within 10 days after the roupe a deposit of 1/5 of the price in a bank to be named.
>
> If the person preferred fails to bring the required deposit or grant security for the price, he shall forfeit the purchase and be libel to exposer 1/5 of the price naming damages.
>
> The exposer obliges himself to relieve the purchaser of said lands of all fue duties and public burdens.
>
> Particulars of property estimated the Lands of Little Tillyrie and Hall Greig on 4th March 1899 as £6724: 2/5d; when inherited by Robert from John Grieg.

A disposition on 10th January 1912 by Robert Greig in favour of Maria Johnston or Reid, widow of David Reid in Thomanean, who with her father Sir William Johnston Bt and her son Robert Matale Reid, bought the lands of Little Tillyrie and Hall Greig for the sum of £8,250 sterling.

The children of Robert and Margaret Greig grew up away from rural life. David was an architect. After training he initially worked in Kilmarnock, later moving to Glasgow where, in 1909-10, he worked from 219 St Vincent Street. Later he became a partner in Mortimer Greig and Henry in Bath Street, who were mainly factors and estate agents. David was obliged to borrow money from his father at some point before 1915, the date of his father's death. David joined the Royal Navy during the First World War, serving as sub-lieutenant on HMS *Satellite*. He returned after the war ended, and was living at 20 Carrington Street in 1920, the year his sister Margaret emigrated to the USA.

John Greig of Nether Tillyrie *(d.1794)*, Elizabeth Low his wife *(d.1835)*, Elizabeth Greig *(d.1880)*, David Greig *(d.1856)* David Greig *(d.1865)* Ann Reddie his wife *(d.1876)* John Greig of Tillyrie *(d.1899)* Robert Greig *(d.1915)* and Mary Elizabeth Peters his wife *(d.1907)* are all buried in a family plot in Orwell Kirk graveyard. On entering the kirk gates turn right along the boundary wall and on your left you will find a table type grave stone with them all named. Beside is the grave of Andrew Greig of Holton, and also a tall gravestone for his daughter Catherine Mitchell Greig (1882-1947) who married Henry Robertson Stark of Ruddon Grange, Elie and died aged 65.

PEARSON DRON-PEARSON

George Pearson and his wife Julia, *nee* Livingstone, bought Berrybrae in 1823 in the reign of George IV. They had two daughters, Euphemia and Christian, and a son, William, who died in 1828. Euphemia married Andrew Reddie of Netherhall, and Christian the Rev Walter Little, Minister at Orwell Parish Church in Milnathort.

Walter Little was born in Jedburgh in 1808. The Orwell Heritors' Minutes show him as minister at the meeting on 28th July 1857. The 1886 Valuation Roll states that the the Rev Walter Little is proprietor and occupier of the manse, garden and offices at Orwell.

Every Heritor having land of £100 Scots valued rent could, by law, vote for minister and the schoolmaster and had a duty to maintain the buildings. They also paid pew rent and were responsible for the poor fund.

In 1873 Orwell Church was in a poor state and in need of many repairs. The Rev Walter Little offered to pay £100 to the cost, and his wife £50 for decoration, which all but two elders enthusiastically embraced and the renovations were then started.

An agreement was made with Sir Graham Montgomery for the Burleigh Wing of the church. He was willing to relinquish the Burleigh Aisle in favour of the Heritors, provided that the aisle would be accepted as part of the church in all aspects, and a portion of sittings in the aisle would be allocated to the Lands of Burleigh and lands in feu from Burleigh Estate, to be binding on Sir Graham Montgomery and his successors.

A report from John Lessels, Architect in Edinburgh, estimated the repairs would cost £482 2s 4d. This would add 1/3d in the £ on value rent. Rev Little informed the committee that the voluntary subscription from church members raised £160, which made it

Rev Walter Little

PEARSON FAMILY TREE

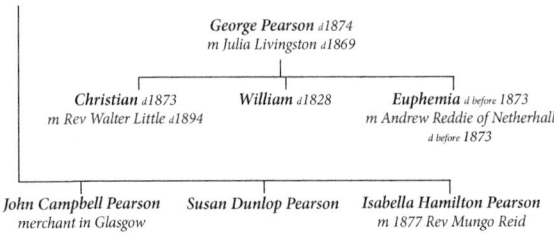

George Pearson *d*1874
m Julia Livingston d1869

Christian *d*1873
m Rev Walter Little d1894

William *d*1828

Euphemia *d before 1873*
m Andrew Reddie of Netherhall
d before 1873

John Campbell Pearson
merchant in Glasgow

Susan Dunlop Pearson

Isabella Hamilton Pearson
m 1877 Rev Mungo Reid

possible for the front elevation and windows with stone mullions and estimates would be obtained for cathedral glass in the windows.

The church was refurbished to last another hundred years and the £50 gifted by Mrs Little was used to put in two beautiful stained-glass windows dedicated to Christian and Euphemia by Rev Little in 1874/5.

There is an Instrument of Sasine dated 1834 in the reign of William IV, giving Mrs Julia Livingston or Pearson, widow of the late George Pearson, and Miss Euphemia Pearson and Miss Christian Pearson his daughters, the former the life rent and the latter two the heirs to the property. Andrew Reddie of Netherhall was Procurator and Attorney, the Baillie David Greig of Little Tillyrye. Witnesses were Robert Reid of Tillyrye and James Stocks ,resident in Kinross, and Alexander Balfour his son residing with him at Tillyrye, signed Michel Balfour on 17 January 1833. The usual feu and double on the new entrant, with the burden of 8 capons, 2 hens, carriages of coals etc to Burleigh House still were written into the Charter of Confirmation from the superior Robert Montgomery Esq, Commissioner for the Trustee of the late Thomas Graham Esq.

By 1869, on the death of their mother, Euphemia was widowed, Andrew Reddie deceased (1859) and she was living at Tillyrie. She and her sister Christian, living at Orwell Manse with husband Rev Walter Little, became heirs to the two rooms of Tillyrie. Again the feu duty of £10 at the term of Martinmas and double at new entrant was due, and receipted a writ of clare constat by Sir G. G. Montgomery Bart in London on 7 April 1869, witnessed by his son Basil Templer Montgomery and George Scott, his butler.

Euphemia died at Tillyrie before her sister, Christian, who in turn died in 1874 leaving a deed of settlement. Neither sister had offspring and so Christian, as sole heir, left a life interest and use to her husband Rev Walter Little, and thereafter to her cousin John Pearson, son of the late Adam Pearson, and his heirs. This was on the condition that he pay each of his brothers and sisters then living the sum of £100. Also:

to Mrs Julia Hamilton Begg daughter of Mrs Agnes Begg or Pearson

Orwell Church, Milnathort

her cousin, £500, also Elizabeth Livingstone her cousin the life rent use of £500, the said sum after her decease to be divided equally between James and John Downie sons of the late Andrew Downie and Margaret Livingstone her cousin or their heirs. To the minister and session of the Kirk of Orwell £100 free of legacy duty, for such poor persons as were resident in the said Parish for not less than seven years. Executors to be John Pearson, James Downie and Rev Walter Little.

In September 1876 there was a Contract of Excambion between Rev W Little, John C Pearson and James Martin, proprietor of the upper portion of Hallgreig. They were wishing to exchange two small pieces of land:

A small piece of ground with the cottage part of the lands of Upper Tillyrye, lying to the North of the Milnathort to Seggie road, and on the East side of the entrance leading north to Upper Tillyrye. On the west a small triangular piece of ground and buildings thereon of the parts of the land of Hallgreig on the north side of the Milnathort to Seggie road and the west of the foresaid entrance north of the road and leading to Upper Tillyrie, and adjoining the farm steading.

John Bogie of Old Fargie agreed to refer the difference in value if any.

The small piece of Hallgreig – £154 18/6d.

The small piece of Upper Tillyrie £151 3/-.

Therefore Upper Tillyrie paid Mr James Martin the sum of £3 15/3d.

The life rent on the lands came to an end when Rev Walter Little died on the 8 August 1890, in the 47th year of his ministry. He is buried beside his wife, and near his in-laws at Orwell graveyard, north-west of the north wing of the church building. This left Glasgow merchant John Campbell Pearson heir to the lands outright.

John C Pearson was a man of substance as a Disposition of Settlement of 13 February 1891 shows:

> *I John Campbell Pearson merchant residing at 5 Lyneloch Place, Glasgow, (First) my sisters Miss Susan Dunlop Pearson and Mrs Isabella Hamilton Pearson or Reid, wife to Rev Mungo Reid minister at the Parish of Mearns, Renfrewshire for their joint life rent and to Susan D Pearson her heirs my land and estate of Upper Tillyrie in the Parish of Orwell.*

> *(Second) To my sisters equally between them the residue and remainder of my estate belonging to me at my death over which I have the power of disposal, including the estates or plantations in 'Jory en Hoop' Picarda and Linglante belonging jointly to me and my friend and partner James Greirson, and also my estates or plantation 'Alfmour' all situated in the Dutch Colony of Surinam, South America and all other estates belonging to me abroad, the whole appurtenance chattels and effects; but under the burdens and condition and others following it; Considering that I and my partner James Grierson are joint proprietors of the said plantations and that we have invested a considerable sum of money in the cultivation and improvement, in the event of my decease the said estates are to be continued to be held & cultivated in the same manner. I therefore provide that it shall not be competent to my sisters to sell my half without the approval of James Greirson, but they shall allow him to manage and cultivate the said estates.*

> *Further considering that I have invested in the firm Adam Pearson and Company, Merchants in Glasgow & London, of which James Greison and I are the sole partners, a considerable sum of money, it may be not convenient for the said James Greirson to pay out my interest in the said business in the term of the contract between us, therefore I declare notwithstanding the terms of the said contract it shall not be competent to my said sisters to demand payment of the balance, but the said balance shall be allowed to remain in the business as a loan for a period of ten years, without prejudice the said James Greirson to repay the balance in whole or part at any time convenient for him.*

> *My sisters and executors shall without being partners in addition to interest at 5% shall be entitled to 1/3 share in any profits, and shall within three months of it being made, receive an Annual Balance sheet*

> *(Thirdly) considering I deposited in the Freehold Investment & Banking Co of Australia Ltd the sum of £100 belonging to Miss Margaret Pearson for five years at 5%, and took out a Deposit Receipt in our joint name, the said Bank stopped payment, and I am desirous that she suffers no*

loss. I direct my executors to make up to her any loss of capital and in-
terest she would have received.

I leave free of legacy to:

Miss Susan Waterston Walker, 9 Nile Grove, Edinburgh the sum of £500
sterling

Miss Helen MacFarlane, 9 Belmont Terrace, Glasgow the sum of £500
sterling

and to each of the four sons of William Hamilton of Greenbank in the
Parish of Mearns £100 sterling.

Sole executors
Miss Susan Dunlop Pearson, Mrs Isabella Hamilton Pearson or Reid,
and James Greirson.

Witnessed
John Andrew Hamilton at 135 St Vincent Street, Glasgow   Solicitor
Bessie Kyle, 165 Shamrock Street, Glasgow   Sicknurse

On 17 September 1877 the following Extract of Registered Ante-Nuptial
Contract of Marriage between Rev Mungo Reid and Miss Isabella Hamilton Pearson was registered.

It is contracted agreed between the Rev Mungo Reid, Minister of the
Parish of Mearns, Renfrewshire and Miss Isabella Hamilton Pearson, 5
Lyneloch Place, Glasgow. That is to say the parties have accepted each
other for lawful spouse and promise to solemnize the Bond of Marriage
with all convenient speed.

For the purpose of making suitable provision for his intended spouse in
the event of his death the said Rev Mungo Reid hereby provides the said
Isabella Hamilton Pearson, promised spouse in the event of her survival
the whole household furniture and plenishing including plates, books,
pictures, bed and table linen, wine, liquors and other such articles for
family use which he may have at the time of his death. Further he finds
himself and his heirs, executors and successors whosoever to life rent
his said spouse in the whole estate which he may die including any life
assurance, but under the burden of the life rent use behoof of Mrs Jessie
Horn or Reid his mother in the event of her surviving him.

Isabella Hamilton Pearson herself hereby accepts as in full satisfaction.
Further the Rev Mungo Reid renounces and discharges all just right of ad-
ministration, right of courtesy to ½ or ⅓ of moveable or other could have
claim and exercise in consequence of the said intended marriage over all
or any part of the lands and other goods, gear, debts, money and effects
generally the whole means, estate etc where ever situated presently belong-
ing or which shall hereafter belong to the said Isabella Hamilton Pear-
son, or which she shall acquire or succeed to in any manner. For which
causes and on the other part the said Isabella Hamilton Pearson consent

of her said promised spouse hereby assigns, disposes and conveys to and in favour of herself the said Isabella Hamilton Pearson, John Campbell Pearson, her brother and James Greirson merchant Glasgow and the accepted survivors and heirs of the last survivor in that trust. But excepting any money at present in her own possession or in the bank in her own name, and also excepting the sum of £300 contained in the 3.69% Sterling Bonds for £100 each of the New York and Canadian Railway Company.

But that the trust always for the sole uses of herself Isabella Hamilton Pearson for behoof of the child or children of the marriage. Failing such children in fee and writing behoof of other person or persons as she shall appoint.

In the event of the said Isabella Hamilton Pearson predeceasing her promised spouse with or without issue of the marriage, in the event the said Trustees shall pay over to the Rev Mungo Reid during all the days of his survivance ½ of the free income of the Trust & Estate.

Both parties consent to registration for preservation and execution. Peter Hutchison clerk to J & J Hamilton Writer in Glasgow 23rd August 1887.

Witness   *John Andrew Hamilton Writer and Peter Hutchison,*
signed   *Mungo Reid and Isabella Hamilton Pearson.*

24th November 1894

There is a Notarial Instrument in favour of Susan Pearson and Mrs Isabella Reid in life rent of all and whole the one half of all and whole of that room in Over Tillyrie purchased by Alexander Dron. The whole of that room of land belonging to Michael Balfour that he sold to Robert Reid.

The same month, they, Susan Dunlop Pearson and Isabella Hamilton Pearson or Reid, with special advise and consent of my husband, in consideration of £4,250 sterling by Mrs Maria Johnston or Reid, widow of the deceased David Reid some time Tea Planter in Ceylon and Railway Contractor, now residing at Thomanean in the County of Kinross, as the price which we acknowledge the receipt, and do hereby sell and dispone to the said Mrs Maria Johnston or Reid and her heirs. All and whole of that room of lands in Over Tillyrie which sometime belonged to Michael Balfour, and all and whole of Berrybrae in Tillyrie that room of land sometime belonging to Alexander Dron.

The Disposition is written by John Laurence Hamilton and signed by Susan Dunlop Pearson, Isabella Hamilton Pearson or Reid, Mungo Reid and James Greirson. George Bogie Solicitor in Kinross did a copy for Maria Johnston or Reid.

The graves of George Pearson and Julia Livingston, his spouse, and son William are in Orwell graveyard in a metal surround, along with their son who died in 1828.

Beside them, behind the railing are Rev Walter Little (*d.*1890 in his 92nd year and 47th year of ministry), and his wife Christian Pearson (*d.*1874). They are north-west of the church.

While researching all the graves in Orwell graveyard with Professor Munro, they found the grave, covered in ivy, of Andrew Reddie of Netherhall (*d.*1859) and Euphemia Pearson his spouse (*d.*1873). They lie to the east of the church beside Reddie graves on the wall including Andrew's father Robert Reddie (*d.*1892 aged 92).

The windows dedicated to the two ladies Euphemia and Christian continue to shine in their glory on a Sunday service at Orwell Church.

REID FAMILY TREE

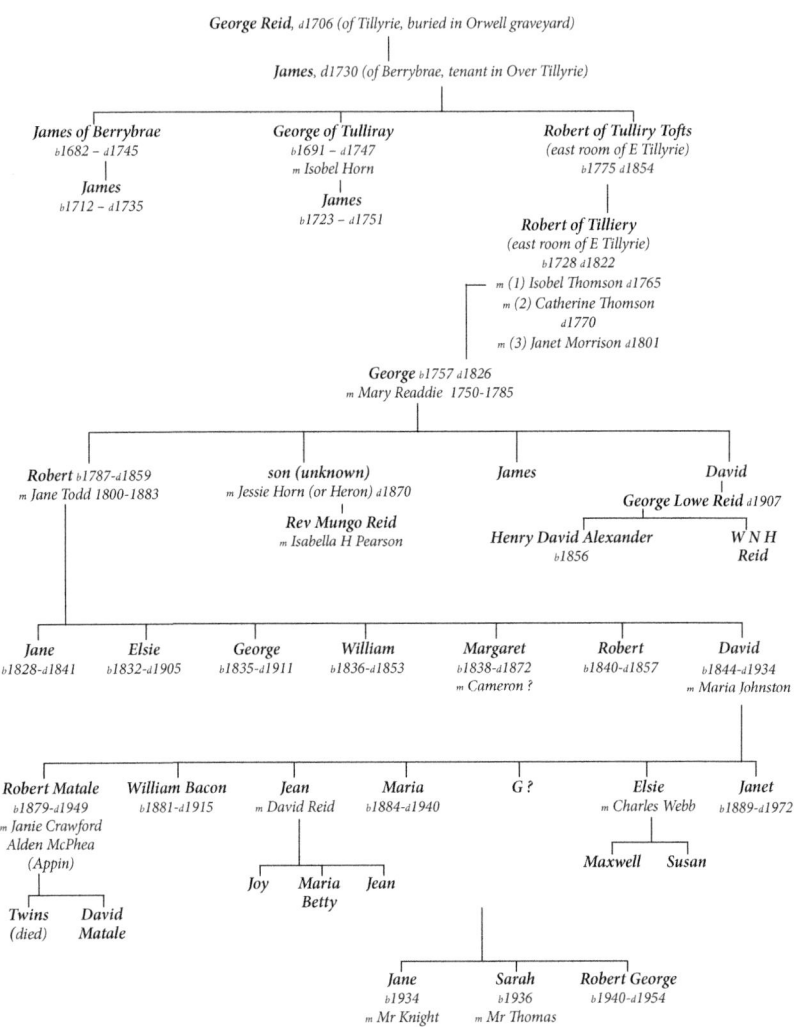

George Reid, *d1706 (of Tillyrie, buried in Orwell graveyard)*

James, *d1730 (of Berrybrae, tenant in Over Tillyrie)*

James of Berrybrae
b1682 – d1745

James
b1712 – d1735

George of Tulliray
b1691 – d1747
m Isobel Horn

James
b1723 – d1751

Robert of Tulliry Tofts
(east room of E Tillyrie)
b1775 d1854

Robert of Tilliery
(east room of E Tillyrie)
b1728 d1822
m (1) Isobel Thomson d1765
m (2) Catherine Thomson
d1770
m (3) Janet Morrison d1801

George b1757 d1826
m Mary Readdie 1750-1785

Robert *b1787–d1859*
m Jane Todd 1800-1883

son (unknown)
m Jessie Horn (or Heron) d1870

Rev Mungo Reid
m Isabella H Pearson

James

David
George Lowe Reid *d1907*

Henry David Alexander
b1856

**W N H
Reid**

Jane
b1828–d1841

Elsie
b1832–d1905

George
b1835–d1911

William
b1836–d1853

Margaret
b1838–d1872
m Cameron ?

Robert
b1840–d1857

David
b1844–d1934
m Maria Johnston

Robert Matale
b1879-d1949
m Janie Crawford
Alden McPhea
(Appin)

William Bacon
b1881-d1915

Jean
m David Reid

Maria
b1884–d1940

G ?

Elsie
m Charles Webb

Janet
b1889-d1972

Twins
(died)

David
Matale

Joy

Maria
Betty

Jean

Maxwell   Susan

Jane
b1934
m Mr Knight

Sarah
b1936
m Mr Thomas

Robert George
b1940-d1954

REID
1680-1911

The Reids feature in the *Extracts from Orwell Parish Minutes* by Rev Thomas Shearer. The following extracts all mention Tillyrie or Burleigh; some are quite amusing. Remember at this time the Minister and schoolteacher are chosen and paid for by the Laird (Lord Burleigh), and the collections in the church go to the poor in the parish and pay towards the upkeep of the church and school buildings. There were two sermons per week, Wednesdays and Sundays, and note *'the stool for ye publick appearance when sinners were summoned by Session on Sabbath Next'*. Orwell village was north of the road near Orwell farm today, and the church was at the loch side, (the loch coming up to the edge of the buildings before the level was dropped in the early nineteenth century). The site of and ruins of the churchyard and manse can be reached from the Loch Leven Core Path between Burleigh Sands and Channel Farm (Loch Leven's Larder). The standing stones to the north of the public road at Orwell Farm would have been just north of the village. The parish boundary was just as it is today, a rather sprawling rural area.

On 22 June 1681 the Rt Honourable Lord Burleigh and Sir William Bruce of Loch Leven met with the minister Charles Mackinnon about the fabric of the church, and ordained that 900 slates, 20 bags of lime and as many nails as shall be judged fit be bought, and 2 marks upon each 100 lib of rent be paid by heritors in the parish to cover the cost.

In July elders chosen included Lord Burleigh, Robert Arnot of Holetown, David Gibb in Little Seggie and Michael Elder in Tulliry.

On 20th September Mr William Dick was called by the parish to be schoolmaster and preceptor. The same day Agnes Morice in Over Tillyrie, being thrice cited on account of swearing, was sharply reproved by session and told to beware of her scandalous sins. £1 10/10d was collected and all distributed the same day to needy persons.

On 10th December 1692 Andrew Black and Janet Horn gave their names to be proclaimed in order to be married. David Black in Tulliquhallie was cautioner for Andrew Black and James Reid in Tulliry for Janet Horn. They were married on 20th January 1693.

Cases that the Session failed to control were sent to Rt Honourable Sir William Bruce of Kinross as *'principle civil Magistrate off ye place to take such course with them as he thought fit'*

Limestone was carted from the foot of the Lomond Hill, and there was a dispute between John Henderson of Middleton and David Thomson of Seggie, the latter claiming the former took away two loads of lime stones belonging to him. Session heard witnesses and William and John Thomson were amongst those interrogated, and William found guilty *'of rising the foresaid scandal, and ordered on Sabbath immediately following the sermon before ye session to express all humility for the injury and wrong they had done'.*

John Stirk in Dalqueich was called and Session finding no ground of fixing that guilt of alleged drunkenness upon him dismissed him with admonitions to take heed to his walk and give no occasion of raising such scandalous reports. (28th August 1692).

On 19th February 1693 Walter White in Tilliry, was summoned upon a report of theft. He told the session he had been coming home from St Johnston, and that on the way he had stolen a hen. He added that he was drunk; otherwise he would not have done it. The session ordered him to appear before the minister on Sabbath next, to express his grief and give satisfaction for his misdemeanours, and also appointed two elders, James Reid and John Simpson in Tulliry, to converse with him twix this and next Sabbath. Walter professed his remorse and hearty sorrow before session and promised the strength of grace to guard against the like evils in time coming. The Session, after reproofs and admonitions, dismissed Walter.

In February 1693 the General Assembly certified that £6 Scots were to be given at weddings, the money for the poor. This was in serious consideration of the abuses at marriages in parishes, such as excessive drinking, piping and occasionally promiscuous dancing and other attending evils by numerous multitudes, and thought fit to restrict persons to 24 on both sides.

On February 7th 1697, James Reid in Tillieray having advanced to a poor man in the parish 50 shillings to help him buy a horse in order to have a means of making a living, was reimbursed by the Church.

16th March Mr David Stirk, having demitted his office of schoolmaster, Session all agreed to Mr John Henderson to take the office. Lord Burleigh signed accordingly, Session and all heritors signing too.

In August Michael Elder in Upper Tulliray was cautioner to a marriage. In September Robert Balfour was mentioned as an elder.

On 11th September Robert Balfour in Burleigh did relate to Session that Jean Arthur, spouse of William Thomson in Milnathort, for a breach of the Sabbath, both by coming from home to his peas on Sabbath morning. She was called to session and said it was between 9-11 pm on Saturday evening, and was rebuked for stealing her neighbour's peas, and exhorted to take heed of her heart and absolved further censure.

1699 was a very poor harvest and considering the very great straits of the poor because of the great dearth and scarcity of food, Lord Balfour was asked and brought forward 3 bolls of bear (gruel) with £40 4 shillings Scots. 6 shillings and 19 merks per boll was distributed by elders Robert Balfour and James Reid to 20 named poor.

On 25th June 1698 a scandal of fornication betwixt William Morice in Milnathort and Mary Craik one of my Lady Balfour's servants occurred. The minister took Robert Balfour and Robert Stark between sermons to talk with William and Mary. The couple desired marriage, and she was put out of her service.

James Reid was in trouble on 6th July. Elspeth and Christian Waterstone and Margaret Henderson reported James had struck his wife on 29th June. None had seen it but had heard of it and Margaret had heard his wife give two wild screeches. James was cited to Session three times and failed to come. On the third day Elizabeth his wife appeared before Session, and told her truth. James had come home weary and tired and asked her to put his horse in the field for him. She confessed she uttered unsuitable words. James had smacked her on the rump. The Session considered this and thought it meet to rebuke her for her miscarriage and exhorted her to be obedient to her husband, to give him no offence and to do as much in her lay to live peaceably with him. James appeared the following day and faced the congregation to confess his guilt in beating his wife and seemed quite affected.

On 22nd October Robert Balfour was given 10s for furnishing things needful for George Robertson's burial. On 10th December to Robert Balfour 'for ale', to John Paton's laying on his deathbed 18s. On 28th April 1700 Robert Balfour is sent to Lord Balfour about victuals for the poor from his annual rent. A list of 29 names were given for distribution of victuals.

In March 1701 James Reid was appointed as Ruling Elder to go with the minister to a Synod, and again in September to Presbytery.

The same September the Councils Act for a voluntary contribution throughout the kingdom for building a bridge at the Gullets on the east end of Loch Leven was needed, and congregations were exhorted to bring next Lord's Day some quite considerable sum for so necessary a work.

Alexander Balfour in Tillierie and John Black in Tilliewhalley joined Session on 5th June 1702. In an inspection on 5th July Alexander Balfour in Meikle Tilliere and James Reid in Tillyrie would in conjunction give the oversight of that toun. Robert Balfour had Burleigh to Orwell village for his area as elder.

In 1703 Thomas Gray in Tulliray is mentioned with five others for being drunk at John Simpson's house in Orwell. They were sharply rebuked and exhorted to be so no more and dismissed.

On 28th May voluntary contributions were requested for John Thomson the younger of Turiff, who was under slavery in Algier. Six libs were collected.

James Reddy, servant to Michael Elder in Tulliry was 'delete' for bringing back from Kinross some goods upon the Sabbath, and summoned before Session. He appeared, confessed and was rebuked.

1707 brought the difficult subject of 'Deacons in Churches' in Scotland. Elders were asked and all refused, so no deacons were appointed. Lord Balfour attended the Synod at Dunfermline in March.

On 7th July Session discussed the Deacon situation, not having had one before, and unanimously agreed if such an officer should be chosen then they may find their government to be more consistent to scripture rules. The August meeting gave the subject more time but by 3rd November three of the persons asked had refused and the fourth had not replied.

In February 1708 the elders in Tilliry 'deleted' Isobel Skinner, a widow woman in Tilliry, being with child and John Gray, son of Thomas Gray tenant there, said by her to be the father. The man consistently denied paternity and the woman as consistently declared he was the father. The case continued for some time. By July the matter was remitted to Presbytery in Dunfermline, John Gray taking an oath of purgation drawn up by them and read to him.

Andrew Horn of Thomean was ordained as an elder on 17th April 1710. In April, Alexander Balfour, James Reid, John Simpson and Robert Arnot were the elders chosen to hold the key to the poor box that year. The money was given quarterly and at times of special need to the poor in the parish.

On 7th February 1709 Margaret Simpson, daughter of the blacksmith in Milnathort, a single woman, was brought to bed of a child. Ordered to appear before Session and asked the name of the father, said it was Robert, Master of Burleigh, who was now abroad. She was rebuked and dismissed until such time as Session would order her public appearance for removing the scandal.

In the present Orwell graveyard, to the north west of the north aisle of the church, the graves of the Reids have been made into a multi-grave monument. The oldest date is of George Reid who died in 1706. On the old (pre-1841) farm house at Upper Tillyrie there was a marriage stone above the wee byre dated 1646. The farmhouse was a stone building two storeys high, with two rooms downstairs and two up a ladder-like stair. There were chimneys on both floors. The room on the right of the front door was the kitchen, with a door on the east to the outside. There would have been a range-type cooker on the left of the east door, and an enclose on the north wall for a box bed. The house stood on the footprint of the present garage between Tillyrie Mains No 3 & 5. It was part of planning consent that the house footprint was maintained. There was a courtyard round the house and a big garden to the west, running right to the end of the buildings to meet the road. There was a double-sided byre for 10 cows or heifers on the right of the house, with a two-box building and then a two-stall stable, and on the left an open shed, joined by a door to a single-sided byre with slate stalls and stone troughs for about eight cattle, and a low chain on the wall without stalls for tying a dog. There was also a reid (cattle court) behind the buildings to the right of the house, which had entrances from the glen on the north and road to the south-east, and

The old Tillyrie farmhouse – converted to stables in 1841

the byre and boxes could be mucked out through a door in the wee byre, and hinged wooded half doors at the back of the boxes into the reid. This was all still there until 2010, but too low for machinery to be used. The old house had been made into a stable with stalls and a loft. When the present Tillyrie House was built in 1841, the floor was cobbled and in our time the building was only a store as it was too damp for stock.

Pre-1841 on the other side of the road (once the main road from Hillfoots and Stirling to Glenfarg and Perth) there were cartsheds, lofts and stables (where the present Tillyrie House stands) and to the west a horse mill. The latter I discovered when trying to plant fruit trees in 'the wash green' in the 1970s, going through layers of stone with a pickaxe! There would be a pair of work horses for each cart archway. Marked on an old map was a well to the east of the reid near the old house and there may have been one at the old stable. There is a corresponding spring directly to the west where Hall Greig stood two fields away, (by the old sycamore tree in the Forty Acre Field). All the buildings were stone, and on the south end of the single byre was a red sandstone pigeon entrance with three arches .

There is a Sasine on 25th December 1730 from James Reid of Berrybrae, life rent tenant in Over Tillieray in favour of his son James Reid, having and holding in his hands:

'a disposition of that date containing the receipt of Sasin underwritten, granted by Mistress Margaret Balfour, eldest lawful daughter of the deceased Robert, Lord Burleigh. Mistress Margaret Balfour saised the same James Reid in life rent and the said James Reid, his son, in fee the said two rooms of land of Over Tillieray and Eeinds, recently pofsest by Robert Reid tenant thereof.'

'Ane handful of Grafs and corn for the said Eeinds. The witnesses were David Greig of Tilliery and Robert Greig lawful son of John Greig of Lethangie, David Walker merchant in Strathmiglo and Robert Pitcairn.'

Unfortunately James Reid the son of James Reid of Berrybrae, died before his father, at the age of 23, *'in the flower of his age'* on 9th March 1735. His father died ten years later.

Then a sasine on 1st December 1746 states:

in the reign of King George II, King of Britain, Ireland and France, in the presence of John Henderson, schoolmaster in Milnathort, Ballie in that part specially constitute to the venture saying James Reid of Berrybrae holding in his hands a receipt of those constate made and granted by Mistress Margaret Balfour in favour of James Reid as heir to the deceased James Reid in Over Tillyire his uncle. (son of James in Berrybrae's brother George) The lands of Over Tillyrie sometime tenanted by James Elder and James Reid together. He is of lawful age and for payment of the sum of £20.00 Scots in ffew, and the said ffew duty double at entry. Heir to the said lands and leading in to the barnyard at Burleigh his port portion and division of the hay from the meadow at Burleigh as wont and this yearly in all time coming after his entry to the said lands, also bringing his grindable grain to my mill at Milnathort and pay the ordinary millusar and duties, particularly paying to the master mill tenant 2 fislots of bear, and drawing water and stone to the said mill, and maintaining his part of the drain dykes and Miln confirm to the same James Reid, paying carriages for upholding the roof of the hail Armoury of Burleigh, and that from the term of Martinmas £1026 confirm to that Ancient Rights and Infoldments of the said lands. Witnesses Henry Simpson, Mathine Young and Robert Young all weavers in Meikle Tillyrie.

1777 a disposition by Mistress Margaret Balfour to James Reid details:

the sale of lands to James Reid, tenant in Over Tilleray paying on 1st May £6720 5 shillings scots (£1726 sterling), all and hail the room and lands of Over Tilleray then profest by the said James Reid tenant. Also that room and lands of Over Tilleray then pofsest by James Elder tenant thereof. The feu, minister's stipends and duties on the said lands £1727 at Martinmas to free James Reid of these public burdens in all time.

In 1781 upon the 15th July:

in the reign of King George III, a public instrument, Ballie Joseph Simpson in Meikle Seggie, for Robert Reid portainor of Upper Tillerye. Also compeered James Reid portioner of Over Tillerie. Underwritten by percept of sasine after in search, and charter granted by George Graham Esq of Kinross. Robert Reid heir of the deceased James Reid, his brother, in the lands of the said James Reid.

Memorials to James Reid and also to his uncle George, below

There follows a Charter of Confirmation from George Graham Esq. of Kinross in favour of Robert Reid portioner in Over Tillyery on 29th December 1786. It is regarding the Easter rooms of Over Tillerye with mansion house, according as the sasine was for George Reid, and Robert Reid of Tofts (youngest brother of George of Tilliray and James of Berrybrae) became the heir. George, born in 1691, was married to Isobel Horn. They had a son, James, born in 1723, but sadly he died at only 28 years of age. George died on 21st July 1747, aged 56.

Heir to both his brothers this Robert Reid, born on 24th December 1728. lived until 1st January 1822, dying at the age of 94. He was owner of Tillyrie Tofts before inheriting both Easter Tillyrie and Berrybrae. He married three times. His first wife was Isobel Thomson who died on 8th March 1765. They had a son George Reid on 4th April 1757. His second marriage was to Catherine Thomson, her sister, who died on 4th October 1770. His third wife Janet Morrison died on 13th March 1801.

Between his birth in 1728 and his death in 1822 the whole world changed. The Industrial and Agricultural Revolutions and war made the world they lived in a different place. There were difficult times when James II and fear of Catholicism pushed the government into requesting the protection of the Orange family to take the throne. Unrest in the time of Queen Anne (1702-14) and the Winter Queen, a sister to Charles I, and when her grandson George I came to the throne there were many uprisings.

The first real change was in 1726 when General Wade built the Great Military Road, which passed through Kinross. This was a blessing as the old road was very narrow and full of 'ruts and dubs'. He also raised the Black Watch six companies which had been offered by loyal Highland chiefs. It was one of the first regiments in service in British Empire 1756 – 63.

In 1736 the first pair of Fanner winnowing machines were introduced to Kinross-shire. At first they were viewed with considerable suspicion, distrust and downright dislike, farmers being loath to make changes on the whole. The winnowing was an ancient method separating the grain from the chaff, or hay from the chaff, simply by throwing the mix so the wind blew the lighter chaff and the heavier grain fell down for recovery. In 1737 Andrew Rodger, farmer on Cavers Estate in Roxburghshire, developed a winnowing machine called a Fanner, which was successfully sold throughout Scotland. Some Presbyterian ministers saw the winnowing machine as a sin against God, as wind was a thing made by Him and artificial wind was an impious attempt to usurp what belonged to God.

In 1740 extreme cold caused Loch Leven to freeze over for a long time, followed by snow in mid January, and again in March. The farmers lost many sheep and cows. This was followed by a bad harvest, leaving many families in deplorable poverty.

1745 saw a great many poor-looking Highland soldiers of the rebel army in Kinross-shire, and it seems they had a knack of serving themselves without assistance of waiters. In 1746 Mr Henderson of Milnathort received a letter on 15th February from David Duncan demanding 'quarters with bread and drink for about 70 or 80 soldiers.'

1748 saw a great famine, so severely felt in Kinross-shire that a relief by contributors of money was made to the poor. The population of Kinross-shire in 1755 was 5,944 of which the parish of Orwell accounted for 1, 891 souls.

In 1763 there was a great drought. Not a drop of rain fell for three months. The Queich burns were dry to the bottom, and Loch Leven's level dropped dramatically.

In the 1760s the Agricultural Revolution began. Fields were enclosed and the run rigs broken down, consolidated strips of stagnant mosses drained, and use of common land changed. Change in crops, including rotations, destroyed forever the traditions of husbandry which dictated the framework for most of the population throughout Scottish agricultural history. It surrenders forever a peasant economy that mainly produced enough for itself in a mainly rural world, where most people were producers. There arose instead a society in which capitalist farmers and landless labourers worked mainly to produce food for the great towns filled with consumers. This they did so well that the farming system in many parts of Scotland became the envy of Europe.

The triumphs of technology were systematically applied for the first time to problems of production; Watts Steam Engine, Neilson's Invention, Arkwright's Water Frame, Crompton's Spinning Mule and Corts's Iron-Puddling Process. These were all key inventions that gave the 1780s their special spurt to the Scottish ability to take immediate advantage of the advances of technology, on the new strength of Scotland's own economy built up before 1780 and on the Union. The prosperity of the cattle trade had provided new money and horizons to many who would be in the vanguard of Scottish agriculture in the next decade.

One of the two greatest areas of advancement was in agriculture between 1770 and 1820. The Scottish population rose by 50% and were much better fed at the latter date. Exports of meat had risen and imports of grain probably had not altered to match the increase of population, therefore giving rise to the likelihood that Scottish farms provided 50% more food than before.

At the time of the Union the population of Scotland was just over a million. It had hitherto grown in fits and starts with generations of stagnation and sudden, if short, catastrophic declines due to famine, disease and war. The growing urbanisation was a direct result of industrial change. By 1832 it had been without parallel in the history of the world.

The earliest survey in 1755 was 1, 265,000 souls. By 1801 it was 1,608,000 souls. By 1811 it was 1,816,000 souls and by 1821 had become 2,091,000. In 1755 half the population lived north of the Firth of Tay and Firth of Clyde. By 1820 only two-fifths lived there.

In 1790 the average number of children born in each marriage was 5-7. They benefitted from a better diet, improvement in child-rearing practices and the elimination of smallpox. The choice of green vegetables, turnips, carrots, herbs, and fresh fruit and an enthusiasm for gardening by the upper classes helped, copied on a smaller scale in the 'kail yards' of peasantry. The arrival of cheap tea and sugar affected a wide and low circle of society in the last decades of the century, and meat became more affordable. Exceeding this was the arrival of the potato as a common field crop. It helped the national diet, eliminating chronic and debilitating scurvy, and for the first time there was an alternative to oatmeal as a staple food. The potato was a lifeline when failure of the oat crop occurred. Famine and death happened in 1740, yet by 1816, when the oat crop had failed on at least ten occasions, people may, without potatoes have been hungry – but not dead.

Diseases were on the increase. Measles caused 1% of deaths between 1738-1788 but 10% by 1807-1812). Diphtheria (or croup) had become the most fatal disorder to which children were liable. Tuberculosis above all was the killer of youth in their teens and twenties, especially in industrial areas. The bubonic plague now withdrew from western Europe, probably because the brown rat had largely driven out the black rat, who had hosted the plague flea. Malaria, which had been prevalent in Scotland, suddenly died out in the late 18th century, possibly due to climate changes caused by cooling periods in the northern hemisphere between 1780-1815. Though seldom a fatal disease in itself, it was a very debilitating one, and contributed to a higher death rate than other causes, especially among children. Smallpox first occurred in Scotland in the reign of James VI, with serious epidemics over a wide area in 1635 and 1641. In Glasgow in 1672 800 children died. One in twelve caught the disease, and 19% of all deaths were attributed to smallpox, while one third of child mortality was caused by it. In 1733 the first inoculation was tried in Dumfriesshire, but it was not until 1765 that it was taken up in Edinburgh and Kinross-shire. Vaccination was devised by Jenner in England in 1796 and almost immediately taken up by Scottish doctors. The vaccination was accepted by the common people remarkably quickly, and the child mortality rate went from 36% before vaccination to 9% after, and by 1813-19 to only 2%.

William Smellie of Lanark in 1752/63 made great strides in the science of midwifery. Puerperal fever that killed so many women in childbirth was hugely misunderstood. The saving was initially restricted to a mainly upper-class section of society. Buchan's *Book of Domestic Medicine*, says 'do not as soon as they are born give babies wine or whiskey, they prefer milk and it is better for them. Do not drop them straight into a basin of cold water, better to bathe them in warm water. Keep children in clean, warm, loose clothing and dry accommodation. Cold kills more than plague.'

Edinburgh Royal Infirmary was founded in 1741 with 228 beds and three dispensaries. From 1760 to 1775 15,600 patients were attended to, of which 11,700 (75%) were cured. Only 750 died.

By 1820 far more Scots lived in towns. In 1750 only four towns had inhabitants of over 10,000 and, by 1820, 13 towns contained 25% of the population. Seven out of ten still lived in rural communities. Farms or villages were still not replaced as a typical social environment in which a man spent his life.

In 1770 the first wheat is said to be sown in Kinross-shire. A bad harvest was recorded in 1783. The victual would not ripen, and there were falls of snow afterwards, known as the 'snawy hairst'. The Highland & Agricultural Society was created in 1784 in order to further the adapting of modern agricultual methods. In 1789 umbrellas were introduced to the area, and they caused astonishment and laughter. In 1792 as elsewhere, the harvest commenced at the end of October

It was a Scotsman named Andrew Meikle who invented the first threshing machine in 1786. Threshing is the process loosening the edible part of the grain from the husk and straw. It is the step in grain preparation after rearing and before winnowing. Hand threshing is laborious, a bushel of wheat taking an hour to produce. In the late 18th century about one-quarter of agricultural labour was devoted to this.

In 1794 another severe frost continued for a long time; Loch Leven and all its feeding burns were frozen solid. In 1796 the Great North Road needed many repairs for the stagecoaches to run on it more easily.

1802 produced a very bad harvest, and a subscription for the poor was taken in every parish. In 1806 the continued high winds in the early part of the year did serious damage to housing, property and trees in the county.

In 1800 the price of cattle and kelp rose rapidly. Kelp, a type of seaweed, was harvested and used as fertiliser and PH corrector in agriculture. The war with France was associated with steep inflation, the rising of grain prices and several catastrophically short harvests. They were not bad years for farmers. Profits rose as well as rents, and change in enclosures and farm techniques took advantage of the buoyant market for food. Wages rose too. The skilled man with a fixed allowance of meat etc had a cushion against inflation. The majority of unskilled workers were less well-placed, paid less than £50 and suffered when the price of corn more than doubled between 1799–1816. No one died of famine but times were hard. The price of oats did not double and, with the introduction of potatoes, oats were less relied upon by the population.

The Napoleonic wars, (1803-1814), ended for a while when Napoleon was exiled to Elba but started again in early 1815 when he escaped, until his defeat at Waterloo in June of that year. He was exiled to St Helena where he died six years later. Kinross-shire saw soldiers return from the war en route to their depots, 'many in a sorrowful state, on foot and in carts'. In 1814 there were rejoicings on receipt of the news of the fall of Paris in March. At the end of that year there was an outbreak of typhus.

News of the victory at Waterloo caused great rejoicings with everyone elated at the prospect of lasting peace. Cattle prices were down at the end of the Napoleonic Wars, but turnips grown in winter for keep was a bonus. The economic situation after 1815 was very grim.

In March 1816 the greatest flood in living memory occurred in Kinross-shire. All the burns were filled to the brim. The South Queich water formed into a deep pool at one side of the Queich Bridge from eight to ten feet deep. It took 400 loads of stones to fill it.

On the 13th August a shock of an earthquake was felt at eleven o'clock at night. Plates rattled on shelves, chairs moved and were thrown about, while beds shook. There was a wet late harvest, with snow on four different occasions, four to six inches deep.

It was 1817 before the next document in the title deeds saga. George Reid, son of Robert and his wife Isobel, who had inherited the lands from his father George, had married Mary Reddie and they had four sons. The eldest son called Robert was born on 12th October 1787.

The disposition in 1817 is by George Reid:

> *'...portioner of Tillyrie in favour for the love favour and affection which I have for my eldest son to Robert Reid and his heirs. All and whole of the Easter Room of the lands of Over Tillyrie with the mansion house therein, houses, bigging's, yards, orchards, mosses, muirs, meadow, commonties, parks, together with the lands parsonage and vicarage thereof as presently posfesfed by myself, and marched and divided from the western room of Mrs Dron relict of the late Alexander Dron, portioner Tillyrie, and also all and whole that part of said farm, including that part of the lands of Nether Tillyrie being the Hill Part of the said farm, including that part called the Glacke, purchased by me from David Greig, bounded by the lands of Holetown belonging to David Walker Arnott of Arlary on the east, the hill part of the farm of Tillywhally on the north, and the lands first disponed above on the west and south, all in the parish of Orwell and shire of Kinross.*
>
> *Further I hereby dispone and make over in favour of Robert Reid all and sundry any whole farm stoking and household furniture as I shall take with me at my removal. But reserving always to me during my lifetime the Dwelling House, barn and byre with the two yards as presently posfesfed by Robert Reid my father, which subjects are to be kept*

and maintained in good habitable condition by the said Robert Reid during my lifetime, further the said Robert Reid and his foresaid shall be bound and obliged as acceptance hereby bind and oblige themselves to pay to me yearly during my lifetime £25 sterling at two terms in the year Whitsunday and Martinmas by equal portion, beginning the first terms payment at Whitsunday 1818. Also to maintain for me two cows summering and wintering, and to furnish me for the said cows besides the ordinary pasture Grafs in summer and straw in winter withy 20 roots of clover grafs for house food in summer and 20 roods of turnips and 80 stones of clover hay for winter food, the said Robert Reid and his forsaids always receiving the dung of the said cows successors or such person as she may appoint the sum of £34 excepting what may be necessary for the gardens hereby reserved, and also to annual delivery to me betwixt yuill and candlemass 8 bolls of good and sufficient oatmeal, one half boll of corn, two and a half bolls of bear (gruel) and ten bolls of potatoes and also to give me land necessary for sowing one peck of linseed and further to drive what coals I may require, likewise to furnish me with a horse to ride when required, and in case Elizabeth or Betty Low my present wife shall survive me, the said Robert Reid and his heirs shall likewise be bound to implement all the obligations prestable on me, and contained in a postnuptial contract of marriage entered into between her and me, and upon the 25th day of August 1815, but in case she shall predecease me then the said Robert Reid is hereby taken to pay her heirs, executer or successors or such person as be appointed the sum of £470 sterling at the first term of Whitsunday after my death, and the legal interest before disponed.

And further I oblige me and my foresaid to free and relieve the said Robert Reid and heirs of all feu Edinburgh on October 1817 and other duties bound to relieve me in all time. "

Witnesses William Brown clerk to Robert Lowe writer (lawyer) in Kinross and Robert Wilson writer.

In 1797 there was a horse tax, the government dictating that for every pair of horses the owner would pay two shillings in tax. Records show George Reid paying 6/- (three pairs of horse), Holeton of Arlary 8/- and Holeton of Burleigh 8/-. Orwell parish had 293 horses working in it in 1780.

The other sons of George and Mary Reid come into the story in later generations. Not much is known about James, but another son married Jessie Horn – or Heron – and are thought to be parents of a son, the Rev Mungo Reid of Mearns. The Rev Mungo married Isabella Hamilton Pearson who, with her sister Susan, had life rent in Berrybrae.

The fourth son of George and Mary Reid of Tilliery, David, was in business in Dunfermline, and it is with his son George Lowe Reid we continue our saga.

George Lowe Reid was born on 6 April 1829. On completing his education at

Glasgow High School, he was articled for five years to Mr Neil Robson of Glasgow who was chiefly employed on railway work. In 1852 George L. Reid obtained an appointment as a Divisional Resident Engineer on the Great Western Railway of Canada, then under construction, and he took up his duties there in April of that year.

In November he was transferred to the headquarters at Hamilton, Ontario, and promoted to Associate Chief Engineer. The main line was opened for traffic in 1854, forming with the New York Central and the Michigan Central Railway the first direct route between New York and Chicago. In the same year George was appointed Chief Engineer of the Great Western system.

He held this office for 18 years, during which he superintended the construction of a number of branch lines, and renewed most of the original wooden bridges in stone and iron. As Chief Engineer of the Detroit and Milwaukee Railway he carried out the extension of that line from Grand Rapids to Lake Michigan. He also erected for the Great Western Company a rolling mill at Hamilton for re-rolling old rails of the main line and branches. The gauge of the Great Western system was 5ft 6in. Much inconvenience was experienced at the frontier termini, where the gauge of the USA lines was 4 feet and a quarter inch, and accordingly a third line was laid. The Great Western main line was under George's superintendence, whereby passenger and goods trains passed in 1866 directly between Chicago and New York. The cars were transported across the Detroit River on an especially-constructed car ferry-boat. In 1868 George was elected a member of the Institute of Civil Engineers.

Between 1870 and 1872 he built the loop line between Glencoe on the main line and Fort Erie, on the Niagara River opposite Buffalo, a distance of 145 miles, affording direct communication between the latter city and Detroit. He visited Ceylon in 1875, and Jamaica in 1883 in connection with railway enterprises of interest with a family connection.

George relinquished the active pursuit of his profession in the former year, and spent much of his time afterwards travelling in Palestine, Egypt and Italy. He was widely read in theology, art and the literature of travel. George died in Brighton in 1907, in his 79th year. He was the father of two sons: HDA Reid, who pre-deceased him, and WNH Reid of the Indian Public Works Department. Both were, like him, members of the Institution of Civil Engineers.

Henry David Alexander Reid, born on 11th May 1856 to George Low Reid and his wife, was their eldest son. Born in Hamilton Ontorio, he was educated at St Andrews and subsequently at King's College, London, completing the engineering course in 1875 with considerable distinction, gaining five prizes for mathematics, chemistry, geology, surveying and art of construction. He was then articled for three years from 1875 to Robert Hodgson of Newcastle, at that time Chief Resident Engineer of the North Eastern Railway. In October 1878, he was engaged by David Reid, the contractor for the Kandy and Matalit Railway, Ceylon, to take charge of the construction of a section of that line. Mr J R Mosse was Chief

Resident Engineer under Sir Charles Hutton Gregory. The works were completed in early 1881. Henry was elected an Associate Member of the Institution of Civil Engineers in December 1881.

In the previous month Henry assumed charge of the construction of a section of the Jamaica Government Railway between Spanish Town and Edwardton for contractors Messrs Reid and MacKay. The Chief Resident Engineer was Mr Valentine G Bell, Director of Public Works, Jamaica. A special feature of this railway was the construction of all the bridges in Portland cement concrete, there being no durable building stone in the district.

On the completion of this railway in June 1886 Henry returned to the UK, and the following December was sent to Venezuela by James Livesey, to survey for the South Western Venezuela (Barquisimeto) Railway, and was afterwards appointed Chief Resident Engineer for the construction of the line extending from the Quebrada Copper Mines to Barquisimeto .

Returning to the UK in November 1889 Henry entered the office of Mr Livesey as chief assistant. In 1891 he sailed for Peru, having been appointed by Mr Livesey as Chief Resident Engineer of the railways of Peru, belonging to the Peruvian Corporation of London. Having completed the summit section of the Great Central Railway from Callao to Chicla to the satisfaction of the Peruvian government, he returned to the UK in October 1893. On 21st March 1893 Henry was elected to the class of Member of the Institute of Civil Engineers.

In February 1894 Henry crossed the sea again, this time to Chile, where he was appointed Engineer and General Manager of the Arica and Tacna Railway in the north of that country. This was a post he held for five years, during which he brought the company out of a state of financial difficulty into a dividend-paying condition.

Henry made a proposed extension to La Paz in Bolivia, a distance of 284 miles, for which the railway company had a concession, and the report and estimated cost met with the approval of the London Board of Directors. Having completed the engagement which brought him to Chile in 1894, Henry accepted the appointment of General Manager and Engineer of the Anglo-Chilian Nitrate and Railway Company of Tocopilla, Chile in 1899. Having spent a week or so inspecting the nitrate works and railway, Henry, as arranged with the London Board of Directors, set out on a three-months visit to England, travelling overland from Valparaiso to Buenos Aires. In crossing the Summit Pass of the Andes, Henry caught a severe chill, which, after he had sailed from Buenos Aires, developed into pneumonia and proved fatal on 20th March 1899, when he was within six days of Southampton.

Henry David Alexander Reid was described as an able engineer, both theoretically and practically, and a man of excellent business capacity, tact, and sound judgement. Of strictest integrity and unbending principle, he was highly esteemed and thoroughly trusted by his several employers and Boards of Directors, whilst his generous and kindly disposition endeared him to a wide circle of friends and to all men under his control, whose advancement in life he had ever at heart. Henry left a widow and four young children.

Returning to Tillyrie, Robert Reid, eldest son and heir of George and Mary Reid, was born on 12 October 1787. He married Jane Todd (1800-1883). Robert lived to be 72 years old .They had seven children; Jane (1828), Eliza – called Elsie by the family – (1832), George (1835), William (1836), Margaret (1858), Robert (1840) and David (1841).

Changes Robert And Jane Reid Would Have Seen In Their Lifetime

In 1822, in a trenching of ground near the 'Gallows-knowe' at Lathro, 12 graves were found, no doubt of those hung by feudal law.

Thirlage, whereby all corn must be milled at the landlord's mill, and the upkeep of that mill was abandoned in **1809**.

In 1828 a reaping machine was invented by Rev Patrick Bell, a Scottish Minister. Tested by the Highland and Agricultural Society, it was judged worthy of a £50 prize. It had a rotating reel at the front which drew the crop as it was cut on to a moving canvas, which in turn deposited it cleanly on the ground at the side, ready to be gathered by hand. The power for these operations came from the motion of the two large wheels as they were pushed by a pair of horses into the crop. It harvested at a rate of 1 acre (o.4ha) an hour. By 1832 there were ten machines in Scotland, and a few were sent to the USA, Australia and elsewhere. There was no production yet on any significant scale, as there was little demand in Britain.

On a more a more local note 1823 saw a great fall of snow that lasted four days, leaving an average depth of six feet, with drifts up to eighteen feet, The roads were impassable for eight days. About 500 people were employed for a week clearing the roads from 1-5 February, although the drifts blew in rapidly behind them.

In 1826 there was a very warm summer, with no rain for 63 days. Farmers had to drive for some five or six miles to water their cattle. The grass burned up and hay sold at 1/6d per stone. Rain came on 20th July. The harvest had begun but many hundreds of acres were reaped by plucking – although the corn, being only about six inches above the ground, could not therefore be sheared. Wheat and potatoes were good crops. Meal could not be got for want of water to drive the mills.

Snow fell again the following winter. Two hundred men unblocked the road this time, but a second fall of snow had them out again in March. A Mr James Foote who had gone to Dunfermline on business and returning on foot by the Cleish Hills was found frozen to death when 50 men went to find him. The drainage of Loch Leven started this year.

In 1831 the population in the Parish of Orwell was 1,772 souls.

In 1832 an outbreak of cholera reached Kinross-shire, a great many people of all ages died. The Kinross-shire Agricultural Society Show was held on 6th August, but owing to the backward state of the hay there were few spectators with a meagre show of stock.

1836 saw a total and annular eclipse of the sun on Sunday at 3 o'clock. Churches closed and there was great excitement.

1837 saw Weights and Measures altered to the Imperial legal notice which arrived in Kinross and was immediately acted on.

1838 A statistical account showed there were 22 thrashing mills in the parish. In mid-winter, with scarcely any ice, only one day's curling was enjoyed all season.

1845 opened with weather bleak but mild. Curlers despaired of having their roaring games. The potato-crop was a disastrous failure, not only in Kinross-shire but throughout the whole country, including Ireland. Collections in Kinross and Milnathort were taken in aid of suffering in Ireland. Harvest was plentiful but in bad condition, while the turnip crop was average. The harvest was late in Kinross-shire as it was in many other places.

The Great Exhibition at London's Crystal Palace in 1851 marked the beginning of a new phase in harvest machinery. With more people finding better-paid employment in towns and cities, many farmers found harvest costs of labour expensive and they took a closer look at mechanisation. Bell's reaper was not at the exhibition, but enormous interest in two machines developed in the USA, where severe labour shortages on the vast new corn fields had a more concerted attack on the harvesting problem. McCormick's reaper was first demonstrated publicly in 1831, but was not patented until 1833. In the mid-western states production increased. In Chicago until 1847 they were producing five hundred reapers a year. Hussey's reaper could not match McCormick's in volume although it did a good job. Both were pulled rather than pushed by horses, requiring a second man as well as the driver to rake the cut crop off the back and to the side of the platform. At the Great Exhibition McCormick's proved better for the damper conditions of Britain. Fired up by the prospect of cutting up to 20 acres (8ha) a day demand was heavy, and a number of British manufacturers made alterations to their own versions of the McCormick and Hussey designs. Over 1,500 machines were distributed by the end of 1853. The intense competition between firms ensured a steady flow of improvements over the next 20 years. To keep pace with these machines, reapers still needed to follow behind to gather the grain into sheaves and arrange them into stooks. A reduction in manpower could be achieved by having two people riding on the reaper itself to tie sheaves that were delivered to them by a moving canvas table, then dropping the sheaves off the back.

Until the railway was established the cattle were walked by drove roads from the Highlands and other districts by drovers; hardy, independent, reliable men. Their word was their bond. They were trusted to pay for cattle once they were sold at the fairs and, as they were working on behalf of the same folk for years, utterly reliable. There was an annual Fair at Cuthil Muir where there was an inn, and stock was bought and sold. Drovers attended similar fairs at the likes of Crieff and Falkirk, and some drove cattle as far as London. These cattle were mature and fattened on the drove, while some had worked as oxen in the fields as they travelled hundreds of miles from Scotland to the fairs of northern England and the fattening pastures of the Midlands, all the way to Smithfield. When the drovers returned some stayed on in the west to help with the harvest, sending their collies home. Visitors to the Highlands remarked on the number of these dogs making their way home, stopping where they had on the way south and the innkeepers were paid for the keep of the dog for the night when the drover next stayed. The coming of rail travel eventually led to a different breed of cattle used that would not have thrived on the drove but could be sent at a younger age. The last of the drovers ended their days in market towns like Milnathort, old men and characters in the mid-twentieth century.

1846 was a wet autumn, with thunder – an early harvest of good corn but much of the late corn injured! There were processions in Kinross and Milnathort to commemorate the abolition of the Corn Laws. There was a great storm; quite a hurricane but of short duration, followed by a deluge of rain. Roofs, chimney pots and trees suffered.

1847 saw a great darkness accompanied with thunder and rain on April 23rd. Extreme darkness lasted from 12.30 till 1 o'clock. The Aurora Borealis was seen in a splendid display on Sunday 7th November between 9 and 10 o'clock. In October and November, typhus and scarlet fever were very prevalent among the young. Half the pupils in the school were absent with the maladies. The North Mail coaches ceased to run on 22nd December. Mail went by railway after this date.

1848 brought a strong frost between January 7th-20th. On the 25th Loch Leven was nearly covered with ice, and the thermometer was as low as -15 degrees. Greenwich Time was adopted in Kinross-shire, as it was in the rest of the country. The suddenness of the change took many by surprise. A heavy gale in the county on 15th December, at about 8 o'clock, blew with a fearful violence; several thatched houses were nearly stripped, chimney-stalks were thrown down and trees uprooted.

1849 brought more storms and the north and south Queich rose to a great height – so much so, the streams united at their nearest point. The South Queich overflowed its banks a little to the west of Burnbrae, travelling north-east by the back of Mawmill until it joined the Stank Burn which falls into the North Queich, the highest spate in 33 years.

There were epidemics of smallpox, scarlet fever and measles among the young, and very few families were not affected. Coaches, constructed to carry ten inside and seven out, were now to leave Mr Walker's hotel in Milnathort, and Mr Rennie's 'Fair Maid' would leave James Glass's Inn. Both would leave at 6am for Burntisland, and the return journey would leave after the arrival of the five-hour 8pm boat from Granton. In October there were a few cases of cholera in Milnathort.

1853 saw the Milnathort Corn Market Dinner held on 23rd February in Mr Walker's Inn, with 47 attendees. The frost was very intense. Loch Leven was one vast sheet of ice, the skaters were enjoying themselves and large numbers looked on.

In 1854 Minathort Town Hall was in the process of being built. Paid for by public subscription, construction began in 1853 and it was opened with a public dinner in 1858. Capable of holding 400 persons, the hall also contains constabulary offices, cells and a keeper room. The steeple, 95ft high with illuminated clock dials and bell cost, in total, £800.

The *Kinross-shire Advertiser,* established in 1847 as a monthly publication, became fortnightly on 13th October with issue number 106.

A branch of the City of Glasgow Bank opened in Milnathort on 5 February **1856**.

In **1858** the Fife and Kinross Railway opened as far as Milnathort in March and to Kinross on Friday 20th August. The bill authorising the construction of the Devon Valley Railway was passed on the 30th June. The railway's arrival in Milnathort led to it becoming a market town in the coming years.

In 1841 Robert and Jane built a new house. The Steading was on both sides of the old road from Hillfoots to Perth via Glenfarg, and the stables, horse mill and cart shed were on the south side of the road. The byres, cattle courts and general sheds were beside the older house with a large garden to the right behind the west byre, and a walled garden with paths and box hedges well set out. The new house replaced the stable, and the horse mill became a grass-washing green and the cart shed was kept at the back of the house, and the old garden was kept in its glory. The new house, completed in 1841 had an entrance hall, two good rooms facing south, and a kitchen, dairy, coal-house, large utility room behind, a drawing room upstairs and three bedrooms. The old house was converted into a stable and hayloft.

The family in 1841 were Elsie 9, George 6, William 5, Margaret 3 and Robert, 1. Unfortunately their eldest daughter Jane died in that year, but a son, David, was born. Jane was only 13 when she died, William died in 1853 aged 16, and Robert died in 1858 aged 17.

In 1859 there is a Disposition & Deed of Settlement by Robert:

'... *considering it to be a duty incumbent upon me for the welfare of any family to settle my affairs in the case of my death. I do grant sign and dispone to and in favour of George Reid my eldest son and his heirs the whole of the Easter Room of the lands of Over Tillyrie, with mansion house therof, biggings, yards, orchards, masses, muirs and meadows. The same passed on to me together with parsonage and vicarage, the same presently possessed by me, and marched and divided from the Wester Room now possessed by the heirs of George Pearson. Also the part and portion of the lands of North Tillyrie being the hill part of the said farm, including the part there called the Glack, purchased by the late George Reid, my father, from David Greig, bounded by the lands of Holton on the East, the hill part of Tillywhally on the North and my said other lands on the West and South. And also the whole of that field or croft of land being part of the lands of Over Tillyrie, which formerly belonged to Michael Balfour portioner of Over Tillyrie, which is situated to the South of the Tillyrie to Seggie Road bounded as follows: On the North by the said road. East and West by the property of Hallgreig. South by the property formerly of John Thomson Esq of Seggie lying within the Barony of Burleigh, Parish of Orwell and County of Kinross.'*

He left all his moveable estate to be divided equally to his surviving children:

Tillyrie, Milnathort, built 1841. Photo: David Millar.

'... excepting always the whole household furnishings and plenishing of every description in the dwelling house in favour of Mrs Jane Todd or Reid, my wife, in the event of her surviving me."

He appointed George Reid, his eldest son, as sole executor, and bound him by acceptation to pay all debts out of the estate along with all funeral expenses. Also:

'... to make payment to the said Jane Todd my spouse in case she survive me of a free annual £50 sterling during all the days of her life. She shall occupy the principal dwelling house and garden upon my lands of Tillyrie rent free, and shall be bound to keep her a cow during summer and winter, and to perform the carriage of whatever coals she may require for her own use.

The said shall be bound and obliged to make payment to David Reid my only other son, and to Mary Reid or Cameron, Eliza Reid and Margaret Reid my daughters the sum of £350 sterling each to be paid the first Whit or Martinmas after my decease. In the event of the said Eliza and Margaret surviving me and my spouse being unmarried then either of them shall in that event be entitled to occupy free of rent the cottage upon my said lands of Tillyrie so long as they or she remain unmarried.'

This was signed and witnessed by George Bogie, writer in Kinross 18 May 1859.

Robert died in 1859 aged 79, leaving Jane a widow at 59 years old. George then took over the farm at the age of 24.

Margaret died in 1872 aged 34 and the widow Jane lived until 1883, passing away at 83 years of age.

George had the usual Notarial Instrument in his favour in 1860 from Sir Graham Graham Montgomery of Stanhope, Lawful Superior, asking for:

> '... feu duty of ten pounds Scots and double on entry. Conditions of all grindable corn grown thereon to and wont. Also £78 Scots for the feu due on the room of land in Over Tillyrie, with service due, and double feu at entry.'

Things went on improving. The intense competition for supremacy between firms ensured a steady flow of improvements in the efficiency of reapers over the next 20 years. The first British version of the self–raking reaper was built in 1860 where the reel was replaced by a cluster of rake arms, rotating on a vertical axis, both drawing the crop on to the cutter bar and sweeping it back off the table in a continuous sequence. To keep pace with one of these reapers four or five people were still needed to follow behind, gathering the corn into sheaves and arranging them in stooks. A considerable reduction in manpower could be achieved by having two people riding on the reaper to tie into sheaves the corn that was delivered by a moving canvas table, then to drop off the sheaves at the back.

The labour shortages induced by the American Civil War (1861-65) caused rapid growth in the USA market, and in Britain there was almost no time to scrutinise this machine before it was overtaken by a new generation with automatic sheaf-binding systems. In the 1870s the first series relied on wire-tying machines but there were difficulties. By 1880 the problem was solved by substituting twine, made from a mixture of sisal and manila hemp. These 'binders' at the close of the 19th-century were used on three-quarters of the grain crop being harvested by machine.

Improvements to binders continued, but the essential features of those used after the Second World War, even some pulled by tractors rather than horses, were hardly altered from their late 19th-century predecessors. The early threshing machines were installed as fixtures within barns and usually driven by horses. There was one at Upper Tillyrie and one at Wester Tillyrie. In 1876 a portable threshing machine was introduced which delivered graded and cleaned corn into sacks ready for market. It was a double-blast machine, which meant that the grain passed through two separate screenings or dressings, each of which was assisted by the draught from a rotary fan.

Haymaking was a labour-intensive time. From the beginning of the 19th century hay rakes and other horse-drawn implements were introduced. The pace increased in the 1850s, when a practical and efficient grass–mowing machine was developed, and during the last quarter of the century mowing machines became widespread once design improvements made them lighter, harder wearing and effective under more uneven field conditions. In 1875 curved hoods were added in front of the revolving rakes, stopping the constant showers of grass on the driver. These machines remained popular into the 20th century, especially where grass was exceptionally thick and swaths of grass were required to be scattered. The ordinary tedder was overtaken by a new device, the swath turner – which, once it reached a reliable form in 1896, was gentler on the crop and was able to invert the swath completely, usually on the second day after mowing, and deposit it on the now dry strip adjacent. A further innovation in the early 20th century was the side-delivery rake, which collected two swaths together into a single row in order to complete the drying before collection began. The process was completed in 1913 with the appearance of a combined machine for the three operations of tedding, swathing and side raking.

In **1860** London merchant James Brand died on 12th June, aged 64, leaving a sum of £350,000. Of this, £200 went to Milnathort to erect a school, his wife Mrs Brand having been born there. In 1861 James Brand Jr contributed a further £200 to his late father's school donation.

In the same year, a steam-powered linen factory was erected in Milnathort – the first in Kinross-shire.

1861 began with severe frost. On 1st Jan Loch Leven was covered with ice of great thickness. There was daily skating and sliding with numerous spectators for about a fortnight. The meal and flour mill of John Ewing in Milnathort was discovered to be on fire about 3 o'clock on the morning of 16th January. The town bell rang, great crowds collected and the Kinross Fire Engine was brought but with little effect. In three hours the mill was a complete wreck.

The Ordnance Survey map, containing the county of Kinross-shire on a scale of one inch to a mile, was published in March. The population census put the county total at 7,759 souls, and those of Orwell parish 2,398. Channel of Pittendreich was exposed for sale at an upset price of £1400, but resulted in no sale. The July fair saw wet weather but a good attendance. The Agricultural Show was held in Market Park in August.

A steam-powered threshing machine was tried on 13th September, on the farm of James Paton, Lethangie. It gave great satisfaction and thrashed 17 bolls an hour. The engine was 4hp and 33lbs psi.

Wages for ploughmen were between £16-£20 a year, while foremen with perquisites earned £20. Hauflin ploughmen received £10-£12 and a hauflin £6-£9. In October St Luke's Fair was held, with the usual cattle, horses and sheep. It also included an apple and onion market.

The *Kinross-shire Advertiser,* which had published fortnightly since 1854, became a weekly paper with issue number 226, published on Saturday 23rd November. News of the death of the Prince Consort was received on 16th December, an announcement which cast a gloom in Kinross as it did across the whole of Britain.

By **1862** agriculture was in a prosperous state, with an increased use of poisoned grain by farmers for the destruction of birds. There was a heavy fall of snow of about nine inches in January. The Kinross-shire Coursing Club held their spring meeting, when 15 dogs were brought on ground. It was a remarkably early spring, the weather in February like that of May. The railway had affected the Let of Tolls on the Great North Road from Perth to Burntisland; there was no competition and they were consequently knocked down. The Agriculture Report said in

August *'the present season has been almost unprecedented for the rapidity and richness of vegetation'*. However the same report later said that *'the prevailing weather during the last three months has been unknown in the present generation, cereals being about three inches in arrear of average seasons and green crops even more'*.

The increase of population in the coal industry was expressed by James Stenhouse Esq when laying the foundation stone of the New Free Church in Cowdenbeath. He referred to his grandfather who had laid the foundation of the first house more than 40 years before, when Cowdenbeath had a population of 1400 including the outskirts. The village developed into a prosperous centre of industrial activity of 17,000 souls.

Applications from all over the country were received for the post of teacher at Brand's School, Minathort, which was almost complete. Mr Whillet of Merchiston School was appointed.

The potato crop was subject to prevalent blight. There was little change in farm wages. The harvest caused anxiety, but as October progressed the weather improved, and good progress was reported. However in November only half the bulk of the crops was partially secured.

On 10th March 1863 there was great rejoicing on the occasion of the marriage of the Prince of Wales. Celebrations included football then dancing at Kinross House. A torch light procession to Kinross House by the Avenue finished the eventful day. In Milnathort Mr John Black Esq of Tillywhally presided over a banquet of cake and wine, while tea, sugar, meal and bread to a value of 2/6d was given to every poor person.

On 30th April the opening ceremony to mark the completion of the Devon Valley Railway from Kinross to Rumbling Bridge was celebrated by a dinner. The extension to Tillicoultry would proceed as rapidly as possible. Mr & Mrs Brand received a warm welcome from the inhabitants of Milnathort. The Rev W Boyd and Mr Whillet (teacher) both gave glowing reference to the elegant gift known as The Brand School. Mr Boyd mentioned the school and its belongings had already cost upwards of £2,000, and to that had to be added the salary paid to the teacher.

In September a Mr Stephens of Carlston purchased a reaping machine. By means of an automatic arm this machine delivered the grain in regular sheaves ready for binding. It could cut 12-15 Scottish acres a day. Successive weeks of wet weather had a disastrous effect on harvest operations and in October difficulty was experienced in securing the crops. In November the price of the 4lb loaf was 4½d, and with the exception of butcher meat, provisions had not been so cheap for many years. Prices of grain were very discouraging.

In **1864** the March Fair horses were cheaper than previously but wages in July were higher. A reaping machine was on show at the Market Park and about 20 orders were taken by the agent. The Luke Fair was well attended, and farm workers who had not been asked to stay went to a feeing market where those looking for labour for the coming year looked for farmers to employ them. It could be that the worker was looking for better conditions. They had all their worldly goods

Kinross House

heaped on carts. It was recorded in the November term day that a cart with a dead child wrapped in only a sheet, who had died of scarlet fever, was conveyed along with the furniture and belongings from South Crossgates to Hilton of Arlary. A closed carriage containing the mother and two other children suffering from the same infectious disease followed the cart. An instance of the reckless manner in which epidemics were spread and the desperation for employment of the family were a sign of the times.

The long talked-about construction of the Forth Bridge had taken definite shape and it was learned in December that a Bill was to be presented in Parliament during the coming session. The estimated cost would exceed £500,000; the length to be 3,887 yards and the height in the deep water channel 125ft clear at the high tide and spring waters.

1865 was ushered in with a snow storm at the New Year. After a severe and stormy spell of cold weather the snow began to disappear at the end of February. Even the curlers were tired of the snowy monotony. Instrumental music in churches at this time had many lengthened protests. The position taken up by objectors was that the innovation was unscriptural and without Divine Authority. The price of wheat was £1 11/1d, best Barley £1 0/6½d, best Oats 16/2d, a bag of 288lbs oats £1 5/4½d.

A public meeting was called in Milnathort by the Kinross-shire Agricultural Society to take immediate steps to meet the ravages of the cattle plague (Rinderpest) which now threatened the district. A meeting of the Justices of the Peace for the purpose of looking into measures against rinderpest was also held. Orders were given to police to inspect byres for cleanliness and ventilation. Mr J Hepburn VS Milnathort was appointed inspector in September. The cattle and sheep markets throughout the county were closed owing to the spread of this virulent disease. The first instance in the county broke out at Mr Beath's farm, Arnot Mill, Wester Fossoway.

The Agricultural Report for December recorded a *'remarkable year for its uniform high temperature, and at close of year pastures as green as if it were April. Crops were abundant and secured in a fair condition. The dread of Rinderpest has however overshadowed the farmer's outlook.'* Rinderpest was an infection of ruminants, especially cattle, characterised by fever, dysentery, and inflammation of the mucous membrane. Death rates among contaminated stock could be as high as 100%. It was mainly transmitted by direct contact and drinking contaminated water, although it could be transmitted by air. (Happily a global eradication campaign in the 1990s had the last confirmed case in 2001, and it is the second disease in history to be fully wiped out following smallpox.)

Back in 1866 rinderpest was a major threat. The grass park lets were affected and in some cases were down 25%. It was calculated that one mound to the south of Tillyochie was 54 yards in length, full of dead cattle. The value of hides deposited could not be less than 30 to 40 pounds. Thursday 29th March was set aside as a day of humiliation on account of the rinderpest. Banks and offices were closed at two o'clock and services were held in the churches from 2pm to 4pm. Alarm was now felt that the dreaded disease had a firm hold in the county. Cattle were infected on farms over a wide area, including Bowhouse, Hattonburn, Brunthill, and Gelvan. All markets for the sale of cattle and sheep were stopped and deaths averaged 1,000 daily.

A meeting of ploughmen was held in Milnathort Town Hall, where bothies were criticised, and codes of rules were drawn up, the most important being shortening of hours worked and payment for overtime. All stray dogs within the county were to be destroyed by police or servants of the occupier of the premises where dogs were found straying.

Protests were raised concerning the cattle plague tax which was being levied on ratepayers. A meeting was held in the Town Hall when it was resolved to resist payment at present. Assessment made in Kinross-shire was two and half pennies in the pound, while for the county of Lancaster it was only three quarters of a penny in the pound.

In October the harvest was greatly retarded by successive weeks of bad weather, half the crop yet unsecured and in jeopardy. St Luke's Fair, the first held since the Cattle Disease Act came into operation, was remarkably well attended. Among the cattle sold were those of Bishop Wilson, Orwell, who parted with 15 cattle at £20 per head.

Alarm was being expressed at the rapid advance of cholera. In one November fortnight in Leven 55 deaths occurred. Public wells were closed and the water supply conveyed by carts.

The wages of haflins were increased by £2 to £4 in October. At close of the year, while the price of provisions remained high, pork was sold at 5d per lb below normal due to the market for pigs being overstocked, potatoes at 4/- per cwt and bread at 7½d per 4lb loaf.

High winds and rainfall prevailed during the last week, and Loch Leven spread over a considerable proportion of the surrounding fields. A severe frost brought the curlers out for a match on Myre Pond.

1867 brought phenomenal weather during the first few weeks of the year. Before the end of the month things took a turn for the worse and the weather became wild. The culmination on 29th January was a severe thunderstorm which broke over the county. On March 20th Loch Leven was ice-bound again. In the middle of May the peak of the West Lomond was covered with snow and large numbers of swallow died. Food prices in May were high. In June Coldrain Farm was purchased by a Mr Fergus for £ 5,700. The July Fair day was very wet and characterised by an unusual amount of pick-pocketing. Servants' wages remained steady at the previous year's rates. Hattonburn was for sale at an upset price of £15,500 but remained unsold. It was later sold to Captain Montgomery for £15,520.

In February 1869 a severe storm of wind and snow caused considerable damage to property and perch were driven ashore in shoals from Loch Leven, while rabbits drowned in their burrows. Fairs prices stuck in 1867; wheat per imperial quarter £3 10/-; best barley £1 16/11½d; best white oats £1 8/5½d and a 280lbs bag of oatmeal £2 7/1½d. There was a measles epidemic in February 1868. Coal was 6/6d a ton.

The hamlet of Middleton had the distinction of being 'a colony of patriarchs', as almost every house contained one inhabitant who had reached the age of 70, and the united ages numbered nearly 1,000.

In 1869 Pirie's double-furrow plough was first used in the county at Gospetry. Mr Tod, one of the most enterprising farmers, spoke in high terms of its qualifications and economical possibilities. Lovely spring weather was enjoyed in April. The Kinross-shire Agricultural Society's Show was held for the first time in Tally-hill Park and, notwithstanding the prevalence of the murrain which affected the show of cattle, the exhibition was remarkably good. This was principally owing to the imposing show of horses of all classes and particularly of work mares. Harvest operations were well underway by the end of August, but on the 29th and 30th the hoar frost was so severe that the growing potatoes in the district were completely blackened in the haulm. A storm of great severity passed over at the end of September, when extensive damage was caused to the grain still uncut, while stooks in the field were blown down and saturated.

At the Kinross Feeing Market wages for first hand ploughmen were £18-£23 a year; second hand £16-£18 and halflins £10-£15. Winter set in early that year. Snow covered the uplands in October.

In 1870 Friars prices stuck at 1869 levels; wheat (per imperial quarter) £1 18/6d; best barley £1 9s 10d and oats £1 2s 2d, while oatmeal was £2 2s 1d. Combined reaping and mowing machines were on show at Stirling. Mr Duff, blacksmith at Burnside, exhibited two horse rakes which were much admired.

A large classroom for girls was added to the Brand School, while news of the declaration of war by France against Germany caused widespread excitement and deep interest. The first journey of any distance on a bicycle from our district was successfully accomplished in July, when Mr John Robertson, blacksmith, covered the distance between Kinross and Glasgow on a machine of his own manufacture. He left at 5pm and reached his destination between 1am and 2am next morning. The Agricultural Show was held at the Market Park and the display of horses excelled all previous exhibitions. Mr Tod, of Lochran, secured first and second prizes, and Mr Young of Lathro was third. Two men were charged with 'furious driving'.

A continued drought in August told heavily on pasture lands, but otherwise the weather had been favourable for harvest operations and these were well advanced in the middle of August. The two streams Queich and Gairney had been dried up for some time. Copious rain fell during early autumn, which revived the drooping pasture lands. The harvest was secured in excellent condition, and farmers were able to commence ploughing by the end of September.

The minimum height of army recruits at the beginning of the Boer War was 5ft 5½in, as it had been since 1793. The last third of the 19th century brought a new diet of cheap imports. While the price of a 280lb sack of oatmeal fell by 37/- to 31/-, the price of the same quantity of wheat went down from 46/- to 22/-. An ounce of tea was down by 64%. Oatmeal became a luxury. The consequence was that many poor families shifted from porridge to a less nutritious diet of white bread and tea. Sugar was cheap, milk a rare commodity and, if they could afford it, some ham was boiled. There was porridge, milk, broth and beef in some houses, but not the poorest.

Life expectancy in 1876 for a male was 41 years and for females 43-44 years. Althorp's of 1833 laid down a minimum age of nine for children working in mills, with a maximum of eight hours up to the age of thirteen. The Mines Act of 1847 prohibited the labour of women and young children below ground. 1863 saw it extended to protect mill workers with the Factory Act. In 1867 the Argyll Commission discovered a fifth of children of school age were not receiving an education, partly due to child labour abounding where the Factory Act was not enforced. The Education Act of 1872 attempted to remedy this by making it compulsory for five to thirteen year olds to attend school.

The arrival of the Saturday half-day came in 1860. Income Tax was introduced in 1789 and Scots paid 68% per head of population compared to 100% in England. By 1867 tax rose to 75% and in 1911 to 95%. Gross domestic production per head went up 1855-1905 by three-quarters. The improvement in real wages in Great Britain had risen by 80%. There was great inflation between 1900 and 1910 in Scots rents, and prices of food and fuel were up by 1912.

Great changes were also occurring in public health legislation. The improvement in infant mortality by 1900 may be attributed to the gradual decrease since 1870 in overwork, malnutrition and other causes of diseases of girls and young women, assisted by 20th century introduction of free milk and medical inspections in schools. These were in addition to improvements in environmental and medical care during and after birth itself.

In 1897 the Public Health (Scotland) Act strengthened the hands of authorities inspecting tainted food and a certification was introduced to control the quality of milk production. A few diseases were wiped out by 1900. The dangers of the typhus group were hugely diminished through improved sanitary conditions. Compulsory vaccination of smallpox paid off, but there was not any more control of measles, pneumonia or bronchitis. Rickets, associated exclusively with urban malnutrition and air pollution, was rife in 1910 but was virtually unknown in the countryside.

The long-awaited Forth Railway Bridge began construction in December 1884 and was opened on 4th March 1890 by the Duke of Rothesay, the future Edward VII. It was 8,094ft long (4677m) and was the longest cantilever bridge in the world at the time. It was also the first major bridge in Britain constructed in steel.

The Royal Highland and Agriculture Society of Scotland published annual transactions from 1868, and Sir Graham Graham Montgomery Bart MA of Stanhope was an Extraordinary Director mentioned in 1700. George Reid Esq. of Tilliery, Milnathort joined as a member in 1871, and had access to all the updates and research. The books were given to us when we took over the farmhouse from Miss Reid. They are from 1870–1952, and they make interesting reading of the times.

In 1895 the school in Milnathort, partly built by Mrs Brand, was completed

Reid Memorial School

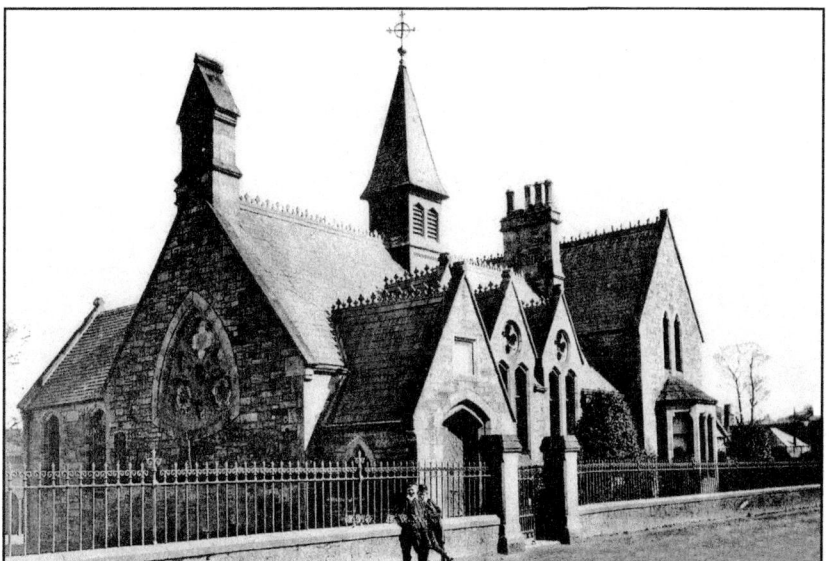

by Mrs Maria Johnston Reid of Thomanean and called the Reid Memorial School.

The Tryst usually held at Cuthil Muir north of Milnathort was, in 1847, held at Gospetry Farm, when 4, 000 lambs were 'stanced' and sold for up to 17/- each. In 1884 the first auction sale was organised by Mr Bethune at Craigo Farm, and top price for fat stots was £22, cows £17, pigs £6 16/- and ewes 13/9d. The Mart south of the railway in Milnathort was opened by Mr George Young of Dollar and soon became known as Young and Bethune, later becoming Macdonald Fraser of Perth. A weekly sale was held on Mondays. On the west side of the North Queich Bridge the rival market of Hay & Co was built on the site of an old woollen mill.

In 1862 George Reid borrowed £2,000 from James Johnston, wine merchant in Alloa, at 5% interest, to be repaid at the term of Martinmas 1893 within the office of the Union Bank of Scotland. The Easter Room of land of Over Tillyrie was used as security. The bond was repaid on 15th November 1872.

In 1881 George Reid's brother David came home from Ceylon with his family and settled in near Milnathort at Thomanean. David and Maria with their family settled locally and David took the shoot at Tillyrie, while Elsie and George enjoyed the extended family.

The Boer War, called the second Boer War or the Anglo-Boer War, was fought from 11th October 1899 to 31st March 1902, involving men of the British Empire countries. This affected prices, as all wars do. George's nephew William Bacon Johnston Reid was in the army and fought in this war.

On 18th July 1892 George Reid made a Trust and Settlement and had as his

Milnathort Auction Mart. Photo: David Millar.

trustees and sole executors Miss Eliza Reid, his sister residing with him, William Tod of East Brackley and William Tod, tenant in Pardovan by Linlithgow. They were to pay his debts and funeral expenses. Eliza Reid was to occupy, during her lifetime, his dwelling house and garden at Tillyrie, and was free to use all his whole household furniture, bed and table wear, linen, china, plate, books and pictures:

> '... that maybe in the said dwelling at his decease, with full power during her lifetime to give away or otherwise dispose of any articles of said furniture or effects or to bequeath the same by last will or deed of settlement. The trustees shall hold the whole residue and means and estate of Eliza Reid in life rent and, shall pay to her annual income at least once a year in her lifetime.

> On the death of the said Eliza Reid (and his own death should she predecease him) the whole and trust and remaining estate to Robert Matal Reid, his nephew, elder son of deceased David Reid Thomanean, on his attaining his 21 years, whom failing to William Bacon Johnston Reid also his nephew and son of David Reid, and failing to the surviving daughters of the said David Reid equally divided on attaining majority or being married which ever happened first.'

He gave power to his trustees either to carry on the leases of any lands which he may tenant at his death or renounce and give up the tenancy as they shall think proper and full power of sale by public roup or private bargain and full power to invest trust funds etc.

He reserved to himself not only his life rent of the whole estate and full power to at, any time, alter or revoke present.

A codicil in 1906 stated 'in the first place considering that Miss Elisa Reid is now deceased and Robert Matal Reid has attained the age of 21'. He recalled William Tod of East Brackley and William Tod of Pardovan by Linlithgow, and

The Ochil Hills Sanatorium

appointed Robert Matal Reid, William Bacon Johnson Reid and Arthur Walker Russell to be Trustees to the same effect.

He also bequeathed £200 sterling '... *payable Whit or Martinmas three months after his death and free of legacy and other government duty*' to his nephew Robert Cameron Reid and niece Mary Ellen Cameron, both residing at Didedin, New Zealand equally or to the survivor.

Witnesses Christina Nicol Graham and Majory Marshall, both his domestic servants. Registered 9th March 1911.

George Reid died in 1911, aged 76.

David Reid and family from 1841 to 1959

David Reid was born at Tillyrie on 11th January 1841, the year in which his parents Robert and Jane built their new house and his sister Jane died, aged 13 years old.

He was first educated at Orwell Parish School and subsequently at the High School of Glasgow, where he gave promise of future success in the profession for which he was being prepared.

In 1856, at the age of 15, he went as a pupil of his relative George Lowe Reid, who was the Engineer-in-Chief of the Great Western Railway of Canada. David spent five years on the construction of that line and its branches.

Early in 1861 at the age of 20, and having acquired much practical knowledge of railway construction, he was engaged by the firm of Lee, Watson and Aiton to join their engineering staff on the works of a section of the Great Indian Peninsula Railway, for which they were the contractors.

When that work was finished he received an appointment on the engineering staff of Joseph Bray, contractor for a section of the same line in the Nizam's State.

In 1869 David entered into a partnership with Messrs Charnock and Mitchell, under the style of Charnock, Reid and Mitchell, for the reconstruction of the bridges on the Great Indian Peninsula Railway between Bhusawal and Nagpur, and for the maintenance of the permanent way.

In 1871, now thirty years old, David with F.D. Mitchell tendered for and was successful in obtaining the contract for the construction of the Ceylon Railway, between Peredenia and Kawalapitya. Before the works were finished his partnership with Mr Mitchell was severed, and the extension completed by David Reid, to the entire satisfaction of Mr E.G. Strong, the Chief Resident Engineer, and of Sir Charles Hutton Gregory, the Consulting Engineer to the Government of Ceylon.

On completion of this work, he undertook the construction of roads in the coffee districts of the island, and the maintenance by contract of many miles of trunk roads.

In 1877 he took in hand the contract for the construction of the branch railway between Handy and Matale, under Mr J.R. Mosse, Resident Chief Engineer. This was executed with great skill and despatch, for which he was highly complimented by the Lieutenant-Governor of the island.

His next public works was the construction, in conjunction with Mr John Mackay of Hereford, of the Jamaica Government Railway Extension, from Old Harbour to Porus, and from Spanish Town to Ewarton, under the direction of Mr Valentine G. Bell, Chief Resident Engineer, and of Messrs Hawkshaw and Hayter, the Consulting Engineers. The line was remarkable for the successful construction of the whole of its bridges and viaducts in Portland cement concrete, there being no durable building stone in any part of the island. The railway was opened for public traffic in the year 1885.

In the meantime David had devoted a considerable portion of his time and attention to the cultivation of tea in Ceylon. The failure of the coffee plant in 1875-78 to disease was a great blow to the island. He bought some abandoned coffee estates and a considerable tract of jungle land. He exhibited his usual energy and spirit of enterprise in this new industry.

Cinnamon was the first crop to receive sponsorship in India, while the island was under Dutch control (1769). Finding cinnamon uptake slow in the slump of the 1830s, the British turned to coffee. In 1870 the plantations were devastated by a fungal disease called *Hemileia Vastatrix*, or coffee rust.

In 1824 tea was smuggled into Ceylon by the British from China and planted in the Royal Botanic Garden in Peradeniya for non-commercial purposes. Further tea plants were brought from Assam and Calcutta in 1839 and 1854.

Working together with D. Reid, E. A. Cooke, John Morsztyn and the daughter of poet Jan Andzeji Morsztn they purchased land in the Dickoya Valley for coffee and tea at the estate called Tillyrie. The first tea seeds were received in Ceylon from Assam by Dr Wallich, botanist in Calcutta, in the 1830s.

In 1840, 240 plants landed at Queens Cottage in Nuwara Elija, property of Sir Anthony Pliphant, Chief Justice of the county.

In 1841 Maurice Worms brought tree cuttings from China, and grew them in his plantations.

In 1896 Ken Rutherford had been in Tillyrie. He was a prominent figure in Ceylon's planting annals. In an article published in 1907, Rutherford described progress made by Ceylon in the plantation sector in the decade just passed. Working together with D. Reid and E. A. Cooke, he had purchased land in the Dickoya Valley for coffee and tea at an estate called Tillyrie.

Tillyrie Estate is 24 km east of Kelani, south of Kandy, capital of the Central Province of Sri Lanka. The humidity, cool temperatures and rainfall in the country's central highlands provided a climate that favoured high quality tea.

Ceylon growers agreed with Rutherford's theories and in 1886 they formed a voluntary syndicate. At the Colonial and Indian Exhibition held in London,

Tillyrie won an award, and this was followed by a certificate award in 1889 by the USA.

Rutherford heard about waterproof plywood being made in Estonia in 1886, and thought it may be suitable for packing tea. He sent his son from Ceylon to Tallinn as managing director of the company Vanessa.

Rutherford published *Ceylon Planters Note Book* and *Times of Ceylon, Colombo 1931*.

David meanwhile met and married Maria, daughter of Sir William Bacon Johnston, Bart, in 1878. Sir William Johnston, born on 17th March 1806, was the son of the seventh baronet, William, and his second wife Maria Bacon, only daughter of John Bacon of Friern House in Middlesex. The baronetcy was an old one, dating from the time of King David (1329-31). Stephen de Johnston, a man of great learning, was given the title of 'clerk' to which normally only the clergy were entitled. He was secretary to the Earl of Mar. Stephen married Margaret, only daughter and heiress to Sir Andrew Garioch of Caskieben near Aberdeen.

The seventh baronet left the barony badly off when he died in 1844, but William inherited his mother's fortune. He had served in the First Royals before 1844. In July 1854 he disentailed the Estate of Hilton and Caskie near Aberdeen, and paid his brother and cousins for their consent.

On 11th September 1855 at St Pancras Church, Sir William married Mary Ann. They had at least two children: their son who became the 9th Baronet of Caskie and Maria who married David Reid.

David and Maria made their home in Kandy. In 1879 their eldest son was born and christened Robert Matale Reid. David was the first tea planter on a large scale who introduced the produce of his estates to the London market, where Ceylon teas in a few years acquired that high reputation which has steadily increased to the present day. His success in this enterprise induced him in 1886 to found the 'Ceylon Tea Plantations Company' now one of the most prosperous undertakings in the island.

David's health caused the family to come home to Britain in 1881, when he was 40. They settled in Thomanean House, Kinross-shire, near to Tillyrie where David was born and his brother George and sister Elsie lived.

The Horn family had been at Thomanean before the 1700s. Andrew Horn was an elder of Orwell Kirk, ordained on 17th April 1710. He was an important heritor in the parish and mentioned often in session minutes. He died on 15th June 1788, leaving a widow with three young sons. She moved with the boys to Dunfermline in 1788, and married again in 1797.

The second husband had no interest in the boys and Andrew, the eldest, joined the army and died at the age of 18 on 5th February 1802. David, the middle brother, went into the navy and died onboard his ship while blocking Martinique, in February 1804 aged 19. This left the third brother John as heir.

John Horn was gazetted as ensign to the 92nd Regiment of the Marquis of

Thomanean House

Huntly on the 12th April 1805. After a hard upbringing an aunt had lent him £40 to buy the uniform. He fought in Ireland until May 1808. After staying one night in 1809 in the empty house at Thomanean, sleeping on the floor, he resolved to live there.

The estate had been for twenty years possessed by minors and during that time the former debt had accumulated to a large amount, and it was necessary to dispose of part of it to satisfy the creditors. The house had been empty since his mother left in 1788.

John went to Thomanean to improve the land, restore the house and pay the debt. He cleared whins and drained Wester Dalqueich in 1811, having bought a pair of work horses. Most of the other farms were let out. He cleared the debt of £7,000 by 1836, and began on other improvements.

In 1812 a road from Milnathort to join the Ochil Turnpike began construction. There had been much opposition to it but, once built and a bridge over the North Queich completed, many saw the advantage and the opposition was dropped. It took a couple of months for the South Queich to have a bridge built as well.

His mother died on January 20th 1820 in Edinburgh. Her second marriage, to a drunkard, had been a terrible mistake.

John moved into the lodge in 1824 for two years while the big house was being repaired, and in 1826 moved back to a 'comfortable' house.

Once the debt had been paid off, in 1841, he commented that he was 'more prosperous than ever contemplated when I took over thirty-two years ago.' In 1849 he bought Mawmill for £5,790, and in 1855 the lands of Deuglie for £3,007 14/9d, as well as Cockairney in 1836.

John never married but he had four children with Belle McEwan – who, when the first son John died in 1836 age two years and three months, was living in Helensburgh. His first daughter was three months old at the time. The surviving children, who lived to be adults, were Margaret, John and Elizabeth.

By 1860 son John was in Edinburgh and Margaret and Elizabeth were living with John Senior at Thomanean. On 18th June 1861 they all went to London to 'The Great Exhibition, and to a cattle show at Bullensay, Sydenham Palace and Windsor Castle etc', returning home on 18th July.

In 1864 on 18th June they all sailed from Leith to Rotterdam, then travelled by rail to Coblenz, and sailed up the Rhine, and after exploring other places arrived back at Leith on 18th July.

John Horn died at Thomanean on 6th April 1865. Previously he had permission from Orwell (he had been a member since 1815), to build a mausoleum in the yard at Old Orwell Church. The building 'was to be built within the 30 square feet, the rubbish removed , the ground levelled and a broken dyke rebuilt' It was also agreed that 'Mr Horn be given permission to plant trees in the Old Orwell Church Yard'. So he was buried in his mausoleum at his old church. In 2020 his descendants gave the key of the mausoleum to Dr David Munro at the Kinross Museum.

David Reid had known the Horn family in Ceylon, and had lent them money when gambling debt hit the family, and they in kind let his family tenant the lovely house of Thomanean, west of Milnathort. The Horn family were short of money, the house needed a lot doing to it and David and Maria enjoyed restoring it to its former glory.

The couple settled into the county, taking part in many public duties. David was elected as a member of the Orwell School Board, Vice-Chairman of the County Council, and Captain of G Company of the Argyle and Sutherland Volunteers. His public spirit and force of character, combined with sound judgement, soon gained for him a leading position in the counties of Clackmannan and Kinross. He enjoyed shooting and held the shoot rents at Thomanean, Tillyrie and Holton.

Robert, born in Ceylon, was followed by one brother William Bacon Johnston Reid (b.1881) and sisters Jean, Maria (b.1884) Elsie and Janet (b.1889).

Along with Captain Thomas Henry Montgomery and his wife Anne Marie of Hattonburn, David and Maria gave generously to the building of St Paul's Episcopal Church in Kinross, which opened in 1875. Maria gifted a new organ to St Paul's in 1892.

In the 1890s the family holiday included a trip down the Nile. Janet remembered this in her old age.

Unfortunately, the strain of those numerous self-imposed labours proved too much for a constitution already weakened by a previous severe illness, and he was suddenly cut off in the midst of a life of unusual activity and usefulness, dying after a brief illness, of peritonitis, at Thomanean on 13th April 1892. David was only 51 years old when he died.

His obituary describes him: 'Mr Reid was a man of unwonted energy, ability, and steadfastness of purpose, and was held in great esteem by all who came in contact with him. Generous and large-hearted, he was ever ready to lend a helping hand to those deserving it.'

Maria was left a widow at 47, with six young children: Robert, William, Jean, Elsie, Maria and Janet. They happily continued to live at Thomanean as a family, and Maria took ownership of the house in 1926.

When they grew up Robert studied land management and, after a spell as a student at Thomanean, was the factor at the Airds Estate in Argyllshire. He married Janie Crawford Alden McPhea of Appin. Sadly she died having twins, and one twin died too. The surviving twin David went to Thomanean to his grandmother and aunts.

William was a soldier through and through, and as a teenager joined the 3rd Battalion of the Seaforth Highlanders. He was in Egypt at the outbreak of the Second Boer War (1899-1902), and the regiment was sent to South Africa. The Seaforth Highlanders fought at the Battle of Paardeberg, and with other Highlanders at many battles with the Boers, which will be looked at later in the history.

The sisters Jean and Elsie married. Jean to David G. A. Reid of Bishops Cottage, Sevenoaks in Kent, a cousin to some degree. Elsie married Charles Webb, a vet who had a practice down south. They had a son Maxwell and a daughter Susan. Maria and Janet continued to stay with their mother at Thomanean.

 William came home with his regiment at the end of the Boer War. The Seaforth Highlanders had suffered heavy losses at the battles of Magersfontein in December 1899 and Paardeberg in February 1900.

The Boer War was the first war where modern weapons were used by the troops, and the enemy vanished on their horses with their smokeless guns giving no visible target to shoot at, and their methods of digging in trenches which withstood bombardments. The spade was a new weapon, 'dig your own trench now – or they'll dig you a grave.' was said on the British lines. The traditional British frontal attack of infantry close together was shot mercilessly to pieces and the square of set battles useless against an enemy who shot from the hill. The range of their smokeless guns was greater than ours.

During the Boer War the British troops learned to spread out, running in spurts covered by fire from others, and to use cover where it existed. Using artillery alongside infantry became common. As the war continued the British, together with soldiers from the Empire countries of Canada, New Zealand, Australia and India, learned to use new tactics to reduce losses with the new type of warfare.

At Magersfontein on 28th December, 3,500 men of the Highland Regiments tramped behind 3,000 men in khaki – no sporrans, no claymores or gleaming coat buttons, khaki aprons hiding the front of their kilts. Three battalions of the Black Watch, Seaforths and Argylls were to storm the kopje at first light.

To climb the steep kopje the Black Watch and Argylls used long ropes, knotted every ten feet, held by the left hand. The men of the Seaforth and Highland Light Infantry groped their way as best they could.

The plain under the shadow of Magersfontein was strewn with rock, holes, ant-heaps and thorn bushes. Despite the deluge of rain and lightning that flashed blue on the rocks, the company kept its head.

At Modder River an aerial reconnaissance balloon was launched to spy out the enemy trenches. At about 400 yards from the hidden trenches, the Black Watch faced a flame of gunfire from the Boers. The Seaforths were hopelessly confused with the Argylls, but had few casualties at this stage. The battle lasted nine hours.

'A movement of a hand, the flash as a canteen tin, even an ankle attacked by ants, then price was paid in muser bullets from the Boer. As shadows shortened, men fell asleep over their rifles and terror gave way to boredom.'

About 200 men of the Black Watch and Seaforths even reached the east face of the kopje, where they were captured or shot, killed by their own artillery.

At one o'clock Lt Col James Hughes-Hallet of the Seaforths found some Boers working round his right flank, and ordered two companies to trickle back a hundred yards. The trickle became a flood and the flood an avalanche. One of the officers said: 'It was a sight I hope I never see again. Men of the Highland Brigade were running for all they were worth, others cowering under bushes, behind guns, some lying under their blankets, officers running about with revolvers in their hands threatening to shoot them, urging some on, kidding others, staff officers galloping about giving incoherent and impracticable orders. The pipe skirled, officers cursed. When the ambulance men went out next day to collect dead and wounded, there were 920 on the British side and 236 Boers.

'The battle of Spion Kop gave General Buller the key to learn how to fight a twentieth-century war.'

The Highlanders who had survived the battle of Magersfontein did not, this time, lose their heads. The thin line grew thinner and by midday the attack had petered out, apart from a few companies of the Seaforth and Black Watch, who had forded the river. MacDonald's brigade was nailed down along the south bank below Knox's brigade and MacDonald, like Knox, had been wounded and taken to the field hospital.

Kitchener had ordered off the Highland Brigade for purposes of his own. Colvile watched them move across the plain. Then one of his staff pointed out that they had wheeled about and were making a frontal attack. Colvile was astonished, but it was too late to recall them – anyway it was out of his hands. Presumably Kitchener had ordered this reckless attack!

'In two senses, Spion Kop was a gruesome anachronism; a relic from the past, a portent for the future. The new-style war was an invisible enemy firing from a distant hill top. It was only in the hospitals and dressing-stations that war had re-emerged in its old brutality. It was the precursor too, the Armageddon in the trenches under the African sun, of a greater one, fifteen years later, in the mud of Flanders.

'The tea time war that was expected to be over by Christmas 1899, had cost the tax payer more than £200 million, and the cost in blood was even higher. The War

Office reckoned that 400,346 horses, mules and donkeys were expended in the war. There were over 100,000 casualties among the 365,693 imperial and 82,742 colonial soldiers who fought in the war'.

'On the Boer side the cost of the war, measured in suffering, was perhaps higher. It was estimated that there were over 7,000 deaths among the 87,365 Boers, including 2,120 foreign volunteers and 13,300 Afrikaners from the Cape and Natal. Nobody knows how many Boer men, women and children died in the concentration camps; official figures vary between 18,000 and 28,000.

'There is nothing civilized in warfare, and never can be, it is a barbarian's game. As Napoleon once said: "Victory goes to the general who makes the fewest mistakes. At the bottom, war is a contest in blunders." '

After the war these models of warfare were introduced to the army, but not without backbiting from the traditionalists and financial cutbacks from governments. The Army recruited men who could use their initiative and not just obey officers who could be killed. The use of officers wearing swords and medals which made them easy targets was discouraged, and uniforms all became less obvious.

This all took time after the Boer War. As the years wore on, generals Roberts, Buller, Kitchener, and younger Lieutenant–Colonels Julian Byng, Edmund Allenby and Colonel Douglas Haig argued their points of view. The rule books of the Army training gradually changed.

William Reid had acquired an exceptional skill in drilling of recruits. At one time he was adjutant of the 1st Highland Cadet Battalion, the Royal Scots, in which capacity he went to Canada with the detachment of Scottish Cadets, who were officially entertained at the Imperial Exhibition in Toronto. He gave his time wholeheartedly to the condition of old soldiers, and for two years he acted as Secretary to the Scottish Naval and Military Veterans Residence Organisation.

On March 26th 1904 William was promoted to Captain in the 3rd Battalion Seaforth Highlanders.

Maria had meanwhile been buying parts of Tillyrie as they came up for sale. In November 1894 she bought Berrybrae and the rooms in Over Tillyrie that been left to Miss Susan Pearson and Isabella Pearson or Reid, for £4,250. Then in 1904 when Little Tillyrie and Hall Greig were sold by roupe, she and Robert went to the sale. The land had been set at an upset price of £9,000, having been estimated at £6,724 in March 1899 when inherited by Robert Greig. Maria, Robert and money from her father William Johnston Bt, purchased the lands for £ 8,250.

Thus the Tillyrie Estate of 880 acres came under the Reid family, with Uncle George owning Upper Tillyrie and Maria and Robert with Little Tillyrie, Hall Greig, Berrybrae and the rooms of Over Tillyrie not owned by Uncle George. Uncle George farmed the lot as owner of much and tenant of the rest.

Robert married in 1907/8 Miss Janie Crawford Alden Macfie of Appin, daughter of William Macfie of Airds, Argyllshire. There is a photograph (below) of the couple leaving outside the town hall in Minathort, a crowd of well-wishers dressed in their finery as the carriage and pair leave, horses lunging forward and the driver in a top hat.

In 1909 Janie died giving birth to twins. One died with her and the other, David, was sent to Thomanean to be brought up by Maria. Robert never married again, and David grew up watched by his father and enjoying the attention of his grandmother and two aunts, Maria and Janet. There is a charming postcard of Thomanean sent by Maria to Mrs Macfie saying she is sending 'a photograph of dear little David'. It was stamped 2.30pm 8th July with a halfpenny stamp of Edward VII, who reigned from 1901 to 1910, so presumably the letter was sent in July 1909.

In 1911 Robert inherited Upper Tillyrie (Over Tillyrie) from his uncle George. He and Maria began planning for a country residence for the family home. They chose the site at Nether (Little) Tillyrie on the south side of the steading and plans show a substantial house, where there may have been a farmhouse, with tennis courts and gardens in the stackyard, incorporating the steading into the garden design.

Unfortunately the First World War intervened before the house was finished in 1914-15, and it was lent to the Red Cross for a hospital until 1919.

William Bacon Johnston Reid was drilling recruits with his usual skill and, to his chagrin, his capacity in this direction meant he was unable to proceed to the front right away.

The British army was not large in comparison with those of France and Germany, being kept mainly for duties in its empire and minor neighbouring wars.

Captain Reid's wedding party leaving the Town Hall, Milnathort in 1907.
Photo: Kinross Museum

The government had not seen the necessity of a larger force so, when war with Germany broke out, a small professional army (the British Expeditionary Force) along with the French, had to hold back the German invasion until men could be trained to help the war effort.

When the unfortunate Franz Ferdinand and his wife were assassinated in Sarajevo the European Powers were already armed to the teeth and ready to mobilise. Triple Alliances were set up between Germany, Austria and Italy on the one hand and Russia, France and Britain on the other. The British were drawn in when the Germans entered Belgium, on their way to invade France. Britain's 1839 treaty with Belgium made her dependedent on trade with this part of Europe, particularly the ports of Flanders. These also made a natural springboard for an invasion of Britain, although Germany hoped the British would stay out of the conflict.

On the evening of Tuesday 4th August 1914, the Great Powers of Europe, with the exception of Britain, were at war, their huge armies already on the march. That very day German troops had invaded Belgium. Sir Edward Goschen, the British Ambassador, saw the German Chancellor. The message he carried was that unless the invasion was halted, Britain would enter the war against Germany. He asked for a satisfactory answer by midnight, failing which Britain would be at war. The satisfactory answer did not arrive and so the two nations were at war.

Germany's Schlieffen Plan was to pour troops through Belgium, race across northern France and capture Paris. The French armies would be caught in a huge encircling movement and France would be beaten. The German troops could then be moved east to face the expected attack of the large Russian armies. It was hoped that Britain, having only a small army, would make peace.

This went wrong for three reasons. Firstly the Belgians fought bravely and slowed down the advance of the German Army. Secondly the French armies, though retreating, were not beaten or encircled and were able to strike back. Thirdly, the British sent their troops across to France with amazing speed, and succeeded in stemming the German advance, first at Mons then at Le Chateau. The Battle of Marne was fought for a week.

Both sides dug into trenches, which would eventually go across northern France from Switzerland to the sea. The Belgians flooded part of the land to stop the German advance, which set them back on their plans.

The 1st Battalion of the Seaforth Highlanders was serving in India as part of the Dehra Dun Brigade in the Meerut Division. They were called to mobilise by wire, at 6am on 9th August 1914. The battalion left Weliva in two troop trains at 9.35am and 2.45pm, and the two trains were joined up at Lakhar.

At 9.15am on Friday 4th September arrived at Alexandra Docks, Bombay, where accommodation was at the Carnac Bandar. On 14th September embarked by half-battalions in the passenger ships Angora and Arancola. At 11am on 16th September left the docks and anchored in the stream. At noon the flotilla left Bombay under escort of HMS Swiftsure, HMS Fox and RIMS Dufferin.

On 2nd October at 5.50pm arrived at Suez. Pickets of Highland Light Infantry and 4th Ghurkhas guarding the canal. Weather very fine and much cooler. Arrived at Port Said at 11.45pm on 3rd October.

6th October left Port Said bound for Marseilles, weather very fine.

At sea October 8th a strong wind blowing, fairly rough, very rough in the night, men sick.

9th October Sea has gone down. 10th October passed Malta at 8am. 11th October passed Sardinia 'bout 11am.

12th October arrived at Marseilles at 7.15 am. Disembarked and formed up in a large shed at 8.30 am – manned with M111 rifles.

Half the battalion was left at the docks for fatigue work, the other half left at 2.45 pm, marching the 10 miles through Marseilles to camp Valentine, arriving about 5.30pm.

After days of heavy rain they entrained at 6.50am at Gare D'Arenc for Orleans. On 18th and 19th they had long halts at Toulouse and Argents, arriving at Orleans at 2am on the 20th October.

The next day a halt to arrange for warm clothing for men and followers. The following day an aeroplane passed over camp about 4.45 pm. On 23rd they marched to La Circotte where rifles were given out, each man to try out his new rifle.

On 26th entrained at 4pm having struck tents and handed over at 8.15am, at 1.15 Battalion paraded and marched to station. Loading carts, wagons, water carts etc with kit ready loaded on them. Train on 27th October, passed Abbeville (1.35pm), Etaples (4.35pm) Calais (8pm) Hazerbock (11pm) and arriving at Merville at 2.30am; detrained and marched to billet in school of Institution N.D. D'esperance.

The strength of the Battalion on leaving Dehra Dun was:
British Officers 9; Goorka officers 17;
N.C.O.s and men 804; groom officers 1

Riflemen 3, total native ranks 826.

Strength of Battalion on arrival at Merville

B O 10; G O 15 N.C.O. and men 728; Followers 41.

Transport Personnel 14; A.S.C. Drivers 7; Mules 46; A T carts 9; Chargers 15; Horses 18; Water carts 2; Cook carts 1; G S wagon 6.

Bicycles 9.

3 men detached at Orleans to act as butchers.

6 men transferred to No 128 Field Ambulance.'

(Taken from 7 Indian Meerut Division Diary)

William Bacon Johnston Reid was mobilised on 7th November and landed at

Le Havre as part of the Highland Division. Whilst there, they were transferred to the 1st Battalion and the Dehra Dun Brigade, where they stayed until the Dehra Dun was transferred to Mesopotamia and eventually ended the war in Palestine in 1918. The Seaforths were transferred to the 137th Brigade of the 46th Division on 6th November 1915.

The Dehra Dun Brigade were at the Battle of La Basse, Armentieres and the Battle of Messinas, which lasted for a month. It took part in the Christmas Truce of 1914.

During this war, machine-guns were used in large numbers, and caused dreadful casualties on either side. The gun positions were often protected by sand bags or banks of earth, as well as masses of barbed wire, and the Germans especially built many concrete emplacements.

The front-line trench would usually be deep enough for men to walk along without being seen. In order to see over the parapet it was necessary to stand on the firing step. Dugouts were cut out along the trench, sometimes barely a depression in the side and others stoutly built to withstand anything but a direct hit. The British built movable barriers of stakes and barbed wire, which were kept in special recesses to be used if German troops entered them.

Night attacks would be lit by 'star-shells' which burst low in the sky to light up all around with a ghastly silver glare. They were often followed by a bombardment of the enemy positions, from guns which were at various distances behind the trenches. Shells whined past overhead, to burst on or near the enemy position, scattering shrapnel and metal fragments in all directions.

Dehra Dun Indian Infantry helping send signals

Dehra Dun troups seeing to horses

To be caught in an artillery bombardment could be a shattering experience, resulting in either death or mutilation.

The second Battle of Ypres started in April 1915. The Germans were trying to capture Calais and Boulogne, cutting off the British supply line for troops and supplies from home, and for the wounded to be sent home. After six weeks' furious fighting Ypres was still in Allied hands and the ports safe. British casualties were great: 50,000 men who could ill be spared and French losses were also heavy. Germany had taken four miles of ground but no breakthrough.

Fighting carried on until the 25th May. It was the first time mass use of poison gas was made by Germany on the Western Front. It also marked the first time that the former Colonial force the 1st Canadian Division defeated a European power (the German Empire) in Europe, at the battles of St Julient and Kitchener's Wood.

A gas cloud wafted towards the allies on a north-easterly breeze and in a moment had them by the throat. They broke and fled, and who could blame them? Dropping like flies, heaving in agony, suffocated by slow poison which caught at the back of their throats, their faces dark. Hundreds of them fell and died while others lay helpless, froth on their lips and racked bodies vomiting.

The Germans reported that they treated 200 gas casualties, who suffered a lingering death of unspeakable agony. The whole air was tainted by the acrid smell of chlorine, with tearing nausea at intervals. They too would later die – a slow, Chloride death. The allies reported 5,000 killed and 15,000 wounded. The dead turned black at once.

Within days the British were advised by John Scott Haldane to counter the effects of the gas by urinating on a cloth and breathing through it. Both sides developed effective gas masks and anti-asphyxiation respirators. The French and British used gas at the Battle of Loos in late September.

War Diary (Strutt's)

May 13th, 1915.

The British bombardment opens with a total of 443 guns and howitzers firing on a 5,000 yard front. The 36 six-inch howitzers would fire on the enemy breastwork parapet, to blow gaps through which the infantry could pour, the 54.4 five-inch would hit the German support line, as would a portion of the field guns. The majority of the 210 eighteen-pounder field guns aimed at the German's wire, firing shrapnel (which was known to be an ineffective weapon for this task, but there was no high explosive available). The bombardment was observed in detail, even early on their reports of a high proportion of dud shells failing to explode, especially the howitzers. Firing day and night, more than 101,000 shells were fired.

May 15th

10.00pm *All units of the attacking battalions are reported to be in position. On the left, the 2nd Division has 6th Brigade (attacking with 7th Kings, 1st Royal Berkshire & Kings Royal Rifle Corps) and 5th Brigade (attacking with 2nd Inniskillings & 2nd Worcestershire), with the 4th (Guards) Brigade in reserve.*

11.30pm *The first-line platoons of infantry leave their trenches and move out into No Man's Land, as the artillery lifts beyond the German support trenches. The advance of the 6th Brigade, west of the cinder track running from Rue du Bois to Ferme du Bois, is completed with few casualties. They occupy the German front and support trenches and begin to consolidate. On the left, between the track and almost as far as Port Arthur, the 5th Brigade runs into a more alert enemy and is hit by heavy machine-gun fire. Some men from the Inniskillings reach the German front line and Brigade dispatches the 2nd Oxford & Bucks in support. The same thing happens to the Gharwal Brigade of the Meerut Division (attacking with 2nd Leicestershire and 39th Gharwal Rifles), which is advancing to conform to the 5th Brigade. They were to form the defensive flank, but they were also cut down in No Man's Land.*

May 16

12.45am *2nd Division orders a further bombardment as planned, to coincide with the attack to be made by 7th Division. The support battalions of 6th Brigade (2nd South Staffordshire & Kings) were unable to leave the British front trench to move up to the captured position due to heavy cross-fire from the area between the two Divisional attacks, which had not been suppressed by the bombardment. German resistance in the*

*area to the front of the captured trenches is stiffening, The support battalions of the Gharwal Brigade (1st/3rd London & the 2nd/3rd Ghurkas) also attempted to move forward, but were immediately cut down
and the movement ceases.*

*2.45am The bombardment intensifies on the 7th Division front, including six field guns firing from the front line, opening gaps in the German
breastwork (a tactic tried with some success by the Division at Aubers),
although in places the lines are only 80 yards apart and great care is
taken to avoid shelling British troops forming up.*

*3.10am The first platoons of the 20th Brigade (led by 2nd Scots Guards
& 2nd Border) left their front line, to close up with the German before
the barrage lifts. Considerable casualties are incurred as they advance
too far into the British shells.*

17 May

*The day dawned with heavy rain and low cloud. Orders were given for
the gap between the 2nd and 7th Divisions to be closed with a view
to continuing an advance towards Chapelle St Roch and Rue d'Ouvert.
The German units in the area between Ferme du Bois and the Southern
Breastwork (opposite Willow Corner) began a systematic withdrawal to
a new line, 1200 yards to the rear.*

*2.45 am British recommence shelling against targets registered the day
before and destroyed enemy positions. The German garrison of the
Quadrilateral is badly hit and the remainder cannot withdraw as ordered. The survivors attempt to surrender, but are cut down by German
shelling as well as the British bombardment which is still falling. Approximately 450 men reach the British line and are captured. Other
German units withdraw or surrender and their front in the area gap,
is giving way fast & walking wounded make their painful way back to
the rear area.*

The following telegram was delivered to R.M. Reid, Thomanean, Milnathort,
Kinross-shire.

*OHMS regret to inform you that Capt W.B.J. Reid Seaforth attached to
8th Highlander reported wounded 16th to 17th May, further information will be sent when received. From Secretary, War Office.*

This was followed by a telegram to Mrs Reid, Thomanean, Milnathort,Kinross-shire:

Deeply regret to inform you that Captain W.B.J. Reid Seaforth Highlanders died in St Thomas's Hospital London on 20th May. Lord Kitchener expresses his sympathy.

*Notification has just been received from St Thomas's Hospital of the
death of Captain W.B.J. Reid 3rd Seaforth Highlanders, who was admitted there at 3.30am today, suffering from severe shrapnel wounds*

of the left foot and right arm, and Toxaemia consequent on the septic condition of these.

An anaesthetic (ether) was administered at 3.30pm, and the operation was just completed at 3.55pm, when the patient suddenly collapsed and died.

The Medical officer at St Thomas's is of the opinion that Capt Reid was wounded on the 16th May.

There is a signature of a Major C.A. Lees from St Mark's College, Chelsea, dated May 20th 1915.

Robert went to London and, with his brother-in-law David Reid of Sevenoaks in Kent, travelled north with the body. Overnight they came, arriving at Kinross Junction with the 8.42am train. Here in the beautiful sunlight of early morning, the estate employees of Thomanean gathered to express their grief at the loss. Covered with the Union Jack, the casket, borne on the shoulders of six estate employees, was carried to a waiting long-cart drawn by a single carthorse. The sorrowful little procession wended its slow way to the Episcopal Church.

There the cortege was met by the rector Rev M.D. Fletcher and the coffin brought into the church. 'The military arrangements connected with the funeral were on a scale befitting the rank of a late Captain. Fully 100 non-commissioned officers and men of 'A' Company 3, 7th Argyll and Sutherland Highlanders, from Alloa (to which company Captain R.M. Reid was attached) provided the escort, under the command of Captain A.W. Russell and Lieutenants D.V. Thompson and R.W. Turner; six A & S 'non-Coms' – Company Sergeant-Major Cotcher, Colour Sergeant Renton and Sergeants Mitchell, Clarke, Beverage and Binnie – acted as pall-bearers. A firing party under Sergeant Mitchell attended. A gun carriage with a team of six horses was supplied by the Royal Field Artillery stationed at Dunfermline; and the Pipe Band of the Argyll and Sutherland, under Sergeant-Drummer Neil Graham also took part.

At one o'clock – fully an hour before the time fixed at which the cortege was to proceed to Orwell Churchyard – a considerable number of the general public had assembled outside the church. The limited accommodation of the building was taxed with a gathering representative of the county. Mr Philip Kiddie, Edinburgh, organist of the church, presided at the organ and sympathetically rendered the following penitential music: 'Blessed Are The Departed' from Spohr's 'Last Judgment', 'I Know That My Redeemer Liveth' (Handel's Messiah) 'O Rest In The Lord' and 'Cast Thy Burden On The Lord' from Mendelssohn's 'Elijah' improvisation in form of Prelude on Dyke's 'Requiescat'; 'When Called By Thee I Gain Thy Portal' (motet by Bach); and Chopin's 'Funeral March'.

Mrs Reid (mother), the Misses Reid (sisters), Captain Robert Reid (brother) and Mr David Reid (brother-in-law) were in the church, and among others were:- Sir Basil Graham Montgomery and Walter

(Foreground) Grave of David Reid

*Graham Montgomery, Sir Charles Bruce G.C.M.C. and Lady Bruce of
Arnot Tower, Mr H. Purvis Russell Montgomery of Hattonburn and Mrs
Purvis Russell Montgomery, Mrs Purvis Russell of Warroch, Mr J.H.
Paton of Lethangie, Major Reid, Whinfield, Mr & Mrs Ramage Dawson
of Balado, Miss Coventry of Shanwell, Colonel Porteous, Mr & Mrs Porteous of Turfhills, Mr W.H. Dobie of Dollarbeg, Mr J. Moncrieff Wright
of Kinmouth, Colonel C.L. Addison Smith, Seaforth Highlanders, Major
Patrick Grant of Kilgranston D.S.O., Major Martin Glynn, Colonel and
Mrs Aitken etc, and a very large attendance of the professional and business men of Kinross and Milnathort. A detachment of twelve veterans
from the Scottish Navy and Military Veteran's Residence, Edinburgh
were present. Several pews were set apart for Thomanean house and
estate workers.*

While the service was proceeding, a concourse had assembled outside the
church. The escort, drawn up in double file, formed a cordon. The men presented
arms, the gun-carriage received its burden, and the military deployed in single file
on either side of the road and the head of the gun-carriage. Immediately preceding the gun-carriage was the pipe band, with the bugler. Drums were draped,
and the Sergeant-Drummer brought up the rear. With reversed arms and to the
strains of 'The Land Of The Leal' the military proceeded in slow march.

Milnathort Station

Carriages were filled with floral tributes and many private carriages and motors with hundreds of mourners on foot, followed the gun-carriage from the Episcopal Church in Kinross to Orwell Kirk Graveyard in Milnathort. Large crowds of sympathetic onlookers lined the streets, while all traffic was suspended, business premises closed, and windows darkened.

On arrival at the cemetery gates the escort drew up on each side of the road-way. With bowed heads, the soldiers 'rested on their arms reversed', and the cortege passed through the lane thus formed into the cemetery.

The Rev Mr Millar conducted the solemn rites at the graveside, concluding with The Lord's Prayer, the Collect and the Benediction. The pall-bearers were:- Captain R.M. Reid, Mr D.G.A. Reid, Mr H. Purvis Russell Montgomery, Mr J.C. Calder, Mr W. Tod, Colonel Addison Smith, Major Reid, and Mr J.A. Ramage Dawson. The sides of the grave had been lined with evergreens by the head gardener of Thomanean, Mr J Pearson.

After the coffin was committed to the grave, the last tribute was accorded to the fallen officer by the troops; three volleys were fired at intervals. Between each volley eight bars of 'Lochaber No More' were played by a piper, and finally the whole lament was played. Thereafter 'The Last Post' was sounded by the buglers.

The *Scotsman* told a short history of William, but it is to the *Kinross-shire Courier* of Saturday 29th May that we turn for a tribute.

> *Today we mourn the death even as we glory in the deeds, of that gallant officer and gentleman Captain Reid of Thomanean. Only a few short weeks ago, for a brief few days, he was amongst us. He looked strong, well and in good spirits, fit, as in fact he was, to go anywhere and do anything.*

He was of graver mien and thought, perhaps (as became one who had so often looked death in the face), than in earlier and happier days. But he was full of faith in the justice of our cause, and in our capacity for accomplishing our task.

Like most keen sportsmen, Captain Reid was the happy possessor of a hardy constitution. He was trained and inured by open air exercise to any amount of hard work or hardship of any kind. He therefore bore the wear and tear of the winter campaign successfully, uncomplainingly, and resolute. Until the end he had never been (except for a week on leave) absent from duty. It was on the 16th of this month that he received the wounds which four days later brought his gallant career to a premature close.

Captain Reid was first and foremost and in all time, a soldier. He was that excellent type of class which does not find its equal, far less its superior, in any Army in the world – the British regimental officer. He never thought of fear except to scorn it. He was devoted to his profession, skilled in its exercise, full of zeal and enthusiasm, willing to face any amount of drudgery, and though a strict disciplinarian, kindly and considerate to his men. As an early example of his devotion, skill, and zeal – his later example requires no words – it is sufficient to say that even before he attained his majority he had done much service in Egypt and during the Boer War in South Africa.

Since these days he had considerably ripened his experience of men and affairs by travel in various parts of the world. He acted only lately as Secretary of the Whiteford House, Edinburgh, and during the whole period performed many highly useful, though unostentatious, military duties. He had acquired an altogether exceptional skill in the drilling of recruits, and his capacity in this direction was so well recognised that on the outbreak of war, he – much to his chagrin no doubt – was unable to proceed to the front.

But the chance came to him in November. He crossed to France then, and in France, except for one brief week, he remained to the end.

That these are no empty words will be seen from the following;- An officer of high rank, writing from the front, after expressing his deep sympathy and personal loss, goes on to say Captain Reid had been of the greatest help, and that his loss was a very great one for the Army, and adds that he was immensely popular with the men, and that all ranks of the 2nd Gordon Highlander (William belonged to the Seaforths but was lent to the Gordons) his influence with his men was as great as if he had spent his life amongst them; that every man spoke most highly of him, and it was a great blow to all that he left them. And in conclusion, the officer in question writes that as one of the old Battalion he would never forget what one of the Seaforths had done for the Gordons.

Maria Johnston Reid gave massively to the war effort. Not only had she two sons fighting, but one of her daughters, Janet, joined the Queen Alexandra's Royal Nursing Corps. She had an account with the local grocer Mr Andrew Muirhead in Milnathort for £48 to be given to the poor, and if it was ever disclosed where it came from she would withdraw the whole of her account. The loss of William, named after her father, was deeply felt.

Miss Janet Reid

The youngest daughter of David and Maria Reid, she was only three when her father died. She was brought up with her brothers and sisters at Thomanean by her mother Maria Johnston Reid.

When the war broke out in the autumn of 1914 she was 25 and, as the minimum age for the Queen Alexandra's Royal Army Corps was 23, she joined up. The QARAC provided nurses for hospitals with 100 beds, and was a registered charity. Queen Alexandra was its president until her death in 1925, when she was succeeded by Queen Mary. It was founded in 1902 at the time of the Boer War and in 1914 was less than 300 nurses strong. At the end of the four years of war it numbered over 10,000 nurses.

Because the British Army was so resolutely opposed to all female military nurses except the Queen Alexandra's Imperial Military Nursing Service, early volunteers from Britain were obliged to serve with French and Belgian forces. Many of these volunteers were from aristocratic families and their servants. Powerful women who ran large families and large estates were well versed in management and saw no great problems in managing a military hospital instead. These gently reared girls walked straight out of Edwardian drawing-rooms into the manifold horrors of the First World War. These girls had to be tough. They worked in flooded operating theatres, where in a big push they might have had four operations going on at once, and ten amputations an hour. They nursed men with terrible wounds and saw them off to convalescent camps, or laid them out when they died. They nursed in wards where the stench of gas-gangrenous wounds was overpowering. They nursed men choking to death as fluid rose in their gassed lungs, men whose faces were mutilated beyond recognition, whose bodies were mangled beyond repair and whose nerves were shattered beyond redemption. The men were often embarrassed by being attended to and bathed by women.

In many instances little could be done but comfort a soldier as he died. They often died of wounds as sepsis set in and continued unabated. Antibiotics were yet to be discovered. Indeed, with regard to sepsis and fevers in particular, good nursing techniques often made the difference between life and death. Undoubtedly in some instances, recovery depended on the immune systems of the individual but infection control, the use of inhalations, poultices and sterile dressings all combined to aid healing. In the Boer War the veldt was a more sterile place, while in Flanders they were fighting on agricultural land aggravated by the waste of the war. Sepsis set in very quickly and was a major killer for wounded men.

As the war progressed, thousands of women began to be involved, serving in a range of capacities. As well as serving in the hospitals, they drove ambulances and travelled on ambulance trains carrying injured soldiers. Pitched into military hospitals, these middle-class women had not much relevant education and were totally ignorant of male bodies. Whatever obstacles bureaucracy put in their way, the huge and bloody tide of casualties arising by the spring of 1915 simply swept them away. Even the British Army's top brass yielded to the combined pressures of need and confident commitment.

A field ambulance was a mobile front-line medical unit for treating the wounded before they were moved to a Casualty Clearing Station. It would include stretcher bearers, nursing orderlies, tented wards, operating theatre, cookhouse, wash rooms and a horse or motor ambulance. The field ambulances set up and supplied Advanced Dressing Stations which were basic care points providing only limited medical treatment and had no holding capacity. The wounded were brought here from Regimental Aid Posts, which were only a few metres behind the front line in small spaces such as a support or reserve trench.

It was realised that a man's chances of survival depended on how quickly his wound was treated. Modern warfare was producing vast numbers of casualties requiring treatment at the same time. Efficient and rapid movement away for treatment was the only way to achieve success. A system was set up known as the Chain of Evacuation. Each section of the chain had its own agenda but the objective was the same – to deal with all medical matters, and to treat the sick and wounded to get them back into the fighting force. This was achieved by the Royal Army Medical Corps personnel working alongside drivers of the Army Service Corps and carpenters of the Royal Engineers in all units. Also in each CCS and General Hospital there were Sisters of the QAIMNS, and nurses of the joint Red Cross, St John's Ambulance Brigade, and VADs (Voluntary Aid Detachments) of the Red Cross.

Here are some quotations from *Roses of No Man's Land* and *Sisters of the Somme*.

> *Military nurses trained or otherwise, were never allowed out without a chaperone, even for the briefest of walks. The tippets that were worn by members of the QAINS were designed to hide a nurse's sexuality, as were the frumpy dresses and pinafores of VAD's, and the blanket coverings were provided by floor length capes.*

Winter 1914

> *...the regulation puttees, which every soldier wore tightly bound from ankle to knee, shrank in the wet, cut off circulation and turned feet black and rotting with frost bite. Lacking drinking water but desperate for a drink of even lukewarm tea, the soldiers skimmed the cleanest seeming*

liquid from the top of waterlogged ditches and trenches without investigating what horrors of ordour or decay might lie in the murk beneath. The result was an outbreak of enteric and dysentery. For the Europeans, hardened to cold if not to exposure, the conditions were appalling. For the Indian troops, they were insupportable. Coughing in an infernal chorus, painfully racked with rheumatism, and bleeding from their wounds, they were brought to the hospital trains that travelled slowly up and down behind the front, from Ypres to Rouen and Le Havre. 'Indian men too cold' moaned a bearded Sikh, shivering on a stretcher. 'Kill more Germans if not too cold.'

Jan 1915

There were six hospital trains trundling up and down behind the Front carrying 400 sick and wounded at a time, manned by two or three medical officers, four nursing sisters and forty RAMC orderlies. It is nearly three months since I sat in a chair, except at meals, and that is only a flap-down seat. I expect we shall be off again tonight somewhere.

It was always 'Somewhere', no one ever knew precisely where. Slow hours of clanking north or inland, punctuated by long waits on sidings while the troop trains or supply trains went through. Then more rumbling through the night, and at last loading up at a shattered station or a wayside halt somewhere in the back of beyond, where long rows of stretchers and huddled groups of walking wounded waited in the wintery weather to board the train. If they were lucky they would unload at Boulogne. If Boulogne was full the train had to go to Le Touquet, or Rouen or, furthest of all, to Le Havre, a journey of 200 miles. When conditions were at their worst it could take up to three days.

Comforts arrived in France by the boat-load. The Red Cross was inundated with gifts that ranged from valuables which could be sold for cash, to the homely, useful items that almost every woman in the country was busy sewing and knitting.

The first six months of 1916 constituted a breathing space for the British Army. It was not particularly noticeable in the hospitals. From December's end to the beginning of May the normal wastage of trench warfare amounted to 83,000 killed and wounded. The casualties flowed in but not all of them flowed quickly out. There was a large backlog of men wounded in the first two years – the blind, the paralysed and the limbless, needing long-term care, and fresh convoys of recently wounded arriving with depressing regularity. The hospitals were being strained to the limit.

It was no easy job manoeuvring the erratic and temperamental motor ambulances up under bombardment to aid-posts in the high peaks, and it was a long, comfortless journey back for the wounded as the ambulances careered down the tortuous rock-strewn roads, for the two-hour journey to safety in the valley below.

Our first warning that convoys were coming was the steady hum of am-

bulances winding down the road as far as eye could see, with scarcely a yard between them. Nearly every case should have a stretcher. Ragged and dirty, tin hats still on; wounds patched together any way, some not even covered.

They were direct from the front and their faces were white and drawn and their eyes glassy from lack of sleep. There were great husky men, crying with the pain of gaping wounds and dreadful discoloured trench feet. There were strings of eight to twenty blind boys filing up the road, their hands on each other's shoulders and their leader, some bedraggled, bandaged, limping youngster.

One ambulance nurse records:

I got quite used to carrying shell shock patients in the ambulance. It was a horrible thing, because they sometimes used to get these attacks, rather like an epileptic fit in a way. They became unconscious with violent shivering and shaking, and you had to keep them from banging themselves about too much until they came round again. The great thing was to stop them falling off the stretchers, and for that reason we used to take just one at a time in the ambulance, because you'd never have been able to cope with four cases at once as you could with the ordinary wounded. Of course, these were the so called milder cases. We didn't carry the dangerous ones – they came in a separate part of the train, and were collected in completely closed up ambulances. They were taken to an asylum for hopeless mental cases.

The question of shell shock was very complex, and as time went on it became obvious that nervous casualties could not be lumped together in a single category. It ranged from symptoms of total paralysis and deaf-mutism to curvature of the spine; from violent hysteria to the type of debilitating nervous weakness which, years later, would be known as 'battle fatigue'.

Shell shock was also called neurasthenia. Shell shock was treated as a wound, so it would qualify for a post-war pension. In 1921, two years after the end of the war, there were 65,000 men suffering from various forms of neurasthenia receiving a pension. By 1922 this had dropped to 50,000 and in 1938 to 30,000.

We were terribly overworked. One sister and I had six tents to cope with alone. The orderly was fully occupied with the men's kits when he wasn't carrying stretchers of the new arrivals. Normally when a new patient was admitted, the orderly undressed him and took his clothes to be de-loused, but in this rush I very often had to see to the undressing of the men myself. Their things were in a pretty foul condition and as all the pockets had to be emptied before they were taken to be de-loused, it was almost impossible to avoid the creatures swarming all over them.

In 1915 at the 2nd Battle of Ypres the Germans used poison chlorine gas. The nurses were appalled as nothing in their experience, nor in the experience of the doctors, had equipped them to deal with wards full of men gasping for breath, with terrible rasping sounds of their struggle, with their blue faces and livid skin; and worst of all, with their terror as the fluid rose higher in their lungs until eventually they drowned in it. The terror was made worse by the fact that most of the men were blind and trapped in darkness in their suffocating bodies.

The Battle of the Somme began on 1st July 1916.

As the guns thudded and flashed through the night a few miles away, lighting the starlight sky with flashes of yellow glare, doctors, nurses, surgeons and orderlies worked flat out. They could only attend to a fraction of the 12,000 wounded who had reached the casualty clearing stations by evening, and fresh convoys of ambulances kept coming all through the night. When the ambulance trains eventually came to the rescue – and eighteen reached the sector the following day – the hospital at bases were equally flooded and equally overwhelmed. It was only possible to keep and care for the most seriously wounded. Others had to go straight to England. In most cases there was not even time to clean them up or even change the first rough field dressing which had been clapped on to their wounds in the heat of the battle many hours or even days earlier.

In the first four days, in 100 journeys, the hospital trains carried 33,392 patients from casualty clearing stations to hospital ships on the river or Le Havre.

It was fortunate that it was fine weather, because sometimes there were so many waiting to go that stretchers were lying all over the quay waiting for a ship to come in. The ships went back and forth all the time, and we could see them even at night passing on their way to embark the wounded from here.

They packed the wounded on to every inch of the hospital ships, not only in the wards and saloons below but into the Sisters' and Doctors' own quarters, and when they were full they laid the stretchers on the deck alongside the walking wounded.

Christmas 1916 saw the belated gift of a week's salary and a special bonus for the year, and two weeks leave for every six months served was given. Christmas 1917 brought large quantities to the length and breadth of the Western Front of largesse from all quarters of the globe. The USA sent shipments of beef, South Africa boatloads of grapes, peaches and nectarines, Canada 10,000 cases of apples and Australia a huge mountain of billycans packed with comforts and goodies.

On 12-13th July 1917 British troops were rocked by a new chemical. The Germans bombarded Ypres with 50,000 mustard gas shells. Mustard gas, when released into the trenches, showed a faint yellow colour, which insidiously seeped through clothing, blistering skin and lungs. The gas stayed on the ground a long time after its release, and anyone touching the skin or clothing of a contaminated person also became contaminated. Some victims initially displayed few symptoms but died later of blistered lungs and enlarged hearts. It was not unusual for men to die two or three weeks afterwards. It was discovered in late July that oxygen therapy worked well on the majority of victims if able to gain access to medical attention soon after the attack. Almost all of these victims continued to experience impaired lung function and chronic bronchitis long after the war ended. My Uncle Bill died at 84 and had poor lungs all his life after being gassed in the Great War. He was fortunate to live.

> The matron was very impressed with the convoy of ambulance drivers (they have a woman's convoy at Etaples). The girls are out on the road bringing in the wounded during the whole time of the raid. (Bombs dropped on Canadian wards next door.) Our own staff and sister, VADs and orderlies were splendid and no one showed the least panic or alarm.

In March 1918 there were 325,000 American troops already in France, by 1st May more than 429,000 and 650,000 still training in the UK or waiting to be shipped across the Channel. This source of fresh troops was welcome.

> In the ambulance convoy the discipline was very strict. Half the time we wore boots and greasy overalls, though we had blue uniforms with tailored jackets and skirts that came well below the knees. We were put on night duty straight away, and being the last arrivals we were given the most ancient and rackety ambulances. Mine was No 896 and I was warned that it had a slipping clutch. We went on duty at eight o'clock and sat round a sort of common-room hut where there is a big stove, waiting for the first call. It came about nine – someone flung the door open and shouted 'Train in. Train in'. We had to rush out and find our cars in the dark, and race down these narrow roads without any lights to see who could get to the railway-siding quickest, because the people who arrived first got the least badly wounded, They kept the very worst ones, the dying ones, until the end and took them out more carefully. There were old orderlies who lifted the stretchers out of the train and into the ambulance, then the section leader would call the number of the hospital you were to go to and you would have to make your way there in the dark, with no lights.

In 1918 the epidemic of influenza that broke out in June seemed to abate but broke out in a new, and more virulent, form in Britain, Germany, and the USA and in ranks of all the armies on rapidly shifting fronts of war.

> It was a terrible epidemic. There was so little we could do for them. The only treatment was to keep an even temperature in the ward. We just had to give them fluid and keep walking up and down seeing if anybody wanted anything. They were all incontinent so you were continually changing beds and washing.

> Even after four years of nursing with awful wounds, the influenza epidemic seemed the worst thing of all. They died like flies. I was the senior Sister, and the surgeon and I spent our whole time going round the casualty clearing station giving the men blood transfusions. We did it for days at a time and it was the only thing we could do to help them, to keep them alive if possible until they got over the main symptoms.

The war had lasted exactly four years and a hundred days. The fighting had ranged from the trenches in Belgium, the barren rocks of Gallipoli, the sands of Egypt, the hills of Macedonia and the plains of Africa to mention just some. For the British army the war finished as it had started at Mons. The last shots rang out on a grey day on 11 November 1918.

> It was a terrible day. Sometimes we had to do fatigues, and it was my turn that day to drive the lorry to take men to the dump to shovel coal. It was a one-ton lorry, which seemed rather big to me in these days because there weren't any self-starters and you had to swing the handle of the beastly thing. We got there and the men were shovelling the coal onto the lorry. I was sitting in the driver's seat and at eleven o'clock these sirens went off and they went on and on. Then the men up in the Bull Ring started to blow the reveille, and we heard the bugles and we knew that it was over.

No patients were admitted after January 1919, and the staff were demobilised. Many nurses did not marry. Thousands of women became elderly spinsters as Britain had lost a whole generation of men. Much recognition of the immense bravery under fire, and everyday dedication to their work over the four years was given. As one ambulance nurse put it: 'If you couldn't laugh, you were finished. At home, in the field and in the trenches, the laughter and the comradeship were the only things that made it possible to carry on at all.'

Janet Reid came home to Thomanean and settled there until her mother's death in 1934, when she and her sister Maria stayed at old Duncrievie House. After Robert died in 1949 she came to Tillyrie and lived in Tillyrie House, but we will meet her again there.

Robert Matale Reid

When Robert inherited Tillyrie from his uncle George in 1911 he was 32 years old. He had plans for a model steading which he built in the stackyard to the east of the dwelling house, and it was so well done that it was still a model steading 70 years later, and lasted almost 100 years. He and his mother had bought Nether Tillyrie and Hall Greig from the Greigs, Berry Brae from the Pearsons and, with what he now inherited, the estate now extended to 880 acres.

He built a steading to house 100 cattle, with cattle courts, calf units, and an indoor threshing mill. The latter had conveyer belts to take the grain to a upstairs granary and the straw to a loft above the cattle court where it could be forked down when needed. There was a stable with 11 airy stalls and a hay shed next door, a feed shed where grain, beans and chaff could be mixed and stored, two byres, and several large individual pens for calving cows and where his Clydes-

Tillyrie and the New Steading 1914 (Photo: David Millar)

dale mares could foal. There was an area for a turnip shed beside the cattle courts and byres, and a cart shed with five square 'arches', as well as three long troughs on the wall of the stable, for the horses to be let out to drink.

The whole building was built in a square, using local brick and faced with a cement-coloured coat. The roof was slate over the beams, with vents built so they could be opened for ventilation for the cattle. All of the wood came from Tillyrie, and a sawmill was set up in the steading at Nether Tillyrie, where the garage for Easter Steadings is now.

At a time when labour was cheap, a cattleman could look after 100 cattle in the well-thought-out steading, and the cattle were well ventilated. A forward thinking plan!

He bred Aberdeen Angus cattle, produced bulls for the Annual Sale at Perth, and regularly registered cattle with the Aberdeen Angus Breed Society. He had Blackface sheep and Clydesdale horses working on the farm, five pair and an orra-horse, and he usually kept a couple of Clydesdale brood mares, who were his pride and joy.

The steading was completed in 1914, about the same time as Nether Tillyrie House. The house was not blessed with the extensive gardens planned and, with war pending, it was arranged to lease it to the Red Cross for the duration of the war as an auxiliary hospital for injured officers. The Red Cross were looking for an auxiliary or convalescent hospital for the county. The capacity of the hospital was 30 beds originally, but an extension was later built for 21 more beds, 42 of which were for patients. A Hospital Committee was set up chaired by Walter G. Montgomery to equip the hospital with furniture, including beds. There was a matron and seven Red Cross nurses, three other nurses and some domestics, and some 32-42 patients. Photos were taken every year, including one of a concert party on 28th September 1918, all of which can be seen in the museum

Annual Concert at Nether Tillyrie with the injured and hospital staff, March 1916

Tillyrie Red Cross Hospital, Milnathort.

in Kinross. A great many local folk helped out, and a surge of knowledge for first aid was driven through the population. Nearly every village had raised a detachment, so there were no staffing problems. 'We took First Aid and Home Nursing classes in the winter of 1914-15 and waited impatiently for the day our hospital could open.'

The first batch of patients from Craigleith Military Hospital in Edinburgh arrived at Tillyrie during the summer of 1915. 'The numbers varied according to whether the war was static or active – the Military Hospitals always cleared their wards to the Auxiliary Hospitals when a push began to make way for a rush of hospital trains.'

'The detachments (of local labour) did a month at a time, in rotation, and were fed and housed, but not of course paid.' Each detachment consisted of six members and took it in turns to do six jobs, which were swapped every week – medical assistant, surgical assistant, house-maid, table-maid, kitchen-maid and the ever unpopular scullery-maid. Everyone had at least one of the nursing jobs on her spell of duty. 'Learning to do other work to hospital standards was very useful to us who went on to further work. Our little hospital was very happy and well-run, and we had a lot of fun, but one's turn didn't come round nearly often enough.'

The ladies of the VAD were a great help, as were many private persons including older people whose commitments prevented them from working there, but they held whist drives, tea parties and other fundraisers, and gave little parties in their homes for out-patients. On 1st January 1916 a long list of VAD who sent gifts included Lady Montgomery, Miss Elsie Reid of Thomanean, Mr & Mrs

Ramage Dawson of Balado, The Misses Simpson of Mawcarse, Mr Black of Tilly-whally and Mr Meiklem of Blairadam. On 8th January a concert was held in Portmoak for the Red Cross and Serbian funds. This kind of charity work continued throughout the war.

The hospital closed in 1919 when the need for auxiliary hospitals dried up. Many of the nursing staff kept in touch, and years later letters arrived to the house from patients or their children remembering the time there.

In the meantime Robert put an agent into Tillyrie and joined up with the 7th Battalion, Princess Louise's Argyll and Sutherland Highlanders. Princess Louise was the sixth child and fourth daughter of Queen Victoria. She married the Duke of Argyll, and gave her name to the regiment at the time.

The advert read as follows:

G.R.

YOUNG MEN of KINROSS-SHIRE!

Your Country Calls You.

Your Country Relies on your Ready Response.

RECRUITS Are Urgently Required to form another Company of Territorials to Complete the Establishment of the 7th Battalion Argyll & Sutherland Highlanders.

Recruits to be from 19 to 35 years of age, not less than 5 feet 3 inches in height, and 34 inches chest measurement.

Terms of Enlistment and other particulars can be obtained on application to:-
Mr A D Richardson,
c/o Falconer & Marshall Solicitors,
and **Sergt. Inst. Ford, Piper Row.**

GOD SAVE THE KING

The 7th Battalion Argyll and Sutherland Highlanders were recruited from Kelty and Kinross-shire. On 22nd August 1914 the use of trains for military purposes was so heavy that normal passenger service was suspended for a day. On 12th September, 40 recruits left Kinross Junction for Alloa.

Dr Murdoch raised the Argyll and Sutherland Territorials. At the beginning of the war he took them all out to France and the bulk of them were killed. He wasn't killed but he never came back to Kinross. He was thought to have suffered from shell shock. In April 1916 he won the Military Cross at Ypres for service rendered to men of the 7th Battalion of the Argyll and Sutherland Highlanders.

The soldiers arrived at the front in the trenches during the middle of the winter. The wife of the Chief Field Marshall John French had a major campaign to collect warm clothing, and in a letter to Provost Murdock Anderson in Kinross she wrote: 'I am collecting warm clothing for the men at the front. It is urgent that they should be quickly supplied... things principally required are mufflers, cardigans, body belts, mittens, gloves, socks and shirts. The most pressing need at the moment is mufflers (2 yards long by 12 inches wide) of which the War Office has asked me to provide 25,000.'

The local press reported on 16th January 1915 that articles of food such as cakes, shortbread, etc would be most acceptable to the troops. As a result a Scottish National Flag Day was held, and 14,880 currant loaves and 14,880 cakes of shortbread were sent to soldiers as a gift on New Year's Day.

Lady Montgomery played a leading role in sending clothing to the troops. Captain Murdoch of G Company wrote from France thanking her for the kindness and added 'we feel a long way from Kinross.'

In a letter to Lady Montgomery dated 26th January 1915 he thanked her for the constant kindness to us and

> *...the articles which have been sent to us by the committee over which you preside have come in jolly useful in adding to the comfort of the men. Of course the Government are bound to supply us with the necessary articles, but the extras which we are fortunate to receive from home help to fill in the gaps which occur now and again. We have been supplied with fur waistcoats and look like a lot of spring chickens when we have them on. The men are pretty fit and keen, and I am sure will do very well. We are attached to a Regular Brigade and are gradually working into the usual routine and taking our share of the Brigade work. We feel a long way from Kinross now with two Reserve Battalions behind us. There have been no casualties in the Company yet though some of them have had narrow escapes.*

> *Yours very sincerely*
> *John Murdoch,*
> *7th A & S. H. Expeditionary Force.*

Robert Matale Reid joined as a Lieutenant of this Battalion. They mobilised at Stirling at the outbreak of war, were sent to Bedford in 1914, and from there to France in December of that year. They were temporarily amalgamated with the 1st/9th Battalion from May to July 1915, then 154th/51st Highland Division in March 1916. They ended the war north of Cambrai.

Lieutenant Robert Matale Reid was made Captain on 7th January 1915. A supplement to the *London Gazette*, 20 February 1915 states that Archibald Porteous (late Captain 7th Volunteer Battalion Argyll and Sutherland Highlanders) was to be made Major, dated 7th January. The under-mentioned to be Captains, dated 1st February, and goes on to name six, which included Robert Matale Reid.

This may have been as a result of the 'Mousetrap Farm' offensive in May when heavy German artillery, including a large amount of chlorine gas, left the 7th Battalion with only two officers and 76 men, but it may have happened earlier in 1915.

The Battle Honours included St. Julien, Frezenberg, Bellewarde, Ypres 1915,

Somme 1916, Bazentin, Poziers, Ancre 1916, Scar 1917, Arras 1917, Ypres 1917, Pilckem, Menin Road, Cambrai 1917, Somme 1918, St Quentin, Bapaume 1918, Aras 1918, Lys, Estaires, Hazebrouck, Bethune, Marne 1918, Soissonnais-Ourcq, Tardennois, Scarpe 1918, Selle, France and Flanders 1914-1918.

Britain entered the war because she had to, and in 1918 it was the British that made the major contribution to defeat the Germans. Field Marshal Haig was congratulated by the King and lauded in the newspapers for winning the war. When offered a viscountcy by Lloyd George, Haig refused any honours until the government agreed financial provision for disabled ex-soldiers. Then, after intervention by the King, Haig accepted an earldom. Haig devoted the rest of his life to the welfare of ex-servicemen, and started the British Legion in the UK and right round the world. He died of a heart attack in January 1928, and was mourned by hundreds of thousands who had served under his command.

One young lad, a farmer's son from Carnbo called Anderson was very fortunate in the war. He was called up in 1917 and when asked if he knew anything about horses said 'No' as he didn't want to land in the calvary. He was posted to the Signal Corps, and with so much to learn about flags and morse codes it was 1918 when the lad sailed from Southampton with his regiment to go to France. They were halfway across the English Channel when news came that the armistice had been signed, and the ship turned back to Southampton. He was demobbed in Kinross, and walked home to the farm at Carnbo.

During the war a wood between Lathro and Gallowhill Farm was cut down for timber for shipping. The Gallows Tree was cut in error, and the chain was retained by someone, but has rusted away since.

When the war ended Capt Reid came home to Thomanean with his mother, son, and sisters, and ran Tillyrie from there. He had many ideas to improve the farm, including designing a cart to take cattle to the market or station (on the way to the Perth Bull Sales) based on the horse ambulances used in the war. It had a ramp at the rear and, when the horse was taken out, the transported animals would unload down the front. It could hold two cattle, or several sheep, or mare and foal. Still in a shed at Tillyrie when we took down the steading in 2010, it was taken and beautifully restored by Ross Kinnaird at Findatie and shown at the Royal Highland Show. It was quite unique.

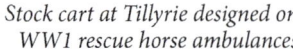

Stock cart at Tillyrie designed on WW1 rescue horse ambulances

In 1926 the sugar beet factory opened in Cupar, and farmers were asked to grow 20 acres of sugar beet for the factory. Captain Reid had a special plough for ploughing the long-rooted beet out of the ground, with a metal label stating it was the property of Cupar Beet Factory. On 8th November 1926 the first beet was cut and 2,718 acres of sugar beet were contracted in the first year. Built at a cost of £300,000 in a location favoured by Cupar Town Council, who promised the water supply to this new venture and, sited beside a good railway system serving all of Scotland from Angus to the Borders, it had good access.

In 1929 Captain Reid built a new bothy for single men, a sore point on many a farm. The new bothy had four single bedrooms, a

Captain Reid

large living room with an open fire, a spacious kitchen with a Raeburn cooker, a bathroom with a WC, sink and bath and a corridor running from the back door round to the bedrooms so people could come and go without passing through the living room. There was also a walk-in pantry, and outside a coal shed and a large garden with a wash line and a piggery. It was a palace compared to the bothy of one communal room, with wooden beds and a toilet in the nearest cattle court of many farms at the time. The new bothy had 'Matale 1929 Founded on Matale 1878-80' on the south-facing front wall. The old bothy at the foot of the garden was used to store grain and grasses for birdseed for his turtle doves for a while.

The *Edinburgh Gazette* of 21st June, 1929 declared that Commissions signed by the Lord Lieutenant of the County: Sir James Charles Calder, C.B.E., J.P. of Ledlanet, Milnathort; Captain Robert Matale Reid J.P., of Tillyrie, Milnathort: William Tod, Esquire, J.P., of East Brackley, Kinross: James Belfrage Black, Esquire, J.P., of Tillywhally, Milnathort, to be Deputy Lieutenants.

Robert was President of Kinross-shire Agricultural Society in 1922, 1929-31, and during the war years from 1939-45.

The Old English Sheepdog Club of Scotland held its first show at Ayr in April 1933, and 25 dogs were benched for the judge Miss McTurk to go over. On 25th September, the club held its AGM where Captain R.M. Reid was elected president for the forthcoming term and the membership stood at 45, which enabled the club to continue guaranteeing classes at the principal open and championship shows in Scotland. The Captain always had some Old English Sheepdogs about him. They were kept in the loft above the garage, and his turtle doves were in the aviary on the east of the house.

In 1933 he had an agreement with James B. Black of Tillywhally, giving him permission to place and maintain an electric line above or below ground belonging to the Captain. 'The rent during the time the electric line is placed across Tillyrie land the first party (James Black) shall pay above ground per annual sums per pole; a) wholly arable land with interference to agriculture 5/- per double pole, 2/6 per single pole and 1/- per stay. b) alongside dykes hedges and fences where no partial interference to agriculture 2/6 a double pole, 1/6 per single pole and 9d per stay. And below ground the annual sum of 1/- each 100 yards or part of. To be paid half yearly Whit and Martinmas.'

'The line was to be as in plans, maintained and used by the 1st party under provision of Electricity Supply Act 1882/1928. It shall be maintained and kept in good repair. The first party answer all claims for accidents damages or injury, and pay compensation or make good any damage or injury. The rent payable shall include any payment required in respect of interference with agriculture, shooting and game rights. The first party shall on 3 days notice lob/fell any trees which obstruct working of line, and pay for any tree felled at reasonable cost which shall be mutually agreed or arbitration if disagree. First party can on one months notice remove his line. The proprietor can give 6 months notice to remove the line. The Arbitration (Scotland) Act 1896 shall apply to arbitration.'

In August 1933 his son David Matale Reid married Elsie Joy Reid, the daughter of his aunt Jean, and her husband David Reid of Sevenoaks in Kent. The Captain and his mother were against the marriage, their being too closely related, but Joy was adamant. Captain Reid expected his son would one day take over from him and offered them Nether Tillyrie House, but Joy had no intention of living near the disapproving relations. They resided at David's Newhall Farm, Chirk in Denbighshire.

His mother died on 2nd August 1934 at Thomanean. She was 89 and had lived a very full life. Life at Kandy must have been exciting with the start of the tea plantations and the making of railways. Her eldest son was just two, and her second son on the way when they came home in 1881, due to her husband's health. Moving to Thomanean their home for the next 53 years, their family grew four daughters, Jean, Maria, Elsie and Janet, and two sons Robert and William.

She saw her daughter Jean married to David George Alexander Reid of Bishops Cottage, Sundridge, Sevenoaks in Kent, a cousin of some degree, and Elsie married to Mr Webb, a vet in the south. Her son William had served through the Boer War and been killed in World War One, and buried at home with honour and dignity. Robert had married Janie Macfie, but it came to a sad end with her death giving birth to twins, the survivor being sent under Maria's wing to bring up at Thomanean. She saw her daughter Janet serve in the Queen Alexandra's Nursing Corps driving an ambulance in Flanders. Maria and Janet lived with her to the end, while Robert and son David grew up at Thomanean.

In her time she had helped build St Paul's Church in Kinross, to which she also gifted an organ and later a sum for its upkeep. There are beautiful staineglass windows there, dedicated to different members of the family. They include her husband's natives in reference to Ceylon, and the colours are beautiful.

The Brand School, started in 1860 with a gift of £200, was opened in April 1863 by which further donations were received from the Brand family, but by the 1900s the school needed investment to bring it to modern standards. Maria gave the money, and the Junior school was named the Reid Memorial School after her husband, and there is a disposition for this in 1914. This was known locally as 'the wee school' (the kindergarten classes) and the 'big school' for older pupils was up Manse Road.

In 1927 her son-in-law David Reid borrowed £7,000 sterling from her, at 5% p.a. at Whit and Martinmas in case of failure. The security for this was that Jean Reid, his wife:

> *...conveyed and made over absolutely in favour of my mother Maria Johnston Reid, the whole of the share of the residue of the estate heritable and movable of the late David Reid, my father, left and bequeathed by him to me under his trust Disposition of 23 November 1886 and with codicil dated 18th October 1887.*

> *Further security of the personal obligations of the said David G.A. Reid written before I, Robert Matale Reid Esq of Tillyrie, hereby dispone to and in favour of the said Maria Johnston Reid the heritable but redeemable as after mentioned: 1. the whole of the land of Little Tillyrie; 2. Hall Greig; 3. 8 merk of lease of Over Tillyrie; 4. Meikle Tillyrie; 5. Spring of Bartwell *in a field of Holton; 6. Easter Room of Over Tillyrie; 7. All of the lands once belong to Michael Balfour; 8. Room of Over Tillyrie once belonging to Alexander Dron; 9. the triangle of land of Hall Greig, lying on the north side of the road.*

> *On default in Payment I, the said Robert Matale Reid, grant power of sale.*

> *Signed: David G A Reid and Jean Reid.*

This massive trust within the family, for something important to Jean and David was discharged in 1930. Maria gave half the sum of £7,000 to each of her unmarried daughters Maria and Janet, while Robert would be relieved of security over the estate of Tillyrie, and Jean of her father's trust of 1886/87.

Maria Reid died on 2nd August 1934 at Thomanean. The Government requisitioned Thomanean House from 1939-45. It was then sold to Mr Bosomworth, a well-known auctioneer who lived there until 1957. The farm was sold in 1935 by Mr Fisher to a Mr Lambie of Dalqueich, and his cousin Alexander Harley subsequently inherited it. Alexander Harley, a local grain merchant, bought the aeroplane hangars a few years later from a shut-down Balado Aerodrome, and eventually bought the house at Thomanean as well. The Harleys, father and son, built an international grain business there, and the family are still at Thomanean. The farm of 310 acres (276 arable) was sold for an upset price of £4,500 in 1935.

There would be many in the county who would miss Maria Johnston Reid, not only her family and friends but also the poor to whom she gave support.

The Captain added to Tillyrie House, and there is a photo taken in 1935 of him and the farm staff in the front paddock, and in the background there are workers putting up the attic. This extended the house, up a stair to an attic the length of the house, with a room to the right taking up about one third of the length, and the attic reached out the back over the kitchens and bedroom above.

The Captain is sitting on the grass with his dogs about him, J. Rugg his greive beside him, and two loons (young lads), then a tractor and with Patrick Stables leaning on it, then all the horsemen with their horses beside them. In the background is the steading as tidy as could be, and not a straw out of place, as good as new.

Patrick Stables was a man from Banffshire who came to Tillyrie in the early 1930s. Taking up his story awhile, he gives a good picture of life on a farm at that time.

> *Farms were often described by how many horses were needed; a two pair was a small farm whereas six pair was a very large farm. There was a well ordered hierarchy over which farm servant was responsible for which pair. In general, the youngest and least experienced employee or Orraman was entrusted with the sixth pair (on a very large farm) and all the way up to the most experienced and capable employee who would take pride in working the first pair. In charge of the whole manual workforce was the Grieve. He was the link between the workforce and the farmer.*

> *The Orraloon means a boy or youth, and was given menial tasks round the farm. Very often this would include taking care of the chickens, mucking out the byre and stables and occasionally helping the kitchen maid or kitchie-deem with her more physical tasks. It was thankless work and every Orraloon couldn't wait for the day when another boy, younger than him would be brought in to take over his role and allow him to move up to the meatier and more masculine job of Orraman.*

At this point, it is worth reflecting on the almost unique style of recruitment involving farm servants at that time in the twentieth century. Because there were no written contracts of employment and terms of employment only usually lasted six months, farm servants tended to move around a great deal, though only within a range of about ten square miles. Consequently, over the period of a full working life, a worker could have experienced the working conditions on as many as 20 to 40 farms.

> *Young and unmarried farm servants were accommodated in a bothy in the farm steading. This tended to be a very basic building with typically primitive eating and sleeping facilities. Farmers were often accused of treating their stock of horses and cattle better. Depending on how many were using it, it may have had one or two double beds which the young*

men were expected to share. Few had running water and any water re-
quired for drinking or cooking had to be obtained from the horse trough
which in some instances could be quite a walk away. Of course, there
was no flushing toilet and the best these lads could expect was a bucket
(pail) with a roughly formed seat on it and located somewhere 'oot the
back'.

The bothies were mostly self-catering, though at busy times of the year, such as ploughing, sowing or harvesting, one or more of the married workers' wives was given the additional task of providing nourishment for the hard-pressed loons.

A kist, a wooded box approx 1200 x 500 x 600mm, with handles at both ends, some internal compartments and usually a lock, would occupy some prominent position in the bothy, mainly as they doubled up as useful seats around a central table. Some bothy loon also had another smaller box called a 'mealer'. This was designed to contain quantities of oatmeal, flour and other grain commodities. One of the perks of the farming industry was to supply each servant with free oatmeal, potatoes and milk. Because refrigerators were still developing in the minds of the inventors, milk was supplied on a daily basis whereas oats were provided every six months.

As an Orraman, his first ambition would be to graduate to the position of Horseman. The most junior employees worked with the least effective pair of horse. His time with the lowest ranking pair would depend on his age, experience and ability. As soon as these criteria were met, he would move up a pair and so on until after many years in a variety of roles and situations he would be entrusted with the very pinnacle of a horseman's ambition – in charge of the first pair!

A horseman's duties meant getting up between four and five in the morning cleaning out the stables, carting the dung to the dung heap, watering, feeding and grooming his horses. He would then go home for his own breakfast, then back to tack up his pair and out to the fields to plough, harrow and cart or whatever the time of year demanded. The horses were 'yoked' at seven and worked until noon, taken to the stable after watering and, after being given a feed, would rest until one. In the afternoon the horses were yoked at one and worked until 'loused' at five for the night. The horses would be watered at the horse trough, cleaned up, bedded for the night and fed. It would be about six before the men ate. In the winter, work started later at eight and finished at four, using the daylight. It may seem a long day for the horses but remember a good Clydesdale never went out of a walk as he was pulling his cart or plough, and the men would stop for a 'piece' mid-morning and again about three in the afternoon, and they were fit horses. On a Sunday a rota was set out for some to water, feed and muck out morning and night. It was a day of rest for the horse so no midday feed was given, but the horse would have more hay for the day, this was to prevent Monday morning disease or tying up.

In 1932 Patrick moved south to work for Captain Reid at Tillyrie. At 37 he was skilled with the horse-drawn plough, and won awards in competitions for the best-dressed pair of horse in full harness and highly polished tack. In addition to his work with horses, Patrick established a much envied skill in building stacks. He was happy here, and indulged his interest in motorcycles again. He courted Flora at Blairgowrie where she worked as a domestic servant at Tower of Lethendy, and they married in November 1934.

After a short honeymoon they moved into a house at Tillyrie, luxurious accommodation reserved for married servants, a 'cottar hoose'. Flora had the job of providing meals, washing and cleaning the bothy along with other married wives on a rota. Their first child Catherine was born on 4th December 1935 in the cotter house, and christened at Orwell Kirk, Milnathort. In 1936 the Stables family moved to a Grieve job near Auchterarder.

Their grandson Don Kinnersley came in 2018 asking about his grandparents who had worked at Tillyrie in the 1930s. We were able to show him the photo of 1935 with his grandfather in it, and we could tell him that Matale was built as the bothy in 1929, so this was the house that Flora kept. Flora was in hospital in Perth, Australia aged 82. He sent the photos he had taken and copy of the 1935 one to her in Australia and wrote to say she was delighted.

Mechanisation with the introduction of tractors used in place of horses were, by the 1930s, much in evidence in rural Scotland. Horsemen were expected to become tractormen almost overnight. Very little training was given to those entrusted with operating these 'noisy, smelly and often unreliable metal monsters'. Patrick said he 'was never warm again after tractors came'. He preferred horses. The sheer physical effort preparing and working horses meant continual exercise and generated body heat for animals and handlers. The early tractors provided none of that, and in summer conditions some benefit for being able to sit down for most of the working day, but in winter and wet days without shelter for the driver it was a long day for the driver. Even wrapped in warm waterproof clothing, he was exposed to driving rain and snow.

In March 1936 Captain Reid looked into the private water supply for the whole estate. He had some time previously sent gauging of springs that make up this supply to D.M. Hutchison, of Smith St Kinross, who were in contact with David A. Donald Esq, of West George Street, Glasgow. After some further exploration into rainfall in the preceding period, an analysis of the water confirmed 'that the colourless of a pure neutral moderately soft water is free from contamination, conformed well above purity standards of bacterial counts and that this supply, in our opinion, is an excellent one and suitable in every respect for domestic and dietetic purposes.'

Seemingly the original source failed at the end of September 1933, and digging for new springs took place in the first week of October, the piping and joining during the second week, and a week was allowed for this to remain open before Hutchison built brickwork round the new supply. There is a book *Improvement of Water Supply to Upper Tillyrie* by A.E. Hutchison & Son, Contractors,

Kinross, detailing all the work and the cost. It runs to 86 pages and the total cost of the work was £2,172 1s 7d.

The water was collected from the three springs to a collecting chamber, where it was piped to a big tile-lined tank in the top of what is known as the Tank Field, from where gravity took it down the side of the fields underground to the glen. In the glen was a valve where the water could be turned off, before following the boundary hedge west of Newton (known then as the bungalow) to the road, where it split to supply Wester Tillyrie and flowed down to Upper Tillyrie Steading. The houses were all on this supply as all were on the Tillyrie Estate.

Over the years the Captain had built roads from Upper Tillyrie Steading, past the duck pond he had built, up past the dipper and along the Earl Haig field, on up to the Holton march (it would have followed the ancient road to Perth to this point in the old days) and on up the side of the Spratis Muir field to the Front Hill. The second road went from the east of the stackyard at Wester Tillyrie and west of Balfour Cottage, up through the Glen Field and followed the burn up the Athron Hall fields to the top of the Quarry Field, and on to the west side of the front hill joining a track on the back hill to Carleith. These gave access to the fields whatever the cropping.

The back hill was ditched and drained and the wet area improved, while leaving the natural heath and flora. A track ran from the west entrance, where there was a sheep-handling area, to the burn at the foot of Carleith Hill.

There are photographs of the Holton side of the front hill being harrowed and sown down to grass (and natural white clover) with Clydesdale horses. There are three pairs harrowing and one horse in the seed barrow. Captain Reid's Old English sheepdogs appear in the background, and in one Captain Reid watching. The hill was 50 acres and went up 200ft in half a mile. These men were fit walking behind these horses all day.

Captain Reid also added another wing to the house, with an upstairs sunny room for a housekeeper, a toilet with hand-basin, and downstairs a walk-in cupboard with shelves and a secure place behind under the stairs, and an outside door opposite a room called the 'dogs room' with a sink, folding table for grooming in a sunny, south-facing location. He also added a bathroom, with panelled walls on the lower half for the housekeeper. This gave him and her privacy.

In 1937 the Bethune family came to Tillyrie, six-year-old James and his parents. Mr Bethune was from Aberdeenshire. The Captain liked to employ men from that area. Mrs Bethune was to milk the 12-16 cows kept to supply the estate with fresh milk. At first the Bethune family was housed at Wester Tillyrie, then moved to the bungalow (Newton) where the maintenance man for the estate used to live. This gave Mrs Bethune less of a walk in the dark in winter, and young James grand places to play in the large garden and outhouses.

The cows were milked in the byre by the old house which held 11 cows with slate stalls, clay troughs and a grip leading to a door into the cattle court for mucking out. The cows would need hand-milked morning and night, and the milk distributed to the Big House and the workers daily. There was a dairy at the rear of the Big House, with stone shelves where the milk would cool, (and cream skimmed off as needed), and probably cans filled for each household.

The Bethune family sometimes stayed in the Big House when the Captain went away on business trips to do with the Ceylon Tea Company, often away in London for days. Sometimes Mrs Bethune helped out in the house, when Captain Reid had trouble with housekeepers.

James Bethune looked after the young horses at Wester Tillyrie. The mares and foals were kept in the stalls next to the old house, and foaled in the main steading in the big boxes. Then they ran in the front paddock with their foals. On weaning the foals were sent to Wester Tillyrie to a cattle court beside the big one. James's job was to bed them with peat, and put them in and out to a field opposite. He said they were well-handled, which was just as well as one night there was thunder and lightning and he just opened the gate and they crossed the road and came in on their own.

Young James had scarlet fever and was taken in the closed hospital ambulance to the fever hospital in Gallowhill Road. In the days before antibiotics the only way to prevent contagious infection was isolation, and the corrugated–iron buildings surrounded by a tall wall, built in the early twentieth century as a fever hospital was the answer. He was weeks lying on his back and the only contact with the outside world was through the closed window. He was happy there except for the food: cold porridge for breakfast and solid, cold semolina pudding for lunch. Once he was more mobile he found the rhubarb patch and gooseberry bushes in the garden.

When asked what Captain Reid was like, he replied 'Captain Reid was a real gentleman, unless you were wrong then you knew about it, a real swearing.'

Captain Reid once almost sacked a cattleman because he had not cleaned out a water trough, as he had had to drink 'stinking' water during the war. He was really angry.

Another incident involved a badger which lived in the Red House Wood, and the Captain kept it like a pet. Donald Urquhart (the forester) shot it one day and the Captain was incandescent with rage. Donald Urquhart stayed working up the hill for days 'til the Captain calmed down.

In 1935 the Kinross and Minathort Rifle Club was opened by Captain Reid on 6th October, which founder member Tom Walker remembered in his book. The Rifle Club stayed at their Rifle Range in Old Perth Road, Milnathort for 70 happy years, with a good membership.

As already stated the Captain bred Aberdeen Angus cattle. He had a herd of pedigree cows and bought good bulls over the years. As a breeder he was always trying to improve his stock, and studied the bloodlines within the country to this end. He registered his stock in the Aberdeen Angus Register, and Rema's Ruby of Tillyrie by Enrocador and Rema's Belle of Tillyrie by Ballintomb Bellman were just two.

In 1937 he won the class for an Aberdeen Angus born on or after 1st December 1934 and before 1st December 1935 at the Royal Highland Show at Alloa with 'Edmonton of Bleaton'. In 1937 with the same bull he won the Challenge Cup for the best bull of any age and also a silver medal, again winning his class on the way. He was also 3rd with a younger bull 'Everlonging of Bleaton' at Dumfries, where the RHS was held in 1938. In 1939 in Edinburgh his cow 'Evening Thimble of Tillyrie' was 4th in her class, and a special £10 award was given to his bull.

The clouds of war were again over Europe, and Captain Reid was 60 years old when war broke out on 1st September, with Germany's invasion of Poland. He was too old for active service, but helped where he could, including the shooting practice at Thomanean. The Home Guard had .22 rifles from Tom Walker, and the experience for some was a first and for others good practice. One commented about Captain Reid: 'there were always lots of dogs, he was a great man for dogs'. He used to produce a bottle after we finished shooting for those who liked a dram'.

Captain Reid was a member of the Milnathort Special Constables with 15 other locals. They were Harry Braid (farmer at Tarnhill), Teddy McCall, Willie Coull (fishmonger), Alexander Duff (headmaster) George Baxter (agricultural engineer) Sandy Harley (seedsman) Steve Young (farmer in Mawcarse) Sergeant McPherson, Jimmy Gordon, John Cowie, Willie Hamilton (butcher), George Fernie (builder), Arthur Morrison and PC Andrew Stalker.

The first Scottish target to be attacked from the air was the Forth Railway Bridge. Fortunately, it was not hit, but as the bombers did not have enough fuel to get home to Germany any extra bombs were dropped before they returned. There were at least eight known bomb-sites in Kinross-shire, mainly in the country and nobody killed, although the one at Tillywhally shattered windows in Milnathort. Known sites included an anti-aircraft shell which landed at Fruix said to have been fired by HMS Hood at anchor in the Forth. A bomb landed at Coldrain Farm only 300yds from Hatchbank, Mawhill, Portmoak Moss as well as Tillyrie, where the crater is still massive despite the ploughing in the 80 years since.

James Bethune remembered the night a doodlebug landmine landed on the march between Tillyrie and Tillywhally, blowing a tree clean out of the ground. The horsemen were quick to have lengths of rope cut off for their lines (reins), and villagers were quick to help themselves to the silk parachute.

The most celebrated false alarm came on the night of 7th September 1940, just as the blitz on London was beginning. The signal "Cromwell" signifying conditions right for invasion was interpreted by the army that the assault had actually begun. The country now in alert, the Kinross Home Guard carried out exercises in preparation for invasion and built up armaments. The fear of invasion was constant in folks' minds.

Kinross-shire did its bit during the war. There was an army camp at Turfhills, an ammunition dump at Mawcarse Station, a Free Poles camp at Arlary, a prisoner-of-war camp at Fruix, the aerodrome at Balado, and anti-aircraft batteries at Orwell, Cleish Castle and Fruix, all within the small county.

'During February 1941 the first sub-machine guns and Northover Projectors were received. Traffic control was started, and owing to the large area covered by the company and to the number of main roads passing through, it was, and remained a heavy commitment.' (*Source: Book About Home Guard*) The cross at Milnathort where the Stirling Road, the road from Perth, and the Edinburgh road via Kinross meet was always a important police block even in peaceful times when prisoners escaped from Perth prison or such emergencies.

By July the Home Guard were part of the Crown Forces and subject to military law. Additional rifles and bayonets were received. Kinross-shire now held 144 rifles, with 10,000 rounds of small-arms ammunition. The operational role of the company was to deny the enemy the towns and villages in the area, to hold certain road blocks and to guard vital points such as telephone exchanges and bridges. Training consisted of Foot and Arms drill and .22 rifle shooting. Great assistance was given by regular military groups such as the Black Watch, stationed in the area.

The first full-scale exercise of the Company was held on 16th February 1941, when 400 Polish troops acted as the enemy, and with Bren carriers representing tanks, attacked road blocks and defence points in the Company area. This exercise was most instructive. Officers of the Black Watch stationed in Milnathort acted as umpires.

In April 1942 the first Invasion Committee was held. In June, two wireless sets were lent to the unit by the Commandant of the Balado Bridge Aerodrome for the purpose of closer communication. On 30th August, an invasion exercise was held at Milnathort which had now become a focal point.

Poles were erected in the flat fields, for example at Turfhills and Balado, to prevent planes or parachutists from landing. They were just a nuisance to farmers.

An Observation Corps – a separate unit – manned 24 hours a day, was on a hill north of Milnathort (on the hill at Nether Tillyrie, in the field called The Hostel), and there were listening instruments to trace aeroplanes the moment they approached, The observer on duty phoned through to HQ at Pitreavie. Members of the Observer Corp included Jack Shepherd, Jimmy Henderson (gardener at Tillywhally), Andrew Mathieson (tailor in Milnathort), George Rollo (hen-farmer at Croft Martin), Charlie Archibald (draper) and Tommy Duncan (blacksmith). George Temple (postmaster) and Arnold Henderson (ironmonger in Milnathort) were both stationed at May Island Observatory Post.

Balado Bridge Aerodrome's contribution to the war was a very large number of highly trained Spitfire pilots, many of them Polish, and many finished up with distinguished war records.

The aerodrome had the minimum of red tape and spit and polish. Morale was high as was the number of hours spent in the air. Some of the flying could be described as distinctly hairy and the instructors felt on many occasions they would be safer fighting the Germans.

The Germans dropped flares at the aerodrome but the planes were all hidden round the perimeter of the fields. They might also have been looking for the railway line, as Kinross was an important junction at the time.

While at Balado the RAF had Spitfires and a Lysander. This Lysander flew out every morning, trailing a drogue behind it, for firing practise. The drogue was at the end of a long rope – a very long rope. Some evenings when it came back there was no target left, only a bit of the end. The Lysander flew back and forward between the Bass Rock and the North Sea, and Hurricanes fired at it. Their bullets were painted with different colours, so they could tell from the holes who had hit it."

Films were shown on Sunday evenings in the Town Hall. Newsreels at the County Cinema (Kinross) were largely concerned with the war and the war effort. One lad remembered seeing his brother in the 51st Highland Division Pipe Band of the Black Watch entered Sfax in North Africa.

Windows in houses and the school were criss-crossed with sticky paper to minimise flying glass due to bomb blast, and blackouts of different materials and construction were used at night.

In January 1944, four anti-tank rifles were received.

During the spring, Exercise Hawk was carried out with the RAF at Balado Bridge to test the intercommunications between the Home Guard and the RAF, and to test the aerodrome defences.

The attacking force, under the Company Commander, consisted of Company HQ's three mobile battle platoons and one mobile sub-artillery unit. The start was at Cleish, and the company moved to contact from there. They were ground strafed by Spitfires. The attack on the aerodrome was at dusk and the defenders used a large numbers of Very lights. Both used these; the ground strafing was very instructive and the objects of the exercise successfully achieved.

During the summer, a course for snipers was run at Blairadam Rifle Range.

Tanks belonging to the Tank Corps suddenly appeared in Lethangie fields camouflaged under the trees, near Milnathort Station. There were men of the Duke of Wellington's Regiment there for a short time, and Poles too. Later the tanks were parked in Baxter's yard, off South Street, and when they were being driven up the street the windows of the houses were broken by stones and mud flying off the tracks.

'The Poles once attacked Milnathort in an exercise. They stormed over the Kirk Hill and captured Burleigh Castle, with top military officers supervising. Sawdust 'bombs' were flying through the air. I saw it all because I lived at Burleigh.' *(Andrew Kerr)*

'The Poles were popular too. We played football with them. They wore hairnets and scent and talcum powder but that was just their way. They weren't cissies.'

'One night the Milnathort unit (about 40 men) attacked the Dump at Mawcarse. There were guards and outposts everywhere – on the bridge over the railway, at their own special siding at the station, and at our siding where we normally loaded potatoes onto trains. We knew this bit of country very well, and we went up the burn very quietly, at one side of the station, then used the wagons as cover to get right up to the house which was the officer's office. When we got near, Dave Croy threw a stink bomb through the half-open window, and they all came running out. But after the stink had cleared away, they invited us all in for a mug of tea!'

During the night in the winter of 1942/43 the men at Tillyrie were woken by the driver of the Sanatorium van at 2am. The steading was on fire. They managed to save most of it, but the middle section with the straw in the loft was lost.

Captain Reid comforted an employee by reminding him that he always had a lid on his pipe when he smoked, so it was not his fault.

Mr Bethune (senior) had a big red tractor at the time, on the Lend Lease the Americans set up as a help to the UK before they entered the war.

The *London Gazette* announced on 3rd November 1942, in a Scottish Home Department, St Andrew's House, Edinburgh dated 28th October: The King having been pleased to approve the appointment of Robert Matale Reid, esquire, J.P., D.L., of Tillyrie, Milnathort, to be Vice-Lieutenant for the county of Kinross, a Commission in his favour bearing the date 24th October, 1942, has been signed by the Lord Lieutenant.

In 1944 the Agricultural Wages Board was instituted by the government, which brought in weekly wages and payment for overtime. This virtually killed off the 'feeing markets' and provided farm labourers with more favourable living conditions.

The building of stacks was an art that few had and many aspired to. The sheaves were flung up to the builder as he worked his way round and up to the crest, and his skill in making it waterproof and finished with a thatch was his pride and joy. On a Sunday the men often went round the neighbours land, looking at their stacks. Many a fisticuffs started at the pub on a Saturday night on a chance remark expressed on the subject.

There was a pond this side of the bridge over the burn as you leave the steading and go down the slope, and white ducks swam and lived there. Every Saturday the horsemen took the horses to the pond and cleaned their feet and feathers (the long hair on a Clydesdale's legs). The Captain didn't like to hear them stamping itchy feet in the stable at night, and Lord help the man who left his horse with dirty legs which could become infected.

One day he noticed one employee did not have much to do and encouraged him to join the army. The chap joined up, and as the war in Europe was about finished, served in Burma.

1947 was one of the coldest winters ever recorded with low temperatures and heavy snowfall. The snow came in February and there were 10ft drifts. Without modern machinery, it brought hardship to all. Folk were shut in for weeks.

After the war the Captain had an American army Jeep, and he and his dogs were a daily sight going about the place. Top dog Bleaton, a well-boned black and white border collie with freckles on his white bits, sat in the front seat beside his master, and the other dogs in the back all enjoying the outings. There are grave-stones behind the roadside hedge, under the holly trees by Tillyrie House of dogs he had over the years, and buried with respect.

He asked John Lawrie in Burleigh to come by the Middleton Road and walk in to meet him in a certain field. When John arrived somewhat bewildered the Captain said 'Young man, I have been watching and I like what you have done at Burleigh and East Brackley. I am getting on and would you be my tenant here at Tillyrie. I have no wish to move out of my house and just wish a tenant to farm it.'

John Lawrie was delighted to come to an arrangement, and further meetings were forthcoming to work out the details. Captain Reid dispersed his Aberdeen Angus herd and the Highland cows on the back hill. He built a byre and dairy unit next to the main steading with a tin hay shed attached, with a plaque 'to the glory of God, Matale 1878-80' on the end above the door. The sheep stayed and all the men except the shepherd were taken on, the shepherd having produced tups for sale. John Lawrie, only having a commercial herd, said the shepherd was over-qualified for his work.

John Lawrie signed the agreement on 14th October 1947, came in as tenant in 1948, and established a herd of pedigree Ayrshire cows. Captain Reid had a good relationship with his tenant, one based on mutual respect.

Captain Reid made his will on 29th December 1948. His trustees and exec-utors were:

> David Matale Reid of Newhall, Chirk, Denbighshire, and William Brown my debts and funeral expenses. Woodlands Kinross, Robert Pearse Anderson Writer in Kinross.
>
> They pay my debts and funeral expenses.
>
> Bequests ; Transfer ordinary shares in Ceylon Tea Plantations Ltd
>
> My Housekeeper Celia Kilgour Campbell, if still in my employment at my death, 3,000 ordinary shares.
>
> The Rev William Norris, 250 ordinary shares
>
> Dr John W. Millar, Ramshawe, Kinross, 100 ordinary shares.
>
> John F. Watson, veterinary surgeon, Ballingall House Milnathort, 100 ordinary shares.
>
> Robert Pearson, 100 ordinary shares.
>
> All to be handed over free of legacy and government duties as conven-iently after my death.
>
> The residue of my means and estate including my estate of Tillyrie and the whole farm stock, crops and implements, furniture and other to my said son and that his own absolute property, And I direct my trustees of

the Rev William Norris should find it convenient to conduct my funeral to pay him in advance the sum of £20 to meet his travel and other expences.

Witnesses: James Milroy (Teller) and Andrew Mitchell Smith (Clerk) Both at The British Linen Bank Kinross

Codicil 1. Cecilia Kilgour Campbell revoke the 3,000 ordinary shares in Ceylon Tea Plantation Ltd, and make over to her 200 ordinary shares in Ceylon Tea Plantation Ltd, if she is in my employment at my death. Dated 10.1.49

Codicil 2. Cecila Kilgour Campbell. Pay her £1000 free of duty in addition to the shares in the Ceylon Tea Plantation Ltd. Dated 15.11.49

Witnesses: Ann Kedar Watson. (Secretary, East Brackley) and Andrew Thomson (Grocer, Milnathort).

Captain Reid died on 24th December 1949 aged 70.

David Matale Reid and his wife Joy had two daughters Jane and Sarah, and a son Robert, who was born with a severe brain injury and never left hospital care until his death at 14. They had continued to live at Newhall Farm, but now moved to The Gelli, Tallarm Green, near Malpas, Cheshire.

In 1951 Miss Janet Reid, had lived with her sister Maria at old Duncreive House after their mother's death in 1934. With the deaths of Maria and Robert she now wanted to come back to Tillyrie and so rented Tillyrie House from David.

The legal agreement which said she was already residing in the house at Upper Tillyrie, states:

...the range of buildings near the house and the ground adjacent, all lying to the south of the service road leading to the Farm of Tillyrie, also with the vegetable garden lying to the north of the said road.

The house and other buildings are to be used for private residential purposes only.

The date of commencement of this let is the term of Whitsunday 1955 being the 28th day of May. The let shall continue until the first term of Whitsunday or Martinmas occurring not less than three months after the date of the death of the said Miss Janet Reid.

The rent for the period of let shall be £100 payable half yearly.

The tenant shall be entitled to all rights reserved to the landlord under Minute of Lease between Robert Matale Reid esquire of Tillyrie, and John Lawrie dated 14th October 1947, and also to take firewood from plantations on the farm.

The landlord will keep the said buildings wind and watertight and will uphold the watersupply and drainage thereof so far as the external to the buildings. The tenant shall have the right to make alterations or im-

provements to the internal arrangements of the house as she may think suitable subject always to the consent of the landlord which will not be unreasonably withheld.

The tenant accepts the subjects as satisfactory in all respects and binds herself to keep and leave the same in good tenantable, habitable and working repair and condition to the satisfaction of the landlord, ordinary wear and tear excepted.

Miss Janet Reid lived at Tillyrie House until October 1973 when she died here. She loved to walk about the farm with her spaniel, way up the hill and 'vaulting' over the gates, as John Lawrie remarked, enjoying her pleasure of the place.

She kept the garden with its box hedges round the two big beds and following the walls giving beds all round about six feet deep. The top border was herbaceous plants with a small greenhouse in the east corner. The big beds contained a large strawberry bed, vegetables and soft fruit; and the other, rows of peonies with clumps of asters for autumn colour and a big bed of roses which had tulips planted for the spring. Donald Urquhart was her gardener. He had worked for the Captain as forester.

As well as her gardener she had a housekeeper Annie Fowles, a daily and the gardener attended to her car. She drove herself, quite something when she was young, but she had her army experience. There were only three cars at Tillyrie in the 1950s. They belonged to Miss Reid, the Cooks at Athronhall and Mr Munro the shepherd at Balfour Cottage, but they were wary of Miss Reid's driving as she collected her papers at Temples, (the newsagents and stationery shop where Heaven Scent is now) and swung round at the Royal Hotel to return along South Street.

When I married and came to live at Tillyrie in 1965, Miss Reid asked me for coffee. I went in and she was sitting in the drawing room in front of the fire as I was shown in by Annie Fowles. She was very charming but it soon become clear she was quite agitated by a local rumour that she was moving out and I was to get her house. I was quite taken aback, never having heard the rumour or thought of having her house. I said so, and asked her to come and see Matale for herself. She came a day or two later and saw what we had done to the bothy, and was so pleased she asked if she could bring some friends to see it, which she did. Rumour can be so hurtful, and I felt she needed some privacy and so stayed friendly but was never too close.

David and Joy visited her sometimes, and when I had my horses in the two loose boxes opposite the back door of the big house, David would sometimes wander over and talk over the loose box doors until called for supper by Annie Fowles. He was a good-looking and charming man, and pleased when my horse won.

One day, when she was about to take her walk she saw the dairyman Jock MacGarva and asked if there were any bulls out in the fields. He assured her there were none. She left him and went round the corner and met 'Sykes Superior', a full-grown, six-year-old Ayrshire bull. She returned to MacGarva and indignantly remarked he had assured her no bulls were out yet she had met one round the corner! Sykes had opened his pen somehow and gone for a wander, luckily he was good-natured and was put back in his pen with no bother.

When she was about 80, after a visit from David and Joy, she found they had arranged for her driving licence be taken from her. She was devastated and cried, as she only drove locally to see her friends and to collect her paper. It seemed unkind to take her independence away. Her gardener at the time became her chauffeur.

Nether Tillyrie House

When the hospital closed down in 1919, Nether Tillyrie House was leased to the Scottish Episcopal Church as a youth hostel. Miss Pat Eadie met a minister who had been a missionary in Africa and was trained at Nether Tillyrie. It must have been in this era that the field to the south of the house was called the 'Hostel Field'.

The house was leased out to Mr and Mrs William MacAdam when they retired from Athronhall Farm in the early thirties. Their daughter Daisy was married from there, to John Lawrie, in 1936. They later moved to Craigowmill.

David Reid and the trustee for Robert Matale Reid, sold the house in 1951 to Alan Campbell McKay for £3,000. The Disposition reads:

'Alan C. McKay residing at The Green Hotel, Kinross sold and disponed to Mr Alan C McKay and his successors the whole and dwelling house, garden and policies surrounding the same known as Little or Nether Tillyrie.

'Land north of the access of the back entrance to the said house and separated from subjects and used as a cesspool for drainage of the said dwelling house. The Whole of the spring water at Bent Well situated in a field on the lands of Holeton, sometime belonging to Andrew Greig, with full control of the said spring and water thereof as will run having an orifice of not more than 1" in diameter, in connection with the cottage at present belonging to us as trustees, and for the purposes and about the existing steading at Nether Tillyrie as at present used, (but not for watering cattle) and for the foresaid sum of £2 sterling annually beginning Martinmas 1951.

'The trustees declaring that the portion of the feu duty of £19 9s 6d allocated up the subjects hereby desponded amounts to £5.

'Further declare for the existing stob and wire fence bounding the subject disposed on the south and the dry stone dyke and wire fence to the east shall be mutual to us and our successors and the maintained at joint expense for all time coming. The stone and lime wall and wooden fence

*on the north side are wholly in the subjects hereby desponded and shall
be maintained wholly by the said despond."*

Signed by David Matale Reid at Chirk 7th February 1951.

Alan C McKay was home from abroad and lived at Nether Tillyrie until 1962,
when he sold it to Mr Whiteman. The Whiteman family came from Fordell, and
only stayed three years.

The next owners were Mr and Mrs Randal and family. He was a vet in Kenya,
working out in the bush. Rumour has it that when he was posted back to Kenya,
even though war had been declared she took a ship and made her own way out via
South Africa. With great difficulty she arrived in Kenya to join him, despite being
pregnant at the time. She was great fun and full of pluck, so it could well be true.

The night they arrived was misty, and when I went to bring my horses in
they got away from me and were gone awhile before returning. They had clat-
tered from the back paddock, past the steading down the road and up the drive
at Nether Tillyrie, and through the archway, round the lawn and home, all in the
mist and darkness of night. I only found out where they had gone, when Mrs
Randal told me that her mother saw the horses, and they all thought she had been
drinking until they found the footfall on the lawn next day. I had some forking to
undo the hoof marks from the lawn! What a way to meet the neighbours, but Mrs
Randal was so funny and charming about it.

In the big January gale of 1968 Nether Tillyrie lost 27 trees. Gospetry lost
one wing of an L-shaped wood, and the whole country was at a standstill with
trees down everywhere, and hen houses blown away. Even chimneys were blown
down.

Mrs Randal was a widow by 1988 when she sold Nether Tillyrie to the Grahams, and went to live at 'Mini Haha' in Milnathort. She still came up with her
black lab to walk about.

In 1988 Donald and Bridie Graham came one afternoon when John and I
were in the garden, and introduced themselves as our new neighbours. Their two
children were with them, the girl Caitriona stayed with them, but Alasdair ran
down to the wash-green to play with the football. It turned out the children were
at the same school at Haddington as my brother Gilmour's children. It was a fresh
and friendly meeting, and has stayed that way to this day.

A tall, powerful man met us in the yard and introduced himself as Angus
Graham. We knew him for weeks before we knew he was a Duke. He was good
company and really interested in all that happened on the farm. As he got older
he came into the kitchen, saying he walked too far and, sat in the leather lug chair
beside the Esse range, chatted away till he caught his breath then went on his way
home.

From his memoirs he was born 2nd May 1907 in London, much to his dis-
gust. As a Scot he would have been happier to be born in a Scots home. He was
the eldest son of the 6th Duke of Montrose and his wife Mary Louise, the only

daughter of the 12th Duke of Hamilton. The 6th Duke of Montrose designed the first aircraft carrier for the Navy.

Hamilton is the premier Dukedom of Scotland and Montrose is sixth in order of precedence. The 12th Duke of Hamilton left his daughter two estates, the Isle of Arran and Easton in Suffolk, but the rest of the Hamilton land and possessions were entailed so automatically went to the nearest male heir.

Angus was brought up at Brodick Castle on Arran, and when the National Trust took it over and kept it as it was in his mother's time, beside her bed is a photo of Angus as a young man. He enjoyed the stalking and shooting, and the Gaelic language which stayed close to his heart all of his life.

He was educated at Winenford, Eton and came down from Oxford with a B.A. (Agriculture). Both at school and at Oxford he enjoyed success in boxing and rowing. At 16 he joined the Clyde Division Royal Volunteer Reserve when leaving Eton, and was posted to *HMS Revenge* to join *HMS Barham* in the Mediterranean Fleet for six months.

On his return from *HMS Barham* he went up to Oxford. In 1927 he and friends, having sailed over on *SS Antonia*, took the train from Quebec to Winnipeg, then worked their way to Calgary. In 1929 he again went on a working holiday in the Varsity holiday, visiting Arizona with visits to Navajo Indians while working on a dig.

When he came down from Oxford with his degree in 1930, he was posted to Rhodesia (now Zimbabwe) to be a general agronomist with A.E.&J, a subsidiary of I.C.I, with special instructions to investigate the question of pasture grasses.

Before he left he married Isobel in a service at St Giles Kirk in Edinburgh. They travelled by ship for two weeks to South Africa.

When introduced to one customer as Lord Graham, he said 'What – are they sending a blood aristocrat?' So after that he was Angus Graham – who, like all Rhodesians, preferred Christian name terms. When they found he was Lord Graham, they were already good friends.

On 1st January 1932 their eldest daughter Fiona was born and Isobel took her back to the UK for a visit.

With a year of the contract with A.E.&I still to go, Angus bought the 1600 acres of Kildonan Ranch, at 16/- an acre. Borrowing half from the bank, he asked his parents to back him. They wanted him to come back home, and refused. However his mother's mother heard, and sent him £2000, for which she was never forgiven.

In 1936 his parents came out to see them in Rhodesia. By now Angus and Isobel were in a brick house they had built on the ranch. The Duchess, her maid, and her daughter Jean stayed in the house, and the rest of the party in the pole and daaga huts on a ridge three-quarters of a mile away, which they had lived in while building the house. The 6th Duke, who had fought in the South Africa War, did not expect much in rural Africa. But however sportingly his wife tried

MONTROSE FAMILY TREE

DOUGLAS GRAHAM 5th Duke of Montrose b1852-d1925
m Violet Graham of Netherby b1854-d1940

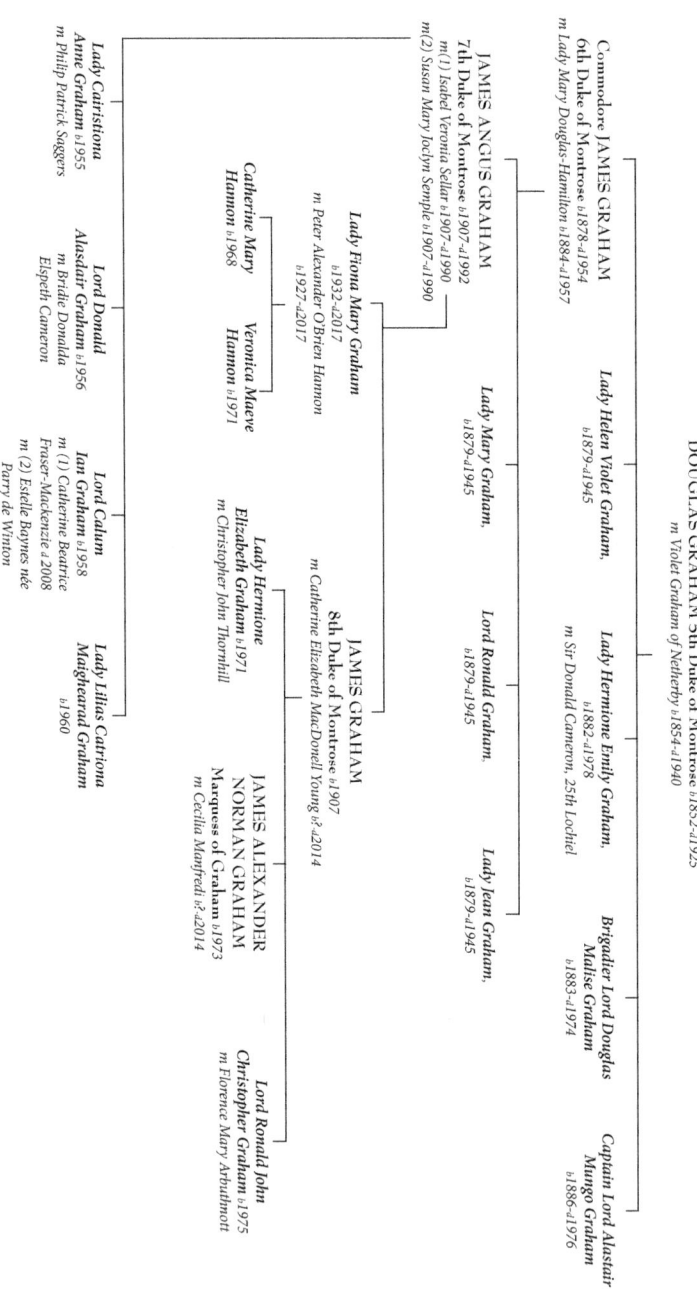

Commodore JAMES GRAHAM
6th Duke of Montrose b1878-d1954
m Lady Mary Douglas-Hamilton b1884-d1957

Lady Helen Violet Graham,
b1879-d1945

Lady Hermione Emily Graham,
b1882-d1978
m Sir Donald Cameron, 25th Lochiel

Brigadier Lord Douglas
Malise Graham
b1883-d1974

Captain Lord Alastair
Mungo Graham
b1886-d1976

Lady Mary Graham,
b1879-d1945

Lord Ronald Graham,
b1879-d1945

Lady Jean Graham,
b1879-d1945

JAMES ANGUS GRAHAM
7th Duke of Montrose b1907-d1992
m(1) Isabel Veronia Sellar b1907-d1990
m(2) Susan Mary Joclyn Semple b1907-d1990

Lady Fiona Mary Graham
b1932-d2017
m Peter Alexander O'Brien Hannon
b1927-d2017

JAMES GRAHAM
8th Duke of Montrose b1907
m Catherine Elizabeth MacDonell Young b²-d2014

Catherine Mary
Hannon b1968

Veronica Maeve
Hannon b1971

Lady Hermione
Elizabeth Graham b1971
m Christopher John Thornhill

JAMES ALEXANDER
NORMAN GRAHAM
Marquess of Graham b1973
m Cecilia Manfredi b²-d2014

Lord Ronald John
Christopher Graham b1975
m Florence Mary Arbuthnott

Lady Catrisitona
Anne Graham b1955
m Philip Patrick Saggers

Lord Donald
Alasdair Graham b1956
m Bridie Donalda
Elspeth Cameron

Lord Calum
Ian Graham b1958
m (1) Catherine Beatrice
Fraser-Mackenzie d 2008
m (2) Estelle Baynes née
Parry de Winton

Lady Lilias Catriona
Maighearad Graham
b1960

to adapt to the rough exigencies of the life they were living – conditions she could never have dreamt of coming her way – the visit was not a success.

When their son Seumas was very ill at just one year old, and Fiona had a near brush with death with appendicitis, it was thought best for Isobel and the children to go back to the UK. Angus would follow when he could. In London they took a small house, and once there he took a job in PR at Rhodesia House. After a while, no longer in love with his wife, he kissed his sleeping children and left to go back to Rhodesia on his own.

With the help of a friend he bought Derry Farm at auction for a cheeky bid of £50 more than the bid of £8000. He then bought ten Trek oxen at £4 each, yokes, trek-chains, a rickety wagon, a plough and a few other tools.

'Boys capable of driving a span of oxen were then considered senior members of a farm gang. Each plough consisted of three twenty inch to twenty-two inch disks which cut through the soil and really turned it over, more like digging than ploughing in the same way as a mould-bored plough would do. One of the ploughs I had bought was really a four-furrow tractor plough, and for eight pounds a head I managed to get sixteen really big Afrikander oxen and the best driver I ever had to handle them.

'There were no roads on the block of arable land which, though later sub-divided, was then one mile from end to end. Each plough had to go five times up and down in the morning and three times in the afternoon and the driver of the four-furrow plough with the big oxen used to like to show off his superiority by overtaking the others and cutting across the unploughed land into the other furrow.

'For those who do not remember the days when sixteen oxen were the main power unit on the farm, let me describe how oxen soon become trained to falling in all facing the same way, and the driver then puts a reim (a rawhide lead) over the horns of each ox. Oxen soon learn to work in pairs that know each other, so the driver would lead out the two lead-oxen first and inspan them, then the two oxen nearest to the plough or wagon (the Aghter oxen) then, pair by pair, the remainder, each in the place to which they were accustomed.

'When all was ready to go, old-time drivers used to have a little bunch of keys on their belt which they would rattle as a sign to the oxen that they must get ready to go, but the modern drivers had other sounds that they employed for this standby movement. Each driver had a long whip with a long lash that he would crack like a rifle shot and then with a high-pitched yell and a crack of the whip, well-trained oxen would, like one, throw their weight into the yoke.

'I remember on one occasion when we were riding maize to the railway siding, a neighbour's wagon in front of mine bogged down. The driver had been lashing away at the oxen with a whip. Some of them had turned round and faced backwards, one or two had lain down and would not get up. In fact the whole team had gone on strike. I asked my neighbour, who was loading the truck if he would allow my driver to take over for a few moments. My driver walked up and down the span, quietly got those oxen that were lying down to get up and those that were facing the wrong way to turn round. He walked up and down again talking to them and then picked up, not a whip but a dry maize stalk and made all the relevant noises to get ready, and let out the starting shout. Every ox jumped forward into the yoke, and out came the wagon.'

It was typical of Lord Graham to understand the men, the training of oxen, and to help a neighbour. He had an interest in every detail of life wherever he was.

In 1939 with all in hand on the farms he went back to the UK. He sailed from Cape Town on one of the Union Castle ships taking a fortnight to get back, arriving on 31st August. He went to his brother's flat in London and, three days later, sat and listened on the radio to Chamberlain announcing that we were at war with Germany.

He and his brother both volunteered and he was given a posting to *HMS Kandabar* as lieutenant RNVR. The ship was about to be commissioned Divisional Leader in Lord Louis Mountbatten's flotilla, the K class fleet of destroyers.

On the 16th May 1940 they sailed out of Devonport, together with *HMS Kingston, Khartoum, Hyperion* and *Hotspur.* Crossing the Bay of Biscay, they refuelled at Gibraltar, went on to Malta and arrived at Alexandria, where they received orders to pass through the Suez Canal and proceed to Aden. They were to be based to convey supply ships up through the Red Sea, for the Italians had eight submarines and eight destroyers based at Massawa in Eritrea.

> 'After a year and a half at sea a letter came from the friend who had power of attorney saying he had to close down my tobacco farm and the Food Production Committee had asked him not to close the maize farm. Another letter this time saying the banks would not advance any more cash to plant the maize crop, and it might be necessary to sell the farms to pay off the overdraft. I replied that if I could only get leave I would gladly come back and see if I could sort things out. However to get such leave I would require a strong supporting letter from the Rhodesian authorities. This might work as I was on Rhodesian terms of service.'

Their usefulness in the Red Sea at an end, the ship moved back to Alexandria and almost at once they were involved in some much more exciting convoy and patrol duties. This included the evacuation of our troops from Greece, after Churchill's design to attack the German forces by advancing up through the Balkans failed. It also included the Battle of Crete, described as the biggest battle of air-versus-sea forces that has ever taken place.

On 13th June he learned his application was given for three months unpaid leave. He '...hitched from Alexandria to Cairo and had to hang around for three weeks after an anti-yellow fever injection before being allowed back into Rhodesia. He then got in touch with some American Air Force chaps about to fly a Lockheed Loadstar down to Rhodesia.' Flying at fairly low altitudes to and over Africa they flew over his farm and landed in Salisbury.

'So unbelievably, on 1st of July 1942, in the middle of the war I found myself back in Rhodesia.'

The bank agreed to extend the overdraft, the Farmers' Co-operative agreed to allow the necessary credit, the Land Bank gave a short term loan and a Highlander friend took on his bond. The staff returned to work with a renewed confidence and things looked up. His farms secure once more, Lord Graham returned to the war.

In March 1943 he was posted as a naval officer to *HMS Janus*. By mid-April the ship was ready to sail, and returned to the Mediterranean. First stop Durban, then Aden, up the Red Sea to Alexandria where they arrived at the beginning of June. They hadn't been long in Alexandria when *HMS Janus* hit a mine in an area meant to have been swept clear, which put her out of further real activity in the war.

'So for the last time down the Red Sea and away south to Durban where we stopped for a couple of days to refuel. I went ashore that evening and ran into some RAF pilots who had come down from Rhodesia to collect a squadron of Oxford training aircraft. Rhodesia was, of course, during the war the principal training area for the RAF and had about a dozen airfields. It was only a couple of days before Christmas and, when I told them Rhodesia was my home, they suggested I fly up with them. I returned on board and asked the Captain if I could have four days' leave and rejoin the ship at Cape Town so I could be in Rhodesia for Christmas. This request was granted.'

After a happy Christmas with his friends he caught a plane and returned to his ship at Cape Town.

They sailed for England the next day and sailed into the Tyne, where the ship was paid off preparatory to the major task of repairing her.

Angus then received an appointment to the Western Approaches Tactical Course in Liverpool, where basic tactics in escorting the Atlantic convoys were taught to 30 officers on each course. On the last few days of the course he received his appointment to Captain of *HMS Ludlow*. The ship was at Rosyth undergoing reconditioning before joining the East Coast Escort Group. During the next two years they took 40 convoys from the Forth to the Thames, 14 to the Humber (mostly from Sheerness), two to Flamborough Head, two to Loch Ewe and two back through the Pentland Firth. Also one to Terneuzen up the Schelde, and a couple of North Sea patrols and numerous short trips. *'It all amounted to a lot of sea time. We had our share of fog, storms and bad weather but most of the time everything went well and according to plan.'*

In 1945, when they were paid off, the Ludlow was to be broken up and Lord Graham managed to source the ship's bell, which he had in his garden, and his cabin chair in his study, to remind him of happy years with some first-class men and officers. Rumour has it Angus asked for Highlanders for his crews, and they had Gaelic spoken onboard except when sending messages out to other ships.

Told he would be lucky to get a passage back to Rhodesia for five months, he got passage on a destroyer in Devonport on 20th September 1945, that was going to Malta. He left her at Gibraltar where he met an Australian pilot flying a Wellington to Heliopolis near Cairo, and hitched a lift. There he ran into the need to have yellow fever vaccinations for the onward passage from Cairo, and had to kick his heels about Cairo and Alexandria for the vaccination to be effective. Thumbing a lift on an army transport to Port Tewfik, he found *SS Capetown* embarking troops for return to Kenya and South Africa. Begging a berth he reached Durban, where his luck was in, and he met some pilots down from the Air Training Fields in Rhodesia, and returning next day. He got a lift with one of them and arrived home within a month and, *'once back, to my veldskoens, khaki shirt and trousers, and the life of Farmer Graham'.*

In 1948 British talk about a Federation of Southern Rhodesia, Northern Rhodesia and Nyasaland woke the interest of Lord Graham to politics. *'The ever-growing chaos in nations up north and the inter-tribal strife made many of us determined to prevent it happening in Rhodesia.'*

'In 1951, after 15 years of asking for my divorce, at last it went through, and I made up my mind it was time to get down to life in earnest. I decided to go back to the UK and find another wife. On my way back to the UK I heard a most charming girl I had briefly met in Kenya at the Nakuru Show Dance before had lost her husband and was now a widow. I carried on with my trip back to the UK, but soon realised that, though I met many charming girls, I would have to go back to Kenya and see again the young widow. I did, and six months later married Susan Gibbs. Susan, who was twenty-three, was the daughter of Dr and Mrs Semple and had a little girl of two, Jocelyn.'

In 1953 they *'went off to Scotland so that Susan could meet my family and I might meet her relatives in Ireland. Her parents were in Malaya.'* They were only half way through their intended stay when a telegram came from the Confederate Party asking Lord Graham to stand for the newly designated Federal Constituency of Umniati. This was the largest of all the constituencies and extended from Chirundu Bridge on the Zambesi to away beyond the battlefields in the midlands, taking a gigantic sweep round his own farm and the west side of Salisbury.

'We all recognised that on the basis of numbers alone, Africans would more and more have to participate in government but the evidence was there for all to see that the rate of handover demanded by them and supported by the British Government meant disaster for one country after another, indeed for the whole of Africa. We determined to oppose this.' Despite sterling work by his wife Susan and friends in December he did not get voted in, and put it down to experience.

So it was back to the farm and the daily tasks of cattle, cultivation and tobacco. In early 1954 his children Fiona and Seumas came for a visit. They were still in South Africa when news came of his father's death on 20th January from a stroke. He travelled to Scotland with Susan and Jocelyn, joining his sister Jean en route from Lusaka, and caught the night train to Glasgow. They were in time for the funeral on the 23rd, and afterwards stayed with his mother at Auchmar. Now Angus was the 7th Duke of Montrose.

Making himself familiar with the estate, with the knowledge of farming in Rhodesia and the help of Bob Hay, then promoted to factor, things looked up. *'I told my mother I thought I could make a go of it, and would renounce any claim I might have to part of the Arran Estate.'* Bob Hay continued to run the estate at Auchar, until it was handed over to Seumas in January 1967.

Leaving for Rhodesia in the middle of May he was asked to give a talk at a political meeting in the local village. There was some confusion as to how he was to be addressed, but to everyone's relief he opted for no change and was 'Lord Graham' for the rest of his public life in Africa.

In 1958 Lord Graham became a member of Parliament and elected a member of the Executive of the Federal Section of the Dominion Party. At this time, Ian Smith was Chief Whip of the United Federal Party, which formed the Government. William Field was the Prime Minister.

In 1959 after a rising of hotheads in Nyasaland in February was contained in a fortnight by the Nyasaland police force and the RAR station there with six fatal casualties among the African population, Lord Graham decided to go over to the UK and make his maiden speech in the House of Lords.

On 24th March he took his seat on the cross-benches, meeting Lord Malvern – who, as Sir Godfrey Huggins, had been for many years Prime Minister of Rhodesia. *As Rhodesians we all pointed out to the British Government how little most of them seemed to know or understand of the African people, and the tragedies that would flow from an all-too-early handover of power to a totally unprepared people.*

'I did my best to explain to their Lordships that what the African nationalists really wanted was never a multi-racial set up on European lines, but an African country with African customs ruled by Africans.' As a result of the debate the British Government appointed a commission under Justice Devlin to report on the Nyasaland disturbances.

1960 brought a referendum in Rhodesia over independence and, with some dubious methods, a Yes vote carried the day. However, when the constitution was finally published it contained two items which had not been in the White Paper at all. One of these items made it quite clear that far from giving Rhodesia independence, it gave the British Government even more authority to legislate for Rhodesia.

In September 1961 Lord Graham represented the Dominion Party at a Conference of the Commonwealth Parliamentary Association in London. *'My main contribution to the debate was in support of the many who tried to warn the British against entering the European Common Market and abandoning trade with preferences with the Commonwealth.'*

In 1962 Field sounded out all those whom he thought genuinely worried about the way things were going in Rhodesia and who were anti-government.

'We met on the 13th March in the boardroom of the Chamber of Mines. To avoid the too-obvious dominance of Dominion Party elements over both Federal and Territorial parties, roughly equal numbers were invited from each group. We discussed a name for the new party and the Rhodesian Front was born.' A committee of four was proposed and once again Lord Graham found himself on a principles and policies committee.

'Later, when Field had gone and Smith became President, most of us realised that any suggestion that the Rhodesian Front was composed largely of old Dominion Party supporters was, to Smith, like a red rag to a bull.'

14th December was surely the wettest of all Rhodesia's polling days but, by the end of the count, the Rhodesian Front were in Government. Lord Graham got the call to be in Cabinet as Minister of Agriculture. On 16th December he started life as the Minister of Agriculture, Lands and Natural Resources.

The Rhodesian Parliament sat four days a week, from 2pm to 6pm and, if there was any urgent unfinished business, it would re-assemble from 8pm to 11pm. *'I was still living on my farm thirty kilometres from Salisbury, and a friend kindly let me stay in his flat when the night session took place.'*

The Ministry of Lands had bought two big estates, where there were already 6,500 purchase farmers. A block of land consisted of roughly 50 acres of arable land and enough grazing for 25 head of cattle. Communal dams were built for fishing and watering stock, and in addition each little farm had a water-point. Roads were put in, boundary fences and communal cattle dip erected and local schools built. The cost of each scheme was divided by three and then by the number of properties to arrive at a cost for each unit. Each property was offered for sale at that price, with payment to be in 20 annual instalments, with no interest due on capital not yet paid-up. Each farm was estimated to provide an 'off the land' living of at least £350 a year. If after seven years the farmer was seen to be successful he could get freehold title. Then, as the owner of property of a value that would more than qualify him for inclusion on the voting registration, both he and his wife could vote.

Sometimes modern science competing with tribal customs failed. When Lord Graham was Minister of Agriculture there were two drought seasons. He tried to get the tribesmen to sell some of their cattle when they were looking well and before the drought took its toll, and put on special sales for them. *'I remember saying to the owner of a particularly large brindle ox that he would get £40 to £50 for it. Your cattle will die if you don't sell them. His reply was "they will not ALL die." The district commissioner told me later "He brought in the ox skin last week and got £3 for it."*

'In the drought-stricken areas the only water available to the cattle was from pits dug in the sand of the dry river-beds. For one or two miles round the villages the land was grazed bare, but I noticed that on the intervening ridges, three or four miles from the rivers, there was still a good cover of grass which, although brown and desiccated, in these low-veldt areas, is still nutritious enough to keep alive game and cattle. The difference was that the game, after coming down to drink, would

move away back to grassed areas, but the Africans were not prepared to drive their cattle the necessary distance away from the village and the water holes. The result was a dust bowl and dying cattle, all within two or three miles radius –and plenty of grass on the ridges three or four miles away from the water holes.'

A born Rhodesian, Ian Smith was the candidate chosen to lead the country into independence. He was not at that time a particularly prominent or popular man with the general public. He was a good sportsman, had a good war record and was politically unafraid to forsake the old establishment when he disagreed with its changed policies.

'We were all loyal to Her Majesty the Queen, and indeed to the British people from whom we came. It seemed to us that the British politicians were jeopardising their own country.'

Field was asked to resign and was replaced by Smith. Very soon they realised that the new man was even more of a lone-wolf than the last. Friends never got close – not even his own Deputy Prime Minister. *'I had experienced little difficulty when Field was Prime Minister in getting Cabinet support for my agricultural proposals and policies. Now I found everything I believed necessary, or wanted to do, was opposed in Cabinet and I soon saw that this opposition was spearheaded by our new Prime Minister.'*

Smith was always quite an artist at double-speak, and seldom made a statement which he could not side-step if later challenged.

Lord Graham was moved to Minister of Defence in the Christmas holiday week of 1965, and started in his new Ministry on 3rd January 1966. The first thing he did was to see the Prime Minister and *'asked what kettle of fish I was being landed with.'* Little did either of them know the head of the CIA was a mole keeping the British well advised of things all the time!

Lord Graham did an inventory of armaments and ammunition supplies, and found to his horror there was only three days ammunition. Assured by Smith that South Africa would let them have any ammunition without delay, Lord Graham asked the Military Attaché at the South African High Commission to go down to South Africa and check this was so. The reply was 'if there was possibility of a British involvement then you had better get anything you need up north of Limpopo without delay.

'In double-quick time two train loads of what was required were ordered and very discreetly unloaded into our magazines at Inkomo and Bulawayo.'

His next requirement was for a supplementary vote to finance the Annual Training Camp for the Territorial Army. *'To my astonishment I encountered considerable opposition, in which the Prime Minister joined:*

"You've already had your share of this year's funds to get that ammunition. You've had your slice of the cake!"

'What on earth is the good of ammunition if we now don't teach the men how to use it?

'Well, in the end I got my funds and, with some modifications for economy's sake, Camp was held.'

Most Africans were on the side of law and order and the Government, and the terrorists could never be sure whether, if they came through populated areas, some fellow Africans would betray their presence. They therefore began their infiltrations through the game reserves, where there were no villages and were unlikely to encounter anyone. The first major infiltration group came across the Zambezi, east of Victoria Falls, in August 1967, and headed through the Wankie Game Reserve. Their presence was discovered and a follow-up ensued lasting five days.

They had to patrol their frontiers and forward camps to which transport could take supplies, and from which a patrol of four or five men looked for signs of entry. On his return from a visit to these camps Lord Graham told his wife of the complete lack of facilities at the camp he had visited. Susan immediately decided to start collecting funds to ameliorate the positions at all forward camps. She got half-a-dozen friends together, and they registered their organisation as 'The Border Patrol Welfare Fund'. This was able to provide refrigerators, stoves, and even small swimming pools, together with recreational gear of all kinds. Lady Susan Graham ran this organisation from their home for ten years and, when she retired, they were asked to a drinks party at which all the forces which had benefited presented her with an inscribed shield indicating their gratitude.

When Lord Graham resigned from Cabinet he had been a Member of Parliament for ten years, six of which were as Minister. With all his Rhodesian funds blocked a pension would have been welcome, but there were no pensions then.

Lord Graham went happily back to farming. His good manager going on to a partnership in another farm, Lord Graham had his hands full. He had just taken over a 27,000 acre ranch, Milsonia. It had a manager but there was still lots of planning to do. He was still growing 60 acres of Virginia tobacco, milking 60 cows, ploughing 800 acres of arable land and fattening 600 head of cattle a year, half reared on the ranch and half bought-in. He also had a stud-herd of Braham cattle, and was building a big shed for grain drying, and (of course) they made all the bricks on the farm.

Other improvements included a night-storage dam with a service area over half an acre. He brought in ESC power to run a pump with an eight-inch pipe from the existing two hundred and thirty-one million dam to fill the night storage dam, from which 75 acres of wheat was irrigated during the dry season.

The ranch was divided into roughly 1,000 acre paddocks, and at one time had 2,300 head of cattle. This was reduced to 1,800 before the two-year drought. He started with Brahman bulls on rough female stock, and after a year or two most were of the cows were Braham-cross. One advantage of this wonderful breed was that they never left a calf behind when being moved or brought in for dipping, a regular job to control the tsetse fly. They did not take kindly to being driven, but would follow if a herdsman walked before them, while two others brought up the rear. The fence had to be solidly cattle-proof, for some old cow would find a weak spot and lead the whole herd out in a rush.

'There was a lot of game on the ranch. In fact there had been five elephants when I took over, but these had to go, as elephants and fences don't go together. There were no buffalo, rhinoceros or giraffes, but almost everything else that you expect to find in that part of the country was there, including two hippopotami in the big pool in the boundary of the river, the Umyati.'

This kept the couple happily busy for the next 27 years, with the births of their four children Kirstie, Donald, Calum and Lilias, who grew up with Jocelyn. The start of the Braham Stud meant they enjoyed many shows with the offspring, and they had a great social life with their many friends in Rhodesia.

Following death threats when Smith's regime ended, the family moved to South Africa and, after two years house searching, the family settled into a small farm in Natal, where they lived, with frequent holidays in Scotland, America and Australia, before the final move to Scotland and Nether Tillyrie House in 1988.

The Duke and his Duchess lived in a small flat at the rear of the house, and had a plaque *'Dukes And Dustmen Only'* at the foot of the stairs. Lord Donald Graham and his wife Lady Bridie lived in the main part of the house with an ever increasing family of Violet (1992), Jennie (1993) and Finlay (1998).

Donald was with Adams Bank in Edinburgh and travelled daily, finding the Megabus (once it evolved) a blessing. He caught it in Kinross and was in Edinburgh hassle-free in half-an-hour and, getting off at the West End, he walked through Princes Street Gardens and arrived fresh at his office, returning when it suited him.

The Duke came to Orwell Kirk twice but found the pews rather small, and so the family were members at Cleish Church. There they were a great asset – Bridie with the Sunday School and Donald became Presbytery elder. For many years Bridie ran a Christmas Nativity Play in locations in Fife, with colourful costumes, real animals and willing volunteers. They were very good and enjoyed by many.

The Duchess was a charming lady who could restore calm in times of trouble with her charm and a little humour to soften the mood. She was a delight to know. She once saw a little box of Matale tea from Sri Lanka and brought it to me, knowing the pleasure she was giving. She always had a cheerful greeting for everybody.

Angus Graham, 7th Duke of Montrose, died in Edinburgh on 10th February 1992, after a year's illness. His love of the Gaelic language ran as an unbroken thread through the whole of his life. Hardly a day passed without him reading, usually aloud, from a few pages, dictionary at hand. He had a wide circle of Gaelic-speaking friends, in spite of spending 57 years in Africa.

His heir Seumas, 8th Duke of Montrose is very like his father to look at, being large and powerfully built. We see him sometimes at Stirling United Auctions selling sheep off his Loch Lomond Estate. Donald, Lord Graham, is finer boned like his mother, but you would know them for brothers.

The Duchess died on 13th March 2014, aged 85.

'She will be remembered by many for her elegance and sharp wit. She is survived by her five children, fourteen grand children and four great-grandchildren.'

The late Duke wrote the following poem to her when alive:

I'll never know the hammer and the tongs
That took you from the crucible of youth
And hammered out the rights and wrongs
On the hard anvil of cold truth
But this I surely know
That heaven's blacksmith blow by blow
Of bright steel forged a lovely girl and gave her life
And she it is I'll love for aye, my own, my darling wife

Lord Angus Graham

Lord Donald and Lady Graham lived in Nether Tillyrie, their family growing up in a happy home with their talents encouraged and appreciated by their parents.

They had a second home in the Highlands near Munlochy in Ross-shire, where they took time out, holidays and weekends, sailing, walking and generally relaxing with their springer spaniels. It was always the plan that when Donald retired they would move up north.

So it was with heavy hearts they put Nether Tillyrie up for sale, and moved away in 2019. They had had over 30 happy years there, but time waits for no man (or woman) and they retired in good health and with plans for the future.

Nether Tillyrie House is now owned by two ladies who combine a mass of knowledge from their busy and interesting lives around the world.

Jina Ramsay, born and educated in Melbourne, Australia, came to the UK and was a company commercial advocate in the 1970s, when she enjoyed the challenges of its male-orientated society.

Veronique von Broekhaven was born in the Netherlands during the Second World War and was brought up in New Zealand. Coming to the UK she practiced as a forensic accountant before retiring. Her love of history, especially the Scottish Civil Wars, drew her to becoming a historian. They are both members of the 'First Marquis of Montrose Society'.

A love of classical music, enjoying visits to the Usher Hall in Edinburgh (the best acoustics worldwide), and interest in books, drew them together 26 years ago.

They moved into Nether Tillyrie house with their collection of over 13,000 books and an equally large collection of music. They are registering a charity with OSCR to form a trust, so that one day the house with books and music can be a national trust for the nation. The library consists of books on history (industrial and economic), intelligence and national security, medicine and biological science.

Their interest in every subject is extraordinary. I left with a book, *Mud Blood and Poppycock* by Gordon Corrigan, and am reading it now. It gives fascinating facts and figures about World War I. Jina found the book right away amongst the multitude of bookcases.

They have plans to extend the laundry beyond the archway up to give a two tier library in keeping with the present house. It is all go, and it will be interesting seeing it all happen.

LAWRIE FAMILY TREE

William Lawrie b1829–d1903 m Isabella Struthers b1833–d1874

Gavin b1857–d1902
m Helen Hamilton

William b1859

James Lawrie b1860
m Agnes Gilmour

Alan b1862
m Ellen Gilmour (twin of Agnes)

Catherine b1891
m Gavin Lawrie

Helen
Catherine
Agnes

Arthur b1894
m Jean Struthers

James
Gavin

William b1896
m Mary Wilson

Jimmy
Jean
Margaret

Isabella b1899
m John Watson

Agnes
Ann

Agnes b1901
m Arthur Braid

Sandy
Agnes
James

John b1903
m Daisy McAdam

Allen b1906
m Margaret Gourdie

Argily
Catherine
Margaret

Constance b1938

Eileen b1941

Dorothy b1942
m John Thompson

John Gilmour b1946

John Mark b1966
m Kathleen King

Jean Catherine b1968
m Euan McGregor

Rebecca Helen b1996

Fiona Catherine b1996

Amy Lawrie b1987

Anna Helen b1990

JOHN LAWRIE

"He would never tell you what to do, just give you advice..."

During the years of plenty, investment in agriculture transformed the landscape. Many farm steadings were built during this time to house livestock, store crops and shelter machinery. Drainage and general improvements to the soil (including lime) were being applied.

With the 1849 repeal laws and the subsequent imports to feed the newly industrialised population in the UK, the economics of agriculture collapsed. As the rich and massive prairie hinterland of the USA opened up, imports of grain in large quantities destroyed the home market. As a direct consequence, the acreage of corn in the UK fell by 25% from 1877-97.

Imported mutton from New Zealand and Australia undercut home production after it became economically possible to ship meat for as little as 2d per 1lb. Similarly, cheap beef from South America undercut the UK market to the extent that there were 20% fewer beef cattle in 1900 than there had been ten years earlier.

Farms fell into dereliction or were reduced to grass as the more expensive grains were abandoned. Many tenant farmers simply vanished, leaving landlords with empty farms.

As they entered the twentieth century, farmers in the UK recognised that their fortunes were dependent not on how they managed their costs, but on how the government controlled imports. Only in time of shortage do governments return to home production and at all other times the benefits of cheap food to the wider economy dominate the political process.

Burleigh Farm, belonging to Sir G. G. Montgomery and tenanted by David Ferguson, was recorded in 1888/9. David Ferguson employed a foreman, a ploughman, a milkman and Isabella Lundy.

David was followed as tenant farmer by his son William, the landlord by 1910 (when William was President of the Kinross-shire Show) being Sir Basil T. G. Montomery. William and his family had two ploughmen, a dairyman and a cattleman working for them.

William and his wife were well-respected members of the community and farmed well, even in the hard times following the war. He guaranteed a friend who went bankrupt, and William's subsequent suicide was attributed to this.

This left landlord Sir Henry Montgomery with an empty farm in difficult times and tragic circumstances.

There was a flow of people in the 1930s and 40s from the west of Scotland to the east and south, East Anglia and Lincolnshire. The economic benefits from the climate, the soils and range of crops were better in the east than the west, and the folk flitting were hardier. The migration, made easier by the railway, made it possible to milk their cows in the morning in the west, travel by train and milk them again at night in their new home in the east. Stock, goods, chattels and entire farm equipment was moved by rail in a day. The saying 'go east for a farm and west for a wife' was very true in many respects.

Burleigh Farm was offered to William Lawrie but he was happy in Clashbenny, Glencarse. However, he said his young brother may be interested.

John Lawrie was the third son of seven surviving children of James and Agnes (*nee* Gilmour) Lawrie in West Newton Farm, Strathavon in Lanarkshire. His father had a herd of Ayrshire cows and was successful with some of them in the show ring. He also had some show Clydesdale mares as well as working horses. John was helping his eldest brother Arthur who was farming Kessington Farm at Bearsden in 1930. Arthur also had a herd of Ayrshire cows and retailed the milk locally. Like his father he was a great showman and he also sold young bulls for breeding.

Born on 4th August 1905, John was 24 when he looked over Burleigh Farm in the summer of 1930. Mr Johnstone, agent for the laird, Sir Henry Montgomery, offered two years rent-free for John to take the farm. An agreement was reached and John became a tenant of the Kinross Estate. The lease also included fishing on Loch Leven in the Burleigh boat – which, as he didn't fish, was not taken up.

John Lawrie

John started at Burleigh on 31st July, and it remained the financial year-end for him and the generations that followed. His sister Agnes came to keep house for him; a happy arrangement as they had much in common. There was electricity for lights in the farmhouse driven by a wheel in the Hattonburn as it passed behind the hayshed on its way to Loch Leven.

The cows were still milked by hand. A good milker could milk eight cows twice a day. As they were tied at the neck by a byre-chain it was a fairly safe occupation, except when a cow kicked with the hind

leg nearest the milker. This could be controlled by hobbling the cow, or holding her tail to control her. A team of milkers, often the wives of the men on the farm, did the milking.

John built up a herd of Ayrshire cows because of their reputation to produce milk under adverse conditions, to produce the milk economically and their ability to calve easier and live longer than most other breeds.

John took over those staff who wanted to stay and, as it was between feeing markets, it was the best way forward. The men were Willam Donaldson, Peter Algie, Henry Crawford and James Downie. John made Henry Crawford his grieve, and there was a great respect from both as they worked together until Henry's death in the 1950s.

As you entered the steading at Burleigh, starting at the entrance from the road, the cart sheds were on the left with six arches for the carts, and chains in each arch to attach the cart shafts. Next to the cart shed was the threshing mill and straw shed, with access out to a bridge over the Hattonburn to the stackyard. Beyond this was storage under a stair up the side of a mill. This took you up to the granary which ran along the whole length above the straw and cart sheds. From the foot of the stairs one could go out to the loading banks for the milk carts, which in turn were behind the dairy where the milk was cooled, and later bottled and stored. This led to the back of the house.

The turnip shed was at the start of the back wall, with the dairyman's house next, then two calf pens, the stable for seven horses and hayshed beyond. Down the last side of the square were cattle courts, a byre and more calf pens. These were all stone-built, the stones maybe recycled from the derelict castle. Later there were two byres built with two bullpens, and cattle pens in front and behind the bullpens. These were brick buildings with a harled finish.

One of the first things John wanted to do when the budget allowed was to renew the horse's worn harness. A potato merchant visited him that winter and introduced himself, saying he knew his father James. John's mother was present and said he should stay for some high tea. John sold him some potatoes in the pit, and the merchant went on his way. As it turned out the merchant was going bankrupt and had bought the potatoes as a hedge, and never paid for them. John never forgave him because he had accepted their hospitality before trading when he knew he was going bankrupt. John always advised 'never to spend money until it was in your hand'. It was two years before he could afford to replace the horse's harness, thanks to the dishonest potato merchant disrupting his budget in the first year.

In 1932 he was offered Lethangie Farm next door to Burleigh, and from then on they were farmed as one unit with two landlords. Mr John Paton of Lethangie was from a family of successful mill owners whose ancestors had bought Lethangie House in 1823, and let the farm to tenants.

Plan of Lethangie, courtesy of Graham Paton of Lethangie

The farms were rotated in a seven-year crop rotation under John Lawrie. Three or four years grass, some potatoes after the grass lay and grain in others, with turnips and cabbage for the dairy and sheep in the final crop before grass again, or the grain would be undersown with grass in the final year. The stooks of grain at harvest time had to be built facing north-west, as that was where the drying wind would come from. Straw returned to the land as dung, and clover was sown with the grass, which improved the nitrogen levels as well as feeding the stock. As John Lawrie said, 'Look after the land and the land looks after you. The soil is the greatest asset a farmer has.'

In 1931 the Agriculture Marketing Board brought some regulation to a very depressed market. Production of commodities like milk and potatoes were regulated for the first time. It also encouraged co-operative marketing. It was not a short-term solution to farming, but did give a long-term solution. While other marketing boards (eg hops and tomatoes) soon died away, the potato and milk boards lasted more than half a century, and the wool board still exists today.

In 1932 the Farm Servants Union amalgamated with the Transport and General Workers Union.

When John Lawrie went to Burleigh many farmers brought milk into the village in carts, and folk brought out their jugs or cans to be filled. John installed a bottling machine. The milk was carried in 5 gallon cans and up some steps to be tipped into the cooling plant. It ran down the cooler and into the bottling plant, which filled one crate at a time into sterilised bottles, and the tops were put on by hand. The filled crate was manually lifted off the machine and replaced by another with sterilised empty bottles. The crates of milk were moved to a large fridge and went out every morning to Milnathort, Kinross or the countryside, with one or two, then three, ponies and milk carts.

John Lawrie on tractor 1930s

The Milk Act of 1934 brought the initial step in control of tuberculosis. The forerunner of a more ambitious undertaking, it was a scheme to ascertain the views of Scottish owners of dairy herds. The owner of an Attested Herd was registered by the Department of Agriculture for Scotland. The launching of the Attested Scheme happened in February 1935, and under section 11 of the Milk Act 1934 it was to supply Grade A(TT) milk to school children to the extent to which it was available. A survey in 1936 showed that freedom from infection in many herds has not only been maintained, but still further progress had been made in eradicating TB.

In December 1934 Agnes Lawrie was married to Arthur Braid in Orwell Church by Rev Millar. They took up residence at Channel of Pittendreich Farm where they had a tenancy from the Kinross Estates. Arthur's brother Harry, who was his best man, lived with their sister Molly at Tarhill Farm. Agnes's brides-maids were her sister Isa's daughters, Nan and Anne Watson.

A story goes that Arthur, his brother Harry in Tarhill, and John were invited as tenants to an evening at Kinross House by the Laird. Arthur was so busy look-ing at the footmen at the door he tripped over the carpet, much to the amusement of the other two.

There is another story about Harry Braid and John Lawrie. They had not been asked to a party in the neighbourhood, so they went to the front door and tied the handle to a tree and rang the bell. They hid in the bushes to see the owners trying to open the door which kept slamming shut.

The markets in Milnathort prospered. They had weekly markets for sheep and cattle and, at the autumn market, thousands of lambs were sold. Perth was the place for pedigree stock, especially the famous Perth Bull Sales. However, the local markets were the backbone of the local industry. Lambs were driven from as far away as Alloa. Newly weaned they were herded into a friend's field for the night, to be driven to the market next day for the special autumn sales. The Market, purpose built beside the railway, was handy for the whole of the country to buy from. Loaded at Milnathort Mart they could go north and south, and then, as the train moved to Kinross, east to west. John's grandfather, who was a flesher

SKETCH OF THE SPECIAL TRAIN WHICH BROUGHT THE LARGEST CONSIGNMENT OF OVER 1,000 SCOTCH SHEEP FROM **JAMES THOMSON** OF HADDINGTON N.B. TO **R.F.POTTER & C⁰** 7, LONDON CENTRAL MEAT MARKET.

in Haddington, regularly bought hundreds of lambs at Milnathort Market, and as there was no refrigeration in his day he had a special routine whereby they were grazed for so long and killed relaxed so the meat lasted. There is a picture of a special train from James Thomson of Haddington of over 1,000 Scotch sheep to R F Potter & Co, London Central Meat Market. Irish store cattle were brought by rail and put in a field over the weekend. Charlie Foley can remember them being driven through the village early in the morning on Monday for the market. While MacDonald and Fraser was beside the rails, Hays market was over the road, and manager Jimmy Steedman paid lads 1/- to herd the lambs or cattle over the road to the railway station . Sometimes lambs were sold at one market and taken to the other to be resold for sixpence more.

The local farmers of that ilk retired to the Royal Hotel after the market, their ponies and traps tied up to hitching rings along the wall in Church Street. So when the farmers wanted to leave, they went to their pony and trap to be taken home. The story goes that a farmer had bought a new pony and, when he returned to his trap the worse for wear, the pony took him to its old home before he knew what was happening.

The 1935 Royal Highland Show awarded prizes and grants, which included one for the invention by Messr Dunlop for a pneumatic land wheel for farm vehicles. Their use enabled a single horse to pull over half as much again as the old standard wheel. There were also prizes and premiums for a ridging & cultivating attachment for tractors, for the cultivation of potatoes, turnips and row crops. It made and split ridges without damaging the crop, at a cost which must have represented a large saving on that of horse-work. Another was a universal draining machine. Agriculture was a ready market for new inventions, which were modified at a great rate.

In 1935 John became engaged to Daisy McAdam, whose parents had retired from Athronhall to Nether Tillyrie House. Mary Daisy was born on 14th August 1908, at Easter Pitcorthie Farm, Dunfermline, the third child of William and Margaret McAdam. She was educated in Dunfermline, taking the tram into town to go to school. She came to Kinross-shire in 1922 when her parents took Athronhall Farm near Milnathort.

Social life in Milnathort then, apart from the Sunday service, revolved around the tennis club and, for the young, the Saturday dance in the town hall. The tennis club had courts beside the golf course, and you had to book a place a week before to get a court because the club was so popular. They had teams who played against Perth and other clubs, but the club they *had* to beat was Kinross. Daisy joked she was in the team because she could drive a car, but she was a good player. So was Thomas Duncan, the blacksmith in Wester Loan.

At the dances, Daisy and her friend Betty learned the Charleston in its early days, and were never short of partners.

King George V died on 20th January 1936. Born 3rd June 1865, he had ascended the throne on 6th May 1910. Wireless communication had come to many

Daisy McAdam married John Lawrie

households and the news came over right away. Edward VIII, Prince of Wales, would now become king.

On 6th June 1936 Daisy McAdam married John Lawrie in Orwell Church. A few weeks before, a friend had kept the groom waiting in the church as she was deliberately very late. John said to Daisy she had better not do that to him or he would not be there. Daisy responded with humour that she would knock on the church hall door when she arrived and he could go into the church.

When his best man, brother Bill, arrived to take John to church along with spats, John said to go to the end of the golf course field and meet him there as he wanted to check the turnips. So they met up at the end of the field, which was on the way to Milnathort and the church, John put on the spats and they arrived at the hall immaculate.

Daisy knocked on the door of the hall and John entered the church with Bill. Daisy's bridesmaids were May Hamilton of Blairnathort and Cissie Young of Mawcarse, and the service was taken by the Rev Miller. The reception was at the Green Hotel. They motored down to Torquay for the honeymoon before making their home at Burleigh.

On 10th December Edward VIII announced his abdication over the radio. The general public were shocked as they little knew of the ramifications that had gone on down south. When it became public knowledge, opinion was divided. Crowned in 1937, his brother David became King George VI with his wife Elizabeth, daughter of 14th Earl of Strathmore and Kinghorne, crowned Queen.

In 1935-36 the government were looking into subsidies for food products from raised import tariffs. The subsidies, however, could not be brought into being immediately because they was still bound by bargains on import quotas which arose from marketing schemes and trade agreements with other nations. The cost of subsidised consumption in the interest of health should be regarded as expenditure on public health and not on agriculture. The situation was further complicated as the population increased from less than 21 million in 1851 to nearly 45 million in 1931. It was estimated that the population would decline in 1950, so there was little hope of an expanding population absorbing increased production.

On 20th April 1938 the Lawrie's daughter Constance Margaret was born. She was christened in the home, as was the fashion. The nurse came in for the home birth, and as the baby was late the nurse drove Daisy up and down the bumpy back road between Seggie and Athronhall. It did no good and was darned uncomfortable. The baby was healthy when she arrived, and a great joy to all.

In 1939 John took the lease of Craigomill from Sir James Calder of Ledlanet. John had been testing his cows for bovine TB. The early tests were hard on the cows and, compared with the better, later testing, too many cows were culled. The whole herd and followers received a TB injection before inspected by the vet a week to ten days later, who measured the reaction. Those cows with a reaction above a certain level were culled.

John separated off culled cows and sent them off to the dairy at Burleigh to Craigowmill, where they were kept until they calved. The calves were removed at birth and bucket fed back at Burleigh, and the cow then culled. This way John did not lose his breeding lines and the calf, never having suckled the mother, was free of her TB. Craigowmill had a good hill and many fields, including one at Finderly.

The house and garden at the north side of the road opposite the Craigomill steading was the new home for his widowed sister Isa and her two daughters Nan and Anne. From there the girls could cycle to Milnathort to catch the train for Perth Academy. Nan was the dux in her final year at Perth Academy, attended college in Glasgow and became a physiotherapist. After spells at Bridge of Earn and Dundee, she became the head physio at Bangour, where her patients included rugby players from the Scottish international team.

1939, of course, was the beginning of World War II. Church bells were only to ring if there was an invasion and signposts were removed from all roads. No lights were to show at night and blackouts were placed in windows.

All livestock markets had government restrictions to ensure the armed forces were fed, and an equal share of food for all. All livestock had to be first graded, before being sold through the ring at the nearest market. The nearest markets for Burleigh were at Milnathort: Macdonald & Fraser beside the railway station and Hays over the railway bridge beside the North Queich burn.

John (reluctantly) was on the War Agriculture Executive Committee for Kin-ross-shire. These committees were formed by the government in all the counties to galvanise the agriculture industry and increase the production of food. Each area was allocated a typewriter, a duplicator and the services of one department secretary to operate them if needed.

As in World War I imported food and supplies were stopped by German sub-marines and shipping was difficult, being needed for the war effort. Farmers were told to plough up fields, especially to grow sugar beet and potatoes. Government thought was that 400 acres (14 hect) could feed 400 people. The acres of potatoes in Great Britain doubled in the war years. In 1939 Fife grew 68,824 acres of pota-toes; by 1942 this had increased to 93,362.

Farmers resisting the £2-per-acre subsidy for ploughing up grassland were instructed by the AEC to plough the area nontheless; there was more land than ever under cultivation.

The Committee also had to decide whether the young men who had been called up were required to stay at home, and 'dig for victory'. In the early 1940s the agenda of the AEC had lengthy lists of those appealing against going into uniforms of fighting forces. Coal mining, steelmaking and agriculture were re-served occupations, and those who worked in them could avoid going to war. The appeal always came from the employer and a variety of reasons were put forward. It could be a 'spare pair of horse were on the farm' and no other labour to work them. Top horsemen were considered a reserve occupation in 1939.

Another of the AEC duties was vermin control. Shoots were held (often weekly) especially targeting pigeons and crows. The government supported this until the late 1950s with grants available for cartridges.

They also had to see existing machinery was put to best use. The government

Kinross Junction

supplied extra harvest equipment and a tractor service and left the AEC to determine how this would be deployed.

There was a standstill order to stop workers changing farms, which killed off the feeing markets, whereby a worker who had not been asked to stay or wanted better conditions stood with his goods and chattels on a cart, waiting for an offer from another farmer. This standstill had to be ratified by the AEC and was not lifted until 1950 to allow workers to be employed outside agriculture.

In 1940, while lifting potatoes in a field beside Kinross Army Camp, James Paterson heard a whistling noise and drew his father's attention to it. His father, who had served in the First World War, recognised the sound of gunshot. Everybody got behind the potato pits, while Mr Paterson went to the camp to stop the shooting. The sergeant in charge of the soldiers shooting with .303 rifles at a butt in a banking, did not believe the shots were going into the potato field and came to see. When they were looking more shots came raining down and the sergeant was not long in crawling behind the potato pits with the others. The outcome was the Army used the outdoor butts at Blairadam, and the tattie squad said they would need danger money.

There was no Royal Highland Show in 1940, and it was 1952 before it was held again, at Inverness. Ration books were issued for clothes and food. Basic commodities such as eggs, butter, cheese, meat and chocolate were rationed until 1952 when they were lifted for the coronation of Queen Elizabeth in 1953. Food rationing was unpopular but successful. In 1939 the UK imported 60% of its food. By 1945, despite imports being halved to 30% of the food needed, the nation was fed from increased home production alongside rationing.

The expected invasion of Britain in the early years of the war was very real to the whole population. The Home Guard was formed, consisting mainly of those who were either too old, too young, or in reserved occupations and did their bit for the defence of the country. Balado Aerodrome was built to train pilots. There was the Free Poles camp, an ammunition dump at Mawcarse, the army camp at Turfhills and a prisoner-of-war camp at Fruix. The army camp at Turfhills, which had been built near the railway for the First World War to carry troops away when trained before being mothballed, was opened again in 1940. It was known for passenger trains to be appropriated for troops when needed.

The Women's Land Army was formed in the later years of the First World War and was remobilised in 1939, even before war was declared. It was only disbanded in 1950.

The winter of 1939/40 will long be remembered for the intense cold. February was the coldest month since 1895 and January since 1881. The mean temperature for the month was more than ten degrees lower than normal. There were gales on seven days between the 10th and 31st, the worst coming on the 15th and 16th when a north-easterly reached 60mph, with gusts of 80mph.

The *RHS Annual Review* published a 17 page article by Sir John Boyd from the Rowett Research Institute in Aberdeen, entitled 'The Effects of War on Agriculture'. It is a very good article and concludes that the slump after the last war is still fresh in the minds of farmers. The government has promised that they will be given a fair deal and will not be let down after this war. He said:

'If we are to escape the post-war slump we should be working now towards a permanent agricultural policy based on national food requirements. When the war finishes, this emergency attempt to get some sort of co-ordinated food policy will come to an end. Harassed as Ministers are with the immediate war problems, it is very doubtful whether they will give much consideration to a long-range agricultural policy, or even to the post-war effects of emergency food measures.

'If we are to have a permanent policy for agriculture, it will need to be evolved not by politicians but by farmers themselves. An exhaustive investigation showed that a food policy based on nutritional needs involves increased home production without a decrease in our imports which would interfere with our exporting industries or overseas investments.

'A national food policy based on human needs would have the support of the consumers and also of social reformers and 'planners', who realise that a flourishing countryside and a well-fed population are the only basis for social and economic stability.'

1941 saw the birth of another child in the farmhouse at Burleigh. Eileen Gilmour Lawrie arrived on 23rd April, and was christened in the drawing room by the Rev Miller.

One morning, while getting up for the 4am milking, John glanced out of the window which faced out to the garden in front of the house. He saw a mass of soldiers in tin hats who were not British, speaking a foreign language amongst the bushes in the garden. '----- Daisy the Germans have landed!' It turned out only to be the Free Poles on exercise – but what a fright they got!

Evacuees came from Glasgow to avoid the bombing. Milnathort welcomed their allotted children and many friendships were made that lasted a lifetime. Daisy and John were sent a man and his three children. The wife had stayed in Glasgow. In a busy daily life they were expected to fit in. However, the man used the farmhouse like a hotel and expected Mrs Lawrie to do everything for them. It was a relief to all when he decided to take them all home to Glasgow.

There was a real need to preserve the livestock numbers in the country and with more land under the plough, therefore reducing grassland, coupons were issued for animal rations. Farmers growing only grain were allowed to keep one third of the crop. No animal feed was now imported. In 1939 there were 1,903,000 tons of animal feed imported. In 1943 only 11,943 tons of fish meal was imported from Iceland. Even St Andrews golf course was opened to graze sheep – and some of the course was even ploughed!

The school holidays were altered as part of the war effort. The summer holiday was cut to four weeks, and the October holiday extended to a month to help with the potato harvest.

Prisoners of war, both German and Italians, were also a labour source. By 1942 there were 37,000 prisoners of war working on farms in the UK, transported daily from their camps. Italian prisoners preferred to stay in camp. John Lawrie used prisoners from Fruix camp, and found the German prisoners (mainly just teenagers) hardworking. Giving food to POWs was an offence, but he gave them scotch pies at 5pm, and a twist of tobacco at the end of the week, which was gratefully received.

A deal was struck in 1941 between President Roosevelt and Winston Churchill resulting in thousands of tractors and hundreds of combines, binders and balers coming to the UK, with payment to be deferred until hostilities ceased. By 1945 more than 200,000 tractors and 3,000 combines had come to the UK in this Lend Lease deal. The AEC determined who received these machines; some decisions caused friction between neighbouring farmers.

In that year the AEC requested that all travelling threshing mills were to have two rolls of netting, no more than half an inch mesh, to encircle the stacks and catch rats as the stacks were threshed. Jim Paterson tells of the threshing mill coming to Gallowhill Farm. A steam engine drove the mill, which they hired three or four times a year to feed the cattle and sheep as the stacks were needed. This time he asked his father if he could have a day off school, which he got as long as he carried coal and water to the engine and chaff away from the mill. Mr Wallace, driving the steam engine pulling the mill and a wooden caravan behind, arrived the evening before. He set up the mill and spent the night in the caravan. Mr Wallace was up next morning at five o' clock to steam up the engine. The young James carried coal and water to the massive engine, and chaff away from the mill all day until they stopped at five for tea, and his father and Mr Wallace enjoyed a dram after the day's work. Mr Wallace looked at James and said he'd done well all day, would he like to drive the steam engine? So James drove the steam engine, pulling the mill and caravan down the farm road, and 'thought the King was his cousin', he was so proud.

On leaving Gallowhill Farm Mr Wallace stopped a while at the Muirs Inn. A police sergeant sought to arrest him for being in charge of a steam engine while under the influence of drink. They went outside where the sergeant saw the great steam engine, mill and caravan in the road, and wondered what he would do with them. He turned to Wallace and told him 'to get in, drive the thing and get the hell out of Kinross-shire!'

On 20th September 1942 a third daughter (me!) was born to Daisy and John. I came in a hurry. The nurse called the doctor at 11am and by the time he arrived at 11.20 I was born. Christened Dorothy after Dr Anderson's wife, it was said that I was always in a hurry as a child. My mother said my father was just as pleased with a third daughter.

In 1941 John Lawrie bought East Brackley, which included the Vane, from the trustees of William Tod. The Tod family owned the lands in 1888 when the census recorded East Brackley as the property of the late George Tod, who employed two ploughmen and a gardener. Vane was owned by Mrs Christian Tod, with a shepherd and a labourer living there. Their son William Tod was the farmer of the whole.

While working for the Tods at East Brackley in 1890, Jim Paterson's grandfather crossed the frozen loch with a horse and cart to bring food to the folk at the farm. He also crossed to St Serf's Island by a causeway of about a cart's width and only two feet deep. This causeway was used in the next century by Arthur Braid to take sheep to graze from Channel Farm, but is thought to have since been washed away in a storm.

William Tod was a Justice of the Peace, a Deputy Lieutenant of Kinross-shire and President of Kinross-shire Agricultural Society in 1911, 1923 and 1933. His mother extended the farmhouse, adding an upstairs drawing-room (with a magnificent view over Loch Leven), and a dining-room beneath it. As he grew older he built the 'White House' for a tenant as he wished to stay in the house he was in to the end of his days.

The fields included one called the 'Covenanters Field', reached by going down the track beside the cottages and past the big wood to a gate that led to a field with a hill. One could imagine the Covenanters using it as a lookout to protect them against army attack, and escape easily. There was a conventicle at Kelty Bridge where 3,000 Covenanters listened to the preacher, but the meeting was surprised by troops and many prisoners were taken, including two ladies' maids from Kinross. They were all condemned to be sent as slaves to the West Indies. This area was strong Covenanting country.

John moved his mother, brother Alan, sister Isa Watson and her two girls into the White House at East Brackley, while Mr and Mrs McAdam moved to Craigomill Farm House.

Aerial view of Burleigh Castle

East Brackley

In the spring of 1942 intelligence information suggested that the Germans were thinking of flying gliders to Scotland, capable of landing on water. Loch Leven seemed to be a likely landing place as it was the only large stretch of water on the east side of the country. A site for a searchlight was made at Orwell Farm. The headquarters of the defence force was to be at Channel Farm, and there were 20-30 regular soldiers billeted there. Sandy Braid said 'I don't remember myself or my family having more than a brief visit to bed during the week of Invasion Loch Leven'.

Before and during the war, pit ponies were used for the movement of coal from the pit face to the lift-cage, pulling wee wagons laden with coal. When the miners were on holiday in mid-July, the Fife pit ponies were brought to the surface, loaded onto railway trucks and brought to Mawcarse station. The 80 tired wee black ponies walked slowly, with some hardly able to see. Neighbouring farmers guarded every roadway and open gateway from Mawcarse station up the road to the hill at Newlands, on to Glenvale and the Lomond hill. Only two weeks later the same ponies had become a lot of frisky ponies of all colours, and were reluctant to be herded back to the station for their return to the Fife pits.

A Hurricane fighter crashed in 3-4ft of water in Loch Leven in 1942, about 100 yards from the front of Grahamstone Farm. Ross Kinnaird remembers the six members of the RAF rescue team who boarded at the farm until the plane was recovered.

By 1943 John had taken the tenancy of West Brackley from Mr Tam Tod,

East Brackley from Benarty Hill

who also wanted to stay in his house and retire. Mr Tod let the land and cottages to John. They enjoyed good discussions on many topical subjects over the years.

The staff at East Brackley were Jim Malcolm (Greive) and his wife Elizabeth; James Collier, his wife Nan and her father 'old George' (as their son was 'wee George'); and Charles Collier (James's brother) and his wife Agnes. There was always a pair of black Clydesdales at East Brackley and the others were bright bays, all with the white feathering on their legs and white blazes on their faces. Burleigh had a pair of white Clydesdales amongst the bays.

In the spring of 1944 the Lawrie family moved to East Brackley House, where they would live for 14 years. It was a beautiful house with five bedrooms, a dressing room, a bathroom, another wee room and a drawing room up some more stairs. Downstairs you entered the house by the front door from the porch which ran along the front, on to a vestibule, then the lovely front hall. The vestibule and the hall had floors decorated with a tiled mosaic and the front stairs with two turns passed a coloured glass window. The two rooms on the right were a small sitting room and an office or gun room. Round the corner on the left of the front door was a morning room and beyond was the dining-room, with a butler's pantry to the right of the door.

At the foot of the front stairs was the swing-door through to the back premises. The back stairs were straight ahead, steeper than the front stairs with one turn by a huge window about two-thirds of the way up. There was a large cloakroom on the left with a toilet and hand basin partitioned off. Along the corridor, as it swung left to the kitchen, was a passage leading to a large dairy with stone shelves, a pantry next door and another room.

McGILLISMITH PASTURES
First year's grass on Burleigh in fine show.

The kitchen, warm with the Esse cooker, had a large window at the far end, the big dresser on the wall behind the door and a large table up the centre. A door led through to the scullery where there was a sink and drying board, another large cupboard and, in Daisy's day, a large double-door refrigerator on the other wall. A further door led to a maid's bedroom. The scullery had a third door that led back out to the passage to the back door and back towards the dairy etc. At the back door the passage turned right, where there was a cupboard, a coal house and a huge washhouse.

The washhouse had a shelf above head height running around the room, two big basins either side of a mangle, with a scrubbing board lying in one. A huge old washing unit sat in the corner, which had a fire lit by hand that heated water in the boiler and the clothes were washed in it. Daisy had a modern machine for washing the clothes. Up the back stairs were two bedrooms and a dressing room, and the landing ran past the bathroom, a linen cupboard, to a door joined to the three bedrooms and the front of the house, and then up the flight of stairs to the drawing room. There was also a big walled garden with flowers, soft fruit and vegetables, outside of which lawns terraced down to a shrubbery which ran up the west side, where a high dyke separated the farm from the garden.

The farmhouse at Burleigh in the meantime was used as a hostel for the single men and a housekeeper employed to look after them. Willie Muir, who came from Athronhall where he worked for Mr McAdam, drove the Milnathort milk cart for decades, first with the bay horse Jimmy then the grey Hector. He had the room off the kitchen. The dining room was used as an office, and Anne Watson was John's first secretary.

1944 also marked the death of Mrs McAdam at 66. She had an inflamed gall bladder and an operation was not possible as her heart would not take it. She died in hospital.

Mr McAdam moved into East Brackley with Daisy and Johnny's family. He had a car and made himself useful running messages and school runs. He visited his son Willie weekly, and enjoyed seeing his granddaughter Christine and her mother Nora, at Bucklyvie Farm outside Crossgates. He was a welcome guest at

Kinross Junction

the White House, taking the children there to admire the lovely garden tended by Isa Watson. Christine remembers:

'If we went to Church (at Orwell) on Sunday with Grandpa we sat in the Athron Hall pew upstairs in the north wing at the very front, and if we went with dad we sat in the Burleigh seat at the back of the east wing, with a table in front of us. Grandpa gave us pandrops during the sermon, to suck not chew! He was an elder at Orwell for a long time.'

When Daisy was pregnant in 1946 he gave her time by taking the children off her hands. Constance was at Dollar Academy and, with Joy and Sandy Braid and Betty Graham, the Muirhead twins and Muriel Sands, caught the train at Kinross. The train was magnificent as it arrived, spewing steam and the odd spark. The carriages had no passages and were opened by a leather strap from the opened window into each individual carriage which held six or eight children. The north bound trains were on the left of the platform, and the south bound on the right as one descended the steep covered passage from the booking office to the station. The waiting rooms were in the middle of the platform, and at the end of the platform beyond the waiting rooms was a concrete model of Loch Leven, all to scale. Details like Castle Island were included. (The model of the Loch is in the keeping of a private individual, and will hopefully be given to Kinross Museum one day.)

Constance's younger sister Eileen remembers: 'Meeting Constance off the train with Grandpa was always exciting.' Eileen was at the Reid Memorial School (the wee school) at Milnathort until she was seven, when she joined the Dollar train with cousin Jimmy Braid from Channel Farm.

During the Great War almost everything that moved or turned on a farm was done by horsepower. During the Second World War the government could and did requisition horses. Heavy horses took munitions and provisions to and from the front lines, and much of Scotland's horse power was reduced. At home the horse's rations were cut, as much of the oats and grain were needed for the market. With a shortage of Clydesdales in 1940 some Suffolk Punch carthorses were introduced into Scotland. John had a cross-Clydesdale Suffolk Punch, called Punch. He was magnificent-looking but quite feisty. Will Tod drove him with a placid Clydesdale called Danny. Work horses had short names like Sport, Clyde, Prince, Jimmy and Tammy. It made working them easier.

In 1939 only a quarter of horsepower was the mechanical kind but the shortage of horses gave considerable impetus to the budding tractor manufacturers. A horse cost £100-200 and lasted for ten years or so. It ate produce from the farm that was not missed in a good year and not worth much in a bad one. As the war continued the horsemen were conscripted to fight and many never returned. Even when horsemen did return, the progress of mechanisation was such that most farms had at least one tractor. Not needing to feed, water and muck out seven days a week, most farm workers learned to lean more to the tractor.

Although the war ended in 1945 there were shortages of almost every commodity for a decade after cessation of hostilities. Blacksmiths found themselves short of coal for furnaces to shoe the horses. Burleigh horses went to Tammy Duncan in Wester Loan, and East Brackley horses went to Donaldson's smiddy at Blairforge. With so many work horses to shoe and ploughs to mend there were two smiddies in Milnathort. Bob Kay had a smiddy opposite the Reid Memorial School on Stirling Road, and there had been smiddies at Seggie, Arlary and Balgeddie as well as those already in Kinross.

Coal was also in short supply for the steam engine threshing machines. The national coal board investigated eight new sites in the East Neuk of Fife.

In 1946 POWs were repatriated to their homelands and, in the harvest, labour proved difficult. Many Poles and some Germans, however, chose to stay.

1946 was also the year that John Gilmour Lawrie was born, on 28th August. This completed the family who grew up happily at East Brackley.

The winter of 1947 was very severe. The big freeze in February saw snow so deep, places were snowed in for weeks. John Lawrie tried to get to Burleigh from East Brackley by Clydesdale. After about a mile, having reached the Fish Tail where a bridge crossed the railway lines and went two ways at the other side (hence the name), the poor horse was so exhausted he had to turn home to Brackley. It is remembered as the worst winter ever. Loch Leven was frozen over and some brave souls even skated over to Castle Island.

1947 brought in The Agricultural Act with policies that would provide subsidies in the form of guaranteed prices and deficiency payments for the farming industry. The aim was to increase home production by another 20% for food security. This widespread financial support for farming helped convert the UK farming industry into one of the most efficient and productive in the world.

The payment levels were determined by the Annual Price Review. It also introduced grants for liming, drainage, fencing, new machinery, buildings and livestock improvement. It was the envy of other industries.

1947 was the year I started at the 'wee school' in Milnathort. The first teacher was Miss Adam, the daughter of the minister in Portmoak. Apart from an exchange visit to the USA after the war she was a fixture there until she married a Norwegian later in life. Anyone who went to the wee school asked, 'Did you have Miss Adam?' and an affirmative answer was treated well. She came home to Milnathort as a widow, and had her 100th birthday celebration at the Green Hotel.

Mr McAdam died in December 1947 at the age of 72. He developed pneumonia and had to be taken to hospital, but it proved fatal. He was so much a part of the family and was sorely missed.

1948 saw the introduction of the National Health Service. Before this it cost to have a doctor's visit. A long-term illness often meant losing the tied cottage, and there was no obligation for local authorities to house homeless people.

It was also the year that John took the lease of Tillyrie at the request of Captain Reid. He built a byre, dairy unit with a turnip shed and beside it a large hay shed for the new tenant. The stack yard was beyond it, and the model steading the Captain had built in 1914 was on the other side. There was a plaque above the door of the byre which read 'By The Grace Of God, Matale 1878-80'.

The two Highland cows on the hill had to go as John was building up a TB-free herd. A dealer, Hugh Dalziel, scoured the herds in the west for good Ayrshire cows for him and John bought some from Dalziel's brother Arthur. One outstanding cow, Lesserlinn Bee, won the dairy show at Glasgow on several occasions. John was not a show man but he let his dairyman Mr Coffee show if he wanted and enjoyed the success. The cow never had a daughter as good as herself, but some of her granddaughters were useful.

J. Rugg the grieve left and was replaced by Jim Malcolm, who had been grieve at East Brackley, where Jim Collier replaced him. Jim and Elizabeth moved into the bungalow (now Newton).

John's mother, my grandmother, died in 1948. A resilient lady born in the 1880s, Agnes Gilmour married James Lawrie in 1898 and they lived at West Newton Farm. Strathavon. When the laird Mr Yule was letting the farm to William Lawrie (John Lawrie's grandfather), the laird said, 'William, with your temper and mine perhaps it would be better if young James had the lease'. So James took the lease of West Newton.

James and Agnes had 16 children, seven of whom made adulthood. The others died aged between two years and four months of gastroenteritis, something that antibiotics would cure today. Women had to be resilient in those days. She was widowed in her fifties and lived into her eighties, greatly interested in her family and all that they did. She was brought up in a family of girls as a Wee Free and religion was important to her. She lived latterly with her daughter Isa at the

White House, East Brackley, but it was her daughter-in-law Daisy who was with her at the end, having persuaded Isa to have a rest.

Farmers applying for extra petrol rations to go to the revived RHS, to be held at Inverness, were turned down as being non-essential travel. To justify a visit to a local town, they often put a bale of hay or a calf in a sack in the boot of the car. In 1948 it was stated that petrol sold for use in tractors was being used in cars and action was taken.

A shortage of sodium chlorate required to burn down the potatoes was reported, so the Board of Trade arranged sufficient supplies. This arrived in huge glass bottles, wrapped in straw in metal cages, and was handled with great care when used to burn the shaws off the potatoes, to prevent blight.

Daisy went to California in 1948 to see her sister and took Constance with her. Jenny had packed her wedding dress in her luggage and went to join her fiancé Bill Richardson in California. Bill, from Dunfermline and unable to get work, went first to Canada and then the USA where he worked as an engineer, bringing water over mountains, through the desert and across massive distances from the Colorado River to California. It took three months for Jenny to sail to California via the Panama Canal. They were married on 26th July 1930 in the little church called 'Wee Kirk o' the Heather'. They were to have three children, and lived through the war in the desert where Bill's work took him. General Patton honed his troops for combat before they went to North Africa (to fight at El Alamein) nearby, and sometimes they had to wait on their monthly trip to collect their messages as hundreds of tanks crossed the road.

Daisy and Constance left from Prestwick, the nearest airport in Europe for the USA, and flew in what they described as a converted troop carrier, noisy and often cold. They landed in Greenland to refuel, flew over the North Pole, refuelling again in Newfoundland, then on to New York, and finally to California. Daisy had to have papers to say Jenny and Bill would keep them for the three months of their stay, for Daisy was only allowed to take £5.

Captain Reid died on Christmas Eve, 1949. The vet, John Watson, came to Tillyrie to put his cats and dogs down. The Captain was seen daily driving his American Jeep, his dogs sitting with him, the top dog a well-boned collie with freckles on his white markings sitting in the front seat and the rest in the back.

John Lawrie arrived as the vet was about to start and they chatted as he also was the vet for Tillyrie and Burleigh. The top dog, Bleaton, jumped into my father's pickup and he said to leave him as he would try to give him a home. John Watson said to watch him as he was known to bite postmen, trying to remove the strip on their trousers.

When they arrived back home at East Brackley my father had meant to tell Daisy the dog was not to be trusted with children. However, Bleaton jumped out of the pickup, up the steps to the back door and straight along the passage into the kitchen. By the time John caught up, Bleaton was pulling Gilmour, who had hold of his tail, round the table. A bond was forged.

Next day, when up at Tillyrie, John stopped opposite the back of the house. Bleaton jumped out and went to the back door, sniffed for a minute and came back to the pickup and jumped in. He never went back to the house in the many times John was at Tillyrie, and was loyal to John the rest of his life, waiting at the gate of the front drive for John to come home when he wasn't taken.

On Sundays we were all taken for a drive round the countryside with Mum and Dad, mainly I suspect so that Dad could see what was being done on other farms. He didn't have many hobbies and motoring was something he enjoyed. In 1949 he bought a bottle-green Bentley from Rossleigh in Edinburgh. We were all packed into it, Constance, Eileen and Gilmour in the back, and I was between the parents in the front with the brake handle to be avoided, and the only view was the dashboard. The smell of the new leather was strong. Aunt Isa said we were lucky to have a father who took us for drives, and as there was no answer to that there was no reply. My parents enjoyed the Sunday afternoon drives, and it was a great relaxation for them.

Dad's love of cars was his only relaxation. Before the war he had a second-hand Rolls Royce and to stop the government commandeering it he had a shooting-brake top made for it. He regretted having to do this because it made the car too heavy and, after the war, he regretfully got rid of it.

The Kinross Show dinner dance at The Green Hotel was always the highlight of the year. Everyone was in formal dress, the ladies in long evening dresses. One person who used to come and stay with my parents was Tattie Tam and his wife Cathy. Tam was from Weatherspoon Donald and Graham potato merchants in Glasgow, with whom John did business. We children were amazed watching Cathy put on her makeup and nail varnish before the night, chatting to us all the time.

Watching the men ploughing with Eileen we noticed Charley Collier's pair

The milk float at Kinross Show

pulling slightly crooked. Tammy seemed eager and was fractionally in front of Prince. It was mentioned to Charlie when he came to the end of the drill. He smiled his quiet smile and said Tammy was getting out of the full weight of the plough by doing this. Prince was willing to pull and Tammy was willing to let him. Charley had a good reputation for ploughing, as one farmer said years later 'Charley always squared off a field, no matter how irregular. He never had a half drill left at the end.'

Jim Collier, the grieve, got a tractor in the late 1940s. A grey Fergy, it could replace two pair of horse and was his pride and joy.

Jim Paterson said as a youngster that he was not yet proficient in the art of thinning turnips, and he and his father were in a 16-acre field and taking forever. A call to Bob Tod sorted it with a gang of Tods and Colliars for two nights after their work. Don Ross's men under Adam Colliar with his brother Will would help out at Tillyrie and Burleigh. It was quite a sight to see all the men working across the field thinning turnips. Jim Paterson became an expert in the Young Farmers and won many medals for thinning turnips, one in an Open Class against a hundred men, for which he won the medal that let him free into all shows in Scotland.

In September 1950 Constance, Eileen and I were sent to board at Craigmount School based at Scone Palace, Perth. There was much sewing of name tapes, Isa helping, and uniforms to be purchased from Forsyths in Edinburgh. There was a half-term weekend, and two out days between it and the expected weekly letter to and from the parents.

In 1951 there was an extreme shortage of both baler twine and coal, which and been in short supply for over a year.

The *RHS Annual Review 1951* stated, in one article headed 'The Food Position Today',

'Our financial resources have been sadly depleted as a result of two World Wars, in which we played a leading part, not only in man-power, but in materials. Apart from coal, we are not rich in natural resources. The greater part of raw materials required for industry has to be imported. And that, of course, falls to be added much of our foodstuffs. Industrial products at one time were dear in relation to foodstuffs. The position is now reversed and this bears hardly on us as a nation. Were it not for the financial assistance given, under Marshall Aid, by our American friends, the position would indeed be desperate. Our financial resources no longer permit of use unrestricted imports as in the past, so that the greatest possible degree of self-sufficiency in food production is not only merely desirable but imperative.

But that is not all. Improved standards of living are now demanded by some of the erstwhile food-exporting countries. Their populations are also rapidly expanding and some foods which in pre-war days were shipped to this country for animal feed are now consumed at home by people. The world's population is increasing at a rate of 20 million per year. Reserves of untapped land are by no means now unlimited, and water and wind erosion continue to take a heavy toll of existing agricultural lands in many parts of the world. Fear of world food surpluses has been replaced by fear of world starvation. We are faced therefore with the urgent necessity of attaining a greater degree of self-sufficiency in home food production in the shortest possible time. The only alternative would appear to be emigration for a large part of the population.'

In 1952 the RHS at Kelso was blighted by an outbreak of foot and mouth disease and there was no stock, just horses, honey and machinery stands. The outbreak meant cows were not allowed on the roads and John Lawrie needed to graze his herd on the opposite side of the road at Burleigh. Willie Ker the dairyman and John 'persuaded' a cow into the burn behind the hayshed and walked her under the bridge to the field. Once they had her persuaded they returned with her and all the cows followed her into the burn, under the bridge and so to the field. The local policeman, 'Jingling Geordie', constantly rode his bicycle to Burleigh to try and catch the cows crossing the road. The funny thing was the cows got used to going up the burn and had to be persuaded to use the road again when the foot and mouth regulations ceased.

By then there were 2,680 members of the Milk Recording Board in Scotland, with 142,914 registered cows. Mr Arthur Lawrie of Kessington and John at Burleigh were members.

Miss Janet Reid moved to Tillyrie in 1951. When her sister Maria had died and Duncrievie House was given up, she first thought of moving to Tillywhally House but, when Captain Reid died, she came to Tillyrie. She took a lease of Tillyrie House from David Matale Reid Esq residing at The Gelli, Tallarn Green, near Malpas in Cheshire,

'...the house and other buildings to be used for residential purposes only, and the ground adjunct for amenity and gardening purposes only. The rent shall be £100 pounds payable half-yearly by equal portions at Martinmas and Whitsunday. The right also to take firewood from plantations on the farm.

The Landlord will keep the said building wind and watertight and will uphold the water supply and drainage thereof. The tenant accepts the subjects as satisfactory in all respects and binds herself to keep and leave the same in good tenantable, habitable and workable repair and condition to the satisfaction of the landlord, ordinary wear and tear excepted.

So the last of the Reids came to live at Tillyrie for the last 22 years of her life.

Great pylons crossed the county of Kinross in the mid-1950s. There was a hue and cry and much objection, but as it was 'for the better of the country' they went ahead. In fact much of the country did not have electricity until then. At Burleigh the cottages had lamps, and Jean Patterson remembers doing her homework by lamp light until about seven years old, when the cottages got electricity. In East Lothian my husband John told me that they worked with generators until the pylons were built, also in the 1950s, at his home in Pathhead, Dunbar. So it was for the common weal of the country at large that the pylons were built through our county.

Small vans came out to the country after the horse-drawn carts were outdated. Grocers, butchers and bakers came, so there was little need to go into the villages for the messages.

When the RHS was at Dumfries, John, Daisy and two friends went down in the Bentley. When they came to the town the police waved them on and they found themselves at the tail-end of the Royal party. On meeting John the Vet, John was greeted with 'We were waved to the side by the police, and there was Lawrie driving along with the Royalty.' It took a lot of living down!

Arthur Lawrie had to come out of Kessington, as it was being developed. Cuthill Towers was for sale near John at Milnathort. Arthur and his elder son James bought it in 1954 and moved their herd there. In 1955 Jim married Jessie and they successfully raised their family at Cuthill Towers.

The demise of the Corn Exchanges was hastened by the arrival of the combine harvester. In the binder and straw stack days, process was more leisurely over the winter months. With the capacity and speed of combines, and two thirds of the crop traded in the six-week harvest period, there was just not time for a weekly grain market. Many of the bigger buyers had their reps who knew what grain was being grown where.

Also in 1954 the Laird, Lt Col Henry Keith Montgomery, died suddenly on 1st October and his son, who had been serving with the Black Watch, came home to take over the Kinross estate. Sir Basil Henry David Montgomery was rather daunted by the task, having had no experience of estate management at that time and, at twenty three years old, he had expected his father to live longer. Mr Johnstone had been the factor for some time so he had some guidance. He said that he was helped by John Lawrie and, if he got it wrong, a remark was enough to tell him so. He and his tenant had a great mutual respect which lasted to the end of their days. Burleigh, although on a 99-year lease, was always coming back to Kinross estate and not handed over to the Lawrie family and John made that clear to them. When the Laird came into the office at Burleigh he would greet John with a good day and remarked he looked well. 'Aye, I am no dead yet' was the reply, and both laughed. It was a good working relationship.

One day Daisy answered the back door at East Brackley and came back to the kitchen saying to John he had better go, that there was a tramp at the door. John went out and when he hadn't returned after 20 minutes Daisy looked out and saw the two of them chatting, sitting on the back door steps.

When John came in he said it was interesting that the chap, Peter Scott, wanted to net the geese and ring them. A large net was to be cast over the geese, trapping them as they grazed. A few days later, however, John was incandescent. 'The b*!?*! let them go again!' John thought they were going to wring the necks of the geese but Peter Scott wanted to ring their legs to track them.

There was a population of 4,000 geese on Loch Leven in those days. They migrated in the spring, returned in the autumn and the long flights, combined with the fact that goose eggs constituted a large part of the Inuit diet, kept the numbers fairly constant. Peter Scott's sanctuary at Slimbridge is a great site to see

Spott House from the rear

birds of all kinds and his paintings, especially those of geese in flight, were very much sought after.

In 1951 Tam Tod died in West Brackley. He requested to be buried on his hill and Charlie Collier's pair of black Clydesdales carried him up to his grave. The Tod family tomb is at Portmoak Church and, though his name is on it, he was buried on his hill of Benarty. Tam Tod left West Brackley to Billy Nelson, and the Nelson family became our neighbours.

The 50 acres at Findatie were, at first, included in the sale of the farm but since the purchaser could not find the money the farm was given to the second-top

Half the byre at Tillyrie

Spott House 1958

bidder, a Mr Kinnaird of Grahamstone. However the 50 acres right next to the farm were not included. A second wife who did not get on with the first wife's family claimed it when her husband died, and left it outwith her husband's family when she died. This had run with West Brackley in Tam Tod's time and, when the sale with Findatie fell through, it was offered back to John Lawrie as tenant.

In 1955 Gilmour started at the nippers (junior school) at Pinkie House, Loretto School, Musselburgh where the Spartan traditions of runs round the racecourse before breakfast and cold baths featured alongside a good education.

In 1956 John asked David Reid if Tillyrie was for sale but at that point David was unwilling to sell. In 1957 John was under-bidder for a farm, Spylaw, at Kelso. He was aggrieved to discover that there had been an arrangement that the final purchaser was to buy the farm just above the best offer.

However, John was happy he had not been successful in getting Spylaw, for a much better farm came on the market the following year. Spott Estate, owned by Sir James Hope, was 1400 acres of undulating strong land in the county of East Lothian. It included Doon, Spott Home Farm and Big Spott. If it had been in good repair John could not have afforded it but, with Tillyrie and Burleigh to support the purchase and East Brackley to sell, it was viable. One reason Sir James Hope chose John Lawrie to be the purchaser was his intention to keep the land together, unlike the consortium of local farmers who wanted to purchase Spott and break it up between them.

David Reid put Tillyrie on the market thinking John would not be able to purchase both it and Spott.

John had always been friendly with David Carnegie, a Milnathort lad whose father had been school master in Dunning. David had done well in banking and was Deputy Head of the Clydesdale Bank, based in Glasgow. They put their heads together and David called in another friend, Alex Mackenzie, who was an international accountant with his firm Whinney & Murray (later Ernest & Whinney). The three of them and Tom Myles, John's lawyer, put together 'John Lawrie Farms Ltd', a family company with capital of 100 £1 shares. John kept 51% of the shares, his wife and three daughters had 8% each and Gilmour the balance. One had to be a blood relation to have shares. Miss Lovey, the secretary at Burleigh, was Company Secretary; she was so good the Inland Revenue wanted to employ her. John was able to buy Spott and Tillyrie.

East Brackley was sold to a Mr Ballantyne – who with his wife, son Quentin and daughter Heather, moved in the November term. A few years later they sold the Vane to the RSPB as a nature reserve.

Mrs Isa Watson moved to Keston, the Muirs, Kinross, which she and John bought between them when East Brackley and the White House was sold. As John travelled up and down from Burleigh, Tillyrie and Spott, never knowing where he would be needed, both Daisy and Isa kept his bed and meals ready on an almost daily basis, and nobody knew when he would walk into a field or byre. Often awake at four o'clock, he could leave Spott and be in the byre at Tillyrie or Burleigh at six and not be home until eight at night. There was no motorway in those days and every village had to be driven through. The ferry ran every twenty minutes from the Queensferry locations. It consisted of three

Dorothy with John Lawrie

An aerial view of North Street, Milnathort showing the Big School and Orwell Church

boats going back and forward all the time, but in busy time there could be a queue. When the Edinburgh Festival was on he phoned ahead to ask about the length of the queue and, if it was particularly long, went round by Kincardine and crossed the Forth there.

Without key men in charge in Kinross-shire, John would not have been able to do what he did. It is said that leadership from the top works as long as the leader retains flair. Johnny Lawrie would not ask anyone to do what he could not do himself. He had mutual respect for his employees, whom he valued. Henry Crawford, who was Greive from 1930 to 1951, Robert Tod (Greive 1951 until he retired), and Willie Kerr (1941 until he retired in the dairy at Burleigh). At Tillyrie, there were Jim Malcolm, Jock Woods and Abe Dewar who were with us from 1948 until they retired. We also had Munro the shepherd and McGarva the dairyman at Tillyrie. These were men in key positions who were reliable and knew agriculture well.

The land at Spott had belonged to the owners of the Fortalice built there by de Spott at the time of Edward I. It was bought by a Mr Sprott, home from abroad, who modernised the house and added to it. In 1812 he put stone drains into the fields, and these drains were still working when John Lawrie did some modern drainage on the estate.

It took John ten years to improve Spott to his standards. There was a gate and a half on the farm, last year's potatoes still in the ground and heaps of lime waiting to be spread. The steading at Big Spott had to be rebuilt, for which Sandy Thomson was brought in to do the work over several years. The land needed feeding and lime and, gradually, this was achieved. Fences were upgraded to be stock-proof, many fields having none at all. This made moving stock a nightmare until it was achieved in its turn, and every field was fenced.

Sugar beet was grown at Spott, extending the harvesting period from late summer for the grain, autumn for the potatoes, then up to December for the sugar beet. The roots were put in the stackyard at Big Spott in large heaps, waiting for the lorries to transport them to the factory at Cupar. Opened in 1926, it was built to refine 400 tons of roots a day. In the 1950s the owners employed 100 men working in eight-hour shifts, with one day off every three weeks, for the three months of the harvest. In the 1960s this increased to 200 men from October to New Year.

The singling of the sugar beet crop was one of the worst jobs, for one had not only to remove weeds and thin the seedlings but also to separate the shoots emerging from multi-germ seed. In 1960 the introduction of selective weedkillers helped kill off the more difficult weeds like knotgrass and mayweed which would tangle round the hoe blades. The greatest step forward was the arrival of mono-germ seed, which only produced one shoot. Unlike turnips, which grow mainly on the surface of the ground, the sugar beet has long taproots similar to carrots, and harvesting is more difficult. The tops were removed as the roots were dug out of the ground by machine and loaded on to a trailer. Mud on the roads was a problem, and a scraper had to be used by sunset to remove it. The beet was graded at the factory and paid in sugar content, normally 16% to 20%, but deductions were made for too much earth, badly cut tops or 'shot' beet.

Binders were still being used at Burleigh and Tillyrie but combines were used at Spott. Two of the men, Robert Lafferty and Ian Sands, had served in the armed forces and were skilled at servicing the combines they drove. The last field of wheat at Burleigh to be bindered and stoked was in the late 1960s in the Golf Course field. After that the potato shed was built at Tillyrie and the sheafs were not needed for tattie pits.

One of the steam-engines Sir James Hope had driven home himself from the factory in Liverpool, had been used at Spott in the steep fields below the Roman Camp Field, with two tractors driving coal to it as it pulled the machines up the face of the hill. This magnificent machine sat along the track from the Home Farm. After a year John asked if he was going to leave it and was rather disappointed when it was moved next day.

In 1959 there was the first Grand Curling Match on Loch Leven since the war. Hundreds of curlers were in rinks three deep out into the Loch and their followers came out to watch them.

In 1962 John, who was an elder at Spott Church, was on the plate one Sunday. The next day he bought the top-priced bull, Townhead Dairy Boy, at the Ayrshire Bull Sales for Tillyrie. He was teased at the church saying the bull was bought with the plate collection.

1963 was the coldest winter since 1740. The worst was three weeks in March, when snow was meeting the waves on the beaches. Eileen and I went to Dunbar

Haymaking (1966)

on horseback twice to get supplies for themselves and neighbours. When the snow melted, we could see the rock plants in the garden had been flowering underneath the snow.

In 1961 Eileen was called home to drive John and help Miss Lovey in the office. There had been a crash and it was thought prudent, with the long hours John was keeping, to have a driver.

Eileen also helped out on the milk cart when the milkmen were on holiday. The Kinross and country runs were by then using vans, which were kept in good order by Les Humphrey of Keirs Garage in Milnathort. However, Milnathort still had a pony, the grey Hector. Hector knew his round and would stop at all the correct places. When he got to Viewfar Road and almost at the end of his run, he went down Old Perth Road to Back Loan without stopping at Victoria Avenue, to the discomfort of those on the cart. Once down Back Loan he stopped outside White the Bakers for a bun, and Lord help the lad who forgot his bun, while the driver checked Giacopazzi's did not need more milk for their ice-cream making.

Once back at Burleigh there was a little bridge to cross to get to the loading bank. This bridge had a big drop down to the Hattonburn and only a rail on one side. It was wiser to let Hector take the cart over on his own as he manoeuvred the bridge to an inch.

The milk boys were a source of amusement: Geordie Hutt, Davey Tod, Charlie Foley and all the other lads who came out to help deliver the milk and collect the money on a Friday. They were great characters, up to mischief and hard-working. One was even known to drive the van when his brother had had a 'late night', barely able to see over the steering wheel, but successfully doing the round and arriving back at Burleigh.

Another source of amusement was seeing the Kinross Fire Brigade on a mission. They were all volunteers in these days and, when the call came, they left their work (butcher, baker and candlestick maker), changed into uniforms and jump edon the Fire Engine, bell going fifteen to the dozen, while one man, still adjusting his uniform, peddled his bicycle madly to catch up with his company.

Jim Malcolm, the grieve at Tillyrie, retired in 1963 and John Lawrie asked a neighbour at Spott if he could have a word with his son John.

Mark Thomson farmed at Pathhead and, having two sons, said there was not room for both to come home so they had better find other employment. John the elder was at the Dick Vet, Edinburgh, and Gyles joined an auctioneers at Reston and Berwick. John was offered the job at Tillyrie. He was to work there in the summer holidays and go back to University for a term and think it over.

The lecturers were disappointed when he left the Dick Vet, as they thought he would make a good vet and he had a way with animals. However, John Thomson came to Tillyrie as a prospect manager, starting at the bottom. He was given the bothy at Matale and often cycled down to Mrs Isa Watson at Keston, for his dinner between noon and one o'clock.

There were 14 folk who worked on Tillyrie at that time. These included Jock Woods, Albe Dewar, Eck Dewar, Bob Alan (all tractor men) Charlie Duncan (horseman) and his son Bob (orraman), Munro (shepherd), Jock Macgarva (dairyman), Rab Summers (cattleman) and the two wives, Mrs Wood and Mrs Dewar.

There were 100 milking cows and their followers plus 500 ewes and their followers. Seed potatoes and seed grain were grown on the 880 acres, which went from 400ft to 990ft, remembering Loch Leven is approx 200ft above sea level.

At harvest, turnip thinning and haymaking, the Burleigh men when free helped out, and vice-versa. Burleigh was more than 200ft lower than Tillyrie, which can mean harvesting a day or two earlier, but in the spring it gets frost that Tillyrie can miss. Turnip thinning, potato lifting and potato dressing saw Don Ross's squad (led by Adam Collier with his brother Will) arriving to help. Normally two farms at equal height above sea level would crop fairly levelly. Every hundred miles further south would mean cropping a week earlier, whereas a hundred feet above sea level would make only a few days difference.

Wedding of Dorothy and John Thomson

In 1963 the grieve at Spott retired, and John Lawrie replaced him with Bob Tod's friend (and second man at Burleigh), Ian Alexander. Ian was an Angus man who, with his wife Julie and family, moved to East Lothian. It took the Lothian men a while to accept an outsider but Ian won their respect with hard work and some humour, and was a first-class grieve to John Lawrie.

The Forth Road Bridge was opened in 1964, after decades of speculation. The ferries stopped running. The bridge cut a quarter of an hour from the Spott to Kinross run, and was a wonder at the time. Over the next decade the motorway was gradually built, and every village bypassed saved time. By the late 1970s to 1980s the time could be cut to an hour's motoring, especially early in the morning.

John Thomson and I (Dorothy Lawrie, third daughter of John and Daisy Lawrie) were married on 26th May 1965 at Spott Kirk and we had the reception in marquees on the lawn at Spott House. Don Ross arranged for Jersey Royal new potatoes to be available, and the meal was served by the Open Arms Hotel in Dirleton. There were 220 guests filling the wee old church to capacity. Old friends of Daisy and John from Kinross-shire, new friends made in East Lothian and relations from both parties were at the wedding. Biddy Thomson's folk from Kent and Paris were present and, as both families had become friends since first meeting in 1958, it was a warm and friendly day.

It was standard practice in farming for holidays to be taken at the end of May (between turnips being sown and the hay ready to cut) or November (after harvest and when the potatoes were up). After a honeymoon in Norway we settled into Matale and down to the work on the farm. One week-end a month the dairyman had off, the next week-end the assistant dairyman, the third was the shepherd's weekend and the fourth was John's, as he relieved the others on their weekends off. For a few years I had been helping Eileen in the office at Burleigh at the end of the week and that continued.

With 50 employees the wages took two days for two staff to prepare. The pages were drawn up at times when the office was not so busy so the wages books were ready for the week each Thursday. The overtime, holidays and extras were noted for individuals, then any changes the Inland Revenue had made, then each person's details, gross wage, tax worked out from a book. The National Insurance contributions were also worked out from a book and the net wage recorded on the page. Then the columns were totalled, balanced and everybody's wage worked out so the required cash was broken into the denominations needed. They were mostly paid about £10-£12 a week, the grieves and dairymen £12-£15 a week and, after deductions, the pounds, shillings and pence had to be worked out so each person got the correct change in their pay-packet. £10 notes, however, were not allowed in the packets as the vans going round the doors may not have had the change. This had to balance with the sum drawn from the bank, and one had to go to the post office and get national insurance stamps and stick them in all the individual cardboard books. The stamps were small and had a revolting glue. They were fiddly to place in the cardboard books, and a sponge was used to wet them to save having to lick them.

On Friday all the money was collected from the bank and checked. Then one could start to make up a set of wages. The wage packets were not sealed until everyone was finished and balanced. In this age of computers and direct debits it seems a lot of effort and energy to make sure the correct wages were paid, and books balanced.

At potato planting and lifting the wages for the tattie squads had to be made up and named depending on how many days the individual had worked. Sometimes, before I married, I took the Spott money home to Dunbar, catching the train at Kinross with a small overnight case, changing at Waverley to the train south and getting off at Dunbar, where I was met. I felt quite safe as nobody would suspect a teenager going home for the weekend and, when the potato squad was working, there was quite a lot of money. Normally Eileen and Mr Lawrie took it home with them.

A bank reconciliation was done every Monday morning for all three accounts. On the fourth week of the month invoices that had come in for the previous month's work were paid. There were the calf registers to keep for the two herds of 100 cows each. The Tillyrie cows were named in families going back to where they came from in 1948. They got their mothers' names with the father named in the registration book. There were Katies, Coralines but the one called Atriaka was prolific and hard to spell. Some families died out, either because they weren't good enough or had no daughters to follow them. It was all rather interesting how some families flourished and others didn't.

Then there was the milk money at the end of the week. On Friday and Saturday the three milkmen and the milk boys collected the milk money, and they brought their book and leather money bags into the office to be counted. The office was open until the last one was in, and the books balanced both up and across the columns on every page and this had to balance with the money. When all three money bags were correct, the money was all put together and checked again before being recorded and put in a nightsafe bag, and taken to the bank. We were lucky to be away by three o'clock. It was sometimes that time before the last milkman came in with his bag. The banks were open until midday and wages were paid to the men at noon on a Saturday.

In the mid 60s the milkmen, thinking of their security on a Friday night once the milk money was collected and folk knowing where they lived, it was decided to take the bags to Matale. The washing machine was a safe place to keep the bags overnight, and it was a good place for a long time. Then one night when they had been out the babysitter said that the washing machine had been making a funny noise, so she had turned it off. The machine must have been left on and bumped into start. All three bags were emptied out and made the "funny" noise. The Raeburn cooker was used to dry the notes before breakfast, and the change was clean and bright, but the leather bags were more of a problem to dry. A new place had to be found to keep the milk money safe overnight at Matale.

When John Lawrie was interviewing a person for a post he always wanted to do so at the person's house and to meet his wife. This ensured they would cause the minimum disruption to good, present employees, and not cause trouble. One prospective employee gave his neighbour's house as his address because it was better kept, but the deception did not work.

On 7th April 1966 John Mark Thomson was born at Perth Royal Infirmary and, when he came home, the snow was still on the ground. He was christened at Spott by Rev Turner and the celebrations after at Pathhead included both sets of grandparents and Biddy Thomson's parents, Charles and Amy Longley from Kent. He was the first grandchild for both families.

In the mid-sixties John and his father went north to a demonstration of a Poldenvale Run-Through Dipper. John ordered one and modified the old dipper at Tillyrie, enlarged it and installed the new dipper. The sheep were dipped twice a year, once after clipping to protect against flies, maggots and other vermin, and again in winter. The new dipper was faster and used half the labour of the old one where the sheep were manhandled into a cruder dipper. The sheep were held in pens, put up a race, stepped into the dipper down steps, (sometimes with persuasion) swam a few strokes and stepped out of the other end into a holding pen to dry off the excess dip. It was a two-man job, one pushing the sheep forward to the race and the other seeing the swimming sheep went under at some point so the head was protected by the dip and that none were drowned.

Jim Colliar had joined the work force at Burleigh and was living at Lethangie. Burleigh men were up at Tillyrie helping out with some work, when one of the men came to the door of Matale in a state, saying there had been an accident and would I come right away. They walked up the road, and by the gate into the west end of the Cottage Park a tractor had hit a telegraph pole. I opened the door of the tractor and saw Jim slumped over the steering wheel and from his colour knew he was dead. Being the man that he was, when he felt the heart attack coming on, he pulled the tractor off the road and would have been dead by the time it hit the pole. I went home and called the authorities and Mr Lawrie at the office. I had known Jim, who was the greive at East Brackley, had played with his son on the roofs and got many rows for transgression from this man. He was part of our everyday life and now the first dead person I had seen.

George Colliar, son of Jim and Nan, started his own engineering business at Balado in the late 1960s. He had previously worked for Bowen near Dunfermline. When he got the Deutz franchise he came to the office at Burleigh to try and convince John Lawrie to buy a Deutz tractor. At one point he said, 'If folk saw a Deutz in your fields they would want one too.' 'Well, you had better give me one,' was the reply. 'Oh! Mr Lawrie you know I can't do that!' The outcome was that Mr Lawrie bought Deutz tractors for years and got good service from George Colliar, with meetings in the Burleigh office and hard bargaining enjoyed by both parties.

1968 saw a double celebration for the family. On 3rd April Jean Catherine Thomson was born and, in September, Eileen Gilmour Lawrie married Jens-Arne Jorgensen. Jean's christening was put back until the autumn, when the great-grandparents who would be north for the wedding from Kent would be at Spott. So in one week in September, Jean was christened at Spott by Rev Turner, with the celebrations at Spott House attended by all grandparents and one set of great-grandparents.

Then Eileen and Jens were married in Spott Church by the Rev Turner. Jens's parents, brother and army friends from his national service days in the Guards

Wedding of Eileen Gilmour Lawrie and Jens-Arne Jorgensen

(still a two-year compulsory service in Denmark) were all in attendance. The Danes all stayed in a hotel in Dunbar over the time of the wedding, and came to Spott House to be entertained. The reception was on the lawn in front of the house in marquees, and a dance in the evening followed the main reception and lunch.

After a honeymoon the couple settled in Jutland on a farm near his parents. They started with Jersey cows and pigs, working their way to a herd of black and white cows.

1969 was a watershed year at Tillyrie. A large frost-proof potato shed was built in the stackyard, with 11 grain bins at the west end. The shed held 60 acres of seed potatoes (approx 500 tons), heaped on the floor. The 11 grain bins were a reception bin, three drying bins and seven storage bins, each bin holding 30 tons of grain. With a 50% government grant available and the interest rates low, the shed was paid off in seven years of trading. Golden Promise seed barley through the 1970s sold for £136 per ton. It was grown for the Scottish Agricultural Industry (SAI) with Mike Silvera as rep and, in the good years, they took every 'pea of barley' they could get and, in a poor year, they looked after their producers. They paid six weeks after the grain was lifted from the farm without fail. This was an improvement on some firms when one was chasing money in May.

This shed meant no more dressing tatties out of pits, and not needing wheat sheaves to insulate the pits. All the grain at Burleigh and Tillyrie could be combined and dried at Tillyrie, and the potatoes grown at both farms could be stored safely, and dressed when wanted under cover. Burleigh potatoes and grain were brought up to Tillyrie by tractors and trailers straight off the field, via Victoria Avenue and North Street.

When the new school was built, and the Reid Memorial School demolished, the children from Tillyrie were eligible to have a school taxi for the first time. Mark started school at Milnathort when he was five. He, Alan Kay and Billy Fernie were the only boys in the class and the teacher, Miss Reid, had no chance of keeping the peace in the classroom with those three.

The sugar beet factory in Cupar shut down on 23rd December 1971. This caused many farmers to look for other crops. Sugar beet was grown on 4,000 acres in Fife alone. Spott was lucky, for East Lothian was able to grow good crops of grain but others had to look for alternative crops. The modern field vegetable industry grew out of this. Sandy Braid at Channel brought in a new vegetable from South Africa called broccoli. His energetic marketing over the years, early runs to markets in Edinburgh and Glasgow, supplying hotels in all areas, then supermarkets when they arrived, made it all a success. He opened a farm shop with his mother. She sold, with great enthusiasm, all the different vegetables: carrots, cauliflower, Brussels sprouts, lettuce and leeks as well as broccoli. He even had T-shirts made with 'Braids Broccoli Builds Braw Bodies' printed on them. Jean wore one while visiting Spott, and John Lawrie said he hoped Jean was being paid to wear it! Sandy's energy was the reason for his success. Many went down trying to establish various ventures.

The East of Scotland Growers, a co-operative of farmers like Sandy and his friend John's cousin, Charles Russell of Muirton Farm, Drem, in East Lothian and other like-minded farmers joined it. Kettle Produce, based in Kingskettle, started in the 1970s and now has a workforce of over 500 and a turnover in excess of £89 million.

An automatic byre mucker was installed at Tillyrie. It was a continuous metal belt that went round the byre in the grip and took the waste out to the midden, which was placed on the road down to the pond, a brick-sided structure which the muck fell down into. This had been used to barrow the waste out of the byre for years, before being emptied with a tractor and bucket into a midden and left in the field to mature.

In October 1973 Miss Reid died. She had had two falls in the last year and broke a hip but with great determination got home to Tillyrie House and Annie Fowles. Annie was housekeeper for decades to Miss Reid, and cared for her when she was elderly with outstanding sympathy. When Miss Reid in her later years had difficulty going upstairs, Annie waylayed John Thomson on his way home to Matale, and he carried her up. They were so discreet that even John's wife didn't know how infirm Miss Reid was. Miss Reid died in her sleep at her beloved Tillyrie.

I had been so careful to be polite to the little old Victorian Miss Reid and not swear in front of her, so when I heard in the eulogy that she had driven an ambulance in Flanders, I thought Miss Reid must have 'heard more swear words than I knew existed'. It was rather sad that after 300 years in Tillyrie the last of the Reids had gone. I remember that Miss Reid left one third of her fortune to St Paul's Episcopal Church in Kinross and another third to the Queen Alexandria Nurses.

Joy Reid invited me down to the big house to see if I would like any of the furniture they were not taking. So I went down to be met by Joy and her two daughters. They took me round the house, pointing out what was available. The younger daughter Sarah, who was tall and elegant and had a slight brown in her green eyes that made you look at her twice, was most kind and gave the children some books about birds. The other, older daughter was plainer and practical. When she was showing me out to the dairy, she could not resist a swipe at my family being lucky to have Tillyrie. I bit my tongue on telling her that if her father had been like my father it would still be theirs. I didn't reply. Meanwhile, Joy told her Miss Reid was falling over the Persian rugs in the drawing room and the big Persian carpet from the dining room was moved to replace the rugs. An old carpet was put in the dining room. Miss Reid, in her will made several years before, left the dining room carpet to a niece, Susan Webb, and Joy thought it funny that they gave the Susan the old carpet and not the big Persian one. Miss Reid's nephew Mathew Webb was left all the crystal in the house, otherwise David and Joy got everything else. I put my name against a few pieces and agreed a price with Joy. I went home thinking how nice Sarah was but was disillusioned with the other two.

One night in November, while Daisy was staying with John and I at Matale, John Lawrie phoned from Keston at 9 o'clock to say if it was too frosty to dig turnips out the ground he would flit us to Tillyrie House the next day. That was all the warning given. So next day, in Baltic weather, Edward Boyle and John came with a tractor and trailer and flitted the household goods to the farm house. The Esse cooker was hard to light at any time but, after sitting off for a month, was really difficult and it was tea time before any heat came off it. All the doors were open to allow the furniture to be brought in and I wrote in chalk which room everything was to go into as it was loaded at Matale. Daisy said she had never been so cold in her life as she was that night. We spent days putting tape round doors in the back premises where the draughts came through the gaps. I was surprised there was no central heating when Miss Reid had been so well off, and it was seven years before John agreed to put it in.

On 15th February 1971 the UK changed its currency. The pound was kept in name and value but instead of the 240 pennies of old, it would now consist of 100 new pence. Goodbye was said to the familiar half-crowns (2/6), florins (2/-), shillings (1/-), sixpences and threepenny bits. Many older people took it badly and had difficulty adjusting. The generation who were at school in the 1950s had learned decimalisation as well as pounds, shillings and pence. They also would have to use kilo, and grams instead of stones, pounds and ounces, and litres instead of pints. All very confusing, but the UK kept the mile and did not convert to kilometres although the inches, feet and yards were replaced by millimetres, centimetres and metres. It was so much easier to move the dot instead of doing the maths.

In 1973 the UK joined the EEC after years on the sidelines, while Germany and France took pole positions within the new community. This introduced a period of rapidly rising prices, and in the first few years we benefitted from the Common Agricultural Policy (CAP). This had been framed in the hungry post-war years and the main agenda was to ensure freedom from hunger. Farmers rapidly responded to a policy aimed at growing more cereals and butter, even on second-grade land and on the continent, tobacco and industrial-quality wine.

About this time John's sister Isa had the misfortune to have a shingles infection, and the doctor said she was not to go upstairs. The upshot was that Keston was sold and Isa came to live at Tillyrie in the bungalow, which she called Newton after the farm where they all grew up. She was always a great gardener and in no time had a beautiful garden at Newton. It was lovely to have her near again, as we ran in and out of her White House at East Brackley, and she was more of a surrogate granny to us than an aunt.

By the late 1970s the media reported wine lakes, butter mountains and bulging grain stores. The brake was put on the latter over-production by 'set aside' whereby 10% of land was taken out of production – running counter to the natural instincts of farmers, but dulled by promises of payments for the non-production policy.

CAP sounded the death knell of the traditional mixed farm. The biggest negative legacy of this well-intentioned policy was that it took farmers away from meeting the demands of the marketplace and into production for production's sake.

1974 was a year of changes. John Lawrie sold the milk runs to Mrs Reekie. The unions in Scotland stopped the sale of fresh milk, no matter how clean and tested and John was not going to pasteurise his quality milk, so he stopped retailing it on 27th October.

Bill at Clashbenny lost some of this tenanted land due to development and open cast clay, and dispersed his famous flock of Suffolk sheep. Bill had been president of the Suffolk Breed Society in 1958-59, which were shown and judged all over, including at the Royal Show and The Royal Highland Show. Buyers came from England, Ireland and Wales to the dispersal, as well as Scots breeders. It was the second oldest flock of Suffolk sheep, founded in 1931. He sold 130 ewes and rams, and a shearling ewe sold for a record 550 guineas. It was a flyer of a sale.

Dorothy and Rebel 'look the sheep'

Tillyrie's smaller lambs went to Spott where on the strong land they grew faster to maturity. We noticed our lambing percentage was reducing, and concluded the smaller lambs included too many twins. So we started to clip the ears of the twin lambs with a different nick from the singles. Twin ability being very hereditary, this sorted the problem and the lambing percentage went up again.

We leased Holton Hill in the late 1960s. They had a flock of big, beautiful Perthshire-type Blackies which we took over. It was remarkable when all the sheep were gathered for the dipping etc, they segregated on the front hill, the Tillyrie ewes went on up to their hill and the Holton ewes turned right through the gate in the march fence to their own hill. Such is the strength of hefting, each returning to where they were reared.

In May 1974 John Gilmour Lawrie married Tessa Ruffman in Newcastle upon Tyne. Tessa, daughter of the late Dr Ruffman and Mrs Ruffman, had followed her parents into a medical career and was a nurse specialising in sick children, in the Middlesex Hospital, London.

In the summer of 1974 the accountants Ernest & Whinney asked Daisy and John to meet them at Tillyrie. There was a special meeting in the dining-room as they realised John's age and that he held 51% of the company shares. John kept one share – the controlling share – and Gilmour could get some tax-free as a wedding present, but I would have to buy shares as there was no way to give them to me. I agreed and they were the only shares ever to be bought or sold to date. This left me with a debt which took years to clear. Gilmour and I were made directors of John Lawrie (Farms) Ltd.

From the Fifties through to the mid-Seventies oil was pretty stable at $30 a barrel. In 1975 it leapt to about $58 as the Arab countries became more important in the industry. It peaked at $120 in 1980. Oil gradually came down to $80 in the mid-Eighties, troughed to $20 in the late Nineties, to peak again in 2010 at $162. It stayed at $100-120 until 2015 then went down to $50-75. The first Range Rover John Lawrie had in the 1970s had cost £2600 and did 15 miles per gallon, which cost a half-crown (15p) per gallon pre-1971. A new Mini cost £300. Inflation was a word we learned in the 1970s and petrol had to be sold in litres once the price rose to 99p a gallon as the indicator only displayed two digits. £1 a gallon meant they would have to be replaced nationwide and it was easier to convert to litres. There are four and a half litres in a gallon.

Wedding of John Gilmour Lawrie and Tessa Ruffman

1975 brought in the the Sex Discrimination Act, and one could not advertise a job for a man. It either had to be for a person or you put in two adverts, one for a man and one for a woman. It did however mean when I applied for a Jockey Club Permit as an amateur trainer to run against professionals, and John said not to put his name on the form, that I inadvertently became the first woman to hold a permit.

As there was no shepherd at that time I looked after the sheep on my home-bred horse, The Rebel and, in the two hours it took, he got all the gallops needed to keep him fit. Rebel was most interested if we stopped for a 'cooped' ewe on the hill, and he would look over my shoulder to see the ewe while she was steadied until her balance came back, and he would carry a sick sheep home over the front of the saddle. We had an Old English Sheepdog called Blue, who was keen to work, but nobody would train him. Blue was the only collie who would work off the horse and, when the Tillyrie 250 acre hill needed its 200 sheep gathered, Blue, Rebel and I could clear the hill of sheep in an hour. We always gathered from the west to the east and off the gate on to the Holton Side of the front hill. Blue was great on the boggy bits where the horse couldn't go. You just said 'Speak to them' and he'd bark, the sheep leaving the boggy area very quickly and, when you told Blue 'Enough's enough', he stopped barking.

One winter day, the snow was lying and I saw a man with a Labrador dog and stick poaching grouse, cowering in cold snow on the hill. Calling to him eventually chased him away, and I sat on Rebel until he left towards the Holton hill. This made me late for collecting the children off the Dollar bus and I jumped in the car in the waterproofs I had worn while looking the sheep up the hill and didn't stop for a hot drink. The school bus was late due to the weather and, by the time we got back home to the warm kitchen it was time for tea. Changing out of the cold waterproofs and making tea on the Esse, I started to feel odd and when John came in I was shivery. It was the only experience of hypothermia I ever had, and from six till after nine I shivered in bed with three hot water bottles. It was not an experience I wanted to repeat.

1975 was a very hot summer. For six weeks it was 80°F by 10am. We had to move sheep after ten at night or early in the morning as the dogs were too stressed by the heat. The Scots potato trade was good as the crops further south failed. Many Scots farmers were able to buy much-needed new machinery because of this. There were fires down south. All it took to start a roadside fire was a cigarette butt thrown from a car window.

A second hot summer followed in 1976, another scorcher with the same ram-ifications. The potato harvest was poor down south and fires broke out all over the place. This began the need for the irrigation of potato crops which, from then on took over as the norm and many huge crops of potatoes were harvested, some with no flavour at all. Some farms in Scotland changed hands for big money.

Up until 1978 the cows were fed Arthur Earlies and Winter King cabbages at Burleigh and Tillyrie. They loved the great big cabbage and would crunch them enthusiastically. When the Burleigh herd went on to cabbage Dr Derek would get a mass of mothers with babies with filled nappies. He would phone Burleigh to check the cows' diet had been changed to include the cabbage, then tell the mothers not to worry as the babies would settle down in a couple of days.

In 1980 Daisy Lawrie, who was never ill, lost a lot of weight and at first was pleased. However in May it had become quite serious, and in June she went into hospital in Haddington for investigation. While she was in hospital Wimbledon was on. This she watched annually as her holidays, locking the door and not answering the phone. If she did pick up the phone she would say 'It's Wimbledon!' and hang up. In the week she was diagnosed with cancer, which was into her liver, and she was given six weeks or six months to live. She was given a blood transfusion and came home.

John Lawrie wanted things to carry on as normal and Eileen was not to come home yet in case Daisy realised how ill she was. When Rev Turner visited she said to him she did not think she would be down the village again. He replied 'Daisy, there is a lot of mischief for you to do yet.' When the district nurse came she noticed some jaundice in her eyes. She saw the Ladies' Championship on the Saturday but wandered in the night and the doctor gave her morphine for the first time. At seven next morning, John gave Eileen and I permission to come to Spott. I was there by ten from Tillyrie, and met the doctor coming down the stairs. He said he'd given Daisy another injection and she would be in a coma for a day or two. Eileen was flying from Denmark and due in at five.

Constance and Biddy Thomson were with Daisy an hour later when her breathing changed, I was sent down to the library where John and Gilmour were talking. They came up right away, and John went to her bedside. Her breathing

Picking potatoes

just got quieter and quieter until she went. We all went downstairs and left John with her.

Eileen was distraught that she did not arrive home in time to see Daisy before she passed away. The funeral, held a few days later, was well attended. Afterwards the folk were invited back to Spott House.

On Aunt Isa's 80th birthday we held a surprise party for her. I asked her out for lunch and, when she arrived, she was shown into the drawing room where all her living relatives were waiting to greet her. She had a ball seeing everyone and it was well on in the day when the party ended. Isa told me off in her mild way, saying that she didn't like surprises. However, she had certainly enjoyed this one.

Mistress Isa Watson, as she was often addressed, died aged 84. Her funeral service was at Kinross Parish Church where she had been a regular member, and then she was buried at Strathavon, Lanarkshire beside her husband John Watson. Aunt Isa disliked being driven fast and the hearse crept out of Kinross but, when it took to the motorway, sped all the way to Strathavon where it went slowly to the cemetery. One cousin said she would have been saying something to the driver about the speed of the hearse on the motorway.

Her daughter Nan, who had retired as head physiotherapist at Bangour Hospital, lived at Newton after her mother.

On John Thomson's 40th birthday (1st July 1982) he was checking stock and saw a heifer lying on her own in Burleigh Sands, while the other heifers and the young bull were at the other side of the field. Being beside a fairly busy road he shut his collie in his pickup, and walked across to the single heifer. Being curious the other cattle came to see what he was doing, and the bull, who had been no bother before, suddenly charged him. John turned to face him and managed to catch the ring in his nose, meaning to stop the bull knocking him down and breaking his back rolling on him.

A tractor driver coming home for lunch down the cut from Burleigh Steading saw the pickup and the huddle of cattle. He drove through the gate and over the top of John, who had been fighting the bull for seven minutes by this time, and had five individually broken ribs, a punctured lung, a broken collarbone and a mangled hand. The bull tried to dig him out from under the tractor, and throwing every tool in the tractor at the bull they somehow managed to get John into the cab. They then drove out the field, tied the shattered gate up, and drove to the doctor's surgery in the middle of Kinross.

I was in the kitchen with the sun shining in, writing a letter while waiting for John to come home for his lunch. The phone went and it was the surgery saying John had had an accident. I asked if he was alive, and the voice just said to come as quickly as possible. I drove to Kinross trying not to panic and, remembering the milkman John Lyon's wife was seriously hurt by a doctor going to an emergency, tried not to speed. However, I was stopped doing 40mph by the police opposite the Green Hotel. I explained that my husband was at the surgery and I did not know if he was alive or not. The police followed me to the surgery where they found John lying on a stretcher with an oxygen mask over his face.

One of the police asked for my car keys and, when asked why, said he would bring the car to PRI so I had a way of getting home. The ambulance had a police escort to PRI. The British police are great when you need them. At Bridge of Earn I saw John move his legs and thought with relief that he was not paralysed.

There followed a never-ending wait as tests were done. Sometimes I was with John and sometimes asked to wait in a waiting room. It was worse waiting away from John as I couldn't assess how he was and my imagination tried to run riot. In the end he was kept in hospital in case of internal bleeding, and I was told to phone at 10am next morning. I phoned his parents from the hospital and got his mother, and had to tell her that John was badly hurt and would be in hospital overnight.

Thanks to the police I had the car to drive home to the children and parents. It was a long night for us all. Next day Dad appeared about 9.30am, to get a beast for the Red Cross charity sale, and he was upset because the hospital had said John was to go home. I said I was to phone at 10am but he insisted otherwise. So I went up for John, who was waiting in the ward, and took him home.

Daisy Lawrie used to say 'You can't go till your number is called'. We reckoned she was up in heaven checking the number, and John was saved.

The next few months were difficult and progress was slow but sure. At first he sat on a wooden chair in the sitting room and, as he could only speak in a whisper due to the punctured lung, someone had to be there all the time in case he needed something, and he'd to be helped out of the chair. At night he had to sit up in bed leaning on pillows, and I slept next door. We arranged a Norwegian cow bell tied to his sheet so if he slipped off his pillows or needed help he could pull the sheet and the bell rang.

Jean and Mark were wonderful, and grew up fast during that time. As the word got out, and the newspapers ran the story the next day, the phone never stopped ringing. We did not know we had so many friends and the children manned the phone all week.

Mark sat his driving test that week. He went from the field with the tractor. He was driving to Sands car park where he met instructor Gay Dees with her car, and the driving examiner. The latter asked Mark what vehicle he had arrived in and Mark pointed to the tractor. As most of Gay Dees pupils did he passed first time, and it was a godsend to us at home. He was able to take himself and Jean to their various tetrathlon engagements, and to Elmwood College in Cupar when it started again.

John was not able to dress himself for weeks and it was November before he was fit to do light work.

Meanwhile the bull, Tillyrie Midas, a son of Miss Burleigh (the only cow to come to Tillyrie when the Burleigh herd was dispersed) stayed in the field for a week. Then he and the Kinross Estate bull were fighting over the fence. When the police found out he was still alive they were angry, and wanted him removed. They asked how we would approach him, and John said he just came! They wanted him tranquilised, which we thought was dangerous. So we arranged for a retired vet from Fife who was a very good shot. The only drawback was that he had Parkinson's disease, but he could control the shakes long enough to shoot the bull.

On the day Jock Woods drove a tractor and trailer with straw bales on it, and the vet was to shoot down to the bull so the shot was controlled. When Jock saw the vet and his shakes he said 'Does he know what he's *!?*&* well doing?' Reassured, Jock drove across the field and the first time the cattle (including the bull) came forward, the vet said to move on so he could get a better shot. They moved forward and the bull followed. We heard the shot before the bull crumpled and fell. The police were furious because we had not tranquilised the bull, but he was safely dead and nobody else was hurt.

John had a clock engraved and presented it to the tractor driver who had saved his life.

After that it was decided to artificially inseminate (AI) the cows and dispense with keeping bulls. That worked with the cows in milk when one could see when they came in season, but was not really any use with the heifers. After a year or so it was decided to buy a Hereford bull as they were good-natured and would give a calf neat enough for heifers to birth. Willie Warnock at Gartfinnan, Forest Mill, had good Herefords and we knew him through the children's tetrathlon at the Pony Club. We arranged to go along, and John was happy enough to go into a field with three young bulls for sale, and bought one that took his eye. When putting the details into the computer, Jean got as far as 'Willie Wark', so the bull was called 'Willie Work' for the rest of his days.

The Hereford-Cross Ayrshire calves were hardy and the bull calves sold well. Two years later we bought a Romanollo bull at Perth Bull Sales. There was only one John liked as too many were short and boxy, but one had the length and scope wanted and was good-natured. He was a blue-grey colour, with eye make-up Cleopatra would have been proud of. He was an Italian breed. The first Hereford cross-Romanollo were born in the following spring, and every year the cows went to the hill in May and came off in October with a calf almost the size of themselves and in calf again. They calved without help and the calves had an inborn instinct to get on their feet and suckle from the cow.

In 1980 they were gathering potatoes at Gallowhill Farm with a mechanical picker, with six women on top sorting stones and soil from the potato crop. One of the woman asked what a mud-covered metal object was and Jim Paterson was able to recognise a hand grenade. He told the police, who sent in an army squad to deal with it. Some of the farm had been used as a training ground for troops in the First World War. The bomb squad confirmed it was a hand grenade from that time and the pin was rusted. Jim said he found one years before and pointed to it under a stone in a dyke. That pin was even more rusted. The bomb squad dug a hole and put sandbags on top of the two grenades. Both were live and went off, blowing the sandbags to bits.

During the First World War the field was in oats and the end rig was hand-scythed, as was then the custom. The horses were fresh after their summer break and did a half-day in the binder till they got fitter, while three other horses did the other half of the day. One day Mr Paterson senior was on the binder when some soldiers started blowing their bugles. The fresh horses took off right across the field, binder and all into the middle of the oats. It was the far side of the field before Mr Paterson got control of the three horses again.

After the tatties were up, one day I saw two men with a greyhound and lurcher dogs, poaching in the Little Dipper field. I asked them who they were and was incensed when one said he was John Thomson. Their bag was full and they tried to make a run for it up the empty drills. I was sitting on Burgundy, who had won four races, so this was a bad choice. On running them down they were told that if they were seen on Tillyrie again their dogs would be shot and, as I was not a very good shot, that could be dangerous. They were not seen again and didn't turn up to pick our potatoes.

Back in 1982 John Lawrie caught mumps and was very ill for two months. While he was in bed his mind was active and he decided to break up the company and have it the way he wanted when he died. He missed Daisy every day, mentioning her daily in conversation.

In the summer of 1983 all the shareholders were to come to Spott. I drove Mr Myles the lawyer and John Lawrie down from Kinross to Spott for the meeting with the accountants, headed by Mr McLennan. Constance was asked in first while the rest of us waited in the morning room. Then we were asked to the library where it turned out John Lawrie wanted to split up the company and share equalled acres and company debt. Gilmour got Spott, Eileen got Meikle Pinkerton and I got Tillyrie. Constance was to be bought out. It took two years for the accountants to work with the Inland Revenue to sort out the what John called 'the divorce', when the one company was made into three companies with the minimum of taxation.

John Lawrie moved back to Burleigh after he started the breakup of the company. The house had been a hostel when the dairy was active and the office was in the dining room. It needed rewiring, painting and generally bringing up to date, and all in a short timescale. The tradesmen he had used for years came and did this at short notice, a sign of the respect he was held in. He always paid for work done within a month of invoice, and had used the same local tradesmen with mutual respect. The office was moved to Balfour Cottage at Tillyrie, where an extra room was built on the east end for an office. Mrs Todd the secretary was to live in the cottage.

Mrs Ann Sneddon, who had helped in the farmhouse at Tillyrie for 11 years, went to help at Burleigh and had a good time helping Mr Lawrie settle in. It all took time but, by November, John Lawrie and his daughter Constance came back to Burleigh to live.

In 1983 milk quotas were inflicted on the industry. Once we got our allocation and things settled down, the government took 20% away from Scotland and gave it to Northern Ireland. It cost us £40,000 to buy enough back to replace it and we were only back to the beginning.

We as a family thought about how the milk quota would affect us. At a meeting with Mr Mackendrick of Bellfield Farm, a well-respected Fresian breeder, we discussed the situation. He advised that we kept to Ayrshires as they were hardier, converted food to milk better and calved easier. Back home, after much thought it was decided to stop using all the herd as potential mothers of replacements. The top third would be the mothers of replacements, the second third would be crossed to Black and White AI and the daughters sold, and the bottom third would be put to beef AI and the offspring sold. The top cows were measured by their milk production, butter fat, calving pattern, confirmation and long levity. We did not condemn cows until their third lactation, unless the first was dreadful. The decision vastly increased the average milk production. Milk recording was the proof. The milk recorder came every three weeks.

Mrs Thatcher encouraged the beef industry to enlarge in 1981 and, just when the extra heifers that folk kept for breeding were put to the bull and calved, she let more imports of cheap South American beef into the UK with no regard to the strict environment, rearing restrictions and slaughter regulations that UK farmers had to meet. Many farmers went out of business, and ones who bought cattle to fatten got their fingers burned and never bought store cattle again.

There were months of 'farmer bashing' in the press and on TV until the start of the Falkland War in June 1981. This climaxed with Mrs Edwina Curry's attack on eggs, which bankrupted the UK egg industry and let cheap unregulated eggs be imported. It did not continue again after the Falkland War was well fought and won.

When Mark left school, he did his year of practical at Spott then did two years agriculture training at Elmwood College. The dairyman Tom Colvin was seriously ill for months, and Mark was up at four am milking 100 cows, before being at Cupar for lectures at nine. John did the afternoon milking until Tom was fit to return.

In his second year Mark was joined by Jean who started her secretary training at Elmwood and, in her second year, stayed with two friends in digs. Both finished their courses with qualifications in agriculture and secretarial studies.

The 1984 harvest was disastrous – wet and windy.

A parlour was built in the turnip shed beside the byre, with an extension for the holding area. The five-aside, built to do six-aside if needed, was especially designed for John's height. The byre was then used as cubicles, with rubber mats for the cows, who were not tied up. The concrete floor was cut in a diagonal pattern to stop cows slipping. The cows from the start were good at using the parlour, some wanting to use the right-hand side, some the left, and some impatient of others wanting in when they had decided it was their turn. Some cows kept their 'own' stall in the new cubicles, and Lord help a young cow who went into the older cow's stall by mistake.

After a year or two, some of the younger cows who had never been tied up were lying in the middle of the floor and not in the stalls. So John and I went down after tea and tied up all the cows with neck chains in stalls. The older cows were no bother but a few youngsters were reluctant, misunderstanding for the first night or two. It was almost a 'water sport' with a difference, roping them and getting them into empty stalls. It took three hours on the first night but by the third all was well, and after that they all used the cubicles with no help.

In the mid-1980s trading in futures markets on food commodities was legal, and some traders played the markets. For years we had sold most of our potatoes to Don Ross of Peebles Brothers. In fact Don Ross and John Lawrie went down to Lincoln, Pembroke, and Yorkshire seeing clients and their crops growing almost annually, and making good relationships with them. Don had retired and his nephews ran the company. We grew potatoes for them and they were well sold, delivered half in November and half in March. David Peebles phoned in November asking for an extension till the spring for all the potatoes. John was not keen as he needed the space to bring cattle in for the winter but, after an hour on the phone, he reluctantly agreed. The potatoes were not picked up in March; in fact they were never picked up. We lost a great deal of money growing the potatoes and the contract was not worth the paper it was written on. The outcome was that we eventually sold our potato quota as the integrity of the people in the trade was compromised. Instead we bought more under the milk quota.

In 1985 Nancy Calder (the secretary) and I went on a three-day computer course as, after the Highland Show, Gilmour and I had decided to computerise the accounts. The year end was 31st July, and we started keeping the different farms on a computer and the first year books were kept as a backup. Wages and VAT were so quick, and the reports and budgeting were a revelation. When John Lawrie heard, he remarked he'd done his budgeting on the back of a cigarette packet. The reply was that if our competitors had computers, it was only sense for us to have them. Keeping books the first year was extra work but, as they balanced with the computer, we happily dispensed with them in the second year. We used Farm Plan by then and they had an office in the Highland Show ground. They were easy to contact with any difficulties.

John Lawrie had used the seed merchants McGill and Smith Ltd of Ayr since 1935, and director John Watson was a welcome visitor as well as a business contact. Their 'Ever Green' booklet published annually with all their seeds, photographs of growing crops and review of the year for plant breeding, extended to 50 pages, and often included a photo of Burleigh cows in front of the castle, and sheep at East Brackley on their clover mix. It also included reports on clients worldwide.

When John Watson retired his son John Watson started his own business. A visit from him in 1985 continued the connection and, on his retiring, Watson's Seeds based at Scateraw near Dunbar, run by his nephew, kept the supply of first-grade seeds coming, a must for good crops.

Tillyrie House, Autumn 1998

Jean married Euan Macgregor on 11th April 1986 and went to live at Falkland-wood Farm, near Falkland, where Euan was working for Mr Shanks. The wedding was at Orwell Church and the reception at the Bridge End Hotel in Kinross.

In 1987 a slurry tower, approx 20m in diameter and four sections high, was built at the end of the byre to take the waste. The grip in the byre was filled in. The area between the byre and the hayshed had been roofed over when the parlour was put in, and gave extra housing for the cows.

A straw shed had been built behind the potato shed, and was longer by three sections. This was used for the first time in 1988 to lamb the sheep inside. Temporary wooden walkways were constructed to go between the pillars of the shed, making pens and feed troughs at the same time. Smaller individual pens were down one side, for newly lambed ewes and for twinning lambs on.

In the 1970s the French shut their markets to horned sheep, which excluded the Blackface Breed, the most prolific of the Scots sheep. John thought a Derby Grit Stone tup an uncontrolled experiment, so he bought me six Derby Gritstone gimmers from Mr Brockelhurst, whom we visited in Derbyshire. These polled sheep we crossed with horned Blacky tups and all the females were polled. The ram lambs by different degrees all had teggs or horns. In the second year we saw a polled (Derby Gritstone cross) Blackie ram at the Blackface Stirling Tup Sales, and bought him from Mr Patterson, a well-known breeder doing the same experiment. He was such a good, well-built ram, with Perth Blacky type fleece and size, that John Lawrie, seeing the batch of three tups we had bought, did not notice the lack of horns and commented well on all the new rams.

We never did breed a polled male, but the females all bred polled lambs. We caused trouble by taking a polled female to Kinross show for two years, especially when we were second in the class the second year. However the experiment ended when the French relented and opened up the market to horned sheep again. But it proved it could be done.

The indoor lambing proved a great success, modified each year, and was the norm from then on. We had lambing people staying in the farmhouse. Some, like Johnny Scott, a shepherd from Gifford, were welcomed annually. We also had a series of Norwegian students from the Dick Vet for about six seasons, as the students from the year before left our name for the next year's students. One lamber came up from Dorset. She and her dog 'Cap' were used to Dorset Horned Park sheep. One stormy day the newly lambed ewes were put into a wood for shelter. Next day Cap and Sarah were trying to bring the Blackies out of the wood to put in a field, and the ewes faced up to the dog, stamping their feet and lowering their horns. Cap, not used to the aggression from sheep backed off. Sarah, exasperated and hassled, said to him, 'If that is all you can do go home!' She was left to get the sheep out of the wood on her own, Cap arriving at the back door of the farmhouse. She laughed about it later and said she would be more careful what she said to Cap in future. She was wanted the following year but married and went to Australia. We had lambers from New Zealand and Australia who played rugby with Mark. One was heard on his phone to his father saying 'they try to save lambs here!' Back home, he said, the farmers sometimes went on holiday and left the sheep to lamb, tidying up when they got home. This way they only kept the easy lambers. Could you imagine UK farmers doing that and the RSPCA allowing it?

Dieldrin sheepdip was banned in the late 1980s. This had been used for generations to keep sheep free of maggot flies by dipping the sheep, while protecting against other diseases like scab. The sheep were dipped twice a year and it was quite a performance as sheep are reluctant to swim down through dipper. I had never seen a case of maggot flies as long as we used Dieldrin, and we had trout living in the burn beside the dipper. We were made to use 'organic phosphorus' to dip the sheep, a nerve agent invented by a German chemist in 1932. Dieldrin was reported to have killed raptors who had eaten fallen sheep and someone worked out that if we ate three tons of mutton in a lifetime it might kill us. The police had to be notified of the days we were dipping and they came along to see that the strength of the new drug was maintained.

Farmers and shepherds were ill with the effects of the drug, in the most extreme cases taking their own lives. After one day's dipping John got up in the middle of the night and put his clothes on. I asked where he was going. He said in a strange voice that he didn't know, but out. I was alarmed at his strange behaviour and said he'd better have a cup of tea before he went. The tea was made, and John's skin was pink and swollen, and for over an hour we sat in the kitchen talking. Eventually he agreed to go back to bed. He did not remember anything in the morning but after that he felt ill near the new dip and handling the sheep. Even well after dipping, the residue was in their wool. When we dipped after that I dunked the sheep under the water with a brush at the dipper and John pushed them in. Too much exposure sent farmers out of their minds – at their worst, they were taking guns and shooting themselves. Doctors dismissed it and soldiers who had handled the 'organic phosphorus' during the first Gulf War brought a case to court for compensation for the way it had affected them.

In 1988 we were offered two farms – Hatton and Pitcruvie – by the landlords John and Valerie Gilmour at Balcormo Mains. We did a three-year budget with Henry Graham of the Clydesdale Bank. After the three years, we were only £100 out except for the bank interest, which had gone from 7% to 17% in that time. John Major was Prime Minister and the export markets were open to us again. Bank interest was lower again, and things were looking up after almost a decade of hard times. All the signs were encouraging.

It was decided Mark would take the tenancy, with John as partner, under the name of Tillyrie Farms Ltd. Two houses were sold at Tillyrie to meet the cost of setting up the project. Mark moved into a cottage at Hatton. When he was ploughing, there were no seagulls round the machine. As he was breaking up the pan, and there were no worms to speak of, the birds seemed to know. It was many years before seagulls swarmed round the plough again. Mark improved the farms and the neighbours commented on the improvements, including the draining of a wet patch which had not been cropped in living memory.

Farmers were encouraged to diversify. Some did bed and breakfast, cottage lets, farm shops etc, but the one that came to Kinross-shire benefitted the county for 18 years. In 1988 three farmers were approached because the land they owned was an island, with roads on the perimeter. The farms of Gallowhill, Balado and part of Mawmill were ideal for the festival which became T In The Park. The deal offered was worth £250 an acre, equivalent to the price of barley without having to grow it. No stock could graze the land because of the danger of E-coli, so the grass was cut as silage and sold to neighbouring farmers with stock to feed. The whole area was herring-fenced weeks before and the land hoovered for drugs, and thousands of folk came and camped for the two (which became three) days of music. There was little disruption locally, many benefits to local shops and a substantial charity gift to the county. It became a national treasure and, when it was stopped, it was unreal. A buried oil pipe passed through the site and, despite planes landing on it at Aberdeen and it being combined over and cultivated in the farms it passed through, such as Tillyrie, we were to understand the threat of terrorists blowing it up with thousands of folk present was considered too dangerous.

John Lawrie died in July 1989. He had left Burleigh to live with Constance in Innerwick Old Manse and while not interfering he kept an eye on, and an interest in, all the farms. He always said he would like to go while working in one of his fields. The day he died Gilmour was at a christening in Newcastle and John went round the fields at Spott, looking at the cattle and testing the grain on his teeth to see how ripe it was and how near to harvesting. He came in joking and in good form at four o'clock and had a bleed. The doctor sent him to hospital where he died by nine pm. We had all been called about seven o'clock and were told he would not live long. After he had asked John about the Tillyrie harvest, he told us all to go away and come back when he felt more comfortable.

His funeral was well attended with the little Church at Spott filled to capacity with friends and relations from all over the country. The refreshment after was held at Spott House, where most people came back and exchanged memories from over the years.

Something he said over the years stuck in the mind. One day, walking home from church at Spott, I asked him why he had been so successful. He replied that after many years of hard work he was lucky that the industry he was in was expanding when he was ready to expand. He walked on a few strides and said 'Mind you, I had the courage to take the opportunities at the time'. In the 1980s, he said, he could not have done what he did because bank interest was high and agriculture in a worse place. His sayings 'Many haws mean many snaws' and 'Never trust a bull, a dog or a man' and 'There is nowhere on a farm for an idle dog, an idle horse or an idle woman. One would chase the stock, one could turn on you and the third spend the money.' The important emphasis on was idle! Another very prudent rhyme was 'When it comes to Candlemas Day (2nd February) you should have half your straw and half your hay.'

Burleigh steading became derelict after John Lawrie gave it up. The land was farmed as part of the Kinross Estate, with the Home Farm and Hatton Burn. Then Mr Kay, a local man who had a business in Milnathort, by turning his hand to house construction made a very good job of keeping the feel of the buildings and turning them into family homes. It took him a long time, as he did the work himself with help from experts as needed. It sits well with the environment and the castle across the road.

Later a developer built houses in the stack yard. This finished the new look of the steading, taking it over the Hatton Burn and filling in the footprint of the old farm steading.

The 50 acres at Findatie, the tenancy of which John Lawrie had kept right up to his death, was only eligible to be continued by blood relation. None of the family in East Lothian wanted it so I took it, having the first instalment for the annual rent in the bank. I discussed what to grow in it with John and decided on seed barley. Luckily my home-bred mare Tycoon Moon, which I had trained on permit at Tillyrie, won a race at Ayr worth £4,000 in January and that solved the financial problem for the project. John was contracted to put the crop in. I rogued the oats out of the grain while SCS contracted the spraying and the combining was contracted to John again. It made enough money to carry on and grow another crop of seed grain again the next year.

In 1992 John Baird of Kirkness asked me to grow potatoes but subletting was not allowed in the tenancy. In 1993 I bought the seed potatoes and contracted John Baird to do the planting, spraying off and lifting, and sold them to him in the autumn. The landlord was not happy, thinking the fields had been sublet, but I owned the crop while it was growing in the fields. The upshot of this was that the landlord offered to buy the lease out. I thought that since the land had been taken away from Findatie Farm by a woman, a woman could give it back. I gave a figure to the landlord that I would release the tenancy for. The landlord said it was a high figure, and I said I would take 20% less if Findatie was offered the land first. The landlord agreed and eventually the land went back to Findatie.

After 17 years training my homebred horses on a permit (a licence for an amateur to train against professionals), I took a professional licence out in 1992. I invested this money in extending my training facilities by building a school 80 x 40 yds and a furlong round, (so eight times round was a mile) and adding a horse-walker. I discovered that when the term 'equine' was added to the front of a word, pounds were added to the cost. The school was built by John Meiklem from Kelty (who did drainage at Tillyrie for decades), for a quarter of the cost of a smaller equine school by suppliers. While we were waiting for loads of woodchip to arrive, Meiklem dug out two ponds for ducks, one up the hill and one in the glen, in a day.

About this time we had to register the maps of the farm to the government and, with Government survey maps and a measuring wheel, and the dining room turned into a mapping room, we did maps for Tillyrie, Findatie, Hatton and Pitcruvie. Fields had to be accurately measured and any water courses and farm roads taken off, woodland and bankings measured. It was some job working out the burns passing through the farms, as the width was not consistent. It took three weeks of full-time work to do. Nowadays it is all measured by satellite and the government tell you what size the fields are. Technology is great!

As the men retired in the 1980s they were not replaced. The bank interest was up at 17.5% and, in the mid-1980s, farmers were selling their farm houses in order to keep their land. Farm workers were paid off and they had to find work in factories or wherever they could, as their agricultural skills were no longer of any use and they were now unskilled workers. Other industries like coal mining and shipbuilding had government handouts when their industries shut down but very few of the many farm workers who were put off the land in the 1980-90s got any government help.

As retiring workers moved into the villages, finding security in council houses, we found some of the cottages empty. At first we let them out but, after a few years, it cost more to do them up when tenants vacated them so we sold them. First Berry Brae to a young couple with two girls, Mr and Mrs Croft; then Wester Tillyrie House to Peter and Jane Tempest; and in 1991, when the secretary moved to Spott, Balfour Cottage was sold to the Barnes family, who are still there and have extended the property beautifully .

In 1987 an agreement was made with Howard Briggs the UK representative for Myhlenber Construction (UK) to develop Wester Tillyrie steading and stack-yard, which was no longer used as modern machinery was too large to fit through the doors. It proved an interesting project and we discovered the hidden history of the building as it was taken down.

The long building and horsemill which became Mill House was built of dressed stone and was a later addition to the rest of the steading. The horsemill

roof was completely rebuilt to make a lovely round room with big windows between the stone uprights. Mr and Mrs Berryman bought it when it was built and
lived there until Mr Berryman's death in 2019, when the house was put up for
sale. It was bought by Neil and Samantha Dupen, who had come from Glenrothes
but were originally from Suffolk and Shropshire respectively.

The next surprise was an older farmhouse than the one across the road, which
we had no idea existed. Planning said the walls of the existing buildings had to be
left. Howard explained that there were no foundations under the old house, and
an accident was going to happen on 'Monday, and the stones used to rebuild the
wall would be finished by Friday'. So foundations were put in place and the house
was called 'The Haywain'.

All the timber came from Finland and Sweden and the workmanship was to
a high standard. Lawrie Cottage was next to be built where the steading jutted
out towards the road. Thorntons were joint sellers of the properties and interest
was shown to both Thorntons and Howard, so both sold the cottage on the same
day. There were fireworks from the underbidder but Howard promised a negative
copy of Lawrie Cottage to Mr Brand, and that became Brand Lodge.

Meanwhile Burnside was built and the Millar family, who are still there, moved
in. The site needed a sewage system and a soakaway was tried in a very wet January and found not to work. So a Clearwater sewage system, including our cottages
and Berrybrae (which had individual septic tanks), was built to do a specified job.
After a year Clearwater sold out to another company and, when our machine was
not doing the job it was bought to do, they would not take any responsibility for
Clearwater's work. Mr D'arcy, the responsible person for Forth Water Authority,
worked with us all the while and, when the Clearwater saga had run its course and
the samples were not passing standard measures, instead of just slapping a fine on

the people using the private sewage system, met with us and brought in Allan Frost. He designed a reedbed which would clean the water after it had gone through the Clearwater plant and would ensure the water would pass the tests. The reedbed was put in place and is still keeping the water clear today.

The Clearwater plant gave trouble in another way, that of users putting cotton buds and condoms down their toilets. These blocked the pump and broke it. To begin with the plant was emptied with a slurry tanker and ploughed into a field. Danny Mackenzie, the tractorman, said after such an emptying 'If we grew tatties in the field they would come out pre-packed!'

As well as a sewage system the water supply was boosted and a fibreglass tank bought that held 10,000 litres. We borrowed a low trailer from Kay the blacksmith and slowly the tractor pulled it up to the tank field site, dwarfed by the size of its load. A hole had been dug and filled with water. The tank was gently lowered and, as the water receded, it settled into place. It was linked to the previous tank in such a way as to keep both tanks fresh.

Mark came over with his combine to help Tillyrie finish the harvest in 1988. A crop of oats in the Mucketland Field was cut in two days with the two combines.

The Romano bull, having settled his 40 Hereford cows, escaped from the hill. Looking for fresh cows, he came through the Wester Tillyrie development unnoticed by the workers there, making for Athron Hall. John, in the big Volvo, got to the west of him when he saw someone walking towards them. It was David Smith of Holton, who was recovering from a heart attack at the time. John said to get in the car. David said he was told to take exercise but agreed to get into the car. John

The fibreglass water tank

drove at the bull to drive him back to Tillyrie, but the Bull had other things on his mind and leapt right over the bonnet. Off he went to Athron Hall and knocking their bull out the way set about looking to the cows.

We collected him the next day and eventually sold him to Gilmour who had 80 Simmental cows to keep him busy. His offspring topped the market at Stirling for Gilmour for years. He was very good-natured and not aggressive, just very determined.

Gillian Forbes asked if we had any buildings she could use for her stone mason work. She settled into the old byre by the old house, opposite the present farmhouse. We enjoyed her work for a few years before she moved to Path of Condie. Her stonework was amazing, whether it was a hand, a ball, a gravestone for a child with Winnie the Pooh images cut into it, or a massive fireplace with a lion's head. We missed her when she moved to her own premises.

I answered a knock at the kitchen door one afternoon. A grey-haired lady was standing there and said 'You won't know who I am', but I recognised her as Sarah, the younger daughter of David and Joy Reid. She was married and wanted permission to show her husband round the farm. It was suggested that it would be even better if they stayed a few nights and looked at leisure. One night, when she was later than him coming down for high tea, he said in conversation that 'his wheels had not fitted her parents' drive when they were young'. Sarah came in and agreed. They met at Pony Club and her parents were disapproving of the friendship. She was sent to Kenya to relations, where she met Mrs Randal who later lived at Nether Tillyrie House. She cooked for dinner parties and events while there. After a few years in Kenya, she was moved to Australia to stay with other relations.

Meanwhile he joined up and went to fight in the Far East and, when he came home, she was not there. Eventually he married and had a happy marriage until he was widowed.

Once he was safely married, Sarah was allowed to come home. Her inheritance was controlled by her parents until she was 50. They met again after he was widowed when they were 60, and had married. They were happy and were living in London, and we kept in touch with Christmas cards for a few years. I wished I asked them more questions now.

In 1993, while in Denmark staying with Eileen and Jens, John and I saw two windmills working at the edge of their village. They were on the side of the road going round gracefully. The village was supplied with electricity by one and the other brought in income. When we got home we looked into getting a windmill for the grain dryer and dairy as electricity was quite expensive. We contacted a Colin Anderson who was looking into this new industry, but there was nothing of a size to do the steading, only larger ones for industrial use. He put us in touch with three companies who developed sites and we left information with Border Wind of Hexham in 1995. We were too busy to take it further and the file gathered dust in the office.

One March we had a blizzard. By midday the snow was up to the hedge-tops and still coming down. After lunch at 1 o'clock, John and our tractorman Danny Mackenzie took a tractor and bucket to dig the way to the hill. A second tractor and trailer with wee bales of hay for the sheep set out for the ewes on the front hill, Holton Side. It was approximately one and a quarter miles up a farm track to where the hayhecks were at the middlegate in the shelter of the Scots pine wood. It took over three hours for them to dig their way up, and they were welcomed by the ewes in the storm. On their return to the steading the house was invisible from the garden gate across the yard, and the road was filled in and only visible as you approached it.

In the meantime the cows were milked by Bill Macdonald the dairyman but the milk had to be stored as best we could. The bulk tank held almost two days' milk. John started to dig the road from the farm end the day after the blizzard and the next day the council snow plough got round to us, but broke down. The third day the cows were milked in the morning and the milk held in big black bags in the dairy sinks, and the cows were not milked until evening that day, when the milk was running out of them. The council snow plough was back again the third morning and John had continued with the tractor and bucket digging from this end. They met and the road was opened in the evening and the milk tanker came in and rescued all the milk. None was poured down the drain and, after the system was washed down and sterile, milking took place, much to the relief of a hundred cows.

Tillyrie Steading 1994

John bought a second-hand snow blower from Dumfriesshire after that and we never had a bad snowstorm for years. John said it was a good insurance! The snow blower was sold when we sold the steading to Muirs in 2010. The two winters after that were bad but it didn't matter so much as, with no dairy, we didn't have a milk tanker coming in daily to worry about.

1990 saw a wave of European workers come for seasonal work on the farms. Many were university students, or already had degrees to their name, and were ready to do manual work. They were hard workers, sending most of the money they earned home to support their families.

In 1990 Deborah Kay and Drew Drysdale bought Nether Tillyrie Cottage, but after a while put it back on the market. Mr and Mrs Halford bought it and moved in with their two children.

In the following year, John had a difficult decision to make. We had a shepherd who did not drive, and a tractor man who was not interested in working with livestock. There was not the budget to keep both and, as neither could do both jobs, it was with a heavy heart that John asked them to find other work.

John asked Euan Macgregor, who was happy at Darno, Falkland Wood with Mr Shanks, if he would be interested in coming to Tillyrie to fill the two jobs. After much thought he, with his wife Jean and daughters Amy and Anna, moved into Matale. Amy started at Milnathort Primary School and was the third generation of the family to attend it. Euan worked away in charge of the sheep and was skilled in all agricultural work. With dairyman Bill Macdonald, Euan and John managed all the work on Tillyrie. Jean helped with the computerised books and the stud.

The machinery ring movement started when Sandy McKay of the Scottish Agricultural College did research about the rings in Germany and introduced the concept to farmers at the annual East of Scotland Agricultural Conference. The disastrous harvests in 1985 and 1986 caused the Border's farmers to set up a machinery ring in 1987 and, by 1990, there were five machinery rings in Scotland.

Machinery rings are a co-operation of farmers who have services to offer, and others who have a demand for services. The ring manager arranges this for a small percentage of the request. The Tayforth Ring was started in May 1989 by Willie Wilson, who had a tractor business in Anstruther. In January 1991 it came to HQ at Newhill with Bruce Hamilton as manager.

Bruce was a whiz-kid on a computer, and the first thing he did was create a database of the 124 members and their machinery. Later, companies who quoted for commodities like fuel, building supplies, biomass, waste recycling, pest control, etc were added as members. Now everything a modern farmer needs for his business is offered and all invoicing, once done by hand, is done online. An annual catalogue, paid for by its advertising, is produced of available services and members.

So this one man, who in 1991 had once-a-week help when needed and holiday relief to cater for 124 members, over the next twenty years extended to seven full-time staff and 1,074 members. The turnover went from £200,000 to an amazing £14.6 million. This is how much the farming industry has evolved to cope with ever-increasing costs and, by cooperation, allowed some to contract out their machinery and help others. In the 1970s we traded the tractors in every three years and the backup industries and traders to agriculture were enormous. There were four big agriculture supply businesses in Kinross and Milnathort alone: now there is one. In 1986 a Deutz tractor cost £18,000 new. By 2020 it would cost £85,000 and now you would not get much change from £100,000. Even a baler is £35,000 nowadays.

Bruce is proud that the Tayforth Machinery Ring, which covers an area from Dundee to the Forth and as far west as Ayrshire, has never made a loss. Most of the girls he has employed over the years have gained confidence and gone on to good high-profile work. There are now a total of nine machinery rings in Scotland.

On 31st October 1991 my son John Mark Thomson married Kathleen Stewart King, daughter of the late Stewart King and Mrs Helen King of Wolfstar, Pencaitland, in the parish church there. The reception was at the Marine Hotel at North Berwick. After a honeymoon abroad they set up house at Pitcruvie Farm, Largo.

In 1992 Mr and Mrs Trevor Croft bought the plot of land between Berrybrae and Newton and built a new house for themselves, very much in keeping with the existing properties. They called it Glenside, and happily they are still there. They sold Berrybrae to two couples who did not stay long before splitting up. Then, in 2003, Phil and Jane Dean lived there. Phil was an architect, and converted the kennels to an office, later extending the house with a wing to the north. He was the architect who drew up the plans when Matale was updated in 2012. He moved to Kinross in 2018 and Berrybrae was bought by Graeme and Morag Duncan.

In November 1992, Tillyrie's application to the Farm Woodland Premium Scheme was accepted and 90 acres of woodland was planted. John chose difficult parts of fields that would make windbreaks and shelter belts. The Tank Field and the Earl Haig Field were planted right out with a mixture of hardwoods; the Forty Acre Field and the Mucket Land Field were planted in strips down the sides, while the Peaket Hat Field had the top in front of the old Scots Pine trees planted. A triangle of hardwoods was put in the corner of the Middle Bank next to the Hostel Field. Part of the Front Hill (which had once been a wood) was planted up with conifers, and extended on to the backhill for shelter. We had to maintain the woods to the agreed standard, and received a grant for planting and maintenance for 15 years.

It was about this time the shooting started under the management of Mal Kepston. Mal bought young birds, which arrived in July each year as pullets, feeding them and putting them in runs at night away from the foxes. The shoots were from the end of September to the end of January each year. There were syndicates, with a given amount of days per season, and individuals who took a day with their friends and returned most years. Some folk came and stayed at the Well Inn in Scotlandwell and combined goose shooting in the early morning with driven birds from 9am. A group from Essex came for more than a decade, a dairy farmer and a flight controller among them. The dairy farmer milked Dutch Holsteins, calved them down at two years, and they were done by five years, all on land reclaimed from the sea by his grandfather. We had good craic over the years with them.

In 1994 the Scottish Milk Marketing Board was disbanded by the Minister of Agriculture John Gummer, causing a free-for-all and an unequal price for milk. The SMMB had paid the same price for the milk, with a bonus for butterfat, so the dairy on Arran or a far-flung farm got the same price as a farm beside an urban area. It also made cheese and butter with excess milk at times when milk was plentiful, it promoted the use of artificial insemination (which originated in communist Russia and was adopted by western countries), and also encouraged the use of milk recorders who came every three or four weeks to record the production and butter fat of every cow. The SMMB had been set up in 1931 and had been successful ever since. Now traders dictated the price depending on the distance from urban areas, causing many farms off the said routes to close their milk production.

Tillyrie had benefitted from the SMMB and our milk, both TB- and Brucellosis-free, was sent to them from the start. When the Brucellosis test came in Tillyrie was one of two farms in Scotland who never had a cow with the disease (the other was in Aberdeenshire). We had to put a scare fence round our march fences so cattle could not contact other cattle.

In 1996 Gilmour phoned us to say he was selling Spott, and moving his family to Queensland, Australia. He could set his children up in Australia in a way he couldn't do in the UK, but he had to go before he was 55. The same week Gyles Thomson phoned John to say he was selling Pathhead. His son was not interested and it seemed pointless to keep going. It was a sad reflection of farming at the time.

Cousin Nan died and was buried at Strathaven beside her parents John and Isa Watson. Newton was sold in 1996 to Jackie Yuill, who later married George Sutherland and they are still happily living there.

1996 brought the export ban of all beef as BSE hit the country. Bovine Spongiform Encephalopathy (BSE), commonly known as Mad Cow Disease caused abnormal behaviour in cattle. It meant they had trouble walking and led to weight loss, later being unable to move at all.

It was thought to be caused by prions, which live only in the nervous system, becoming changed to abnormal prions and causing a disease of the brain. It could not be transmitted contagiously or by infection. It is thought it was spread by the parts of cattle not intended for the human food chain being ground up to a powder and used in a variety of ways, including in animal feed. About the time BSE appeared an Act of Parliament allowed the temperature of meal processing at a new factory in the south west of England to heat the meal to a lower temperature than it had previously. There was also an outbreak of scrapie in sheep in that area and therefore a greater infected volume was going through the slaughter process around that time. Whether these were factors in the equation is anybody's guess.

BSE can take four to six years to develop and show symptoms from the time the abnormal prion infects the cow. Once the incubation period is past and symptoms start to show, the cow dies in two to six weeks. There is no treatment or vaccine for BSE, and no reliable test for it while the cow is alive. Once dead the brain is found to be spongy. Sheep, goats, mink, deer and elk all have their own version of BSE. Cats get feline BSE and, according to our vet, it was around at the time of the pharaohs. The UK had 78% of the cases of BSE, while the USA, France, Spain, the Netherlands, Portugal, Ireland, Italy, Japan, Saudi Arabia and Canada also suffered. Measures were taken to prevent it from entering the human food chain: since 1997 it has been illegal to use parts of cattle to make food for other cattle.

Human beings can get a disease called Creutzfeldt-Jakob (VCJD) a rare and fatal brain disease. Three cases occurred in people who lived in or visited the UK in the ten years the ban lasted. Neither BSE or CJD are contagious, nor can they be spread by drinking milk or eating dairy products.

It was a disaster to the whole of the cattle industry. The government announced it was giving £300 compensation to those who lost cows. This became the standard price for all cattle sold. We were getting over a thousand pounds for the spare heifers from the dairy, and now they were worth three hundred, less than the cost of production. The worst off were tenant farmers, whose overdrafts were borrowed on the valuation of their herds of pedigree cattle, now greatly reduced. Many went to the wall. There wasn't BSE in Scotland anything like England, and it mostly seemed to affect Holstein cows that were pushed harder and younger than other breeds. Also Scottish feed mills were older and used a chemical-based system. The ban lasted ten years, and was not removed until May 2006.

However, 1996 was a good year for the family. On 14th April 1996 Rebecca Helen Thomson was born to Kathleen and Mark at Pitcruvie, and her christening was in Lower Largo church, with all the grandparents and Great-Granny Thomson present. In 1997 the minimum wage was introduced.

In 1998 on 10th January Fiona Catherine Thomson was born at Pitcruvie and once again we attended Lower Largo for the christening. Both families, Thomsons and Kings, met afterwards at Pitcruvie.

The dairyman was away by then and John was both milking and doing the outside work. In early December 1998 John came in at breakfast time with a terrible pain in his chest. When it didn't go away after half an hour the doctor was called. Dr Richmond was wonderful and, thinking it might be a heart attack, said to take him up to PRI. There John was wired to lots of gadgets and I was told to come back at two o'clock. Never had Christmas shopping been less fun. When I returned to PRI John was sitting up in bed looking pleased with himself. The treadmill had been turned up further and further and they had never had it so high. There was nothing wrong with his heart and the doctor diagnosed angina and said he'd to take an aspirin a day.

The upshot was that the dairy had to go. We decided not to sell the cows at a roup as the older ones would go for slaughter. The cows were sold as they came up to calving and the older cows were given the summer at grass, with each given three Angus cross-heifer calves to suckle. Alex Cousar, a dealer with whom we had been working for years, bought the calves to start a suckler herd and the old cows romped round the field with their new calves like youngsters. Some of the cows went into good herds and we heard of their offspring doing well. It helped with the wrench of putting the dairy off. We received 23p a litre for decades, and the milk price had gone down to 18p. After we stopped producing the price dropped to 14p for a while. I was shocked to find that milk cost 67p per litre in the shops. There are only three dairies left in Kinross-shire now: Holton, Cuthill Towers and Wharlaw Hill near Carnbo.

Before all this, in September 1989, we had a party to celebrate both our 50 years in Tillyrie and Eileen and Jens' 25th wedding anniversary. We put up a large tent in the front paddock, which we thought was flat until the flooring went in and it was uphill from the bar when dancing later. We asked the people who had worked for us and with us at Tillyrie and Burleigh, as well as friends and relations who had been at Eileen and Jens' wedding. It was a good night shared and there were a few sore heads in the morning.

In 1998 Alistair Cook bought Nether Tillyrie Steading from a couple of lads who were going to develop it but never got round to it. When we were emptying it we moved 17 different kinds of ploughs, and kept the best one of each, some of them at Matale now. The steading had been used to store things in case they came in useful or the new one did not do the job as well as the old. The old sawmill, used when the new steading was built between 1912 and 1916, and the wood for the rafters and fittings, which came off the estate, was covered with ivy. A cross-cut saw used in 1929 by Bob Tod and Donald Urquhart was taken and restored, and shown at Kinross Show.

Alistair was an architect and developed the steading beautifully, keeping the charm of the place while making two superb houses, and giving gardens to each. He and his wife Sheila lived in the East House, until she tragically died. He was going to move away, but fortunately did not and is still with us today. He took up woodwork, sawing and drying trees, and creating furniture in a most artistic way, using the burrs in the wood included in cupboard doors, and imaginative furniture like his dining table with a glass centre through which candle light could shine. He is very gifted.

The Wester Steading conversion was bought by James and Lorna Barr. James, a former marine, served his country in Aden and Burma.

Mark came home on 28th November 1999 when he gave up the tenancy of Hatton and Pitcruvie, and the family Mark, Kathleen, Rebecca and Fiona moved into Dower Cottage.

With half our income going when the dairy went, we started to look for other ways to make money. The file on the windmills was still there and we contacted

Border Wind at Hexham who had shown interest. Border Wind had been bought over by AEMC, an international firm. Colin Ormiston of AEMC did not know they had our file but, on finding it, was interested in the site. We had several meetings with them and visited the planners in Perth. They put up a wind monitoring mast in 1992.

Unfortunately, AEMC got their fingers burned in some small ventures in England and, as a policy, decided not to do more smaller sites, but to concentrate on big projects. However, Colin said the Tillyrie Hill Site was a good site and to carry on.

I visited Perth Planning Department and met with Mr Esson, who suggested I attend a two-day wind conference. There I met with many people wishing to lease the site, one of whom suggested developing the site in partnership with him; he would do the planning. The conference was very interesting about the wind industry in general.

Steve Mackin of Lomond Energy had had years of experience in wind energy and was enthusiastic about the project, and we embarked on what was to become a long-term partnership to develop Tillyrie Hill with five wind turbines. By developing the site ourselves, instead of leasing it to a big company, we kept the turbines for our partnership. After ten years they would be paid for.

I found it quite an experience to find out so much about Tillyrie. Hydrology, archaeology, nature, landscape and visual assessment, noise, telecommunications, aviation and military interests, and social economic and environmental benefits all had to be reported in detail.

The first application was made in 2004, and the Planning Committee was split on the outcome. Steve gave a presentation and six folk made objections. It was mainly objectors who said their water supplies were in danger or their paid agents. One even said his water supply was in danger when his water came off a different hill. The Development Committee were split 50/50 on the application and the chairman, with his casting vote, said the hydrology had to be sorted out before any decision could be made.

We resubmitted a modified plan to suit Scottish Natural Heritage at Battleby, and we visited all the water supplies with a geologist and took photographs to prove our findings. That was in November 2006 and, when we had not heard by January 2007, we got our local councillor to bring the matter to the attention of the Development Committee. The Development Committee demanded the Planning Committee should hear our application. As there were council elections due in May we wanted our application to be heard again by the present council. There was no movement so I made an appointment (with great difficulty) to see the Head of Planning, and took Mark along as a witness. Having expressed surprise at our being there, after half an hour of asking why our application was not going forward, he suddenly said it was because he had made an arrangement with another party not to put it to the Development Committee.

We then went to the Government to appeal on the grounds of 'non-determination' of the application by PKC, and PKC thought we would win. The appeal was held at the Windlestrae Hotel in Kinross on 12th December 2007. The Reporter visited all the sites mentioned on day one, and listened to presentations, witnesses and objectors in a court-like manner, with QCs acting for both PKC and ourselves, until 19th December. The Reporter returned to the Ochil Hills Hospital on 3rd January 3rd, and other viewpoints were referred to him in February 2008.

The Reporter sent his decision, which we received on 26th February. He turned down the application. Ten years of hope and work, while good in the learning, were very disappointing. If the loss of Calais was in Tudor Queen Mary's heart when she died, I felt windmills would be the biggest regret in mine. At times it was a close-run thing.

John retired from farming in 1999. EEC rules, especially set-aside, really got to him. To do only 80% of a job was wrong. After a fortnight he was bored and started bruising oats on a small scale, which led to a full-blown grain roller-mill business. He had clients from Dunblane to Dunkeld, Perthshire, Fife as well as Kinross-shire, and even went to the Borders twice. He did some fencing when the grain rolling was finished for the season, and bought a post chapper in 1999 to do this.

He sold the grain roller business and goodwill in 2012. Getting home at eight o'clock at night, having left home at six or seven in the morning, became tiring and, at 70 years of age, he decided the fencing would keep him busy enough. This had been steady work and also grew to take another man on in 2016, but

in 2019 he tried not to work weekends. He ordered a new, updated stob chapper at the Highland Show in 2019 so obviously meant to carry on.

In February 2001 a foot and mouth outbreak was declared. The 1967 outbreak was confined to a small area in Northumberland and, as soon as it was identified, the animals were slaughtered on the spot the same day and the carcasses buried in quicklime. This stopped the outbreak.

Since the 1967 outbreak there had been significant changes in farming methods, and the closure of many local abattoirs meant that animals for slaughter were now being transported greater distances. In 1980 the treatment of foot and mouth disease passed from the UK Government to the European Community Directive, which set out procedures such as protection and surveillance zones, the confirmation of diagnosis by laboratory testing, and that the EU and its standing veterinary committee had to be consulted on any actions taken. An earlier directive, 80/68, on the protection of ground water, gave powers to the Environment

Agency to prohibit farm burials and the use of quicklime unless the site was authorised by the agency.

The 2001 outbreak started at Burnside Farm, Haddon on the Wold, in Northumberland, when untreated swill from army barracks, restaurants and local schools was fed to pigs. The pigs were sold through the market in Carlisle and the first case was found on 19th February at an abattoir in Essex. Cases were then reported in Devon, Northumberland, Buckinghamshire, the Isle of Wight and North Wales. We put a map of the UK on the kitchen wall and added a red sticker for every new case daily.

Racing was stopped for a week, and when it started again racecourses were expected to continue with their programmes as if nothing was wrong. This meant some owners told trainers that if they didn't run their horses, they would remove them to a trainer who would. This put stress on trainers to run horses. The lorries were hosed down with disinfectant when they entered racecourses, and the horses went through disinfectant walks into the stables, and the public had to walk through disinfectant. Our lorry was next to trainer Howard-Johnston's lorry, and his cattle were being put down with F&M that day. When Jean told me, I was angry and phoned the Department of Agriculture in Edinburgh, They would have nothing to do with it and told me to phone DEFRA. DEFRA only had unmanned answering machines. So I phoned the head vet at the Jockey Club, and said there should be a restriction within five miles of an outbreak. He agreed and said he was meeting Tony Blair and the head of DEFRA next day, and he would suggest it. The answer we got back was 'there was a general election due in March and the folk in the cities must not know that anything was wrong in the countryside.' So nothing was done until May, and the election was eventually postponed until 5th June.

Meanwhile the Northumberland trainers were saying that, in the previous November, the government had been asking about supplies of railway sleepers and coal. The whole thing seemed to be badly handled, and those who remembered previous outbreaks of foot and mouth, quickly contained and the animals dead and buried the day the disease was diagnosed, could not understand how it had got so out of hand.

By the end of March there were up to 50 new cases a day. MAFF officials called the army for assistance and their military discipline was a great help in getting the necessary action taken. At that time there were 80,000 to 93,000 animals a week being slaughtered.

Scotland had a bad outbreak in Dumfries and Galloway. The bunker used for the Lockerbie air crash was used as a headquarters. One of our vets took his holidays to go and help, and was very frustrated by having to wait until eleven o' clock every morning when Westminster had met and given the orders for the day. The vets were each given two farms to visit, then had to phone in for more orders, and were passing each other going to farms. Despite this the area was cleared of the disease after it having wiped out many herds of cattle, including many pedigree Galloway cattle and almost all the pedigree Dun Galloways. Scotland was clear of foot and mouth and applied to the EEC to resume exports. Exporting was expected to start at the end of the week when, on the Wednesday, yet another case was found on government land near Hexham. That put a stop on the export markets for Scotland.

By September there were 'only' five cases a day reported, and the last case was in Cumbria on 30th September. Restrictions were kept in place until 2002. Halted on 1st October the disease had cost the UK eight billion pounds. The Lake District in particular was badly affected by the drop of tourism and the Cheltenham Festival, worth hundreds of thousands of pounds per day, was cancelled. The culling, not only of infected animals but also those in surrounding areas, meant that six million cows, sheep and goats were killed, and Cumbria was the worst affected area with 893 cases.

Several cases of F&M were reported in Ireland and mainland Europe following the unwitting transportation of infected animals from the UK. The Netherlands was worst affected, suffering 25 cases. Vaccinations were used to stop the disease and no vaccinated cattle were slaughtered. Then 250,000-270,000 cattle were later destroyed, significantly more than in the UK, because of the density of cows on a holding. The use of vaccine was repeatedly considered during the outbreak in the UK, but the government decided against its use after pressure from the National Farmers Union. France had three cases in March. Belgium, Spain, Luxembourg and Germany carried out some precautionary slaughters which in all cases eventually proved negative. False alarms came to nothing in Finland, Sweden, Denmark and Italy. All European countries imposed livestock restrictions from infected countries.

Many farmers never recovered from the stress of seeing all their stock shot and them not being allowed to leave the farm for days after. Some began again the long slow job of building a new pedigree herd from where they could find the right beasts. We were very lucky, sticking the red dots on the map of all the cases, that it never came near our area. However, we had many friends who were not as fortunate and were devastated by it.

On my 60th birthday, in 2002, I retired and handed the Jockey Club trainer's licence over to Jean. We had a big party with the owners and staff, I had a good send-off and Jean got a warm welcome. Mark had given up the tenancy at Leven and returned home. The Thomson MacGregor Partnership was set up with Euan doing the sheep enterprise and Mark the cattle and grain. Mark's wife Kathleen took over the company books. Everybody had a place in the company.

Mark started with a mixed herd of sucklers, the Aberdeen Angus crosses we raised on the Ayrshire cows and cows Alec Cousar bought for us, and Mark used a Simmental bull over them. There was only about 100 acres of grain.

In 2004 John and I took seven weeks away to let the youngsters get on with the company. We went round the world visiting the cousins in California for two weeks, three days in the Cook Islands, five days in New Zealand and on to stay with Gilmour and Tessa in Queensland for two weeks. A quick visit to Cairns to

Jean with Anthenion wins at Hamilton. Libby Brobie (headgirl) leading up with Jockey

see the coral reefs, back to Perth via Ayres Rock, a few days at Perth to meet Gay Senior (whom we hadn't seen since 1963) and to Singapore for three days, and then a thirteen-hour flight home. Austravel had a special deal an owner told us about, four stops for £800. We stayed with relations on two stops. Dandy, a horse I bred, won six races. I got money as the breeder ever time he won and used £1000 to upgrade to business class on the long flights. The only contact the youngsters had was email at relations, but they never used it. For folk who had few holidays it was very special.

Mark had been farming with a mixture of cows, and in February 2008 visited Castle Douglas for the pedigree Luing Sale. Messrs Cadzow started in the 1970s on the island of Luing to breed a cow that would be hardy, easy to keep, easy calved and good to handle, being good-natured (any with nature problems were culled). They crossed the native Highland cow with a Shorthorn, and established the genes until they had a breed which bred true. This breed, called Luings, could live outside in most climates, and had the scope to be commercial. They were in demand to cross with the Simmental, and the offspring Sim-Luing were great mothers for herds on lower ground.

Mark went with enough funds, he hoped, to buy three heifers and, in a buyer's market, came home with five. The next year it was a seller's market and he bought two. We thought it would take ten years to establish a herd. However, a

top breeder and his brother fell out and
a third of the herd was sold in the Cal-
edonian Market, Stirling as commercial
cattle, but the Luing Society said they
would provide pedigrees of the cows
from tattoos if asked. Mark bought ten
cows of mixed ages, with heifer calves
at foot and in calf again. A further
lucky sale occurred a while later when
Mr Cadzow died. The cousins split and
again a sale of one third of the cows
from Luing were sold (with pedigrees)
at United Auction Market outside Stirling. With an understanding bank manager, Mark bought another 14 cows of
different ages, with heifer calves at foot
and in calf again. So his herd of Luing
cows was established within a much shorter timescale.

Mark Thomson

The Kinross Area Local Plan 2001 encouraged development in the countryside as well as villages. There were 29 maps of country sites available for development, including Balado, Craigomill, Cuthill Towers, Hattonburn, Mawcarse,
Middleton, Netherton, Ochill Hills Hospital, and Upper Tillyrie. It was only realised that our steading was included in the intended policy when negotiating
a wayleave for a water pipeline between ourselves (represented by McCrae &
McCrae) and Scottish Woodlands Ltd (agent for The Beaverhall Partnership Ltd)
in June 2001.

Contacting PKC Planning Department, the planner Mr Macfarlane came out
and walked round the steading. As the buildings were brick and steel he agreed
that they could be demolished and developed into houses on the footprint of the
steading and stackyard.

There were 11 offers from interested parties and, with the help of McCrae
& McCrae, it was found that Muir Homes submitted the best offer. This was accepted and the next seven years were a rollercoaster. Forth Water and other water
authorities joined to form SEPA, which was to control the whole of Scotland. Unfortunately they had no structure or policy, and it took over two years for them to
reply to Muir about water and sewage. SNH at Battleby twice agreed to planning
matters with Muir Homes but didn't inform PKC planning department for six
months. So over three years were lost once the plans were registered. There were
disputes about street lights, which the present hamlet won, and a bus stop was
put opposite the farm house near a blind bend. Except the sanatorium bus when
the Ochil Hills Hospital was open, the only bus to ever come up our road was the
school bus when the children were collected from their doors all on one side of
the road, and the new hamlet, called Tillyrie Mains, has the children picked up
and let off at the entrance to their houses, so the bus stop is surplus. There were

lots of problems that over the years were solved, and building finally started in the winter of 2009-10.

All through the deep snow of November until the spring they worked away taking down the potato shed and the straw shed, before tackling the hay shed and dairy unit. The main steading was next, with the hundreds of pigeons perching on an ever-decreasing roof, and the older buildings at the back door last. The walk up from the stackyard seemed longer without the buildings on the way.

They built the houses nearest the entrance first, with a show house slightly further down at the first cul-de-sac. The first house was sold in 2011. All were finished by spring 2012 and the last house sold by 2014.

Meanwhile in 2008, just as lambing was starting, Euan broke his leg. With 800 ewes to lamb it was a crisis. However, his father Allan and friends rallied round, and gave us time to find Tom Bowe, who came from the Wicklaw Hills in Ireland to help, and what a find he was. He helped out that year and the next, and neighbour Rab Bell was pleased to get Tom's help with his lambing too. Tom comes over at Highland Show time and looks in and it is always a pleasure to see him. It was a frustrating time for Euan having to stay in the house with his broken leg, which eventually mended well.

When Muir Homes knocked down the steading, replacement buildings were needed. It was decided to put the racing at Wester Tillyrie in the Mucket Land Field. A stable with 16 boxes was constructed by Peter Dale whose father had put up the potato and straw sheds many years before. The Monarch horse walker and most of the straw shed were moved to the site from the previous locations at Upper Tillyrie. The site was levelled and the road made by John Meiklem's firm.

Mark settled on a site on the old farm track built in 1948 by his grandfather

Luing cows

from Nether Tillyrie out to meet the Holton-Middleton road from Milnathort. The road was made up and the site for buildings levelled by John Meiklem. Three sheds were planned but the sale to Muir Homes was worth 40% less because of the time wasted at planning as the cost of steel and other materials had gone up and so, with no grants, so only two sheds were constructed. The cattle shed had no outside walls and a handling area up the middle, so the cattle could be fed round the outside of the shed, and handled inside in the dry. It made for a well-ventilated shed. The other shed was a general purpose shed that could store implements or straw, or even be a lambing shed as the time of year dictated.

Neither Mark nor Jean wanted the farmhouse, which I had loved for forty years. I decided to move by my seventieth birthday as the housekeeping was becoming burdensome. Tillyrie House was put on the market in the autumn of 2010 and sold in ten days to Gordon and Katie Smart. They were living in London at the time. He was interviewing celebrities for The Sun newspaper. We were to be out by December for them to be in for Christmas. However events proved otherwise. We were waiting for Jean and Euan to build a house at the new steading at Wester Tillyrie, and moved to a log cabin at Findatie in the interval. The phone-hacking scandal at the Sun brought promotion to Gordon Smart, and it was two years before he was able to return to Scotland as editor of the Scottish Sun.

In the meantime Gordon's uncle (who was an architect) designed changes to Tillyrie House, which changed it from a farmhouse to a residence without losing character. It is beautiful and functional for the charming couple who moved to live there in the late autumn of 2012. They had hoped their daughter Laurie would be born at Tillyrie, but the house was not quite ready. It would have been the first child born in the house since Robert and Jane Reid had their sixth child David in 1841, and as that was the year the house was finished there is no record of whether David was born in the new house or the old house that year.

Gordon and Katie are local to Kinross-shire and were educated at Kinross School. It turned out that, when they were looking at Tillyrie House in 2010, his parents lived in Keston, Muirs, Kinross, the house that Isa Watson lived in from 1958 until she moved to Newton at Tillyrie. When we sold them the house I said to Katie to put their stamp on it as I had thought of it as Miss Reid's house for the first three years after I moved in. It is lovely to hear their children playing and the house happy. It reminds me of our time with children growing up there.

About the same time as the Smarts moved into Tillyrie House, John and I moved back into Matale. Jean and Euan had built a lovely house at Wester Tillyrie, and Mark and Kathleen had almost finished building their new farmhouse at Nether Tillyrie which they called 'Carleith', after the grassy hill at the back of Tillyrie, on the march with Whitehill and Shire End Farm.

The Thomson McGregor Partnership had run its course, and now Mark was to run most of Tillyrie. Jean and Euan were at Wester Tillyrie, with Euan also renting Templands, his late father's farm by Falkland, and taking winter grazing for sheep locally. He also contracts for other farmers and, being highly skilled and a grafter, is in great demand both locally and in Fife.

In 2017 the hill was sold to the Woodland Trust, and planting started in the spring of 2018. They were able to get the stone for the roads from quarrying on site, and made little disturbance in planting. The whole area was deer-fenced and the trees are growing well. Bobby Edgar, who has had the shooting at Tillyrie since Mal Kepston's death, is also engaged to keep the deer and vermin down.

Agriculture has changed vastly in the two decades since the millennium. EEC rules, environmental care and now climate change are challenging, never mind the vegan attacks.

We have always used clover in the grasses and farmed traditionally, using modern innovations as they proved themselves useful. From 2016 Mark used GPS mapping and by 2019 the whole farm was GPS mapped, allowing the amount of fertiliser needed in the fields to be measured to the individual square foot, and similar for lime. This reduced the fertiliser use, is economical and keeps the soil in good heart. The animal dung, well-rotted, keeps the humus content right, which in turn keeps moisture in the earth and helps with drainage. Soil, being the farmer's best asset, has to be kept in good health. Modern science has proved cattle grazing on grass with clover is environmentally friendly.

Nowadays farms with huge tractors and massive machines have no place for anyone other than farm workers, who are mainly the sons of farmers. Those with agricultural skills are in high demand. They work extraordinarily long hours during sowing, harvesting, lambing and so on. Often they operate machinery worth more than a hundred thousand pounds, and use sophisticated electronic gadgetry that would leave their forebears gasping. With so few on the ground, their output is a hundred times that of their forebears. They also work mainly alone, and that can be dangerous or cause mental health problems.

Since the eighteenth century farmers today are at the mercy of their government not to import goods that do not meet the standards of home-produced food products. The farmers can be as efficient as possible, but they cannot compete with imports of cheap foods that are substandard when they are fenced in with welfare rules. In an ever more suburban society, with no contact to rural life and no understanding of good agricultural practices, it is a challenging time.

Now in 2020 we enter unknown territory, and only time and history will tell whether decisions taken today and tomorrow are correct. Brexit is decided and negotiations ongoing about conditions for leaving the EEC. Climate change and now the pandemic is challenging the world. The world and man has changed through centuries of evolution. What will tomorrow bring? God willing, it will be good.

Bibliography

Arbuckle, Andrew *Footsteps in the Furrow,* 2009
Brigden, Roy *Harvesting Machinery,* 1989
   Ploughs and Ploughing, 1984
Corrigan, Gordon *Mud, Blood and Poppycock,* 2004
Cuthbert, Margaret, *Kinross-shire A century of Stories,* 2011
Graham, Angus (7th Duke of Montrose) *Master of None,* 1999
Horton, Charles *Stretcher Bearers,* 2013
Johnston, Arran Paul *Blood Stain'd Fields. The Battles of East Lothian* 2013
Jones, Spencer *From Boer War to World War II 1920-1014, Tactical Reform of the British Army,* 1981
Kinross Historical Society Booklets
Kinross Museum *(Photos and Maps)*
Oliver, Neil *A History of Scotland,* 2009
MacDonald, Lyn *Passchandale,* 1993
   Roses of No Man's Land, 1993
Mackay A.J.G *Fife and Kinross,* 1895
Magnusson, Magnus *Scotland A History of Nation,* 2001
Massi, Allan *The Royal Stuarts,* 2013
Milnathort Golf Club *A Hundred Years of Divots*
Moffat, Alistair *The Wall,* 2008
Morric, Marc *Barony of Kirkness by courtesy of the Baird Family of Kirkness Castle,* 2003
   William Wallace, 1995
   A Great and Terrible King (Edward I), 2005
Munro, David *Loch Leven & the River Leven. A Landscape Transformed,* 1994
Pakenham, Thomas *The Boer War,* 1992
Paterson, Jim *350 Years of Kinross Curling Club*
Reid, Stuart *Crown Covenant and Cromwell,* 2012
Robertson, Rev Thomas (Minister of Dalmeny 1799) *Mary Queen of Scots,* 1799
Shearer, Rev (minister in Orwell in 1950/60s) *Notes of Minutes of Orwell Session Meetings from 1681*
Shukman, Ann *Bishops and Covenanters. The Church in Scotland 1688-91*
Smith. *Research into the fallen WW1 in Kinross-shire* (Kinross Museum)
Smout, T.C. *A Century of Scottish People 1830-1950,* 2010
   A History of Scottish People 1560-1830
   A Tour Through Great Britain Book IV

Spencer, Charles *The Killer of the King,* 2014

Starns, Penny *Sisters of the Somme,* 2016

Starkey, David *Fatal Colours,* 2012

Stevenson, David *A Hunt for Rob Roy,* 2004

Tranter, Nigel *The Patriot* 1981

Walker, N.H *A History of the Kinross-shire Volunteers,* 1988

Weir, Alison *Mary Queen of Scots,* 2003

Winyard, Tom *Burleigh Castle and the house of Balfour* (Kinross-shire Historical Society No.6)

First World War and an Army of Occupation War Diary: 7 Indian (Meerut)Division, 19 (Dehra Dun) National Archives. 1990.

Indian Division and Brigade 1/9 Battalion Ghurkha Rifles. 9th August to 30th November 1915.

The Annals of Kinross-shire AD 490 to AD 1870, 1990

The Title Deeds of Tillyrie 1730-1950

Transactions of the Highland & Agricultural Society 1872, 1879, 1900-1930

Printed in Dunstable, United Kingdom

70376178R00178